DR. AC PRESENTS

HIDDEN HORROR

A CELEBRATION OF 101 UNDERRATED AND OVERLOOKED FRIGHT FLICKS

EDITED BY AARON CHRISTENSEN

DISCOVER THE HORROR

Kitley's Krypt - Chicago, IL

ISBN 13: 978-0-9911279-0-0

DEDICATION

To my incredibly beautiful and supportive wife Michelle, who shares not my shameless completism and is more than happy to walk out of the room when a flick fails to move her. Love you more than Godzilla loves stomping miniature tanks and buildings.

ACKNOWLEDGMENTS

HorrorHound's Aaron Crowell and Nathan Hanneman, for giving my scribbling a place to live and breathe for the past five years.

Fangoria's Tony Timpone and Chris Alexander, and *Rue Morgue's* Dave Alexander and Monica S. Kuebler, for being the leaders genre fans need and deserve. Thanks for coming aboard, gentlemen and lady.

Brett Harrison, for his amazing cover art. Good god, man. Your talent is mind-blowing and we are not worthy.

Bill Lustig, for all he's done both as a director and champion of unsung oddities. Thank you for your impassioned and articulate foreword—there's no one I'd rather have serving as our ambassador.

Jason Coffman, Adam Rockoff, Thomas Sueyres, Fans for Living, Dan Kiggins and Justin McKinney, for their invaluable assistance in tracking down several hard-to-find nuggets of cinematic joy. Special thanks to Justin for supplying some of the unforgettable imagery found herein.

Craig J. Clark and Ken Johnson, for their sharp-eyed proofreading acumen.

John Pata, who bought the very first copy of *HORROR 101* and then had the questionable judgment to cast me in his first feature *Dead Weight*. Your skillful layout is a beautiful bounty of blood, boobs and beasts. Thanks for always pushing for the best results rather than the easy or expeditious ones, amigo. Looking forward to the next burrito 'n' movie night.

Finally, deepest thanks and heartfelt appreciation go out to blood brother (and publisher) Jon Kitley of Kitley's Krypt. Over the past decade, you've been an invaluable source of inspiration and encouragement, and it is no exaggeration that I would not be the fan I am today were it not for your steadfast and unerring guidance. I am blessed to call you master, mentor and dearest friend.

CONTENTS

HIDDEN HORROR

FOREWORD

Earlier this summer, I received two emails: one from former *Fangoria* Editor Tony Timpone and the other from Dave Alexander, Editor-in-Chief of *Rue Morgue* magazine, each saying that they had recently contributed an essay to a new book on overlooked fright flicks. They also mentioned that the gentleman heading up the project ("a good guy," they assured me) was interested in having me pen the foreword. I was flattered, of course; the subject of obscure and underrated horror is certainly one close to my heart, having acquired and/or produced nearly 400 DVDs for Anchor Bay during its formative years (1999-2003) before creating my own home video distribution company, Blue Underground. I'll also admit to being slightly impressed that this fellow had procured such estimable talent for his worthy cause – I learned that Tony and Dave were joined by 99 other seasoned souls, each celebrating a forgotten celluloid treasure of terror. How could I say no?

I've been a fan of scary movies as far back as I can remember. In the town where I grew up (Englewood, NJ), there was a cinema that played horror double features; my school bus route went right past it, and every day I would see what was playing on the marquee. (Some of the titles were better than the actual movies!) I later became friendly with the manager, and on Tuesday nights, I would carry the four print cans down from the projection booth to the driver in the lobby, and then carry the four new ones back upstairs. In exchange, I got to see all the movies I wanted for free. I was in heaven.

As a youth, the films that made the biggest impressions on me were the derivatives of *Psycho*, movies like *Hush...Hush, Sweet Charlotte* and *Die! Die! My Darling*. I also loved Christopher Lee as Dracula and sought out every one of his and constant companion Peter Cushing's films. I found many of these and other crazy gems courtesy of my local TV horror program, *Chiller Theatre*, with its six-fingered hand coming up out of the swamp and ominous intonation, "Chillllleeeeerrrrr." Each Saturday night, I found myself discovering bizarre new favorites like *Curse of the Faceless Man*, *The Monster of Piedras Blancas* or *The Return of Dracula* with Francis Lederer.

While it's easy nowadays to connect with like-minded film fanatics, I was often on my own in a pre-internet era. I had friends who would sometimes accompany me to the theater, but there wasn't anyone around as crazy about these movies as I was. Instead, horror reference books and *Famous Monsters of Filmland* proved faithful companions, helping to shape my opinions about certain titles and guiding me toward new ones. After my brother Jason got older, he became my frequent companion – he often reminds me that I brought him to movies that he probably shouldn't have seen and that it traumatized him for life. (He's a lawyer now, so I keep waiting to get sued.) After I got a little older, I began spending more and more time in New York City, where in 1969 I discovered 42nd Street and Robert Downey Sr.'s *Putney Swope*. My world exploded.

A great horror film makes an indelible impression. You remember the time of the year, weather, theater, where you sat and especially the audience reaction. I've never really been attracted to mainstream Hollywood movies; the beauty of a true independent film is its ability to tackle convention, to find ways to push the envelope even when done for commercial purposes or shock value. To my delight, nearly all the films profiled in *HIDDEN HORROR* originate from outside the Hollywood machine; the few studio efforts on hand tend to be the "oddballs" of the bunch; I think there's something about that that sets them apart.

Nowadays, pretty much any film you ever wanted to see, or ever heard of, is available on DVD (especially the studio burn-on-demand labels) or Blu-ray. *HIDDEN HORROR* is here to guide the hand and heart of a younger generation of upcoming horror fans ready to head into deeper, choppier waters. Thanks to aggressive studio marketing, viewers tend to focus on the shiny new object of the month; as a result, they often overlook older films not being dangled in front of them. A book like the one you're holding opens our eyes to films from years gone by. The more we talk about these older efforts, the more people will seek them out and continue to talk about them in the process. There's an audience out there for these gems; maybe not the type of audience that shatters box office records, but an audience nonetheless and an appreciative one.

These 101 films cover a wide expanse of subgenres and periods of cinema and countries of origin. For me, foreign features have always had something special. From the camerawork to the music to the overall atmosphere, there is usually an artistry on display that transcends mere genre. In the way different types of exotic foods stimulate a different part of our palate, a really well-done piece of foreign horror lights up our brains: "Wow, I've never tasted *anything* like that before. I don't even know what that *is*." When the Italians and Spanish did their versions of Hammer gothic or George Romero's zombies, the distinctive flavor made them beautiful, extraordinary and unique.

That's the spirit of *HIDDEN HORROR*, to develop new viewers' tastes for fare outside the mainstream. Hollywood will keep cranking out fast food because it's cheap and easy, but true artists create things that we'll never forget. Love maybe, hate possibly, but remember always. If this book can tempt fans to travel outside their comfort zone and sample a few exotic buffets, all to the good.

As with any list of this nature, there are a few items that raised an eyebrow or two. For instance, I wouldn't have initially regarded my own *Maniac* as being "under the radar," especially since I've been so close to it for so long and seen it widely distributed. But upon further reflection, I realize there's a new generation of horror fans out there—especially if they've only sampled mainstream horror—that might never have heard of Frank Zito or Joe Spinell. In that respect, I'm pleased it's being showcased and in such fine company. On that note, there are quite a number of titles on the *HH* roster that I haven't seen (or in some cases even heard of) myself! DVDs and Blu-rays that I actually have sitting here at home that I've just never gotten around to, ones that I'm kind of excited to watch right now, films like *May*, *Dark Night of the Scarecrow*, *Alucarda*, *Fascination* and so on....

Let the adventure begin.

Bill Lustig
Los Angeles, CA
September 2013

A WORD FROM THE DOC

There's a phrase that every seasoned horror fan loves to hear, no matter how many times it comes along:

"Have you seen _____?"

The moment those three words drop, our ears perk up, brains tingle, and cinematic salivary glands begin to drool as we await the title in question. If we've encountered the film, our inner thesaurus starts scrambling to adequately express our sentiments. If not, we immediately put it on our "to-see" list, knowing all too well the curse of being the sole witness to an unforgettable piece of screen terror. The double blessing of any great scare flick is not only the thrill of engagement, but the ability to recommend and/or commune about it with blood brothers and sisters near and far.

As Mr. Lustig so accurately points out in his foreword, it wasn't always so easy to find one's own tribe of loonies. But today, with the tap of a keyboard or swipe of a screen, it's possible to chat with fans from all over the globe, gathering recommendations and sharing spirited discussions any time of day or night. Over the past decade, through the IMDb message boards, Facebook, horror conventions, and film festivals, my secret circle has expanded from a precious few to literally thousands; my friends have become my idols and my idols have become my friends. I'm honored to find myself in such esteemed company and thrilled to share their bounty of knowledge.

There is no denying the embarrassment of riches within this genre we love; the problem is often the effort required in extracting these gems or the ability to recognize them as such. For the horror veteran, word of mouth is the divining rod of choice, the method by which we select how to spend our next 90 minutes. It's not the critics' picks or box office tallies that get my juices flowing, but rather the urging of a like-minded soul. I count myself incredibly fortunate to be surrounded by some of the best, boldest, and bloodiest out there.

The inspiration behind *HIDDEN HORROR* is simple: To showcase an assortment of fright flicks my international band of gooble gobble geeks feel have been denied their rightful place at the terror table. Movies that go missing when the annual October lists circulate, but about which everyone shouts, "Oh yeah, that one's *awesome*!" whenever they finally get mentioned. Celebrating these unsung greats among far-flung friends whose opinions I admire and respect has been an unqualified joy; the choices are as surprising and varied as the contributors themselves, ranging from old to new, from a broad sampling of countries, each with a personality all its own. It's a carefully curated checklist for the fans...by the fans.

Now, some of these "hidden" titles have been doing so in plain sight. In other words, the 101 films showcased herein are not intended to represent the "most obscure movies you've never heard of." I even questioned whether some of the titles proposed were "underrated and overlooked," assuming classics like *Werewolf of London* and *The Devil Rides Out* or exploitation masterpieces such as *Humanoids from the Deep* or *I Spit on Your Grave* to be already highly esteemed and firmly imbedded on fans' radars. But the fact that my fellow informed aficionados believed these movies to be deserving of renewed recommendation intrigued me; it didn't take much convincing for me to want to give them a boost in visibility for a new generation. More than anything, I was once again reminded just how subjective our experiences are, and of the thrill in being the conduit for discovery. There is nothing—NOTHING—like turning someone on to a flick that blows her mind and/or turns his stomach. I think you'll find our inmates have done a fine job of running this particular asylum.

Be advised: This is also not meant to be a comprehensive list of alternative titles. In fact, quite the opposite is true. Its intent is to open doors and minds, stimulate taste buds, and expand boundaries. The best way to approach this compendium is as an epic pot-luck movie party where everyone has brought a favorite dish and wants you to give it a try. It's meant to be the beginning of the journey rather than the end; to provoke thought, challenge expectations, and reward courage. Even if you've seen every movie mentioned between these covers—and you have my unqualified admiration if that is the case—you're bound to acquire some new tidbit of trivia or insight after reading the corresponding essay. Of course, if we manage to tick you off, that's okay, too.

Finally, in addition to acquainting you with unfamiliar titles, we hope *HIDDEN HORROR* inspires you to break out those fondly remembered faves gathering dust and introduce them to your own dark minions. In fact, I bet you're creating your list right now. And I, for one, want to read that list. Keep sharing the scare, fellow fiend.

Enough of my yakking – down in front and on with the show!

AC

ALUCARDA 1977

BY NATE YAPP

Alucarda is not a film one simply watches. It sneaks up when least expected, infecting the viewer with its insanity. Once experienced, it burrows deep into the brain, a hysterical fever of sex, screaming, and sacrilege.

"Surely," you say, "this is exaggeration. Over-the-top hyperbole to entice viewers to check out the movie in question." Yes—and yet these are the only appropriate terms by which to discuss Juan López Moctezuma's masterpiece, because these

> **"AND THIS IS WHAT THE DEVIL DOES: HE GRANTS US VIRTUES TO EXPAND HIS KINGDOM, THE ONLY VALID ONE."**

are the rules of engagement Moctezuma establishes from its earliest scenes through to the manic end.

Alucarda's descent into madness begins with an old man delivering a child in a decrepit crypt. The mother (Tina Romero) asks the man to take the child to the local monastery, pleading, "Don't let *him* take her away." As the old man departs, the mother is assaulted by strange noises from all parts of the crypt and finally cries out. Fifteen years pass, whereupon we see the recently orphaned Justine (Susana Kaminski) arriving at the monastery to meet her new roommate, the strange, intense Alucarda (Romero again). The two form an obsessive relationship, quickly separating themselves from the other girls. In their explorations, they discover the aforementioned crypt. After Justine falls ill during a hell-and-brimstone sermon in the monastery chapel, Alucarda blames the church, invokes Satan, and initiates herself and Justine into his service via a super-Sapphic ceremony. Things only get weirder from there.

Writer/director Moctezuma was an associate of Alejandro Jodorowsky, co-producing the renowned avant-garde filmmaker's *Fando y Lis* (1968) and *El Topo* (1970), and the surrealism that pervades those early works is very much a part of Moctezuma's style. However, where Jodorowsky applied the lessons of Luis Buñuel to allegory, Moctezuma uses them to breathe new madness into established horror structures, especially those of Edgar Allan Poe (as in his 1973 film *Mansions of Madness*) and Hammer's vampire films.

Alucarda, in particular, shows strong influences from 1960's *Brides of Dracula*, where another home for young girls is invaded by a malignant force. Eventually a man of reason and learning arrives to defeat the evil, something achieved in part with a makeshift crucifix. However, *Brides* is couched very much as a conflict of good vs. evil, innocence vs. corruption, life vs. death. There are no such easy delineations in *Alucarda*. There are just a bunch of people in a mess. Well, and there is the Satan thing.

Ultimately, Moctezuma is using (however intentionally or unintentionally) the narrative of the Hammer film as a framework upon which to nail his own vision. *Alucarda* dispenses with such niceties as internal logic and clearly delineated protagonists and antagonists. Demonic influence and the power of the Catholic faith are interchangeably treated as hysterical delusion and stark reality. When reason eventually meanders onto the scene, in the form of local physician Dr. Oszek (Claudio Brook), it is championed at first before being rendered impotent by supernatural occurrences.

The key scene (and Moctezuma's masterstroke) occurs when Alucarda and Justine give themselves over to Satan. It is delightful, delirious madness that begins with Alucarda's screeching invocation of the various names of the devil. After a German hunchback (also played by Brook) appears from the shadows and guides the girls through a ceremony of mutual blood-drinking and nudity, they are led to a field where a goat-headed man invites them to join his orgy already in progress. Intercut with this are scenes of the one sympathetic nun in the monastery praying for the girls' souls and bleeding from every pore.

Although Moctezuma's vision is clearly the driving force throughout, Tina Romero's performance is the eye of the whirlwind holding it together. Her wide, seeking eyes seem to pierce the veil of the mundane, as do her fits of hysterical screaming. She projects the wounded naiveté of a girl seeking fulfillment in forces she cannot fully grasp (first love, then Satan). It's telling that when her character steps out of the spotlight briefly toward the end of

the second act, the momentum flags, then comes roaring back with a fiery passion upon her return.

While there are indications that Alucarda's pact with Satan is part of her own loss of sanity, Catholicism is linked to a madness of its own, namely the madness of repression. Held in sway by Father Lázaro (David Silva), the religious order within Alucarda's monastery rejects all earthly pleasures. Even the human body is disdained and considered little more than a potential gateway for the devil. Repression trumps even personal hygiene, evidenced by the large crimson stains emanating from the pelvic area of the nuns' gauze-like habits.

The level of zealotry in this monastery is apparent from the first time we see the church, which is not the stereotypical paean to the wonders of God. There are no stained glass windows with sunlight streaming in across the pews; this house of worship is a dank, dark cavern, lorded over by a giant, grotesque crucifix. Behind that, seemingly hewn into the rock, are numerous echoes of the same image of Jesus Christ on the cross, eerily lit from below by rows and rows of melted votive candles. It's a perverse exaggeration of the central image of worship in Christianity—a mostly naked man dying in agony.

Standing before this gruesome spectacle is Father Lázaro, delivering a sermon of hell and damnation against the dangers of the devil using the organs of the human body to enter the soul. We first see him at a distance, enough that he seems to be part of the tableau. This allows us to know him completely even before his first words are spoken. When his first reaction to being intimately touched (after a crazed Alucarda comes on to him) is to gather the members of the order for a round of bloody flagellations, we are not surprised at all.

It would be simple for Lázaro's outrage and zealotry to be merely a sublimation/transference of his own repressed desires, the very demons he rails against scapegoats for his self-disgust. However, Satan and demonic possession are very real parts of Alucarda's universe; we are shown that there is some necessity to the Father's vigilance. However, the fact that he and the other members of the clergy are right about the cause of Justine and Alucarda's bizarre behavior does not justify their eventual response: a horrible, sadistic exorcism-cum-torture session. Both girls are crucified and Justine is stripped, humiliated, and stabbed with a long needle (shades of the death of Christ here).

This complexity—sympathetic characters drawn down the path of evil, ostensible forces of good becoming monsters in their own right—coupled with Moctezuma's dogged refusal to allow things like logic get in the way of his storytelling might lead readers to believe *Alucarda* is a difficult film to watch. Nothing could be further from the truth. *Alucarda* is best experienced by giving over to the bizarre visuals, manic energy, and shocking violence. It is not, by any means, a *simple* experience, but it is a highly enjoyable one that leaves one subtly but unmistakably changed.

Nate Yapp begged his parents to buy him The Cabinet of Dr. Caligari *for Christmas when he was eight, which pretty much sums the guy up. He was editor-in-chief of Classic-Horror.com (R.I.P.) for thirteen years. Currently, he lives in Los Angeles with his spouse, two cats, and more DVDs than he could hope to watch in his lifetime.*

AT MIDNIGHT I'LL TAKE YOUR SOUL 1964

BY JONATHON LUCAS

"DESTROY ME! I BELIEVE IN NOTHING! I WANT PROOF OF DIVINE RETRIBUTION!"

1964 marked a tumultuous time in Brazil's history, with its democratically elected government forcefully overthrown and replaced by military rule. Always a very strict Roman Catholic country, the new authoritarian regime furthered restrictions on its citizens, enacting new laws that stifled freedom of speech and increased censorship of all media. Not the most fertile cultural climate for horror cinema to flourish in, right? Nevertheless, this was the year that Brazil's first horror movie, *At Midnight I'll Take Your Soul*, was hurled like a celluloid pipe bomb into the midst of so much conservatism and religious piety.

Our star is a suave gentleman indeed, name of Coffin Joe (played by director/co-writer José Mojica Marins). He enjoys the simple things in life like strong drink, good smoke, and the company of beautiful women, but he's a connoisseur of darker pleasures like murder, tyranny, and mocking the misery of others. He also rocks a sweet top hat and cape—who doesn't love to see a bold fashion choice pulled off with aplomb? More than anything else, Coffin Joe wants a son to carry on his bloodline. A man of high standards, he feels that only the most perfect woman is worthy of carrying his child; unhappily married to a barren woman, he sets his sights upon his only friend's wife. Relentless in his goal, Joe has no qualms about eliminating any obstacles—if the dream girl cannot be wooed with soft words, then forceful menace and clenched fists will suffice.

Inspired by classic Universal horrors, *Midnight* is a curious blend of the traditional and the groundbreaking. On one hand, it looks, sounds, and feels like a film from the '30s or '40s with its ghoulish soundtrack, broad character-izations, lusty overacting, and gothic graveyard sets with smoky mist billow-ing across the screen. But then striding into this old-school horror landscape, not just subverting it but *perverting* it, is the figure of Coffin Joe. He's a force of almost pure amorality, taking gleeful sadistic relish in every murder and mu-tilation. It's all displayed with a certain level of over-the-top low-budget charm that somewhat undercuts the ugliness, but Joe's leering grin as he chops off a man's fingers with a broken wine bottle or the lecherous joy he shows when licking a soon-to-be rape victim's blood off of his lips remain remarkably nasty stuff, even a half-century later.

Marins' intention with Coffin Joe was to create a horror icon unique to Brazil, one that his fellow horror fans could call their own. Whilst most horror movie villains tend to lurk in the shadows or at least be shrouded in an air of mystery, *Midnight* puts its monster front-and-center from the first frame to the last. He doesn't just dominate the screen time, but the film's entire ethos. Even though it's made clear early on that Coffin Joe will eventually meet his comeuppance, his tyrannical presence and Nietzschean philosophies hold sway throughout. He's part fascist abomination, part figurehead of protest. In 1964's Brazil, the blasphemous sight of Joe devouring a lamb shank on Good Friday while mocking a religious procession was highly taboo. Even more so is the spiritual climax where he defies the heavens, railing against

both God and Satan, denying not just superstition, but the entire ide-al of any authority outside oneself. This is horror cinema used as a voice of rebellion against an op-pressive regime of thought restric-tion. Valuing personal power and self-belief above all else, Coffin Joe is the mouthpiece for Marins' rage at the state of his country, where government and church attempt-ed to reduce his fellow citizens to groveling insects.

Born on Friday the 13th (yep, seriously) in March of 1936, Marins grew up living in the movie theaters that his father managed, and his first forays into directing were the comedies and westerns popular in Brazil at the time. Intent on follow-ing no rules but his own, his deci-sion to make a horror film was met with ridicule from his filmmaking peers; with little support, it was predestined to be a low-budget affair. But fancy production values are no substitute for passion—Marins attacked his work with a fervor that ranged from the inventive to the eccentric to the downright psychopathic. Considering Coffin Joe's persona is so intertwined with Marins' own, it's remarkable to think that he only took on the role after the original actor quit the project. No one else could have inhabited the spirit of the character quite so purely.

Even after selling his house and car to finance the film, there was still such a severe lack of funds that everyone involved had to adhere to a torturous filming schedule of 16 hours a day every day. At one point, when exhaustion had reached a breaking point, with cast and crew ready to walk off the set, Marins held a gun to a cameraman's head and threatened to blow the guy's brains out unless the scene was completed. This was years before Werner Herzog famously pointed a loaded gun at Klaus Kinski, so I'm comfortable in labeling Marins the pioneer of this revolutionary directorial technique.

Marins' conviction reached its pinnacle when funds allowed for only four more days of shooting. Rather than settle for whatever ended up in the can, he split his cast and crew into 12-hour shifts. Meanwhile, he himself stocked up on cheap, over-the-counter amphetamine pills and downed them a dozen at a time, continuing to both act and direct for 96 consecutive hours to complete the movie.

Coffin Joe's reign of terror continued for several more movies, among them a direct sequel in *This Night I'll Possess Your Corpse* (1967) and the experimental *Awakening of the Beast* (1970), a mockumentary exercise in meta-horror stylings that predates *Wes Craven's New Nightmare* by nearly three decades. The films grew wilder and more provocative, and so too did the behind-the-scenes mayhem. As related in the documentary *The Strange World of José Mojica Marins*, tests were devised to prove cast and crew's dedication to the material. Auditions reportedly involved having real tarantulas, snakes, and scorpions crawl over one's body. Or eating worms and cockroaches. Live burials. Severe electrocutions. Teeth removed without anesthetic. And so on.

In 2008, a 72-year-old Marins returned to give Coffin Joe a suitable send-off. Had age somehow managed to mellow the man? Not a chance.

Embodiment of Evil is an abject lesson in growing old disgracefully, the sheer extremity of its content putting today's Splat Pack of young gorehound filmmakers to shame. Coffin Joe quite literally goes out with a bang.

But it all started with *At Midnight I'll Take Your Soul*. When the film opened in Brazil, it was outright banned in some states while wildly popular in others (a theater in São Paulo played it for four months straight). Its unique recipe of camp theatrics, dark philosophy, and salacious sadism is most certainly not for everyone. But those willing to look past its technical imperfections will be rewarded by the highly personal vision of a true provocateur, manifested in one of the most magnificently malevolent monsters ever to grace the silver screen.

Jonathon Lucas, a horror fiend whose love for the genre predates his brain's ability to form memories, currently resides in a sunshine wonderland with his lovely wife, noisy toddler son, ever-hungry cat and a mountainous pile of unwatched DVDs. His musings on horror, pornography, art and life can be found at filthodyssey.blogspot.com. Just keep the kiddies well away from there. Actually, most adults should probably steer clear too.

BAD TASTE 1987

BY ADAM MUGFORD

In a world of orcs and elves, lovely bones and big hairy apes, a proud, bearded man looms over all that is and once was and could have been even more.

"WHAT ARE YOU DIRTY WHORES DOING ON MY PLANET?"

A night of boredom, a stroll down a barren aisle, a middle finger to my face—that's all it took. To be fair, any right-minded horror fan would be hard-pressed to ignore VHS box art featuring a suit-sporting, machine gun-gripping, bird-flipping alien-freak-monster, but at the time I was under the impression that films like Peter Jackson's *Bad Taste* simply didn't exist. Could there really be something so radical? Something so utterly bodacious? It would take the swipe of a worn-down video membership card and the slapping down of a hard-earned buck eighty-seven to find out the truth.

Allow me to introduce, as I was so joyously introduced to them those many moons ago, The Boys: Barry (Pete O'Herne), Frank (Mike Minett), Ozzy (Terry Potter), and Derek (Jackson). However, these aren't your typical blue collar chaps. Aptly named the "Astro Investigation and Defense Service" (yes, A.I.D.S.), The Boys are in fact part of a secret government department wrangling all things E.T. and space-based. And, luck be true, in the small, fictitious seaside community of Kaihoro, aliens have touched down with disturbingly sinister motives aimed against the region's hapless citizens. These particular intergalactic interlopers are of the psychopathic/cannibalistic variety, here to slice and dice *Homo sapien* flesh to suit their home-world taste buds—in addition to making a quick buck. Lucky for us Earthlings, The Boys are more than up for an unfair fight, with their fumbling, bumbling, brave, and brainless (literally at times) captain leading the way—he's a Derek, after all, "and Dereks don't run."

Bad Taste's shadowy stature in horror cinema is not due to one reason, but rather a trio. First and foremost, *Bad Taste* is a 1987 "cult" horror movie—from *New Zealand*, no less—a term that garners a mix of hesitation and confusion amongst moviegoers. Why take a chance on something so different that it is given cult status? Less adventurous viewers prefer comfort and stability—not straying from the norm, which this film does in spades. Secondly, consider its reputation as the undernourished, imperfect, gangly older brother of Jackson's own *Dead Alive* (aka *Braindead*) (1992). Why would cinephiles want to watch a less gory, less polished effort? (All you grainy, low-budget-loving horror fans are the minority, so shush.) Last, let us take into account the expansive resume of its creator. Why would a budding movie/horror buff start with *Bad Taste* when they can watch an exercise even more subversive in *Meet the Feebles* (1989), much bloodier in *Dead Alive*, or hell, one with greater star power in *The Frighteners* (1996)? However, these three elements conversely act as plusses for hardcore horror veterans, eager to experience the raw, unfiltered pleasures of an artist not yet caught in the Hollywood machine and its sway.

Yet, even within many horror circles, the movie is rarely mentioned; even stranger is that when it is invoked, the response is unwaveringly positive. *Bad Taste* is an anomaly—a respected debut feature condemned to the amateur league. It's not as gory as an early Olaf Ittenbach flick or as low-budget as *Basket Case* or a financial revelation like *The Blair Witch Project*. It's not as exploitative as *Pink Flamingos*, as cult-heavy as *Eraserhead,* or as splat-stick as *Evil Dead II*. So where does *Bad Taste* fit in? The answer: first in line. It's not numero uno in any single category, but next time you're asked to share a low-budget horror movie with heart and gallons of low-budget gore to spare, please do everyone a favor and recommend *Bad Taste*, a celluloid pizza with all the fixings.

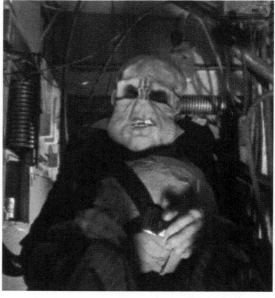

This crazy Kiwi treat has stood the test of time and still delivers on many a front, especially of the comedic variety. Yet within the slimy brains, bowls of green vomit, and beautiful New Zealand scenery, there is one element that sprouts higher than the rest. It's the dual performance of Peter Jackson as not only our fearless nerdlinger-commando, but also the scruffiest of aliens, "Robert." This latter character plays an integral role in the ensuing alien mischief, and the unabashed enthusiasm Jackson conjures as Derek is the stuff of which dark comedic gold is made. Whereas the majority of the cast is a

little damp behind the ears, Jackson's acting chops are nothing less than perfection—over-the-top yet entirely under control. Basically identical to his weirdo undertaker assistant in *Dead Alive*, in some odd way, Jackson's turn serves as an audience guidepost, showing how the movie is best ingested (and digested): simply let go, accept the imagination, and enjoy the insanity.

Bad Taste remains a fairly forgotten gem, not catching flack but most assuredly gathering dust. With a gestation period of four years, here is a feature that defines "labor of love" (as seen in the 1988 documentary short *Good Taste Made Bad Taste*). With Jackson's Mum and Dad offering their support (in addition to random kitchenware), the loyal cast and crew volunteered their free time to the project and their friend in whom they shared an undying trust. Initially intent on qualifying for a local film festival, they were soon blown away by the swell of positive response. Lucky for us, that was just the beginning. The movie eventually earned exuberant applause at the prestigious Cannes International Film Festival and around the globe. Through friendship, creative juice, and a burning passion for celluloid storytelling, *Bad Taste* stands as one of the greatest inspirational tales in the annals of low-budget cinema—and should be remembered and honored as such.

As the bearded man gazes out over his life's work, he scratches his head in deep thought. His eyes squint, his brow furls, and he mumbles softly. His eyes go blank for a brief moment, and then he smiles. He nods, turns, and walks away, whispering about a boy named Derek, alien madness, and of untold amounts of chuck and blood.

Adam Mugford was born and raised on the North Shore of Massachusetts. An identical twin, he sought his own unique identity and promptly discovered that he, well, liked weird shit. Knowing not the allure of Kool-Aid, but rather preferring the broth of a bubbling bowl of slime, his passion for the horrific is as unhealthy as ever. He can be found dwelling in Salem, MA, with a couple of disobedient mongrels named Koko and Jug.

THE BEAST MUST DIE 1974

BY PAUL HOUGH

> ## "ONE OF YOU SITTING IN THIS ROOM... IS A WEREWOLF."

Some of the fondest memories of my childhood were the frequent occasions that my dad drove my brother and me to Highgate Cemetery—to this day one of the scariest, most overgrown, and haunting of environments. After letting us out, he would challenge us to see who could walk the furthest within those dark gothic gates. Probably not what most families do for family bonding, but for me these were truly magical experiences. One particularly pitch black night when we were eleven and seven, with the full moon high in the sky, he put on a werewolf mask and jumped out from behind some trees, sending us screaming into the cemetery. Later, after we'd recovered from our trauma and my brother had gone to bed, my dad let me watch *The Beast Must Die* on television. The impact of that film on that special evening has never left me—I'll remember it forever.

A gripping, endearing, and entertaining journey full of apprehension and intrigue, *The Beast Must Die* takes the premise of an Agatha Christie who-dunit and elevates it from "Who is the murderer?" to "Who is the werewolf?" A game-hunting millionaire (Calvin Lockhart) invites six suspects to his secluded estate for a weekend (sharp-eyed viewers may recognize the set from many other films shot at Shepperton Studios). Upon their arrival he eloquently imparts his theory that one of them is a werewolf; by the end of the weekend, he states, he intends not only to expose the werewolf but also to kill it. He goes on to explain that the grounds of his stately home are completely covered in microphones and tracking devices so there is no way out. With his guests held captive, tension is perpetually increased one notch at a time with many fluid and exciting action scenes to follow.

Beast was UK director Paul Annett's first feature, having impressed Amicus producer Milton Subotsky with his 1969 documentary *The Battle for the Battle of Britain*. On the MPI DVD commentary, Annett explains that due to his television background and the tight schedule and budget (250,000 pounds), the film was meticulously planned out before cameras rolled in 1973. Though well lit, with gorgeous set and costume designs, the most successful elements are the gripping dialogue set-pieces brought to life by a superb ensemble which includes the great Peter Cushing, Charles Gray, Anton Diffring, and Michael Gambon. Michael Winder's script, based on the short story "There Shall Be No Darkness" by James Blish (and given an uncredited polish by Annett and Scott

Finch), allows this venerable team of professionals to deliver some great lines. While there is a lot of humor, the characters take themselves seriously, thus we take them seriously.

As our werewolf hunter, Lockhart could be described as a black version of Clint Eastwood. Oozing with charisma, cool as hell in his shiny black leather suit, this is someone whom we seriously believe will get the job done. Though the character was not written specifically for an actor of color, with blaxploitation cinema's popularity riding high, the talented, classically trained Lockhart landed the lead. While reportedly not the easiest performer to work with, the end result was a superb leading man who carries the story with finesse and intensity.

One questionable choice was to have the werewolf be more of a wolf than the traditional man-in-wolf's-clothing. To achieve this, a large dog was draped in a "wolf-skin" costume. The result is somewhat effective although by today's standards it feels more cheap and/or charming than chilling. (Even as a kid, I knew my dad's werewolf mask was the scarier of the two.)

But ultimately the movie is best re-membered for its "Werewolf Break." Shockingly, Annett had nothing to do with the gimmicky narrative device added by Subotsky in post-production. According to the director, Subotsky considered him-self not only a producer but an editor of sorts who would "save" films in the edit-ing room—whether they needed saving or not. However, in the case of the Werewolf Break (inspired by the "Fright Break" used a dozen years prior in William Castle's *Homicidal*), he struck gold.

The movie opens by zooming back from a set of gleaming bared teeth, revealing a freeze frame of a werewolf's face followed by onscreen credits which read, "This film is a detective story—in which you are a detective." A captivating voiceover (famous radio personality Valentine Dyall) then asks, "Who is the werewolf? After all the clues have been shown, you will get a chance to give your answer. Watch for the Werewolf Break."

When I saw this, *I was blown away.* Never had I been so engaged and enticed to watch a movie to the end. By speaking directly to the audience, as Alfred Hitchcock had done for his TV series, Subotsky immediately involved the viewer as a participant rather than a passive voyeur. (The "Who is the Werewolf?" tagline was also used in the marketing campaign, imploring patrons not to reveal the ending—another Hitchcock gambit.) There are very few films where I've known I was experiencing something magical while watching; the impact of the Werewolf Break as a kid has stayed with me ever since.

Once the introduction concludes, Douglas Gamley's fantastic '70s score erupts over a shot of Lockhart running for his life through a forest. As the movie progresses, Annett's skillful use of camera angles, placement, and actor staging make us feel we are right in the action. Because of the director's visceral approach, there is an added sense of danger; one sequence (pre-*Twilight Zone: The Movie*) shows a helicopter hovering incredibly close to our lead actor, while at other times the camera is positioned in an action vehicle inches away from the cast members.

As the onscreen action played out, I observed everything as closely as possible, trying to figure out the clues as any keen detective would. When the Werewolf Break finally came, I remember shouting my answer at the screen, hoping and praying I was right while simultaneously second-guessing myself and on pins and needles for the final revelation. Watching again as an adult, the anticipation is *much* more effective than the actual event—since there are really no clues to be solved, the manufactured denouement is very apparent and the conclusion somewhat lacking. (I also know now that if Annett had knowledge of the device, he likely would have done things differently to work up to it.)

When the movie was over, I remember going to sleep both satisfied and sad at the dark and untraditional ending—a true testament to the successful collaboration of Annett, Subotsky, and their worthy cast. But what struck me most was that this film had *moments*; moments of tension, moments of suspense, moments of thrills. To create something that stays imbedded in someone forever is a remarkable achievement. That enduring memory of *The Beast Must Die* inspired me (and continues to do so) in ways I didn't know movies could.

Paul Hough directed the horrifying multi-award-winning documentary, The Backyard, *about kids who violently wrestle with insane homemade weapons. With award-winning shorts and music videos to his credit, Paul's debut sci-fi/horror feature* The Human Race *premiered at Fantasia to rave reviews.*

THE BLOB 1988

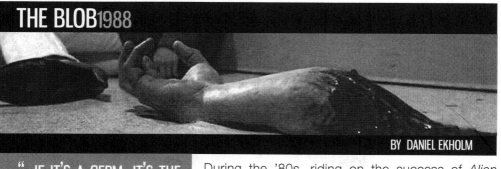

BY DANIEL EKHOLM

"...IF IT'S A GERM, IT'S THE BIGGEST SON OF A BITCH YOU'VE EVER SEEN."

During the '80s, riding on the success of *Alien* (1979), audiences witnessed an explosion of sci-fi/horror flicks the likes of which not seen since the late 1950s. Most were based on concepts that had been around for decades, but a few were bold enough to literally remake some classic horror efforts, with predictably vary-ing degrees of success. I usually don't care for remakes, but in the hands of skilled directors and craftsman, films like John Carpenter's *The Thing* (1982) and David Cronenberg's *The Fly* (1986) prove that remakes could be made equally well, or even better than their predecessors. Chuck Russell's reworking of Irvin S. Yeaworth Jr.'s 1958 sci-fi-classic *The Blob* belongs among this celebrated company.

Like Carpenter's *Thing*, this retelling of an ever-growing, all-consuming amorphous terror from space was a failure at the box office, earning only $8 million during its U.S. release (not even half its $19 million budget). Much blame has since been laid on distributor Tri-Star for insufficient promotion, but it's difficult to determine why *The Blob* failed to find an audience. Even on home video and cable, where it was later discovered by a few more devotees (me among them), the film has consistently struggled for recognition, harshly evidenced by Sony's mediocre DVD release in 2001.

"The original *Blob* was a special film, and I got obsessed with doing my own version of it, of updating it and using some of the expectations from the original. I think it shook people up so much because it's so pri-mal," Russell stated in a 1988 interview with *GoreZone*. "It's a monster in its simplest form. There is something about this thing that can slide under your door or squeeze through an air vent or quietly dissolve some-body in the next room that's very elemental. It just makes monstery sense. It's fear of the worst death—being eaten."

The Blob marked Russell's second run at the director's chair, following 1987's successful helming of *A Nightmare on Elm Street 3: Dream Warriors*, and he brought one of his co-screenwriters on that project, Frank Darabont, to aid him in bringing this new vision to life. Heading up the huge special effects teams were Lyle Conway (creature designer), Tony Gardner (makeup supervisor), and Hoyt Yeatman (visual effects supervisor). Together, these five brave men set out to pay tribute to a classic by raising the bar as high as it could go.

Call it nostalgia for a time when most special effects were not pro-duced on a computer, but during the '80s people still embraced the words "movie magic." Conway's Blob was made of silicon and other translucent materials, while Yeatman's crew mixed blue-screen and stop-motion tech-nologies to give the creature life. They also designed a motion-controlled tentacle, allowing precise movements to be pre-programmed by a com-puter, photographed at very low speeds, and repeated exactly. This meant that different elements could be shot separately and then lined up exactly when being optically composited.

These joined efforts also led to a multitude of creative ideas and solutions. "If you shoot upside down," Yeatman revealed to *Cinefantastique*, "you can get some very interesting effects with the tendrils or the Blob itself. When you put that together with a background shot normally, the gravities are different, which gives a unique look."

Thematically as well as technologically, both *Blob*s are clearly products of their time. The '50s version is as much a propaganda film against dangerous unknowns like the Soviet "red menace" (note the monster's color) as it is a straightforward creature feature. The remake, by contrast, is more interested in exploring the explicit distrust of our own governments. The '80s version also provides an in-depth backstory regarding the Blob's origins. While some might feel that the creature's genesis should have been kept ambiguous, I disagree. In the original, we know nothing about what drives the creature nor of its origins—whether it kills for pleasure or for survival or merely instinct. It may have no consciousness whatsoever, an innocent organism that happens to be at the wrong place at the wrong time (for us, at least). The only thing known is that it crashed on Earth inside a space mineral of sorts. In Russell's version, which I find much scarier, the creature is specifically *designed to kill* and there's nothing anyone can do to change its mind.

Born as it was during the golden days of practical effects in the late '80s, several visceral death scenes are handed out for our gruesome pleasure, but they rarely feel gratuitous thanks to Russell's focus on having them serve the drama as opposed to being showcased for their own sake. The gory reveals, with bodies twisted and torn inside out, often act as payoffs to a suspenseful sequence, providing both jump-scares and gross-outs. "I looked at the Blob as a giant stomach that got larger and larger as it ingested things. In the beginning it's like a smaller parasite eating away, so things look raw and bloody because it can't consume everything," Tony Gardner explained to *Cinefantastique*. "By the end, it's literally sucking people dry and turning them into gum. We went for a clean look, not a blood-and-guts look, because

there wouldn't be any left. We really stylized it to be fascinating rather than gross. Some of the stuff actually looks like weird modern art pieces, in a twisted way."

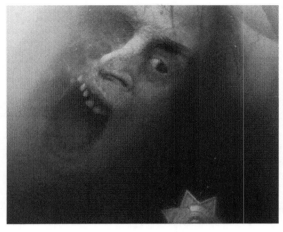

The characters (especially Meg, played by the beautiful Shawnee Smith) are also more believable than their '50s predecessors without losing any of the small town atmosphere. In the original, it's clear these are adult actors trying to pass for teenage characters and that the mischief-making "kids" are relatively harmless, so any failure to pay attention to their warnings falls entirely on the ignorant grown-ups "who just don't understand." In Russell's movie, Kevin Dillon's character is a genuinely troubled rebel who has earned every bit of distrust. None of the '80s kids are 100% innocent, which makes them much more realistic, as is their need to maintain a facade towards their parents and authority figures, which in turn gives a credible reason for the adults having doubts. The original portrays kids how adults think they should be, while Russell shows the reality behind the facade.

Finally, none of the remake's characters are completely safe. In most horror movies, we can tell who will survive to the final reel, but Russell—taking a page out of Hitchcock's *Psycho* handbook—doesn't hesitate for a second to sacrifice characters we've grown to like; a breath of fresh air in an often predictable genre.

Horror is completely subjective, but while some people are more terrified by slasher films or thrillers because of their "realism," it is the supernatural and the unexplainable that get my heart racing. For me, a threat that cannot be escaped, hidden from, or reasoned with is much scarier than an off-his-meds human being with a knife. *The Blob* definitely deserves a place of respect and recognition alongside the 1980s reinterpretations of *The Thing* and *The Fly*, confirming the notion that remakes—in the hands of the right artists—can exist for reasons other than making a quick buck.

Daniel Ekholm, born in 1982, is a Swedish journalist and film theorist who's had a special interest in horror films ever since seeing Gremlins *in the late '80s. Daniel has worked as a film critic for several magazines and hopes to be able to continue doing so for one of the major newspapers in Sweden. He also wants to write his own book about film in the future.*

BLOOD FOR DRACULA 1974

BY MICHAEL VARIO

> "MY BODY CAN'T TAKE THIS TREATMENT ANY MORE. THE BLOOD OF THESE WHORES IS KILLING ME!"

We are all familiar with Dracula, the vampire count created by Bram Stoker. There have since been innumerable celluloid manifestations of the infamous undead bloodsucker, many done with a humorous twist. But none have ever matched Udo Kier's enduring, endearing portrayal in Paul Morrissey's *Blood for Dracula*.

While I have been a horror fan as far back as I can remember, I did not see this film when it was first released. Being but an ignorant suburbanite 16-year-old at the time, I assumed—based on the "X" rating the MPAA had seen fit to slap upon it—that it was just some trashy bit of pornography. Twenty years would regrettably pass before I experienced this overlooked gem of horror, comedy, and exploitation.

Accompanied by Claudio Gizzi's haunting theme music, the opening scene of Dracula applying his makeup (in front of a mirror casting no reflection) with a flash of fang sets a tone of comedy mixed with beautiful melancholy. We learn Dracula is dying and can only be saved by the blood of virgins; "tainted" blood only makes him sick. Being so well known in his Romanian homeland (and owing to a shortage of virgins), his overbearing servant Anton convinces him to travel to Italy—being a Catholic country, it surely must have many virgins, right?

We are next introduced to a titled but poor family of Italian aristocrats. The Marchese and Marchesa have four daughters: one a spinster, another still a child, and two that the Marchesa would like nothing more than to marry off to a wealthy suitor. Also residing at the villa is Marxist farmhand Mario, who happens to be bedding the two marriageable daughters. A comedy of errors follows the Romanian count's arrival as Dracula works his way through the deflowered sisters presented to him as virgins, becoming progressively more ill. Unbound by class proprieties, it is Mario who sees Dracula for the monster he is. The ribald finale includes a dubious rescue-by-rape followed by an axe-wielding shower of blood and limbs reminiscent of Monty Python's parody skit, "Sam Peckinpah's Salad Days."

The comedy is not slapstick, but subtle farce offset by horror and gore, with Dracula presented as both ridiculous and sympathetic. On another level the film is an allegory for the clash between the aristocracy and the working class, evidenced by Mario criticizing the bourgeois and prophesying the coming Marxist revolution whilst bedding Saphiria and Rubinia. This common laborer puts an end to Dracula and literally subverts the aristocratic family from the inside out. Set in the 1920s with an eye on the '70s counterculture, there is also a clear message contrasting traditional and modern values, Dracula and the decaying villa representing the old ways in opposition to the young daughters and especially Mario and his distaste for social classes.

Originally released as *Andy Warhol's Dracula*, the artist's name was little more than branding. Morrissey was a member of Warhol's Factory and had gained notoriety with his films *Flesh, Trash,* and *Heat*. It was decided during pre-production discussions with producers Carlo Ponti and Andrew Braunsberg for his next project, *Flesh for Frankenstein* (aka *Andy Warhol's Frankenstein*), that Morrissey would direct two films in tandem. The same day that principal photography for *Frankenstein* ended, he began filming *Dracula* with much of the same cast and crew. While *Frankenstein* was over-the-top and campy, shot primarily in studio and in 3D, *Dracula* is more restrained, poetic, and lensed on location at a villa outside Rome. As opposed to the flat cinematography and muted colors seen in contemporary offerings, both films used vibrant colors and direct lighting, something I much prefer aesthetically.

Produced in Italy, it was financially prudent to use a mostly European cast and crew. There is no doubt that the star of the show is the great German actor Udo Kier, no stranger to horror and exploitation fans for movies such as *Mark of the Devil* and *Suspiria*, though his four-decade career has spanned all genres. This is my favorite of all his performances; at times extreme and hilarious, at others sad and sympathetic, yet  always imbuing the character with style and grace. Interestingly, he was not Morrissey's first choice for the role. Srdjan Zelenovic, the Serbian actor who played the monster in *Frankenstein*, was originally cast, but passport problems led to Kier's fortuitous last-minute casting.

Street hustler-turned-underground film star Joe Dallesandro plays Mario the sexist, socialist gardener, having previously appeared in Morrissey's *Flesh/ Trash/Heat* trilogy. An actor of limited ability, though with some measure of sex appeal, Dallesandro's New York accent is amusingly incongruous within the story's setting, though it does serve to highlight the character's earthy, working class nature. Another performance worth noting is that of Arno Juerging as the servant Anton, shifting deftly between drama and comedy as required.

The rest of the European cast is more than capable and the lovely actresses portraying the Di Fiore sisters (Milena Vukotic, Stefania Casini, Dominique Darel,

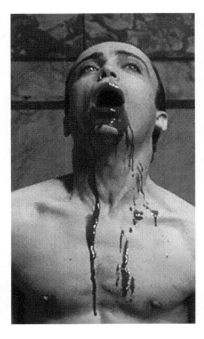

and Silvia Dionisio) are not too shy to supply an ample number of nude scenes. For the role of the Marchese, producer Carlo Ponti recommended the great Italian director Vittorio De Sica (*Bicycle Thieves*, *The Garden of the Finzi-Continis*, *Umberto D.*). De Sica had some reservations when informed of plans to shoot without a script (this was later to change), so he asked if he could write his own part with the assistance of longtime screenwriter Cesare Zavattini. Morrissey quickly assented.

Unbilled second unit director Antonio Margheriti is also well known in the horror community for his films *The Long Hair of Death*, *Seven Deaths in the Cat's Eye*, and *Naked You Die*. Morrissey's friend Roman Polanski also contributed a cameo for a comedic pub scene; the famed director was shooting another film in Rome and stopped by for a day when Udo Kier was unavailable.

When I finally discovered *Blood for Dracula* about a decade ago, I loved it immediately, finding Morrissey's wholly original take on vampires rivaling that of French director Jean Rollin. On another level, the movie is wonderfully funny, often in a comedy-of-manners way. As a fan of exploitation cinema, I was not disappointed by the abundance of female flesh on display. (Those disposed towards the opposite gender will also find plenty to enjoy.) Above all, the film earns its horror pedigree. While there are no real scares, the final act gifts us with plentiful gore and dismemberment courtesy of special effects maestro Carlo Rambaldi.

The fact that Morrissey created a genre piece more European than American in flavor, as well as its 1974 time-stamp, small budget and lack of famous stars, have all contributed to *Blood for Dracula* falling between the cracks for many contemporary horror fans. Even the Warhol label holds less allure than it might have 30 years ago. For fans of '70s horror and exploitation movies, especially those that are "different," I wholeheartedly recommend watching this unique treat, specifically as a double feature with *Flesh for Frankenstein*. You will not regret it.

Michael Vario was weaned on both classics and schlock supplied by Chiller Theater *and* Creature Features *since his childhood in 1960s New York. When home video came along, he found the floodgates opened to all the horror and exploitation movies he could find. Michael worked in the IT industry in NYC for many years and is currently living in the backwoods of the Poconos, pushing Linux on the locals.*

BRAIN DAMAGE 1988

BY JASON HERR

"I DON'T GET A BRAIN, YOU DON'T GET MY JUICE. WE'LL JUST SEE WHO CRACKS FIRST."

My introduction to writer/director Frank Henenlotter's brand of oft-overlooked screwball-splatter came via his 1982 feature debut, *Basket Case*, which I caught on USA Network's series *Saturday Nightmares*. For several years, I religiously watched the weekly showcase for obscure mid-'80s/early '90s horror fare, unearthing some really strange and influential (to me, at least) slices of cinematic memorabilia along the way. Gravitating towards anything that looked sleazy, cheesy, or just plain weird, I soon developed a soft spot for low-budget and lowbrow horror and exploitation films.

As soon as I was old enough to obtain my own rental card, I haunted the local video store, often returning weighed down with literal armloads of VHS tapes. It was during one of these first exciting and liberating solo flights that, after seeing Henenlotter's name on the front box art and having so enjoyed his first film, I immediately snapped up a title called *Brain Damage*. Although *Basket Case* will always be my nostalgic favorite, this 1988 follow-up revealed a surprising maturity and darkness, one still unmatched by the director's subsequent works.

The film begins as Brian (Rick Hearst) awakens to discover that a semi-phallic, turd-like parasite has taken up residence in his body. The creature, named "Aylmer," initially tries to calm Brian's obvious bewilderment over his newfound station with hippy-dippy platitudes such as "I am you, Brian. I'm all you'll ever need," and "From now on your life will take on a whole new light, and all you have to do is look into the light, and listen. Listen to the light, Brian. Just listen to the light." But the only platitude that Aylmer really needs to bestow comes in the form of a trippy blue liquid injected through a hole in his host's neck. The fluid leads directly to Brian's brain, acting as a euphoric and hallucinogenic drug...one that proves highly addictive.

But the juice comes at a cost. See, Aylmer needs to feed on human brains to survive, and it's up to Brian to locate food sources to satiate his new pal's appetite. As he strolls from one dark corner of New York City's underbelly to the next, in search of Aylmer's next meal and his own next fix, the young lad journeys through an unceasing parade of punk-rock dive bars, back-alley trysts, and junkyard scavengings. All the while, we watch helplessly as Brian's addiction transforms him from a seemingly normal city-dweller to a full-blown blue-juice junkie.

Henenlotter's sophomore effort is another screwy and darkly comical ride, albeit one with a decidedly more sinister air. Where the second and third *Basket Case* films (1990, 1992), *Frankenhooker* (1990), and *Bad Biology* (2008) veer off into unabashedly gleeful ridiculousness, *Brain Damage* portrays a realistic descent into full-blown drug addiction...even if the method of receiving the fix is outlandish by real-world standards. I'm not surprised to see Henenlotter, a director who eludes critical notice except in underground circles, tackle this thinly veiled allegory; the man is, after all, an NYC native who lived in and around the 42nd Street scene during its '70s and '80s heyday. One can be sure that run-ins with junkies, prostitutes, and all manner of criminal elements were a daily occurrence, and anyone who has witnessed the unfortunate, inevitable decline and erratic/obsessive behavior of an addict can testify to its harrowing nature. That said, the film is filled with outrageously humorous, typically Henenlotter-ish splat-stick moments. (The infamous "fellatio" or "brain pulling" scenes, anyone?) Even while tackling hard-hitting subject matter, the man retains a deep-seated love for the bizarre and the grotesque.

The basic idea for *Brain Damage* came to life while Henenlotter was being courted by production companies seeking a slasher flick. Since that particular genre wasn't really his forte, he started conceiving a storyline involving a parasitic creature that would leave its host to kill. (The addiction angle was later incorporated to provide a Faustian soul-selling element.) Even though the $600,000 budget was considerably larger than the mere $35,000 he'd had on *Basket Case*, the purse strings remained tight all the way through production and post-production. The movie was largely panned by critics and viewers alike during its "almost non-existent theatrical release," according to the man himself, but later found a cult following after being rolled out on VHS. (As there are currently many versions floating around in different degrees of "chopped," the preferred edition to seek out as of this writing is Synapse Films' uncut 2007 DVD release.)

Working from a rough drawing by Henenlotter, the Aylmer puppet was created by f/x artists David Kindlon and Gabriel Bartalos (who has worked on all of the director's films since). The cute fella's distinctive voice was provided by John Zacherle aka "Zacherley the Cool Ghoul," a staple of East Coast TV horror programming dating from the late 1950s. Zacherele, who later became a NYC disc jockey, also has a brief cameo as a weather man—in full Zacherley regalia—in *Frankenhooker*. Now in his 90s, the much-beloved horror host

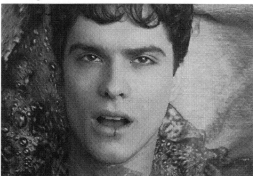

still makes regular appearances at New Jersey's Chiller Theater horror convention.

Despite the heavier ideas at play, Henenlotter manages to skillfully balance his disturbing subject matter with playfulness. (*Basket Case* fans will immediately recognize a few cameos and locations, including a memorable subway train encounter and a notorious little hotel.) Even as the third act drifts into pitch black territory, Henenlotter lightens the tone of one particularly dismal scene by having the latex one burst into "Aylmer's Tune" (a catchy little jingle). More so than his other efforts, *Brain Damage* demonstrates Henenlotter's deft hand at offsetting a potentially depressing storyline with the campiness and gory eye-candy that true exploitation film-lovers crave.

Though Henenlotter has only directed six feature-length films (to date) over a 30-year career, the fact that all of them are near-classics in the eyes of serious underground-horror/exploitation fans is a fitting tribute. We appreciate a man who only involves himself in labors of love, and will be lining up for whatever he gives us in the future even if mainstream audiences won't.

Jason Herr is a lifelong horror fan whose area of expertise lies in shock/gore/extreme horror, exploitation, and "roughie"-era porn films. A professional tattoo artist by trade, as of this writing he applies his craft at Temple Art Tattoo Studio and Art Gallery in Hagerstown, MD. Jason lives in Martinsburg, WV, with his wife, Karen (who he met on the IMDb horror message-board), and their cat, Karma.

BRIMSTONE & TREACLE 1982

BY MICHELLE TRUDEL

"There resides infinitely more good in the demonic than in the trivial man." — *Kierkegaard*

From the opening credits of *Brimstone & Treacle*, where pieces of parchment are seen floating from a gargoyle's mouth while a children's choir sings a happy tune, it's clear that something is awry. Seconds later, we meet Martin Taylor (Sting). Emerging from a church amidst a horde of altar boys, Martin looks out of place and sinister from the get-go, and his first words ("Which one? Which one will it be?") don't set our minds to rest any. But who is he? A homeless grifter, a well-dressed pickpocket, a psychopath, or maybe something...*worse*? Averse to the sound of church bells and clearly in need of a square meal or two, Martin is on the prowl...

> "I NO LONGER ACCEPT THERE'S SUCH A THING AS A LOVING GOD. IF HE'S THERE, THEN HE'S JUST A CRUEL BEAST, A VICIOUS OLD BUGGER."

...and Tom Bates (the wonderfully irritable Denholm Elliott, reprising his role from the 1976 BBC teleplay) is today's catch.

Martin begins the game by convincing Tom that they've previously met. From the older man's bumbling, uncomfortable responses to the encounter, Martin is able to gain sufficient information to convincingly claim to be an old friend of Tom's now-bedridden daughter, Patty. Tom briefly escapes, but the tension only escalates when Martin finds his way to the Bates' home that night.

Forlorn but devout Norma Bates (Joan Plowright) is worn down from caring for her daughter Patty, the victim of a hit-and-run accident. Patty (a fearless Suzanna Hamilton) is severely disabled, unable to speak, and completely dependent upon her parents, but there are hints that she can hear and possibly even understand what is happening around her. Imprisoned in her own body with no means of communicating or asking for help, Patty tries unsuccessfully to sound the alarm upon Martin's arrival at the Bates' dreary, suburban home.

Not only does Martin claim to have been a friend to Patty, but he soon insists that they were secretly engaged, while she can only incoherently twitch and moan in response. Tom will have none of it, but Mrs. Bates—exhausted, lonely, and desperate for a miracle—sees Martin as a godsend. The wheels are set in motion: as Patty thrashes helplessly in her bed, Martin charms Norma while randomly repeating words and phrases deeply personal to her husband. It's clear that things are about to go from weird to worse.

I love this little treasure of a movie. I love the acting. I love the pervasive sense of dread and slight scent of perversion throughout its lean 87-minute running time. I love the excellent soundtrack, which includes songs from The Police, Squeeze, and the Go-Go's. I even love the fact that so few people knew what I was talking about when I would mention it by name back in the '80s.

Some will find the film overtly, deliciously blasphemous. Especially enjoyable are the almost giddy repetitions of religious overtones, both in words and purposeful visuals, including a very quick shot of an angelic Patty staring past a white dove hanging over her bed and Martin smirking as he passes the creepily lit portrait of Jesus in the hall. Uttered not once, but twice is the phrase "You could be the devil himself."

No kidding.

In interviews, Sting has said that he chose to play Martin as if he were truly an incarnation of the devil—a choice I like because it simply adds to the grotesque nature of the proceedings. If we buy into the idea that Martin is, in fact, a "fallen angel" (as he calls Patty), rather than just a common sociopath, then the stakes rise enormously. Terrible things are surely going to happen

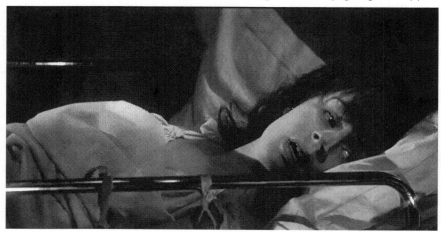

within the Bates house now that Martin has arrived and has insisted on staying to "help." Sting's performance is not subtle in this regard—he practically winks at his audience and dares us to hang on for the ride. All we can do is guess what form the evil will take and how bad it will be.

And what a perfect family for Mr. Mephistopheles to visit! Mrs. Bates is deeply religious, praying daily for Patty's recovery and calling Tom "wicked" when he reveals the sheer depth of his own loss of faith. Tom is, ironically, employed as a verse writer for the "Evangelist Press" and is not only a bitter ex-believer engaging in his own form of wickedness at the office but, unbeknownst to Norma, is indirectly responsible for Patty's seemingly irreversible brain damage. Through flashbacks, we learn exactly why Tom spends his days wracked with guilt and self-loathing; this is a family torn to shreds, riddled with tragedy, secrets, blame, and daily misery. Let's not forget that Patty is young, beautiful, and completely vulnerable in her bed. The devil has hit the jackpot.

When Dennis Potter's drama was first produced in 1976 for the BBC's *Play for Today* series, it was pulled from the schedule by programming director Alasdair Milne, who called it "brilliantly written and made, but nauseating." After several subsequent stage productions, the BBC version finally aired in 1987 and is now currently available on DVD and on YouTube. (We've obviously come a long way from the censorious standards of the mid-'70s.)

But Potter felt *Brimstone & Treacle* would be most fully realized as a feature film (and having secured the lead singer of The Police to play his antagonist couldn't have hurt, either). Director Richard Loncraine (*The Haunting of Julia*) coaxes superb performances from his cast of four, especially Elliott, whose Tom is a lost soul who flips from deep mourning over his daughter's condition to petty complaints over what's being served for dinner to lustful behavior at his place of business to deep fear that his life has no meaning at all. The man is all over the map and it's a pleasure to watch him squirm when Sting's Martin literally slams into him on the street and worms his way into his house.

Kierkegaard's opening quote takes on more meaning after a viewing or two. Are Potter and Loncraine implying that Mr. Bates, the trivial man, is more to be blamed than the devil, since the havoc Martin wreaks results in what could be seen as the answer to Norma's prayers? Can a visit from the devil actually be a blessing in disguise? Loncraine devises several wonderful fantasy moments— such as an over-the-top prayer vigil with Plowright and the dead-sexy dream sequence featuring a naughty, half-clothed Sting (fuel for many adolescent fantasies)—all of which kept me coming back for countless late night showings on HBO.

Horror isn't just about gore and jump scares; a fright fest can take many forms. Words that could be (and have been) used to describe *Brimstone & Treacle* include: *dark fantasy, controversial, twisted, macabre, disturbing, nightmarish, claustrophobic, squirm-inducing, bizarre*... There is also a healthy dose of humor added to this potent stew, and at the conclusion of Martin's adventure with the Bates family the question is clearly posed: What if Norma was right and God really does exist? If that's the case, then He's been watching, and his fallen angel Martin has some serious explaining to do.

Michelle Trudel is a yoga-obsessed Reiki practitioner, live music fanatic and wellness coach-in-training, currently residing in Chicago. When not espousing the virtues of love, peace, great nutrition and moving meditation, she prefers to watch her favorite horror flicks next to her favorite guy and thinks a good scare is good for your metabolism.

THE BROTHERHOOD OF SATAN 1971

BY DOUG LAMOREUX

"ARISE AND COME IN, CHILD. ENTER FOR YET ANOTHER LIFETIME IN THE BROTHERHOOD OF SATAN."

At midnight, the teenager I was in the '70s tip-toed to the TV set. Keeping the sound low so as not to wake the family, I twisted the antenna and crossed my fingers. (There were only three networks and, depending upon luck, weather, and snow tolerance, five or six channels.) I'd circled the fright flicks in that week's *TV Guide* in anticipation and that night's offering, as I settled on the floor inches from the screen, was something called *The Brotherhood of Satan*.

It opened on an obviously toy tank and I could see it wasn't merely poorly done *kaiju*—it was meant to be a toy. Sitting beside an empty Coke bottle for scale, the tank's gun turrets flashed and its treads clicked forward. An unseen mother and father cried out in terror. Then the heavy treads of a *real* tank ground up and over a family car, crunching metal and shattering glass. A fire broke out and blood, just a touch, dripped from the wreck. A small boy in cowboy hat and six-shooters left the decimated car, followed the full-sized tread marks and, at the top of the roadside ditch, picked up the tank—now a toy again. He carried it through the smoke to a waiting group of children led by a blonde girl holding a music box playing an eerie melody. It was an opening I remember nearly forty years later.

The Brotherhood of Satan is a Columbia picture and, more importantly, an LQ/JAF Production, the oft-unsung company formed by two men deserving of praise. They are actor, producer, writer, and director L.Q. Jones, best remembered as the crazy "Three-Fingered Jack" in *The Mask of Zorro* (1998), and actor/producer Alvy Moore who found fame as the bumbling Hank Kimball on the sitcom *Green Acres*. Together they made three marvelous movies: the awesome no-budget horror *Witchmaker* (1969), our *film du jour* (based on a story by Sean MacGregor), and the 1975 classic *A Boy and His Dog*, adapted from Harlan Ellison's post-apocalyptic novella.

Back to our feature. Ben (Charles Bateman), his eight-year-old "birthday girl" daughter K.T. (Geri Reischl), and fiancée Nicky (Ahna Capri, *Enter the Dragon*) are traveling to grandma's through New Mexico. They discover the crushed car from the opening sequence and hurry to nearby Hillsboro to report the accident. Upon arrival, they are inexplicably attacked by rioting townsfolk, half of whom are happily screaming, "It's over!" while the rest angrily shout, "You took them!" The sheriff (Jones) arrives but, rather than take their report, demands at gunpoint to know how they got into town. The three escape these lunatics but wreck their own station wagon just miles away after swerving to avoid—wait for it—a blonde girl with a music box. When the dust clears, there is no sign of the girl; Ben and his family have no option but to walk back to town.

Hillsboro has a terrifying secret. Over two dozen people, from six different families, have been slaughtered in accidents over the last three days. Additionally, nine children from those families—all between the ages of six and nine—have gone missing. No one has been able to get out of town and, until now, no one has been able to get in. The beleaguered sheriff, his deputy Toby (Moore), the local priest (Charles Robinson), and the town doctor (Strother Martin) want to know what's happening and how Ben, Nicky, and K.T. got into Hillsboro. Meanwhile, the "accidents" continue and K.T. disappears.

Bit by bit, director Bernard McEveety and screenwriter William Welch (with assistance from an uncredited Jones) let us in on the mystery. A coven of Satanists (called witches here) are at work. And what a group! Like the disciples in *Rosemary's Baby*, we're dealing with nasty senior citizens. But, while Polanski's octogenarian Satanists are sweetness and light as they pave the way for the precious new arrival, the old folks of Hillsboro are vicious monsters selfishly serving evil. These frightful witches cheerily commit serial murder, killing the adults of Hillsboro by using black-magic-actuated toys. Following each horrendous slaying, the newly created orphans are led to an abandoned house in the hills. Why? I can't tell you. But I can tell you this: in one sequence, a witch (Helene Winston), the wife of their minister, no less, is called to account for straying from their dark lord. "Weighed and judged" for her crimes, including the Christian baptism of their child, her capital punishment is meted out by the bare hands of her frenzied former colleagues.

McEveety, a veteran sci-fi television director, delivers bang for the buck in his first feature while cinematographer John Arthur Morrill juxtaposes brilliant colored lighting—reminiscent of the Spanish horrors of Naschy and Ossorio—with long master shots that seem to be recording very real events. The two are assisted by a smart script and gritty visuals (a psychedelic nightmare sequence in a temporary morgue, where bodies lie next to hanging beef, rivals the celebrated dream scene in Hammer's *The Plague of the Zombies*). Going by Hitchcock's rule that music works best in horror when it's cut off, Jaime Mendoza-Nava (*The Legend of Boggy Creek*, *The Town That Dreaded Sundown*) provides a divine original score using only a ghostly music box theme and a children's choir. Several sparing wind and percussion instruments take a brief

bow in the third act to heighten pursuit but otherwise the silence is broken only by rain, thunder, and the despairing, mournful howl of a dog.

Performance-wise, it's screen veteran Martin who leads the pack. As kindly Doc Duncan, he's restrained, retired and tired, but when the sun sets, his iron-fisted minister of all that is sinister steals the show. You believe that he believes. Remembered as Captain ("What we've got here is...failure to communicate.") in 1967's *Cool Hand Luke*, Martin's genre efforts include the 1973 cobra creeper *Sssssss* and *Nightwing* (1979) but, for my money, his gift to horror is this performance. He noshes some scenery, yes, but does so with relish.

The rest of the cast range from great to believable to serviceable. As is often the case in horror, the heroes have little flash but the supporting characters shine. Winston is delicious as the ill-fated Dame Alice, Robert Ward mines our sympathies as a traumatized parent of a targeted child, and Judy McConnell is hellish as the lovely coven initiate Phyllis. Outside of Reischl's K.T., the children are played by the filmmakers' and friends' offspring; three McEveetys, Moore's daughter Alyson, and so on. They're kids, they're fine, go with it.

The Brotherhood of Satan is of its era. There are few flashy special effects and those looking for outright gore will find precious little here (though plenty is implied). What they will find is a thought-provoking shocker that requires, and deserves, attention. Sit close to the screen, give yourself over, and prepare to be creeped out. Evil may well be right beside you...eating a blood-red snow cone.

Doug Lamoreux grew up trading letters with "Uncle Forry" Ackerman from Famous Monsters of Filmland *magazine. He never outgrew the monsters. Doug appeared in the fright flicks* Hag *and* The Thirsting *(aka* Lilith*). He authored the novels* The Melting Dead, The Devil's Bed, *and* Dracula's Demeter *(2012 Lord Ruthven Assembly fiction nominee) and contributed to* HORROR 101: The A-List of Horror Films and Monster Movies.

CARNIVAL OF SOULS 1962

BY SHELLY JARENSKI

The iconic 1963 horror movie *The Haunting* ends with the chilling "...and we who walk here, walk alone." The film's core themes are encapsulated in that line, uttered by the misfit heroine Eleanor Lance. Hill House is the first place Eleanor has ever felt at home, and the line suggests that she'll be happiest as a ghost. At the same time, the contrast between

> "I DON'T BELONG IN THE WORLD. THAT IS WHAT IT IS. SOMETHING SEPARATES ME FROM OTHER PEOPLE."

the communal "we" and "walking alone" introduces an ominous ambiguity. Eleanor may be joining a community of female ghosts, or she may be walking the halls of Hill House in isolation and despair.

While Robert Wise's haunted house chiller became a classic of the genre, the equally atmospheric and arresting *Carnival of Souls* languished in obscurity due to a dubious distribution strategy by the corrupt Hertz Lion Company. The film was dumped unceremoniously onto the creature feature drive-in circuit, where its quiet eccentricities were out of place, and was all but forgotten until its theatrical re-release in 1989. By then, immeasurable damage had been done both to its reputation and distribution rights. Even its rightful induction into the Criterion Collection in 2000 was undermined by its ubiquity amongst the dreck on numerous "50 Greatest Horror Classics" boxsets.

Despite its cult status, *Carnival of Souls* can be understood as a corollary to the more famous *The Haunting*. It essentially portrays what being part of the community of the dead, while simultaneously feeling utterly alone, looks like. We follow another outcast female, and the sole survivor of a tragic car accident, Mary Henry (Candice Hilligloss). Characterized as unfit for the mundane world, Mary is "tough minded," troubled, and unusual. The people in her home town are perplexed that she is not more "humble" in the wake of her accident, and that she approaches her new job as a church organist with a pragmatic irreverence. Leaving her hometown, she declares, as have misfits everywhere, "I am never coming back." Mary is not traditionally feminine; she's hardened and impious. She also doesn't belong; tenuously connected to a world where everyone else feels comfortable. We are not surprised when Mary declares, "I have no desire for the close company of other people."

"Uncanny" is a term that originated with Freud, describing that which is familiar but out of place. (The original German has it as *unheimlich* or "un-home-like.") The sensation of encountering the uncanny is one of deep disturbance; a singularly ambiguous psychological experience that is nearly impossible to define. Like Eleanor Lance, Mary never feels she belongs to the world. Everything seems familiar to her, and yet she feels an inexplicable sense of separateness.

These scenes introduce the question of Mary's sanity; when she becomes haunted by a mysterious, pale-faced stranger (played by director Herk Harvey), the viewer experiences everything that follows through a fog of unreality and dream-like discomfort. (Gene Moore's organ-inflected score only increases this sensation.) In addition to being stalked by the menacing and ethereal figure, Mary is inexplicably drawn to a rotting old bath-house/ballroom/carnival and repeatedly goes there to prove that her foreboding attraction is just a harmless trick of her imagination. She begins experiencing odd spells, illustrated as some of the creepiest, most disturbing, and painfully moving scenes in the horror genre. The nature of *Carnival of Souls'* terror lies in its atmospheric oddness, and worse, in its ability to make one question the reliability of perception.

These qualities—I'm sure psychologists have a name for this kind of fear, but I always just call it *"Twilight Zone* syndrome"—are what tie me to this film. The idea that one cannot trust his or her own reality has always been most terrifying to me. Questioning our perception means, as Mary is forced to do, questioning the entire nature of our being. For years I had nightmares in which the people around me could not see what I saw, in which I had vital information that could prevent the end of the world, but no one would acknowledge my presence. *Carnival of Souls* captures these sensations of anxiety, despair, and existential crisis in a way I have seen no other work of art accomplish.

Both Harvey and screenwriter John Clifford were employees at the industrial and educational film company Centron Studios. This institutional background served them well in terms of familiarity with equipment and execution, but severe financial limitation ($30,000) led to a more guerrilla style of filmmaking. According to Hilligloss, interviewed in Tom Weaver's *Double Feature Creature Attack*, Harvey would randomly wander around, saying, "'We need a department store, and this looks like a very good one. Let's go in.' We walked in, looked around…found a saleswoman. Herk said, 'Listen, for twenty-five dollars, would you keep people out of the dressing room area?'"

Even on its limited budget, excellent use is made of the varied locations. Clifford was attracted to the exposed musical pipes at the Reuter Organ Company in Lawrence, Kansas, while Harvey was inspired by an abandoned ballroom within the Saltair amusement park on the shores of the Great Salt Lake in Utah. Obviously, there's nothing much creepier than an abandoned carnival and/or ballroom, and Mary's explorations of and hallucinations about this space are played to great effect. Some of the more haunting scenes, though, take place in mundane spaces such as department stores, city parks, and train stations. Having terrible, inexplicable things occur in these familiar, often sun-drenched locales enhances the viewer's deep unease and is an effective engagement with the uncanny.

This engagement brings up the theme of sexuality. As noted, Mary is characterized as an unfeminine woman, and some of the strangest moments come from her encounters with her lascivious housemate, John Linden (Sidney Berger). A generic fear of sexuality, especially female sexuality, could be noted here; however, I think it is important to categorize *Carnival of Souls* as queer horror. To describe something as queer means less that it is definitively gay or lesbian and more that it is non-normative; that what is being portrayed challenges our sense of clear dichotomies of human sexual expression. Both Mary Henry and Eleanor Lance struggle with their sexual identities—Eleanor, a virgin, is confused and frightened by the advances of the androgynous, bi-sexual beauty Theo; Mary alternately flirts with and recoils from Linden, and overreacts to a doctor's query about whether she has a boyfriend: "No, and I have no desire for one!" For gay and lesbian individuals, much less for people whose sexual identities don't clearly fit into any category, the social experience for much of the twentieth century could be characterized as a living death, unrecognized at the level of representation or equal citizenship.

Being unable to fit in except with female ghosts or wandering the world unseen and unheard, wondering why you don't understand other people and they don't understand you—these are fitting metaphors for what it means to be queer. While I believe strongly that *Carnival of Souls* needs to be understood as queer horror, it also remains a compelling, deeply empathetic picture for anyone who has ever struggled to fit in.

> *Shelly Jarenski is a college professor living in Ann Arbor, Michigan. She was raised as a horror fan by her mother and aunts by consuming a steady diet of* Tales from the Darkside *and* Dr. Who *until she was ten years old.*

THE CHANGELING 1980

BY DON SUMNER

> "THAT HOUSE SHOULDN'T HAVE BEEN RENTED. THAT HOUSE IS NOT FIT TO LIVE IN. NO ONE'S BEEN ABLE TO LIVE IN IT. IT DOESN'T WANT PEOPLE."

Ghost stories are some of the most difficult horror films to get right. So easily can a tale about rambunctious spirits become overly cheesy or worse, extremely boring. Every horror villain has a backstory of some kind, but ghosts usually come complete with a full-fledged mystery filled with plot twists and hidden motivations. To make matters worse, most displaced spirits don't simply appear in a mirror somewhere and explain their tale of woe in gory detail, but instead drop little hints here and there, make objects float around, maybe cause noises in the night, and then wait impatiently for the living to figure the whole thing out. *The Changeling* has the advantage of Academy Award-winner George C. Scott at the helm as the living detective, and he does a great job putting the pieces together while delivering a commanding performance that sustains our attention between apparitions.

When composer John Russell (Scott) has car trouble on a winding snowy mountain road, there just happens to be a phone booth nearby so he can call for assistance. While in said roadside booth, a freak accident occurs when a truck slams into his stalled station wagon, leaving his wife and daughter dead. After months of grieving, John eventually moves to Seattle to teach a college course and try to get his life back together, but he quickly finds staying with friends too confining for a famous composer given to tinkering on the piano until the wee hours of the night. John follows a lead about a house for rent managed by the local historical society; while certainly too big for one person to live in, it has a music room and will allow him time with his thoughts and music.

It doesn't take long before the house and its contents assert themselves with a clear consciousness. Whatever it is lurking in the house's shadowy confines has something to say...and will not be ignored.

The Changeling is one of the best ghost stories ever committed to film. There are not a large number of "jump scares" and the effects certainly reflect their timeframe, but haunted house tales are all about the sleuthing necessary to track down the source of the unseen specters and discover what in the (after) world they are trying to say. In that regard, Hungarian director Peter Medak and screenwriters William Gray and Diana Maddox (working from Russell Hunter's story) hit every single nail squarely on the head. A good ghost story contains equal parts tragedy, mystery, crime, and retribution. In some cases, the cause of the haunting is delivered in the form of a grand reveal, such as *Poltergeist*'s housing-project-on-ancient-Indian-burial-ground. However, the pieces of *The Changeling*'s haunting puzzle come out one by one, and our hero, tirelessly spurred on by clues presented by the specters themselves, pursues the leads.

For John, the disturbances begin after he moves into the old house with a single note playing on the piano by itself, but the "innocent" haunting presence soon progresses to rhythmic thumping. By the time faucets start coming on by themselves and the vision of a young boy appears in the water of the bath tub, it is clear that random bumps in the night are not on the agenda. There is an untold tragedy that must be revealed if the tortured spirit is ever to rest.

The characters and performances are strong throughout, and Scott carries *The Changeling* through to the bitter end. There was a time in cinema when "big name actors" could do all kinds of films, and Scott was always a bit of a Hollywood rebel. He is paired with the lovely Trish Van Devere; the two met on the set of *The Last Run* in 1971, and married the following year. The duo would go on to appear in several projects together including *The Day of the Dolphin*, *Movie Movie*, and, of course, *The Changeling*.

The tone and mood are very unique for a horror story in that they are so… normal. The house is certainly big and imposing, but many of the scenes— shot outside or in very bright light— aren't oozing with dark foreboding ambiance. The entire film is presented very matter-of-fact, really. The advantage to that style, in this case, is that it doesn't seem particularly strange that John resists running screaming from the house the first time something otherworldly happens, or that he goes to such great lengths to fulfill the requests of the spirit seeking acknowledgement and retribution for a past wrong. There are some excellent shots, including an aerial view through the top of a house with the floor cut out and a focus on the face of a dead man through his broken windshield after an auto accident, but the overall tone is not one of overt "atmosphere." It is as if Medak decided to let the performances and script tell this story, aided by some subtle yet effective scares, without making the whole picture dark and dreary and forced.

It is interesting that *The Changeling* should be a "Hidden Horror" rather than a recognized household classic. The film swept the (Canadian) Genie awards, winning Best Picture, Actor, Actress, and several technical awards, and returned fair U.S. box office receipts ($12 million against its approximately $600K CAN production budget). Still, it under-performed when compared to other 1980s Canadian horror efforts and remains lesser known than its brethren to this day. For example, that same year's *Prom Night* had the benefit of rising scream queen Jamie Lee Curtis while David Cronenberg's *Scanners* featured a game-changing head explosion. *The Changeling*, by contrast, was a slow-burn, no-nonsense dissection of a decades-old mystery orchestrated by a creepy ghost in a historic mansion...not necessarily sexy. Perhaps the lack of a particular stand-out component is to blame for its having slipped into obscurity with all but the most dedicated horror fans.

Ostensibly a whodunit with ghosts, *The Changeling*'s performances and story are what elicit positive reactions from horror aficionados rather than any mind-blowing visuals. The music, characters, intrigue, and well-cultivated suspense keep our attention to the end and the film in our thoughts long after the credits roll. Hunter claims his story is based on actual events he experienced living in the Henry Treat Rogers Mansion in Denver, Colorado. In interviews, Hunter claimed that even after the building was demolished, the ghost followed him to his next dwelling and had to be exorcised by a priest. Whether the author was the victim of a long-standing and violent haunting himself, or just has the kind of vivid imagination necessary to be a good writer, we will never know. The film adaptation of his story, however, is ours to enjoy as a classic of the horror genre and one of the best cinematic ghost stories of all time.

Don Sumner is the editor-in-chief of Best-Horror-Movies.com and author of Horror Movie Freak, *the book George A. Romero called "an excellent guide for Horror Freaks and aspiring horror moviemakers." Don has written about the connections between horror movies and horror comics for the* Comics Buyer's Guide, *horror movie locales for* USA Today *and is a regular radio guest nationwide talking about horror, Halloween, and all manner of spooky things.*

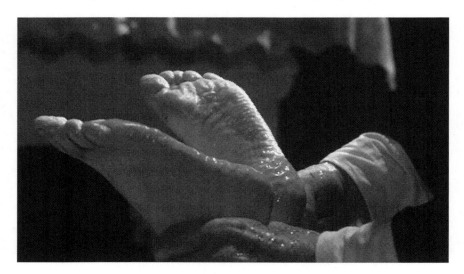

THE CITY OF THE DEAD 1960

BY ALAN TROMP

The City of the Dead, or *Horror Hotel* as I originally saw it, has great sentimental value to me. It's one of the very first fright films I can remember watching as a child on the TV late show in Cleveland, Ohio, so there's a very good chance I was jokingly ushered through the thrills by horror hosts such as Ghoulardi

> "THE BASIS OF FAIRY TALES IS REALITY. THE BASIS OF REALITY IS FAIRY TALES."

or Big Chuck and Houlihan. Years later, back when you could only get some of these memorable B-movies on videocassette from other collectors, it was one of the very first VHS tapes I bought. Recently, I found a *Horror Hotel* one-sheet movie poster online at a decent price, and bought it for its hideous green-tinted depiction of rotting cemetery ghouls and cheesy tagline, "Just ring for doom service!"

In the movie's prologue, Elizabeth Selwyn (Patricia Jessel) is burned as a witch in 1692 Whitewood, Massachusetts. She swears a pact to Lucifer and places a curse on the entire village. Fast forward to contemporary times, where history professor Alan Driscoll (Christopher Lee) encourages his star pupil, Nan Barlow (Venetia Stevenson), to travel to Whitewood and write a term paper on the diabolical goings-on there. The proprietor of the foreboding Raven's Inn, Mrs. Newless (also Jessel), bears a striking resemblance to the legendary witch, and a sinister hitchhiker, Jethrow Keane (Valentine Dyall), is the double of the witch's former lover. Nan is warned to leave by the town's blind reverend and his granddaughter Patricia (Betta St. John), but the very-much-alive witch cult manages to abduct her. When Nan fails to return, her boyfriend Bill (Tom Naylor) and her professor brother Richard (Denis Lotis) investigate and wind up battling a coven bent on sacrificing Patricia to their infernal master.

To say the movie is atmospheric is a gross understatement. There's so much fog swirling around the cursed town, it looks like the surface of Venus. Many scenes are accentuated by the chiaroscuro of flickering flames, and the eerie chanting of the Satanists, like a church choir gone awry, completes the aura of menace.

While fairly bloodless by today's gross-out standards, the film is still chock full of wild stuff, including stabbings, stranglings, animal sacrifice (off-screen), corpse-strewn crypts, reanimated dead who can vanish in the twinkling of an eye, burning apparitions that appear in the middle of the road, the magical "hour of thirteen," some pretty naughty black lingerie, and a total conflagration at the climax.

Authentic parts of folklore and religious ritual are also woven into the plot, such as the Black Mass, the feast day of Candlemas, mystical plants (woodbine), and sympathetic magic similar to voodoo. The iconic image of sinister, robed figures has been featured as far back as early gothic thrillers like Matthew Lewis' *The Monk* (1796), *Weird Menace* pulp magazines, and EC Comics, as well as Bergman's *The Seventh Seal* (1957), Ossorio's *Blind Dead* films, and even *The Da Vinci Code* (2006)!

The chills are balanced with macabre humor. A shot of a descending blade during a human sacrifice cuts to a pastry knife plunging into a cake, a handy satyr-faced faucet washes away unsightly bloodstains, and while bullets won't stop a witch, throwing the empty pistol at them makes them duck (just like in *Billy the Kid vs. Dracula*). It's also funny that the movie's American distributor, Trans-Lux, later brought us *Speed Racer*! By the way, there are no records that we ever *burned* any witches in America. (Hanged, yes; burned, no.)

Lee, Jessel, and Dyall do a superb job as the ringleaders of the coven. One minute aloof and cordial, the next they are grinning or laughing hysterically about their plotted carnage. They take great pleasure playing cat and mouse with the two young women whose blood they plan on drinking to continue their undead existence. "A living descendent of those who were cursed," muses Dyall about one victim. "It somehow seems to make it better." Some reviewers have suggested, however, the toughest acting challenge faced by the all-British cast was pulling off convincing American accents.

Phil Hardy, in his *Encyclopedia of Horror Movies*, notes that the film has a style reminiscent of H.P. Lovecraft. There's no Cthulhu or Yog-Sothoth, but the movie definitely shares the cult pulp author's affinity for subterranean passages, damned books, atavistic cults, and decaying backwater New England villages. Nan Barlow is very much a Lovecraftian character, unable to resist the lure of forbidden knowledge even when it puts her very soul in peril.

City of the Dead's legacy may be even greater as a launching pad for some really talented individuals. Lee, of course, is still a horror and fantasy star of the first magnitude, while this was director John Moxey's feature film

debut; he went on to a stellar television career, directing everything from the celebrated *The Night Stalker* TV-movie to episodes of *Magnum, P.I.* and *Murder, She Wrote*. Screenwriter George Baxt penned such unusual thrillers as *Horror on Snape Island* and *Circus of Horrors*. Valentine Dyall's rich resume included being "The Man in Black" narrator on BBC Radio, acting in *The Haunting* and *Dr. Who*, and dubbing the voice of bloodsucker Mike Raven in Hammer's *Lust for a Vampire*.

Executive producer and story author Milton Subotsky and producer Max

Rosenberg were Americans who met in 1954. At the end of the '50s, the pendulum of fantasy films was swinging from giant atomic monsters back to gothic terrors. The duo, emboldened by the success of Hammer Studios' sexy, colorful remakes of famous creature features, decided to jump on the British horror bandwagon. *City of the Dead*'s success

inspired Subotsky and Rosenberg to relocate to England, and their creativity and business acumen led to the founding of Amicus Productions, which spawned such beloved shriekshows as 1965's *Dr. Terror's House of Horrors* and 1972's *Tales from the Crypt*.

In modern fright films, the powers of good seem pretty feeble compared to those of darkness, and survival often hinges on a lucky break. In *City of the Dead*, the explosive conclusion refreshingly demonstrates that faith packs a considerable wallop. Although Christianity plays a role, the punishment meted out to the witches is strictly eye-for-an-eye, fire-and-brimstone stuff right out of the Old Testament.

I personally think *City of the Dead*'s place is secure as a cult favorite, particularly among baby-boomers. Clips show up in Rob Zombie and Iron Maiden songs and videos. However, it may be underappreciated by the latest generation of horror fans, being overshadowed by more famous witchcraft films like *Curse of the Demon*, *Black Sunday*, *Witchfinder General*, and *Mark of the Devil*. The good news is that the film is readily available on bargain DVDs, primed to shock young boils and ghouls adventurous enough to sample its diabolical delights.

In this age of remakes, it's no surprise to find *City of the Dead* bandied about on the list of titles slated for a "reimagining." So, good luck with your new project, cinematic resurrectionists, but if you screw up this childhood favorite of mine, I curse you with the reverend's bitter words: "Creatures of salt! I adjure thee by the living God!"

Alan Tromp is a technical writer/instructional designer living near St. Louis, MO, with his wife Patty and his giant dog Bella. He's written several articles for Twilight Zone *and* Filmfax *magazines, and once acted as a zombie priest in a stage version of* Night of the Living Dead. *He is doomed to walk the earth until he gets to see that lost jewel of macabre movies,* Voodoo Heartbeat *(1975).*

CITY OF THE LIVING DEAD 1980

BY DAVE KOSANKE

"The soul that pines for eternity shall outspan death. You dweller of the twilight void come Dunwich." Those words appear on a tombstone in the opening shots of Lucio Fulci's *City of the Living Dead* (aka *The Gates of Hell*). Released overseas in 1980, American audiences had to wait until 1983 to enter these titular gates—ones that opened onto a mythical town populated by rotting cadavers, howling shrieks, persistent winds and the lumbering dead—but rest assured, it was unlike anything we had seen to that point.

When *Dawn of the Dead* became a major success worldwide, the Italians had a stake in the matter since horror icon Dario Argento was one of the producers. Back home, the trimmed-down movie was rechristened *Zombi* and soon became a lightning rod that dramatically altered the horror landscape, with filmmakers all over clamoring to ride the coattails of its success. Fulci was first out the gate in 1979 with his own rendering on the undead mythos, *Zombi 2,* a not-so-subtle attempt to sucker patrons into thinking it was a sequel to Romero's splatter opus. *Zombie*, as it was known in the U.S., became an international box-office smash; once again producers were itching to capitalize on its success. Enter screenwriter Dardano Sacchetti, who told *HorrorHound*'s Mike Baronas, "After the island in *Zombie*, there was a need to take the story into the city, a small city, whereby places and old legends could cross over in an almost classical way."

City of the Living Dead (which has a poster design eerily reminiscent of the U.S. one-sheet for *Dawn of the Dead*) centers on Mary Woodhouse (Catriona MacColl) who, during a séance, receives a vision of a priest, Father Thomas (Fabrizio Jovine), hanging himself, thus causing the gates of Hell to open. The final resting place of Father Thomas, the moody town of Dunwich, doubles as a passageway to the Underworld, the entrance of which must be closed before All Saints Day lest the dead rise and claim the Earth as their own.

The specter of Howard Phillips Lovecraft hovers close overhead, having inaugurated the fictitious village of Dunwich into pop culture lore with his 1929 story "The Dunwich Horror." The celebrated author's vision of a barely inhabited town whose sole inhabitants are suspicious and superstitious echoes several *City* plot points. Much like *Zombie*, the movie's atmosphere and eerie edge create a profound unease, but this time Fulci amps up the nightmare illogic to extremes. Things often happen for no reason other than to unnerve and unsettle the viewer (a device the director would employ again in 1981's *The Beyond* and *The House by the Cemetery*). The photography, courtesy of frequent Fulci collaborator Sergio Salvati, is shrouded by layers of fog and mist (and in some instances maggots!), giving an otherworldly vibe to the Dunwich environs. We do learn through several dialogue passages that this particular Dunwich was built on the ruins of the original Salem witch burnings (which would logically place us in Massachusetts, though this is never mentioned in the film).

The gore quotient in a Fulci horror flick is always consistently high, but after the visual assault of *Zombie*, effects specialist Gino De Rossi (not to be confused with the equally venerable Gianetto De Rossi) was looking to once again out-gross the competition. De Rossi and his team whipped up a small group of the living dead whose preferred M.O. was to squeeze their intended victims' (including leading man Christopher George's) cranial cavities until their brains oozed out! Several scenes even featured a mixture of real maggots and worms being blown onto the actors faces, and an undisputed highlight occurs when a drill bit meets one end of poor Bob's (Giovanni Lambardo Radice aka John Morghen) head…and pops out the other side! (Incidentally this is the only murder committed by a *living* person during the film's 92 minutes.) Yet speaking to *L'Ecran Fantastique* magazine, Fulci said Bob's death scene meant a little more: "… [the scene] in which the young Bob undergoes a trepanning is a cry against a certain kind of fascism. […] The father of this girl kills Bob because Bob is a different marginal being: a terrified victim who doesn't understand the hostility which is unleashed upon him."

While we are on the Gore Score, another full 10 can be dished out to the scene where poor Rose Kelvin (Daniela Doria) vomits up her entire intestinal tract. To accomplish this majestic feat, Fulci exclaimed, "We had to use the entrails of a sheep that had just had its throat cut which really had to be swallowed by the actress and which she then had to vomit up. Horrible, isn't it!" (Indeed, Lucio, even though a fake head is clearly employed to finish off the gag.)

Aside from all the splatter, the final ingredient that cements *City of the Living Dead* into a masterpiece of visceral horror is its eerie musical soundtrack. Fabio Frizzi had already created the unforgettable "zombie march" for *Zombie* simply by combining the banging of his hand onto a microphone with the use of the

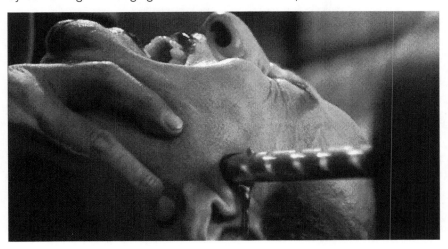

mellotron keyboard, the latter of which would become synonymous with Fulci's best efforts. Here, Frizzi again uses a modified version of the zombie march, as well as deep percussion beats to signal the arrival of impending doom.

The worldwide success of *City of the Living Dead* ($13 million according to Motion Picture Marketing founder Lon Kerr who handled U.S. distribution duties) meant that plenty of audience members were caught off guard during one of its many international runs. However, even more gorehounds became aware of it via videocassette. Back in the days when fans could easily find bootleg dubs of VHS tapes at flea markets, one such dealer had a copy of *The Gates of Hell* (along with *Psycho II*) which I snapped up, my interest piqued by the coverage in *Fangoria*. Needless to say, I was blown away for all of the reasons mentioned above—I had never seen anything like it up to that point...and still haven't for that matter.

While its reputation has grown exponentially over the years, *City of the Living Dead* still seems to take a backseat to other Fulci classics like *Zombie* and *The Beyond*. Most modern critics conclude that it doesn't hold up as well, mainly because the story makes no sense (including the indefensible final freeze frame as young John John runs towards the camera, with screams on the soundtrack as the film stock rips apart). Yet for me, and countless others, *The Gates of Hell* will always remain open no matter how many times we visit Dunwich.

Dave Kosanke has been self-publishing Liquid Cheese, *"the fanzine of movies and music to mangle your mind," for the better part of 20 years, and been on the writing staff of* HorrorHound Magazine *for the past five. He has also written for such notable publications as* Ultra Violent, Midnight Marquee *and* Scary Monsters.

THE COMPANY OF WOLVES 1984

BY KEVIN MATTHEWS

"OH, THEY'RE NICE AS PIE UNTIL THEY'VE HAD THEIR WAY WITH YOU. BUT ONCE THE BLOOM IS GONE... OH, THE BEAST COMES OUT."

It's sometimes very easy to recall my first encounters with certain movies that fired my passion for cinema and it's sometimes very, very difficult. I can easily envision the Hammer double-bills on TV that I was allowed to sit up and watch if I didn't distract the babysitter from taping the best albums from my parent's impressive selection of vinyl. But *The Company of Wolves*...well, I can't remember the specifics. Released in 1984, I can only guess that I was 10 or 11 years old when I saw it for the first time on British TV and that initial encounter is lost in a muddled collection of memories—but that's almost as it should be. Writer/director Neil Jordan's second feature so consummately captures the atmosphere of dreams that any sharper memory would be at odds with the way it seeped into my mind, seemingly melding its imagery with pre-existing thoughts already rambling around my subconscious. *The Company of Wolves* is a dream caught at 24 fps, and the impression it made has stuck with me forever.

Upon mentioning this title to seasoned horror fans, I usually get this reaction: "Oh yeah, that *is* a great movie. I always forget about it." Why? Why is it so often forgotten? Is it the deliberate way everything is stylized — constantly reminding viewers they are watching a presentation of fictions? Or did it just have the misfortune to come out only three years after a great trio of lycanthrope films: *Wolfen*, *The Howling*, and, of course, *An American Werewolf in London*? Or is it a combination of both?

Jordan's blending and filtering divergent shapeshifting fables through the mesh of human sexuality stands up (thanks to his superior direction and the source material from Angela Carter, with whom he collaborated on the screen-

play) as one of the finest werewolf movies, one of the finest British horrors, and a modern classic full of memorable moments, potent imagery, and surreal visuals. It's also a fantastic celebration of storytelling and the power of tales that can enter our lives at any time and stay with us forever. Oh, that may sound a bit flowery, but even as a very young lad I could spot many scenes and moments that referenced legends and stories I was already familiar with. Despite its strange (but oh-so-impressive) atmosphere from start to finish, almost everything onscreen serves as a reminder that these stories retain their power and moral lessons even when we all know that they're "just" stories.

Events ostensibly take place within the dreams of a young girl, Rosaleen (Sarah Patterson), allowing for a number of disparate and yet subtly linked vignettes covering a range of traditional werewolf stories and dark fables. They are as follows:

1) A traveling man who weds a woman goes outside on their wedding night to answer nature's call...and ends up answering a call of nature; 2) a young man, upon meeting the devil in the middle of the woods, is given a transformative potion; 3) a wedding party of carefree noble folk is cursed by a woman formerly abandoned by the groom; 4) a village hunts a wolf, but confusion and fear ensue when a severed paw doesn't remain a paw; 5) Little Red Riding Hood, of course, and 6) a feral girl looked after by a kindly priest cannot resist the lure of her wild roots.

Most of those tales are related to young Rosaleen by her gran (Angela Lansbury, absolutely wonderful) although the young girl gets to tell a couple of her own. Every segment is entertaining enough on the surface, but writhing beneath almost every line of dialogue and startling image is an undercurrent

of psychosexuality. The ebb and flow of the different narrative strands are perfectly paced, not allowing the whole enterprise to feel like a simple anthology movie, which it could easily have done.

Company of Wolves was quite well received when released, with a number of critics (including Roger Ebert) lauding the visuals and disturbing content, and while it was far from the year's biggest money-maker, it did return a profit. Lavishly executed, the movie mixes some of the very best artistry and design ever seen in the werewolf movie subgenre with a clever script delivered by a superb cast. Despite the ever-watchable likes of Stephen Rea, Brian Glover, David Warner, Jim Carter, and Terence Stamp, it ends up being Danielle Dax (best known as a rock musician) and a dancer named Micha Bergese who steal the show as stars of their separate tales.

Christopher Tucker's special effects may not be quite as impressive nowadays as they seemed back in 1984, but they make up in creativity and wonderment what they lack in realism. Despite ambition occasionally exceeding resources, every big FX moment ends up being memorable for all the right reasons. This is a grim Grimm fairy tale, a bloodied *Le Petit Chaperon Rouge*, accentuated beautifully by Anton Furst's astonishing production design and a haunting score by George Fenton that, come the darkly magical finale, will have goosebumps appearing all over your arms.

Literary types will also appreciate how the movie effortlessly evokes Angela Carter's distinctive style. Take the following excerpt: "They will be like shadows, they will be like wraiths, grey members of a congregation of nightmare; hark! His long, wavering howl…an aria of fear made audible." It was Carter's vivid poetry that obviously drew Jordan to the material, inspiring in turn so many beautiful visuals.

Jordan's other works that have even one toe dipped in the genre (*Interview with the Vampire*, *Byzantium*, *In Dreams*, *The Butcher Boy*, and, um, *High Spirits*) demonstrate that he is well aware of the trappings of on-screen horror/fantasy and relishes the opportunities to embrace the tropes while also transforming them. On the superb DVD commentary, the director states that *Company of Wolves* doesn't work as a horror movie because it doesn't deliver what is expected from such a film. With the greatest of respect, I beg to differ. It may not work as a *standard* horror movie for those wanting bloodshed, gratuitous nudity, or other easy pleasures but it's most certainly a haunting classic. I invite you to approach Jordan and Carter's shared vision with an open mind; eyes and ears alert to every detail, nuance, and delightful thread in a tapestry that covers a hell of a lot of ground concerning the nature of the beast inside us all.

> *Kevin Matthews still lives in Edinburgh and still really, really likes it there. He regularly writes for Flickfeast, tries to contribute daily to his blog, For It Is Man's Number, and spends as much time as possible watching movies (mainly horror, of course), writing about movies and generally diverting as many conversations as possible toward the subject of movies. Fortunately, he has a very understanding wife.*

CRIMES AT THE DARK HOUSE 1940

BY ROBIN SCHUMAKER

If one were to watch a lot of low-budget, inexpensive, public domain films, and especially if those titles were to be found on those cheap 50-100 disc sets, it would safe to assume that one has watched a lot of bad movies. Since many of these have no redemptive

"I'LL SQUEEZE THE LIFE OUT OF YOUR GREASY BODY!"

qualities while others can only claim dubious entertainment value, it would not be unreasonable to wonder why someone would subject themselves to such misery. The answer is quite simple. Sometimes, every so often, while sifting through the dreck and tedious trash, a hidden treasure emerges, one that makes sitting through the rest worthwhile. Such are the films of Tod Slaughter, including the little-known *Crimes at the Dark House*, directed by George King.

The 1930s were a great time for horror movies. In the United States, Universal Pictures was having much success with their classic monster pictures such as *Dracula* and *Frankenstein* (both 1931) and their ensuing progeny. But while the Count was draining the blood of his victims and the misunderstood Frankenstein Monster was rampaging through the countryside looking for friendship and understanding, a series of (onscreen) murders were taking place in Great Britain. The perpetrator of these crimes was Tod Slaughter.

Born in 1885 in Newcastle-upon-Tyne, Norman Carter Slaughter (oh, how even his name is suggestive of his destiny!) started his acting career on the stage, performing various roles in the popular Victorian melodramas, and continued to do so until his death in 1956 at age 70. Fortunately for future generations, he later went into film acting and, together with producer/director George King, made a series of low-budget melodramas.

While his debut feature was *Maria Marten, or Murder in the Red Barn* (1935), based on an actual murder case in Britain, Slaughter is probably best known for his role as Sweeney Todd in the 1936 production of *The Demon Barber of Fleet Street*, a non-musical version of the story and the first of his collaborations with King. The duo would ally forces six more times: *The Crimes of Stephen Hawke* (1936), *It's Never Too Late to Mend* (1937), *The Ticket of Leave Man* (1937), *Sexton Blake and the Hooded Terror* (1938), *The Face at the Window* (1939), and, of course, *Crimes at the Dark House*. Slaughter was almost always the villain in these period films, and he over-played these roles with gusto and flair.

Crimes at the Dark House is one of the more entertaining entries in Slaughter's filmography. Like many of the Universal horrors, it is loosely based on a Victorian novel; in this case, *The Woman in White* by Wilkie Collins. It is essentially a tale of identity theft, set in a period when such a crime had a more romantic and glamorous image. The modern day identity thief just uses a computer and numbers to commit the deception. The false Sir Percival Glyde had to go through the trouble of murder, marriage, and mayhem in order to perpetrate his wrongdoings!

Crimes opens with a murder in Australia, with Slaughter seen sneaking into a tent and driving a stake through a prospector's head. While rifling through the victim's belongings, he finds a letter stating that the victim is Sir Percival Glyde and that he has inherited the estate of Blackwater. Slaughter decides to impersonate the dead lord, return to England, and seize the Blackwater estate

by masquerading as the newly offed nobleman. Fortunately for him, none of the servants have been employed long enough to remember the real Sir Percival's youth. Taken with a comely lass in his employ, the false Sir Percival twirls his mustache, licks his lips, and has her reassigned as chambermaid (i.e., in his bedroom) rather than the parlor maid. Meeting with the family lawyer, Mr. Merriman, he learns that the estate is in great debt and that he is, in fact, penniless. His deception is nearly discovered after the lawyer asks to see a mole on his hip, but the solicitor backs off when Slaughter roars an indignant "Damn it, sir, are you asking me to remove my trousers?!" Merriman then suggests that a marriage to a rich noblewoman—already arranged by the deceased father—may be a way to get out of debt. Of course, the path to the money may require murder and committing certain ladies to an insane asylum, but all's fair when you are an aristocrat. But who is that ghostly figure in white that seems to haunt him?

The main narrative is reasonably straightforward, but with plenty of twists and turns to keep the viewer intrigued. In some movies, such convolutions can bog down the narrative and result in a loss of interest. Fortunately, *Crimes* moves along at such a rollicking pace, with necessary dialogue well interspersed with scenes of action, that it never gets boring. Indeed, it is a bit of a roller coaster ride, and given its short 69-minute run time, it has a surprisingly high body count.

But Slaughter's bombastic performance is really the film's *raison d'etre.* The rest of the cast performs admirably, but they are only props the overripe thespian uses to ply his trade. The style of acting is certainly dated—one can envision Slaughter as an older silent movie villain tying his victim to the train tracks. He delights in his dastardliness and relishes his evil role. Physically impressive, Slaughter towers over most of the rest of the cast, hamming it up to heights seldom seen in modern cinema, complete with maniacal laughter, gleefully rubbing his hands, and, of course, twirling his mustache. But when he later employs more subtle facial expressions to complement these overt mannerisms, one can't help but be impressed. The florid dialogue (by H.F. Maltby) suits the star perfectly, providing juicy lines ("I'll feed your entrails to the pigs.") for Slaughter to deliver with unfettered zeal. His is the grandeur of the stage and the silent era transferred to the talking picture. While his performances lack the realism of modern cinema, his full-blooded portrayals of such thoroughly despicable characters simply add to the overall charm.

From the opening (stake in the head!) to its fiery climax, *Crimes at the Dark House* is a wonderfully entertaining film, and a product of a sadly bygone era. A multitude of creative murders, a dastardly villain who doesn't spare anyone, and some remarkably risqué themes (for the time) all contribute to its virtues. It represents the last of the King/Slaughter collaborations, and as such has a bit of a nostalgic feel to it. Some of the dialogue had become familiar, and Slaughter's mannerisms had become iconic. For some this may make it a bit stale, but for me, it just adds to the fun of it all. The performances of this maniacal Englishman are at least the equal of those of Boris Karloff, Bela Lugosi, and company on the other side of the Atlantic, and certainly warrant discovery by a new generation.

Robin Schumaker has enjoyed frightening movies since seeing the Wicked Witch in The Wizard of Oz *as a child and* Halloween *in the theater. In his regular life, he has been covered in as much blood as Carrie White at the prom and as much vomit as Mr. Creosote's unfortunate waiter, and has held a human heart in his hand like Mola Ram, but prefers to relax and watch movies with his family.*

THE CURSE OF THE WEREWOLF 1961

BY REENE KNIPE

> "OH YES, THAT'S RIGHT. THEY CHAIN UP WILD ANIMALS. THAT'S WHAT I AM... AN ANIMAL!"

There's a shot late in *The Curse of the Werewolf* in which the eponymous lycanthrope—teeth protruding over its upper lip, heavy brow atop red-limned eyes—stalks the camera while shadows play across its face. It's a beautifully atmospheric moment giving us our first real look at Roy Ashton's superlative wolfman makeup, and for that, it's become the most famous shot in the film. No doubt this is why it was featured prominently in the opening credits and commercial tags of the Saturday afternoon creature feature program that played on the local Detroit station when I was kid. Over the course of many, many Saturdays, it became indelibly etched upon my brain and it remains, to my mind, one of the most iconic images in all of horror movie history.

That memory feels like it's always been with me. I've even been known to claim *Curse of the Werewolf* as my "first horror movie," which can't possibly be true. In fact, I clearly remember comfortably watching it from the floor of our second home—the one my parents took over payments of from my grandparents—which means I could not have seen it any earlier than the ripe old age of four or five, by which time I was already an old hand at the monster movie thing. It was, however, my very first *werewolf movie*, and its effect upon me was profound; as a child struggling with issues of identity, the transformative power of the werewolf was equal parts fascinating and terrifying. To this day, werewolves remain my favorite of all monsters, and *Curse of the Werewolf* stands at the very top of my list of such stories.

The prologue sets up a couple of the film's essential themes: That the actions of others can shape the soul, and that the soul can shape the body. It opens with a beggar (Richard Wordsworth) arriving in a tiny Spanish village to find a celebration in full swing. He calls upon the local lord, Marques Siniestro (Anthony Dawson), hoping to be fed, but is instead treated like a dog and imprisoned in the dungeon. In time, he succumbs to his circumstances, becoming more and more bestial. Only a mute serving girl (Yvonne Romain) treats him with any kindness. It is, unfortunately, kindness not to be repaid; when she later repulses Siniestro's lecherous advances, he imprisons her with the feral beggar, who rapes her. She escapes and avenges herself upon the Marques, then flees the household, pregnant with the beggar's child.

The girl tries to drown herself in a pond but is rescued by a gentleman, Don Alfredo (Clifford Evans). Hers is a temporary respite, however, as she dies giving birth to Leon on Christmas Day. Soon after, during the infant's baptism, the image of a gargoyle is seen reflected in the water...a bad omen if ever there was one. God has turned away from this unwanted child born on His son's birthday, and in the absence of His gaze, a bestial spirit has taken up residence in Leon. Don Alfredo is advised that weakness and vice (and the full moon) will weaken Leon's defenses and let loose the beast in the boy's body, while love will strengthen the soul and gird him against evil. There's a brush with a shepherd, his flock, and a local hunter, but Don Alfredo's fatherly affection (and a set of thick iron bars on Leon's bedroom windows) reins him in and keeps him (and the villagers) safe.

That is, until Leon (Oliver Reed) reaches adulthood and, believing himself cured, sets out to build a life of his own in the nearby village. In no time at all, he finds himself gainfully employed and enamored (reciprocally) of his employer's very beautiful daughter, Cristina (Catherine Feller). Life is good, but happiness is short-lived, as wine and a visit to a brothel with his randy coworker bring the beast lurching to the surface.

Curse of the Werewolf is an archetypical Hammer film in many ways. It's a period piece, shot on the Bray Studios backlot, replete with gorgeous gothic sets recycled in that classic Hammer way from pieces built for another picture. Terence Fisher, Hammer's go-to guy, is on hand to direct Anthony Hinds' script (adapted from Guy Endore's classic *The Werewolf of Paris*). The blood, as always, is a garish red, and the usual Puritanical morality is in place (spoiler: The Church is pure and good and you do not want to be a sexually available woman in this film).

But the ways in which it differs are telling. It's a sweeping story (we first meet Leon's mother when she's still a child, and Oliver Reed doesn't even appear onscreen until the halfway point), lending it something of an epic, timeless quality. And there are moments that seem, in the words of one of my viewing companions, "almost Disney-like" (a mustache-twirling aristocratic villain named Sinister; a leaving-home-for-the-big-wide-world scene that practically screams for singing bluebirds). But this isn't Disney. What my friend is feeling is something older, something that might have dripped from the lips of the Brothers Grimm themselves. That may be the most distinctive thing of all, because unlike many Hammer films, there are no happy endings on the horizon here.

Werewolf movies, as a genre, tend to be cynical. In *An American Werewolf in London*, our afflicted protagonist's horror movie lore tells him that he can only be slain by someone who loves him. He's wrong, but he's onto something: what werewolf films are really telling us is that *love can't save you*. It's a message that warms the cockles of this skeptic's heart, and which *Curse of the Werewolf* plays with explicitly, positing as it

does a hope for salvation...and then undoing that hope at every turn. Worse, Hinds' screenplay suggests that cruelty is more powerful than love; when Larry Talbot succumbs to his curse in *The Wolf Man*, it is simple misfortune, the whims of an uncaring universe. But in *Curse*, suffering always results from the human failing of not being able to love enough: The mute serving girl's kindness can't shield her from violence, Don Alfredo's affection is an impermanent sanctuary reinforced with iron bars, and Cristina's love runs deep but not wide enough to envelope Leon the way he truly needs. They want, like all of us, to believe in love...it just fails them.

Still, if this were any other fright flick, the monster's death would at the very least grant some reprieve. But *Curse of the Werewolf* plays for keeps, saving the greatest horror for its closing moments. I'll leave you to discover it for yourself, saying only this: the film begins and ends with our werewolf crying, haunting images that serve as the perfect bookends for Leon's tragic story.

Renee Knipe is a lifelong horror fan who would like nothing better than to someday craft the definitive werewolf film. She studies video production in Ann Arbor, Michigan, and lives in nearby Ypsilanti with her cat, Rufus. (Yes, named after the cat in Re-Animator! *How kind of you to ask.)*

CURTAINS 1983

BY MARK ALLAN GUNNELLS

"HAVE YOU EVER WANTED ANYTHING SO BADLY YOU'D DO ANYTHING FOR IT?"

When I was a kid, I watched every horror movie I could get my hands on. Some were great, some mediocre, and many were downright wretched. Of these, there were a number that I continued to watch often well into adulthood. A few I never wanted to see again. And then there were a handful that I never saw again after the initial viewing but always remembered fondly.

Among these was a film whose title I could never remember and therefore was impossible to track down. I remembered bits and pieces of the plot, but one image stood out more than any other: a killer wearing a creepy "hag" mask ice-skating across a frozen pond, bent on decapitating a young woman with a sickle. Long after I had forgotten many of the specifics, that scene remained burned on my brain. What better compliment can a film receive than to have produced a moment that someone finds unforgettable?

Later, with the rise of the internet, I visited an online horror message board, posted what I could remember of the plot, and asked if anyone knew the title. I received an answer almost immediately—the 1983 Canadian feature *Curtains*. At the time, there was no official DVD release, but I did manage to locate it on YouTube. In many cases of revisiting a childhood fright flick as an adult, I've often been disappointed; cheap and silly with bad acting and effects, they do not live up to my rose-colored memory. As such, I approached my re-watch with trepidation. To my delight, I found it just as enjoyable decades later.

Starring John Vernon of *Animal House* fame and Samantha Eggar from *The Brood*, *Curtains* tells the story of several actresses who spend the weekend at a director's mountain cabin during a snowstorm to audition for a role in his next production. Each actress has her reasons for desperately wanting the part...and one of them may even be willing to kill for it.

According to Caelum Vatnsdal's *They Came from Within: A History of Canadian Horror Cinema*, filming on *Curtains* began in 1980 but the project,

 amidst rewrites and reshoots, wasn't finished until 1983. It is suggested that a lot of the problems stemmed from producer Peter Simpson who, having produced the Jamie Lee Curtis vehicle *Prom Night*, wanted another straightforward horror flick. Director Richard Ciupka, on the other hand, chose to go against the established slasher grain, bringing a more European sensibility to the production. The original screenplay even had a supernatural element, with a creature designed (but never used) by makeup legend Greg Cannom. A year after the first cut was delivered, Simpson himself directed many reshoots, whereupon Ciupka demanded to have his name removed from the picture. The onscreen directing credit was eventually given to "Jonathan Stryker," the name of the fictional director in the movie.

There was some recasting as well. Most famously, Adam Rockoff reports in *Going to Pieces: The Rise and Fall of the Slasher Film* that Celine Lomez was originally cast in the role of Brooke but was fired over her unwillingness to do full frontal nudity and replaced with Linda Thorson. Ironically, no full frontal nudity is featured in the completed movie.

Lost in the early '80s glut of slasher films, *Curtains* was not a great financial success upon initial release, overlooked by the majority of moviegoers. But it certainly made an impression on this horror fan. Re-watching it recently, I was impressed by how well it stands up all these years later. Ciupka directs his first feature film with a sure hand, giving it a great look and atmosphere, that European sensibility that upset Simmons so. The setting is highly effective; I've always been of the opinion that snowstorms are more frightening than thunderstorms and make a much better backdrop for horror. Budgeted under $4 million, the film has some great production values. Even via a poor video transfer watched on a laptop, *Curtains* still looks *good*.

In addition to the ice skating kill that made such an impression, there

are many other standout moments in this well-paced and exciting movie. A dream sequence involving a life-sized doll is truly creepy, and an extended chase scene with one of the unfortunate actresses culminates with the seemingly perfect hiding place becoming the perfect deathtrap. The ending manages to provide an unexpected and interesting twist, and the final shot is both disturbing and darkly amusing.

The actors and actresses involved vary in the talent department, but all the characters have distinctive personalities and are well defined. For me, the standout is Lynn Griffin as quirky stand-up comedian Patti. Griffin bristles with personality and charm—in the scene where she auditions alone for Vernon, she shows real steel and fire. Eggar also impresses in the prologue, a stunning sequence where her actress character checks herself into an asylum to get into the mindset of a deranged lunatic, only to end up understanding insanity a *little* too well. It is a fine line for an actress to tread, and she straddles it perfectly.

I love horror for its escapism and adrenaline rush, but what I love most are fright flicks that strive for more than just mindless murder. *Curtains* has ambition, delivering thrills with style and intelligence. It's unfortunate its initial release proved such a bust and that so few modern horror fans have even heard of the film. In the end, it seems the creative disagreements between Simpson and Ciupka and its subsequent late entry in the slasher race doomed the picture to obscurity.

To wit: as of this writing, *Curtains* has never received a proper DVD release. In 2010, it was included in a compilation set (*Midnight Horror Collection: Bloody Slashers*) with three recent straight-to-DVD horror movies Over the years, there have been several online petitions by fans urging Echo Bridge to re-release *Curtains* as a stand-alone DVD with a better transfer and some special features. However, so far there has been no movement on that front.

Even though some might find its hard-to-locate status daunting, I strongly urge fans of the slasher genre to watch this film. With an intriguing plotline, interesting characters, memorable kills, and a satisfying conclusion, what more could you want? Whether you find the Echo Bridge compilation or watch it on YouTube or Hulu, it deserves to be dusted off and rediscovered. Let's open the curtains again on *Curtains*.

Mark Allan Gunnells has been writing since he was 10 years old. He has published over 15 books over the past 5 years with various small press publishers. He lives with his partner Craig A. Metcalf in Greer, SC.

DARK NIGHT OF THE SCARECROW 1981

BY DAVE FUENTES

> "DON'T YOU KNOW WHAT HE'S DOING? HE'S PLAYING THE HIDING GAME."

My world would never be the same after *Dark Night of the Scarecrow* made its October 24th, 1981, debut. I was eleven years old; too young to see scary movies at the theater and my household bereft of the newfangled innovation of home video. This made-for-television feature, however, sidestepped these obstacles and its arrival was nothing short of monumental. My enthusiasm was not in vain and I remained a devoted fan of Hollywood's first killer scarecrow for years after it entered obscurity. I carried the memory of its pulse-pounding final seconds well on into adulthood, inspiring a lifelong desire to one day procure it for my horror library. While '70s and '80s television horror did have a few bright spots (e.g. *Salem's Lot* and *Duel*), none achieved the lasting impact that this film had on me.

Written by J.D. Feigelson, the story takes place in a small, rural town where the developmentally challenged Bubba Ritter (Larry Drake) innocently plays with his young companion, Marylee Williams (Tonya Crowe). This cross-generational friendship doesn't sit well with a few of the locals, especially the town's diabolical mailman, Otis Hazelrigg (Charles Durning), who's convinced the relationship is anything but pure. After Marylee is injured by a dog, rumors spread that she has been killed by Bubba whereupon Otis summons his red-neck cronies faster than you can say *Of Mice and Men*. Bubba's attempt to disguise himself inside the family scarecrow proves unsuccessful and his haunting first-person plea, "Bubba didn't do it!" goes unheeded. The makeshift firing squad responds with a barrage of bullets with the revelation of Marylee not only alive, but having been rescued by Bubba, arriving moments too late. The town's kangaroo court allows the killers to walk free amid the screams of Bubba's grieving mother (Jocelyn Brando). "There are other kinds of justice in this world," she cries, "besides the law!" Her words prove prophetic as the assailants each begin to meet their untimely deaths.

This compelling, revenge-from-the-grave tale was reminiscent of the popular EC Comics that proliferated during the '50s. These stories often provided lurid and graphic narratives of earthly injustices being rectified by the supernatural. *Dark Night of the Scarecrow*, though neither lurid nor graphic, achieves even more hair-raising results by using clever filming techniques to accompany its well-written screenplay and stellar cast. While many fans balk at the notion of an effective horror tale being created for a general audience, this film represents the rule's exception.

One reason it stands apart from most TV offerings was director Frank De Felitta's refusal to ever approach it as one. Abandoning techniques reserved for the small screen, cinematographer Vince Martinelli used wide angled shots providing full view of the character's surroundings, something much more common in theatrical releases versus commercial broadcasts at that time.

This same consideration was given to the film's soundtrack. De Felitta bypassed traditional composers in favor of Glen Paxton, despite his having no experience in horror. On the 2012 Blu-ray commentary, De Felitta states that this decision was based on Paxton's ability to "get into a picture." The result is a truly chilling score so effective that it often provides narrative in scenes otherwise devoid of dialogue. This is illustrative in the moments following the killer's discovery of Bubba's innocence; as the men stare guiltily at his blood-soaked body, the macabre notes, accompanied by a sudden breeze, alert viewers of a supernatural presence just as effectively as John Williams' famous chords heralded the arrival of the shark in 1975's *Jaws*.

De Felitta would also prove highly deft at maneuvering around a medium that prohibits gore. Take, for example, the moments following the death of a character who finds himself in the wrong end of a wood-chipper (the first on-screen utilization of this device as an instrument of death). Just as the victim

falls in, De Felitta immediately cuts to the next scene featuring a close-up of strawberry preserves being dabbled onto a breakfast plate. Although not a trace of blood was ever visible, viewer impact remains the same.

The novice cast provides brilliant performances, especially a then-unknown Larry Drake. Feigelson felt that casting a familiar actor would hinder the illusion of Bubba's disabilities and this proved a keen decision as, for years afterwards, many speculated if Drake really was mentally challenged. His character becomes an unlikely hero as he protects Marylee and wards off potential trouble, customary of the effigy he'd become.

Dark Night of the Scarecrow also marked the first starring vehicle for Charles Durning, a role he did not relish due to his view that the character had no redeeming qualities. (Feigelson specifically chose his occupation as a postman because "no one's afraid of the mailman.") Otis, a man who hides his inferiority by adopting a superior stance, fashions himself as a General of sorts, his postal uniform aiding in his delusions while deceiving most everyone around him. He feigns noble intentions in his concern for Marylee despite subtle clues that his true feelings are far less savory. Regardless of his imposture, he's unable to conceal his true nature from Mrs. Ritter who doesn't hesitate to remind him, "The only official thing you've ever done is lick stamps!"

At the center of the drama is Tonya Crowe's Marylee Williams who, despite her age, shows extraordinary talent displaying a mature range of emotions.

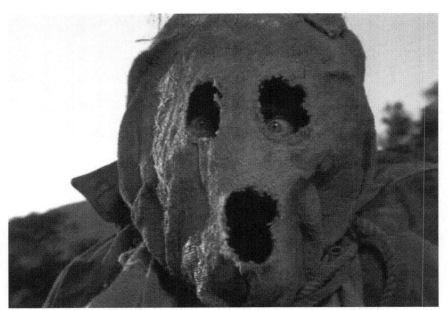

While most kids claiming to commune with the dead would doubtless appear creepy, Crowe manages to do so while fully retaining her character's innocence.

Killer scarecrows have appeared in many films since *Dark Night of the Scarecrow* but few designs would ever prove as striking. Appearing more as a symbol than a protagonist, its mere presence sends chills. Feigelson clearly understood that the simplest designs can be the most effective when he created it in his own studio. "I designed the scarecrow after writing the script, then I got together with art director Bill Griffin and he constructed the head first before we added the body," says Feigelson. "It went through a few minor revisions including doing away with a nose. Our final creation was the one eventually used in the movie."

Though well received by viewers—including Vincent Price who told Stanley Waiter in the book *Dark Visions*, "...it was mar-vel-ous! I was terrified!"—the film remained scarce for the next thirty years with only a brief VHS release and a cult following of bootlegging fans keeping it alive. Its perseverance surprised Feigelson though not Drake who told me in 2011, "...it endured [because] it was a great story; I knew that it would have legs." The film was finally given a digital upgrade in 2010 followed by a Blu-ray release in 2012—the same year Paxton's score also became available. Despite these innovations, it remains generally unknown to the average horror fan and is absolutely worthy of their attention.

In the end, *Dark Night of the Scarecrow* teaches us that a loving friendship not only transcends death, but trumps evil. Over thirty years later, it still holds up today despite its initial TV limitations. In this regard the picture is not unlike Bubba, where sometimes an imperfect package can yield the greatest of treasures.

Dave Fuentes resides in Chicago, Illinois, and is co-blogger of the Rondo Award-winning "Terror from Beyond the Daves." He's written for Horrorhound Magazine, G-FAN *and* Scary Monsters Magazine. *Fuentes recently participated as a judge in the Madison Horror Filmfest.*

DARK WATERS 1993

BY GERT VERBEECK

> "FOR THOSE WHO ARE BLIND SHALL SEE THE TRUE FACE OF THE BEAST AND FOREVER SUFFER IT IN THEIR SOUL."

During the nineties, my desire to absorb as much cinema as humanly possible led me to several rental stores across our small Belgian country; shops that would go the extra mile in offering imported VHS tapes, hidden gems that might otherwise have never found their way to our viewing market. At the time, my interest and love for Italian horror was growing strong and steady (thanks to discovering the works of masters like Dario Argento, Michele Soavi, and Lamberto Bava), and it was thus that I came across Mariano Baino's *Dark Waters*. In retrospect, the nineties are considered a thoroughly lame decade for the horror genre. But people who claim nothing decent or original came out during that time simply aren't making an effort. *Dark Waters*, alongside Bernard Rose's *Candyman* and Richard Stanley's *Dust Devil* (both 1992), is a prime example of a filmmaker daring to explore new ground or at least tread it differently.

Some viewers have described *Dark Waters* as being in the tradition of Argento and Mario Bava. I beg to differ. For starters, Baino uses completely different aesthetics to shape his film on virtually all levels. Tangibly flavored with H.P. Lovecraft's Cthulhu Mythos, religion—and its possible condemnation—is the strongest theme running throughout (as well as the undeniable power of money). These aspects are rarely found in any film by Argento or Bava, clearly differentiating Baino from his contemporaries. This youthful director delivered a picture with a consistently grim and eerie tone, while at the same time introducing us to a compelling mystery—the kind that once you dive in, you never come out...at least not the same way you entered.

Appropriately titled, *Dark Waters* incorporates themes that shun the light of day, with Baino showing us a mere tip of the proverbial iceberg. This approach keeps much of the mystery intact, indicating that the depths presented here are more abyss-like than one might imagine. Notions such as money being a necessary evil, used to feed, breed, and maintain more evil while the users are convinced of its greater good, or the idea of humans spawned by hidden ungodly mothers walking among us in ignorance. These are fertile concepts, yielding authentic and original cinematic nightmares.

While Baino's magnum opus is a tight and solid film, the genesis of this *pièce de résistance maléfique*, a Russian-Italian-British co-production shot largely on location in Ukraine, was far from smooth. The struggles with getting his first full-length feature completed reached near-mythical proportions, with reels of film stock disappearing (read: being re-sold on the black market) being one of the more mundane problems encountered. Foremost was the cultural clash between the local crew and Baino's English corps of collaborators, a rift which would represent the source of many misgivings during the three-month shoot. The local crew members' enormous consumption of vodka was problematic and the local production manager would often promise much the night before…and deliver nothing the next day. If one ever needed proof that perseverance prevails, they need look no further than the production of *Dark Waters*.

In light of all that went wrong, it's somewhat miraculous that one particularly complex scene from the film's opening sequence went right on the first take. Shot with multiple cameras, we see a chapel being flooded. Walls collapse and a priest nearly drowns before ultimately being impaled by a giant cross through the throat. The prologue also introduces the isolated island setting, a convent with a sinister order of nuns, and a strangely repulsive artifact: a sculpted seal incorporating a demon's head. Devoid of dialogue, it's an impressive opening that puts all the key elements into place and sets the foreboding tone for the rest of the movie. (*Dark Waters* relies heavily on mood and atmosphere, inarguably strong assets that are established early on and maintained throughout. Its sometimes glacial pace is an appropriately chilling one.)

We are then introduced to Elizabeth, played by the gracefully beautiful Louise Salter in her debut role. Her reasons for traveling to the convent are twofold. Her friend Theresa (Anna Rose Phipps) resides there to sort some things out, staying in touch via letters. But even more compelling is Elizabeth's recent discovery of her father's twenty years of regular payments to the order of nuns following his sudden religious conversion. With the convent harboring a terrifying secret, Elizabeth's journey into this macabre world very much becomes one of self-discovery, eventually undermining the established psychological/ emotional strength of her character and providing the film's primary conflict.

In terms of acting, Salter is well-matched by Venera Simmons (whose appearance in *Dark Waters* remains, like co-star Phipps, her sole screen acting credit). Simmons plays Sarah, a young nun who cherishes her wish to visit England some day (which results in a fine moment between her and Elizabeth when the latter remarks "You'd hate it, Sarah," and nonchalantly offers a cigarette to the naïve youth). While clearly inexperienced, Sarah's role will become pivotal in guiding Elizabeth through her ordeals. The other supporting characters aren't required to bring a great deal to the acting table (their roles are relatively minor), but all are exquisitely cast based on their looks and charisma.

Alex Howe's astounding cinematography elevates the film immeasurably. Opting between static framing, liquid camera movements, and the occasional Steadicam shot, the action within each frame is well-choreographed and the lighting put to supreme use. Thanks to Baino's keen vision being executed by a

capable crew, viewers bear witness to some truly haunting imagery throughout (such as the two girls standing before the crucified *monja sin ojos*). Rarely has such dark and twisted religious symbolism been rivaled onscreen.

To support and enhance the madness, one-off movie composer Igor Clark provides a suitably moody score, whether it it is ominous analog synth soundscapes or the more grandiloquent main theme. Ivan Pulenko's tremendous production design is also worthy of note, even going so far as to building a small coastal village. And the pre-CG special make-up and monster effects during the film's final morbid revelation are ghastly enough to contort any horror fan's facial features into a devilish, appreciative grin.

As with many debut efforts, *Dark Waters* is not without flaws. Baino and co-screenwriter Andrew Bark's dialogue feels a bit artificial at times, yet this strangely suits the otherworldly environment of the island-based convent. In the third act, there's a somewhat less-than-effective fight scene between Elizabeth and a knife-wielding killer nun, but the brutality portrayed works nonetheless. One might also nitpick the chronology of certain smaller events. Yet again, none of this detracts from the overall accomplished result.

Even with his limited CV, Mariano Baino remains a unique and visionary filmmaker and is without a doubt amongst the most intriguing directors to have emerged from the nineties European *cinéma fantastique* landscape. Baino seems a man preferring quality over quantity, steadily building an original body of work drenched in supernatural profundity and I, for one, eagerly look forward to what he unveils next.

Gert Verbeeck resides in Brussels, Belgium. The driving forces in his life are music (his first love), movies (the woman he wants to marry) and writing (the one that keeps coming back to him). Being a musician, he remains active in the Brussels music scene. As a writer/director, he is currently working on his first feature-length screenplay, a genre-blending anthology movie. Gert is also the co-founder of Cult Reviews, a website dedicated to cinema a little more out-of-the-ordinary.

DELLAMORTE DELLAMORE 1994

BY DAVE GRAY

Dellamorte Dellamore is the best Italian zombie movie ever made and arguably the best film out of Italy for the past couple decades. Got your attention? Good. Let's get the basics out of the way. Directed by Michele Soavi from a screenplay by Gianni Romoli, the film stars Rupert Everett as Francesco Dellamorte, Anna Falchi as "She," and François Hadji-Lazaro as Gnaghi. Next, a brief summing up and then on to the good stuff.

> **"OH, COME ON, GNAGHI. THE WORLD'S FULL OF GIRLS LIKE THAT, AND THEY'VE GOT BODIES, TOO."**

Dellamorte started out its life as a novel of the same name by Tziano Sclavi, who would take many of the themes presented in the book as a blueprint for his *fumetto* (graphic novel) *Dylan Dog*. *Dylan Dog* is as influential on Soavi's film as the original novel and while Sclavi had no direct involvement with the production, his hand is everywhere. To wit: Franco Dellamorte from the novel is melded with Dylan to make Francesco Dellamorte who, as already noted, is played by Rupert Everett...on whom Dylan's character design was modeled for the *fumetto*. Not that Sclavi is the only influence; there are allusions to everything from the 1973 biker horror flick *Psychomania* to Rene Magritte's *The Lovers II*.

Soavi spent most of the 1980s as one of Dario Argento's army of protégés, an assistant director on *Tenebrae*, *Phenomena*, and *Opera* and second unit director on Lamberto Bava's *Demons* and Terry Gilliam's *The Adventures of Baron Munchausen*. Soavi's first feature, *Stagefright* (1987), was a solid slasher that suffers from a bit too much Argento influence. In 1989, he took the helm of *The Church* from Lamberto Bava at the last moment, while 1991 brought a team-up with Gianni Romoli for *La Setta*, released in the States as *The Devil's Daughter*. While still too Argento-flavored for my tastes, Soavi starts to come into his own with some wonderfully haunting dreamlike images, including one that would carry over to *Dellamorte*: a snow globe.

We are introduced to Buffalora Cemetery's caretaker Francesco Dellamorte— whose job is more about keeping the dead in the ground than keeping the grounds well maintained—trying to have a nice, normal, everyday talk on the phone. But the damned freshly risen zombies keep knocking on his door like a rotting parade of Jehovah's Witnesses and magazine salesfolk. What else would you expect from a graveyard with the inscription "RESVRRECTVRIS" (Latin for "They Will Resurrect") above the gate? *Dellamorte* is structured more as a series of connected sketches than a sustained narrative, a tack that gives the running themes of carnality and charnality full rein, as well as accommodating the tonal

75

shifts from morbid romance to surreal nightmare to dark comedy, all with a vicious streak of cultural criticism and psychological richness throughout. You can have your blood, guts, and intellectual stimulation too.

At its core, *Dellamorte* is about Francesco dealing with the twin emotions of love and death, attraction and bereavement. To make his predicament with this duality even more personal, we have his surname Dellamorte, a play on "*della morte*" meaning "of Death," and his mother's maiden name Dellamore, a play on "*dell' amore*" meaning "of Love." So the deck is stacked pretty well against Francesco from birth. Early on, our dour caretaker falls for a beautiful, veiled woman (known only as "She") and in an unsurprising turn of events, things only get worse from there. Francesco's inferiority complex puts an early damper on things when confronted with She's devotion to her departed lover, leaving Francesco unable to spark her interest until she sees the vault. Some people like roses and wine, some like oysters and avocado…She likes corpses and bones. She finally welcomes Francesco's advances in the ossuary but only after he's veiled. Which begs the question: Who is she really embracing? Francesco and the new life he represents, her dead husband, or Death itself? She breaks it off before things go very far, her guilt for perceived infidelity personified in the empty staring eye sockets surrounding them.

Since it's a movie, She returns and they try again. Only this time her husband actually does rise from the grave and their intimacy turns to violence via her vengeful undead spouse. Four more encounters with She, in different guises, before it's over, with each renewed life only stirring memories of past loss while adding more scars. Should anyone be surprised when the philophobic and gynophobic fallout leads to a killing spree? Francesco's loss becomes so great that he can no longer see the difference between living and dead. He's killing not because of misogyny but because of disillusionment and misguided self preservation. True, it makes no difference to his victims but it should to viewers.

In *The Great Dictators: Interviews with Filmmakers of Italian Descent*, Soavi explains: "*Dellamorte* represents a major step […] because it deals with important contemporary issues. […] I tried very hard to explain this parallel between his world—closed within the cemetery walls full of life, green, and animals—and the outside world which is supposed to be living but is instead full of boredom." Outside the psycho-sexual themes of the main story, what else could he possibly be talking about? For that we'll have to look at the risen dead. The zombies Francesco encounters are all archetypes of segments of Italian society; some in the past, others still hanging around. There are fascist scouts, corrupt politicians, nuns, and the leader of a young biker gang. The film plays heavily on the Italian love of reverse affirmation of their faith and cultural tides. The key to why the country's moviegoers embraced the undead subgenre lies above the Buffalora cemetery gate: RESVRRECTVRIS.

But why is *Dellamorte* a hidden horror outside of its land of release? First let's look at October Films' mishandled distribution, whose title change to the generic and boring *Cemetery Man* and marketing it as an exploitation flick with the tagline "Zombies, Guns, Sex, OH MY!!!" didn't do it any favors. Secondly, while now (finally) receiving its due critical praise, at the time of its initial release most U.S. and UK critics simply did not understand it or weren't willing to look beyond its horror aspects. Stephen Holden's *New York Times* review grumbled, "For all the repulsive goings-on it's oddly unscary, and after a certain number of zombies have rattled around the old graveyard it all seems terribly repetitive." Finally, Anchor Bay, who has released many fantastic editions of films that wouldn't have gotten a nod elsewhere, issued a lackluster DVD in 2006, years too late for it to register for anyone outside of its small group of existing fans.

Beautifully shot, with a literate script well served by a cast who all deliver superb performances, *Dellamorte* is a unique experience that will raise some strong feelings. Soavi's artistic voice sings as it eloquently explores themes that have eluded others well versed in working in the genre. There are many ways to see every moment, many interpretations for everything. One could walk away from it meditating on the psychosexual tangles or only see a steaming plate of misogyny or a great zombie ride or be completely baffled by it all. There are no easy answers to be found. That, for me, is the highest praise that can be given.

Dave Gray is a former heavyweight sumo wrestler and pet psychic. Created in an experiment to create the ultimate warlord based on Leonardo Da Vinci plans, he dreams instead of floral arrangement. Residing in Maryland (too far from the Bay) with the love of his life, a retriever named Phineas, he scribbles game and tech reviews. When talking about himself, he invariably and heavily lies.

THE DEVIL RIDES OUT 1968

BY MATTHEW DOUGLAS HODGSON

Witchcraft. Mumbo jumbo. Black magic. Concepts that seem more silly than scary in today's technological age. However, these were ideas that once struck fear and paranoia into the hearts of many. I am every bit the sorry skeptic often portrayed in our beloved genre

"I SHALL NOT BE BACK... BUT SOMETHING WILL."

as a stubborn dolt, but even if I don't believe in dark esoteric powers, many do. Dennis Wheatley, the prolific author of 1934's *The Devil Rides Out*, was no exception. The sensationalist dust jackets of his occult novels reveal Wheatley's purported belief in black magic and its secret practitioners operating in 1930s England. Perhaps it was this belief or fear that enabled him to conduct such careful and detailed research into the subject, leading to one of the most serious and informative fictional treatments of the black arts. *The Devil Rides Out* turned out to be his most popular novel, one which had Christopher Lee, Wheatley's neighbor at the time, pounding on the Hammer Studios doors to adapt it into a feature film.

The story begins with two old friends, the Duke de Richleau (played by Lee) and Rex van Ryn (Leon Greene), meeting for their annual reunion. Having shared a number of harrowing adventures, the comrades truly cherish these get-togethers, but Simon Aron (Patrick Mower), the youngest member of their party, is peculiarly absent. It strikes the friends as odd that he would merely

have forgotten, so they pay a visit to his country home to ensure his good health. Unfortunately, the situation only becomes murkier, as they find Simon entertaining guests—a party of 13. The number and Simon's sudden interest in astrology cause the Duke to suspect something sinister of the gathering. His hunch proves correct as Simon is discovered preparing a black magic ceremony alongside a dangerously powerful man, the evil Mocata (Charles Gray), and his minions. The Duke and Rex prepare to combat these occult practitioners, stopping at nothing to rescue their friend from the clutches of darkness, the power of light their only weapon.

Re-titled *The Devil's Bride* in the U.S. (for fear American audiences would think it was a western), the film is widely regarded as one of Hammer's best productions, and as such it might seem an odd candidate for an underappreciated horror film. However, the popularity of Hammer classics has waned over the years, seemingly ignored or undiscovered by new genre recruits. Many titles offer little more than nostalgia—that classic "Studio That Dripped Blood" look—but this is where *The Devil Rides Out* stands out from its Hammer brethren and other 1960-70s fright flicks in general. Rarely has such a venerable ensemble of creative giants been assembled for a single feature film.

Despite its popularity, there is little in Wheatley's novel to enthrall or frighten the modern reader. Maybe it's a product of the times or perhaps it's Wheatley's florid style, which anathematizes the building of any suspense. Fortunately, Richard Matheson, hired to adapt the novel for the screen, displayed considerable talent as a storytelling surgeon. Whether it was the judicious replacement of "monkeying" with "meddling" in one of the Duke's most memorable lines, or the excision of a scene in which the Duke and Rex prepare for a showdown with Mocata by marking each of their "nine openings" with holy water, by discarding numerous irrelevant and absurd elements, Matheson's storytelling experience elevates the content of Wheatley's novel to new heights.

Onscreen, Lee and Gray command our attention as the respective personifications of good and evil. Playing the mastermind Mocata, fashioned by Wheatley after notorious occultist Aleister Crowley, Gray steals almost every scene despite his limited screen time. Already an accomplished TV actor, Gray was just starting to break out in the film biz, having appeared in *You Only Live Twice* and the Nazi murder mystery *Night of the Generals*. Even so, most cult aficionados will probably recognize him as the criminologist and narrator in 1975's *The Rocky Horror Picture Show*.

Lee, by contrast, rarely found himself in the heroic role, having starred as memorably villainous characters such as Fu Manchu and Dracula. As evidenced in an open letter to his fan club, Lee felt that his portrayal of the Duke would convince everyone once and for all that he was capable of playing a "normal" character, not just monsters. The rest of the cast are satisfactory with Leon Greene as Rex the only questionable casting decision. His Australian accent was deemed too difficult to understand and his lines were dubbed by frequent Hammer horror actor Patrick Allen.

Meanwhile, Terence Fisher, director of *The Curse of Frankenstein, Dracula*, and countless other memorable Hammer classics, used his keen editor's eye and directing acumen to allow for an abbreviated shooting schedule, a boon given the £285,000 budget. Fisher's extensive experience was not the only factor making him a good match for Wheatley's material. While not necessarily devout, Fisher believed in the real-life balance of good and evil, easing the author's worries that his work would be turned into an unabashed horror movie.

Fisher had been criticized throughout his career for his reliance on static shots, but a viewing of *The Devil Rides Out* will convince even the harshest detractors that Fisher's reserved camera movements did not translate to inert onscreen action. In fact, two of the most effective scenes feature an almost still camera, the first being when the Duke and Rex crash Simon's party. Fisher allows Lee to lead the camera as he wanders amongst the guests, eavesdropping and acquiring ominous hints regarding the nocturnal meeting. This unobtrusive camera movement in one long take allows Lee's movement and facial expressions to tell the story and build suspense.

The second example, involving Mocata and the Duke's niece, begins innocuously enough but turns malevolent as the occultist imposes his monstrous will. Here, Fisher uses a very slow, almost imperceptible zoom to create an emerging power imbalance and a feeling of claustrophobic dread—all without the actors even leaving their chairs! James Bernard's powerful score and Bernard Robinson's magnificent set design, faithfully recreating 1920s England, complete with an astounding collection of vintage automobiles, only add to the skillfully crafted atmosphere.

The FX-heavy ending is the major reason the film does not finish as strongly as it starts—one scene in particular with a creepy crawly on a miniature set is laughable today and was probably disappointing in 1968. Yet the masterful first act, combined with the momentous task of adapting a novel as ornate as Wheatley's, is a testament to Matheson's skill as a screenwriter.

I don't remember whether I discovered the novel or its screen adaptation first; either way they were purchased in a dusty old second-hand shop where such treasures are often found. Looking back, I can't think of a more fitting location to discover a film that on the outside looks like nothing more than a B-movie, but on the inside features a powerhouse of talent behind and before the camera, treating with the utmost seriousness a historically frightening subject...one whose devilish grip is loosening on the world with each passing year.

Matthew Douglas Hodgson is an aspiring screenwriter and fiendish lover of all things horror from the mysterious to the macabre. He's hoping to make his two latest feature horror scripts, Rec Me *and* The Thing in the Woods, *realities sooner rather than later. He lives on the outskirts of downtown Toronto with his partner in crime, Heather, carefully planning a life free from offices, bills, quotas, and bosses.*

THE DEVILS 1971

BY DON BAPST

"PAY NO ATTENTION TO THESE TEARS; THEY ARE THE DEVIL'S TEARS."

Few films have managed to retain their shock value as well or as long as Ken Russell's *The Devils*. Even the late director, upon viewing an uncut version of his notorious "Rape of Christ" scene (once thought lost but recovered in 2002 by critic Mark Kermode), exclaimed, "My God, this is obscene!"

The Devils is far from the most violent film ever made, though the scene of Father Urbain Grandier (Oliver Reed) getting his legs crushed by an overzealous exorcist is as deeply disturbing as any slice of 21st century torture porn. Nor is it the most sexually graphic, though at the time there had never been so much full frontal nudity in a major studio picture—even a European studio. But when one considers said naked bodies were unfrocked nuns writhing on an altar, you

can imagine why some viewers had issues.

The scandal started during production as word of the diabolical goings-on at Pinewood Studios was leaked to the press. Stories of nun orgies and black masses drove conservative Christian activists in the UK to protest the film before seeing a single frame. Upon completion, the British Board of Film Censors hacked a couple minutes out of it, while Warner Bros., the picture's U.S. distributor, chopped another four minutes and then some. (Thankfully, the somewhat less manhandled UK release of the film is available on DVD, with an accompanying documentary that showcases additional missing scenes.)

But besides a few naked nuns, what exactly was all the fuss is about? After all, just two years later, Linda Blair would be plunging a crucifix into her prepubescent privates in an Oscar-winning picture hailed as the biggest recruitment campaign for the Catholic Church in history. (Especially ironic is the fact that The Exorcist was also distributed by Warner Bros.) The plot of what is technically a historical drama only hints at the controversy.

During the 17th century, the fortified French town of Loudun thrives in an atmosphere of religious tolerance under Father Urbain Grandier, a benevolent leader who happens to be a womanizing libertine. Meanwhile, back in Versailles, the Catholic Church's power-hungry Cardinal Richelieu (Christopher Logue) wants King Louis XIII (Graham Armitage) to drive the Protestants from France and merge the Church with the State. The flamboyant King agrees, though he wants to keep Loudun out of it simply because he promised to.

Determined to crush all Protestantism in France, Richelieu's minions find another excuse to defrock the town's peace-loving priest and bring down its walls: the testimony of hunchback Sister Jeanne (Vanessa Redgrave). Jealous over handsome Grandier's do-it-yourself marriage to another woman (and his indifference to her love letters), Jeanne testifies to being raped at a black mass while possessed by demons. As her exorcism goes public, Jeanne's fellow Sisters are driven to blasphemous extremes by Church leaders eager for incriminating testimonies. Despite having just turned over a new leaf with God, Grandier is found guilty of heresy, brutally tortured and burned alive at the stake.

Russell's version of the true story is based on John Whiting's 1961 play of the same name as well as the 1952 nonfiction book *The Devils of Loudun* by Aldous Huxley (which was itself inspired by an account in Alexandre Dumas' 1840 *Crimes Célèbres*). However it is told, the story of Urbain Grandier is a terrifyingly timeless tale of the abuse of power and the tyranny of masses corrupted by religious fanaticism.

Though its historical events are based in fact, Russell is more concerned with an emotional, visceral truth than a literal one. More than any other source can be felt the influence of Krzysztof Penderecki's 1969 effort, *Die Teufel von Loudun*, which tells Grandier's story as an opera. In Russell's film, the cacophonic score by contemporary composer Peter Maxwell Davies appropriates Penderecki's discordant, unsettling atmosphere while ratcheting up the tension a couple more notches. Like the industrial noise of *The Texas Chain Saw Massacre*, the aural tapestry of *The Devils* leaves no harmony or stillness in which to hide.

Also operatic are Shirley Russell's lavish costumes and expressionistic production design by Derek Jarman, who would go on to become one of the most celebrated directors of experimental cinema. The heightened landscape of Jarman's onscreen Loudun lends a nightmarishly present quality that keeps viewers from confining the story to the past.

But what ultimately leaves people so disturbed by *The Devils* is not its striking images and sounds, nor the masterful performances by Reed and Redgrave, but its assured mixture of horror and humor. Audiences are kept on the edge of their seats, squirming with awkward laughter and physical tension from start to finish. Like Father Mignon, masturbating in the church rafters as naked nuns writhe on the toppled crucifix below, there is (guilty) pleasure in being a complicit voyeur.

Critic Alexander Walker (who, like many others, loathed the film at the time of release) captures its inescapable essence: "The physicality of the film was a thing that struck me when I saw it. It looked like the masturbation fantasies of a  Roman Catholic boyhood."

Isn't that exactly what the twisted world of bigotry—of any stripe—looks like? Ultimately, the subject of *The Devils* is vulgarity itself. When church and state leaders abuse their power to dominate and torture the citizens they are supposed to protect, they break the ultimate taboo by committing the ultimate heresy. The greatest downfall of Russell, who actually converted to Catholicism in the 1950s, was his success at creating images so scathingly and uncomfortably immediate in their satire of sexual, political, and religious hypocrisy that they cannot be mistaken or ignored.

Russell's is not a cinema of words or suggestions; his is a hyperbolic moving picture accentuating all that is dark or disturbing with the most garish colors, the most visceral textures. While others might leave them to viewers' imaginations, Russell explicitly dramatizes Sister Jeanne's tormented sexual fantasies. Grandier appears to her as Christ on the Cross, allowing her to lick his stigmata. (Guilty over these impure thoughts, she beats herself with barbed whips and gives herself stigmata with the cross on her own rosary.) This is the closest she'll ever get to him....

Well, until she finally has her flesh-and-blood hero burned at the stake. In a scene cut from even the most complete prints, Jeanne receives the charred femur of Grandier following his execution and, once alone with it, masturbates with the blackened relic: The ultimate act of jealous loneliness driven by superstitious fanaticism.

The Devils is a gorgeous but difficult film to watch because it leaves little to the imagination, which, because of its subject matter, is precisely what it needs to do. One can read other accounts of Grandier from the comfort of their armchair and imagine the darkness of religious oppression relegated to the past. But in watching *The Devils*, one cannot help drawing comparisons between the historical figures onscreen and modern day zealots crying for dissenters to be stripped of rights and freedoms. These complex characters are presented as neither heroes nor demons but as flawed individuals caught up in a crazy moment in history. But first, viewers must deal with its urgent physical presence, navigating this hell of a world where religion has killed reason and madness reigns.

Don Bapst is an award-winning filmmaker, playwright and author of several novels including The Hanged Man, *a mystery thriller about the secular origins of the Tarot.* The Guardian *recently called his translation of Gabrielle Wittkop's* The Necrophiliac *"a masterpiece." For more info, visit donbapst.com*

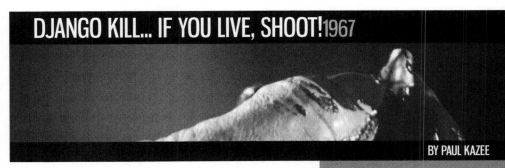

DJANGO KILL... IF YOU LIVE, SHOOT! 1967

BY PAUL KAZEE

Django Kill... If You Live, Shoot! is not technically a horror film. It's a spaghetti western...or maybe an experimental art film. Whatever it is, it's just as likely to be appreciated by fans of horror and horrific exploitation as by fans of westerns or cinematic art. Many spaghetti western fans actually do not know what to

"WHICH DO YOU PREFER? DESERT SNAKES, VAMPIRE BATS OR THE BLACK LIZARD OF DARKNESS?"

make of *Django Kill*, at one moment a decidedly standard cowboy yarn, the next a twisted, sadistic nightmare featuring—not only bats and lizards—but death by molten metal, a gruesome explosion of man and animal parts, and a pale, mysterious madwoman locked-up behind an iron-barred window. Yet, sadly, horror fans remain largely unaware of this film's dark, smart, and horrifyingly nasty appeal.

Further frustrating appreciation is its misleading title. Django does not appear in *Django Kill*, nor is he even referred to. Fresh off the international success of Sergio Corbucci's *Django* (1966), the famed character's name was merely tagged onto the title in an effort to better sell it to unwitting American audiences. Unsurprisingly, director Giulio Questi disliked the change, preferring the direct translation of the original Italian title, *If You Live, Shoot!* Speaking of translations, please note that—unless otherwise indicated—all quotations herein refer to the improved subtitle translation provided with Blue Underground's 2012 Blu-ray release.

Perhaps best known to horror fans for his role in Lucio Fulci's *Don't Torture a Duckling* (1972), Tomas Milian stars as "The Stranger," a handsome half-breed who is revealed clawing his way out of an open grave as the film opens.

Believing him to have returned from the dead (and perhaps he has), a pair of Indians take him under their care, asking only that he eventually share with them any special wisdom he may have gained on the other side. In the meantime, they will aid in seeing each of the cruel palefaces who put him in his grave laid to rest in one of their own. To this end, the Indians melt down the modest cache of gold they find The Stranger to be carrying and from this forge several bullets. Gold bullets are "deadlier than lead," they note. (The English-dubbed version adding, "Go deeper.")

In a flashback, we learn that The Stranger and these nasty gringos were former partners. Along with several of The Stranger's Mexican *compañeros*, they ruthlessly robbed a Wells Fargo stagecoach of its gold and murdered a regiment of bathing Union Army escorts—literally catching the soldiers with their pants down. However, the American bandits quickly dismiss any intention of sharing the gold with "dirty Mexicans," claiming it was already enough having put up with "the stench of your greasy skin." The half-breed and his friends are forced to dig a mass grave before each is shot dead...

...and this is where things take a wide left turn. I first saw *Django Kill* in NYC as part of a week-long festival of spaghetti westerns, and while I enjoyed several of the other features, when I arrived at this particular point in the film I realized that nothing else in the festival would ever compare.

Cut to the band of murdering *gringos*, each one meaner and uglier than the next. After surviving a long trek across the desert with little or no food and water, they arrive at a quiet western town. Too quiet. Something in this town is even uglier than they are. The air is filled with dread, with evil. In the dubbed version, one of the bandits remarks, "Even God wouldn't stay here." And indeed, there is no evidence of anything holy in this town.

The first thing the men see is a lone naked child, standing in a puddle of his own urine. Nearby, a girl maliciously pulls the hair of a young boy, while spit-

ting in his face (in the dubbed version, it is inexplicably made to appear as if the girl is merely taunting the boy, not spitting on him.) Another girl, crying for release, is observed being violently squashed under the boot of an abusive uncle.

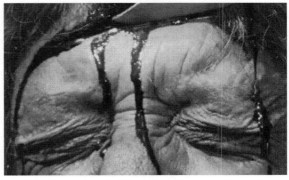

What kind of hellish place is this? "I don't know what the white men call it," one of The Stranger's Indian companions later explains. "Our people used to call it The Field of Anguish" (or rather ridiculously, "The Unhappy Place" in the dubbed version). Is this place—in fact—Hell? Perhaps The Stranger truly is among the walking dead? "...you can't leave this town as long as you still have bullets," the Indians explain suggestively. "You have many left to shoot."

Hell or not, the Indians lead The Stranger to this godforsaken place, knowing that the American bandits had to have passed this very same way. By the time the trio arrives, however, the fate of all but the double-crossing bunch's leader has already been soundly settled by the decidedly inhospitable locals.

Rather pointedly, when one of the local cowboys first spies the gold, the camera leads his eye from the saddlebags in which it is stashed to a wonderfully suggestive close-up of a horse's ass. Questi claims this cowboy, dressed almost fetishistically in metal-studded black, is—along with his identically dressed companions—representative of Italy's fascist militia against whom he fought as a partisan youth. And it is from this civil war experience that the director's seemingly pitch black view of mankind may have been derived. In his short film *Visitors* (2006), for instance, Questi (playing himself) is visited by the ghosts of the soldiers he killed, and these men beg him to please kill himself so that they—and he—may be freed from "the hell of being remembered."

Clearly, Questi and his co-writer, Franco Arcalli (*Last Tango in Paris, Once Upon a Time in America*), have more than a simple western on their minds. This approach likewise applies to their remarkable giallo collaboration, *Death Laid an Egg* (1968), a fascinating (and equally under-appreciated) critique of capitalism wherein a company works to chemically breed a headless, wingless chicken...a throbbing blob of soft meat that the writers compare to modern man.

With *Django Kill*, the two similarly gaze into the twisted soul of man, revealing...? Racism. Greed. Sadism. Criminal Sexuality. Horrifying Indifference.

When a man has his belly pumped full of gold bullets, the townsfolk lay him out for emergency surgery, not to save his life, but to retrieve the precious metal. ("I've searched for gold in vain my whole life, and he's full of it.") When the black-clad cowboys take a pretty teenage boy hostage, they invite him to share in a perverted orgy of food, after which they turn their increasingly sinful appetites toward him. Then there's the manipulative and uncaring bar girl who unashamedly cuckolds her man when he hesitates — only briefly — to put his son's life at risk in a deadly gamble for cold-hearted, selfish gain.

In the end, creators Questi and Arcalli leave us with a sobering final comment on the horror and obscenity of human existence by returning us to the children, two of whom are seen growling and distorting their faces in a competition to be acknowledged the more grotesque. ("I'm uglier than you are," one of them adds in the dubbed version.) Both readings speak to the same concern: When even our children have the desire to be monsters or freaks, hope for humanity is lost. And with this the attentive viewer recalls an earlier scene in which one of the townsfolk says of the woman who will be his undoing, "She wouldn't hurt anyone. She's like a child."

Paul Kazee has dedicated his life to film, a pursuit proven to have a market value of precisely $7.35 per hour. Paul has written for Joe Bob Briggs, founded a popular genre festival (New York Asian Film Fest), and currently programs horror, sci-fi & cult film in upstate New York. In the past year, Paul watched over 325 movies – 312 inside a movie theater as God intended. When not watching movies, Paul sleeps. Alone. In an open grave.

DUST DEVIL 1992

BY J. LUIS RIVERA

> "NO, MY FRIEND. THAT WAS REALITY. YOU ARE DREAMING NOW."

"For me, *Dust Devil* is about magical reality," explained South African filmmaker Richard Stanley to film critic Mark Kermode for *Sight & Sound* in 1992, a seemingly antithetical statement but one that best summarizes the essence of a film set in a land where myth and reality are one and the same. Regretfully, this could not have been said of the hacked 87-minute version crafted by distributors for its original release, one that rendered it an incomprehensible, substandard thriller. Fortunately, Stanley eventually recovered the rights to his film and the cult classic can now finally be seen as originally intended.

Robert Burke plays a nameless hitchhiker roaming the highways that run across the Namib Desert in South Africa, killing those who pick him up in a series of bizarre ritual murders. However, this man with no name is not a common serial killer, but rather a supernatural being that the natives call the Dust Devil, a spiritual creature trapped in a human body with the mission of collecting souls. As the slayings continue, police detective Ben Mukurob (Zakes Mokae) takes the case, intent on proving this mythical demon to be a flesh-and-blood human being. Meanwhile, a

young woman named Wendy Robinson (Chelsea Field) abandons her abusive husband and heads towards the desert…where she'll soon encounter true darkness.

Richard Stanley based his story on the real case of the Nhadiep, a Namibian serial killer that was never caught and whose unknown identity led to stories about a supernatural origin. This marriage between reality and legend is ever present in his screenplay, as the story works both as a serial killer mystery and as a tale of supernatural horror. It is also the link to Stanley's other main influence: the western. "When the legend becomes fact, print the legend," states John Ford's 1962 classic *The Man Who Shot Liberty Valance*; *Dust Devil* takes this notion one step further. Within this mystic world, legends *equal* fact and magic is a force of nature to be feared.

Mysticism abounds in *Dust Devil*, giving the film a distinctive identity of its own. Even though deeply rooted in South African mythology, the nameless hitchhiker roaming the highway possesses an iconic universality. He is a symbol of the dualities of the world (man and spirit, life and death, reality and dream) and an echo of those mythic links between the spiritual and the corporeal. This superhuman shapeshifter's mission is to ease the pains of those seeking death, even if they don't know it.

Wendy and Ben are two lost souls whose futures seem as bleak as the desolate Namib landscape that serves as background for their stories. Wendy is fleeing an unhealthy relationship while Ben seeks escape from his profound melancholy following the death of his only son. According to Stanley, both of these protagonists represent the problems of South Africa: sexism and racism, two very real demons colliding directly with the supernatural Dust Devil. Once again, the duality of reality and magic comes into play ("There is no good or evil, only spirit and matter," intones Burke at one point) and this mixing of harsh realism with oneiric spiritualism is among the movie's most interesting elements—one essentially lost to the editor's shears during the initial 1992 theatrical release.

It's impossible to discuss *Dust Devil* without referencing its notable post-production problems. After enduring a difficult shoot on location in the Namib Desert, things began to fall apart when Stanley's original cut (clocking in at 120 minutes) was rejected by the production company, Palace Pictures.

Additionally, since the movie dealt with a serial killer, something akin to 1991's smash *The Silence of the Lambs* was desired. To that end, *Dust Devil* was butchered, removing all the mysticism and substantially reducing its run time. Soon after, adding insult to injury, Palace Pictures filed for bankruptcy.

Miramax, the American distributor, took control and trimmed the film even further, cutting it to a mere 87 minutes without any involvement from the director. The result was a confusing and somewhat incoherent storyline that hard-

ly resembled Stanley's original vision. Unsurprisingly, initial reviews of this mutilated version were less than stellar, prompting Miramax to dedicate little effort to active promotion. *Dust Devil* promptly sank off the radar and into obscurity. Fortunately, in 2006, Subversive Cinema released Stanley's "Director's Cut" to DVD, allowing fans to finally witness his supernatural serial killer roaming through the desert as intended.

Yet this is no typical story about a psychopathic murderer, as Stanley's use of horror genre conventions to highlight more metaphysical concepts is actually what sets it apart, making it one of the most interesting efforts from the 1990s. Beginning in familiar horror territory, it soon moves away from standard police procedural trappings and glides into a different shade of reality, as if the characters were entering a nightmare come to life. An exercise in symbolism, the film not only shows but also evokes, giving new life to old myths by mixing them with the modern legends of popular culture (for instance, the shaman character lives at the local drive-in). Again and again, we encounter the constant juxtaposition of the old and the new.

That pairing of opposites could even extend to the two existing versions of the feature—Miramax's "commercial" cut and Stanley's more personal, idiosyncratic one. Further coupling lies in the fact that while *Dust Devil* is, of course a genre film, it could also be described as an attempt to capture a nation's essence (or better said, a dark aspect of it). As the movie that finally brought Stanley back to South Africa after having spent time in the United Kingdom (the site of his mainstream breakthrough, 1990's sci-fi/horror *Hardware*), it's not difficult to see parallels between *Dust Devil*'s narrative themes of fighting one's personal demons and its problematic theatrical release.

There's something mesmerizing about the formidable landscape of the Namib Desert, simultaneously beautiful and haunting, that this unique cinematic artist has managed to capture and transmit perfectly. To me, the success of *Dust Devil* lies in its ability to play with myth and reality, blurring the boundaries in one single vision of darkness. With great care, Stanley crafted a powerful horror film that represents what he most loves and hates about South Africa. Such is its duality. It is said that in the desert one can find either God or the Devil; in *Dust Devil*, we find that they are one and the same.

J. Luis Rivera is a Mexican-born cinephile who has been in love with horror films ever since he watched Cronenberg's The Fly as a small kid. While life led him to become an engineer, he has also managed to find time to become a film critic and a filmmaker in his own right. It's hard to forget your first love.

EDEN LAKE 2008

BY JUDE FELTON

Released in the UK in 2008, *Eden Lake* didn't reach the States until January the following year (via The Weinstein Company's Dimension Extreme imprint). Purely for the fact that it was a new horror movie from my home country of England, my interest was immediately piqued. At the time, it seemed that as soon as I

"LISTEN, YOU HAD YOUR FUN. LET'S JUST CALL IT QUITS..."

left in 2005, there had been a serious resurgence in the quality of genre output back across the pond. I knew I had to get my hands on a copy.

But when the closing credits rolled on my first viewing, I found myself physically and mentally drained. The opening scenes had hinted at, but by no means had prepared me for, what was to come. When the final frames came round, I hated writer/director James Watkins for what he had done to me... even though it was a terrific and chilling conclusion to the harrowing events that had gone before. *Eden Lake* was, and remains, a visceral exercise in which the oppressively brutal action rarely lets up.

Four years before he took Daniel Radcliffe out of Hogwarts and thrust him into a confrontation with *The Woman in Black*, Watkins conceived a tried and trusted horror formula, following a young urban couple, Jenny (Kelly Reilly) and Steve (Michael Fassbender), as they travel to the north of England for a romantic getaway. Not long after arriving at the titular destination, they find themselves in confrontation with a group of local kids, a conflict which escalates into incredible violence.

However, there is more to the equation than immediately hits the eye. Made at the beginning of the so-called "hoodie horror" boom, *Eden Lake* and other UK horror flicks such as *F* and *Cherry Tree Lane* (both 2010) dramatized the growing social fear of kids with bad attitudes and too much time on their hands. You see, the common perception is that everyone in the southern parts of England is incredibly well educated and cultured; it's only when you move up North, to the more working class areas, that intelligence levels drop and violence is seen as the solution to all problems. For example, Jenny is seen teaching a group of very well-to-do-looking preschoolers in the opening scene, and later, when the couple are traveling, their car stereo plays a radio show where various people are heard complaining about the state of education and the lack of its availability to some kids today.

The film makes it very clear from the outset that Jenny and Steve are intended to be our heroes. They're good-looking, smart…why wouldn't you like them? Watkins is a sly fox though, which his storytelling clearly demonstrates. These "heroes" are the interlopers, and while we might initially perceive them as unwitting victims of senseless juvenile violence, they actually fuel the fires on multiple occasions. An accusation in a local café, breaking into one of the kids' houses, confronting the kids on the shores of the lake, they are slowly digging their own graves.

Even if the kids are obnoxious shits, Jenny and Steve are the outsiders. They do not act like guests; even with the welcoming locals, they try to impose their "civilized" presence—at first in subtle fashion, then more overtly as tensions rise. Unfortunately for Jenny and Steve, the kids push back, and push back hard.

Watkins is clearly playing upon England's north and south cultural divide, while at the same time maintaining a cloudy ambiguity regarding his protagonists' "innocence," an approach that reveals an even more frightening picture upon subsequent viewings. Northern stereotypes are played up, with mothers beating their children, brash beer-drinking men, children running wild in the streets. But it isn't for Jenny and Steve (or the viewer) to tell them otherwise. This is how they live, right or wrong. Watkins does not paint his younger characters as saints either, a fact that becomes all too apparent as the clock runs down via some truly unsavory scenes. The point is, if you arrogantly barge into someone else's home territory, you should be prepared for a conflict.

This is a gritty, violent, and at times brutal excursion into the darkest heart of human horror. Yet the tension and atmosphere generated are just as important, if not more so, than the more visceral encounters on display. Watkins manipulates his audience perfectly, knowing exactly when to get in our faces and when to pull back—the most disturbing scene is seen by the viewer from a distance,

but it is this restraint that allows us to stay invested in the characters' fates. (You would not want to see this particular scene up close, of that I am sure.)

What distinguishes *Eden Lake* from the wealth of "survival horror" offerings is that the escalating violence between the protagonists and antagonists feels justified, truthful, and well-charted. It will make you think—more importantly, it will make you question your own beliefs of right and wrong.

There are no masked figures slashing up victims, no disfigured monsters getting ready to jump out, no nubile final girls—Watkins leaves it to each individual viewer to work out who the heroes and villains really are.

Of course, this would all have been in vain if not for Reilly and Fassbender's sympathetic and charismatic lead performances. While Fassbender's Steve is the instigator of dramatic events (and he plays the part perfectly), it is Reilly who really carries the movie's full emotional weight. Credit also has to be given to the young supporting cast, who alternate between terrifying ferocity and pitiful innocence, reacting accordingly to events in the only way they have been brought up to respond.

When conversations turn to great modern UK horror, I always hear the same films mentioned: *The Descent, Dog Soldiers, Shaun of the Dead,* and more recently, *Attack the Block.* Yet rarely do I see *Eden Lake* mentioned and, quite frankly, this baffles me. Sure, there is almost no humor to offer reprieve from the bleak onscreen events, and one could argue that the thick English accents and unceasingly dark tone might scare away a less daring American audience. But, on the other hand, you also have the inclusion of rising star Fassbender, an actor who came to prominence with Steven McQueen's *Hunger* the same year as *Eden Lake* and who has since gone on to such high-profile Hollywood exercises as *Prometheus* and *X-Men: First Class.* I would have thought that this aspect alone might have given such a superb chiller more exposure, but no such luck.

It's rare that a director can blend genuine tension and scares with a graphic approach to horror, but Watkins manages it here with great gusto. *Eden Lake* is a solid punch to the gut and while I still hate its creator for how he made me feel, I also thank him for bringing this incredibly good slice of fright to life.

Jude Felton currently resides in Northeastern Pennsylvania by way of England. Contributing to various movie review sites since 2005, he now focuses on his own site, The Lair of Filth, as well as writing for HorrorHound magazine. Having been a fan of horror and dark cinema since he was a wee one, he still gets that special thrill each time he puts a movie on.

THE ENTITY 1982

BY SERENA MORRISON

Years ago, following a particularly grueling shift at the local library, I arrived home, checked my mail and was delighted to find—among a stack of bills and junk mail—my recently ordered out-of-print DVD for *The Entity*. I had been previously unaware of this cult staple until a friend whose taste in cinema often runs parallel to my own began chatting it up. After hearing its basic plot, including the infamous "ghost grope" scene, I was sold.

Like many a well-marinated genre fan, at this point there is little that a filmmaker can roll out that leaves me profoundly disturbed. I make this claim not as a badge of honor, but to properly celebrate this underrated classic. *The Entity* had such a profound effect, I distinctly remember every aspect of my first viewing—specifically Charles Bernstein's pounding and insistent musical score—and its power has not diminished over a multitude of repeat viewings.

Though the '70s and '80s were littered with genre efforts featuring the dubious preface "based on true events," this scorching film's claim carries more weight than most. In 1978, Frank De Felitta penned a "factual novel" based on Doris Bither, a woman living in Culver City, California, who claimed that she was being terrorized by three different supernatural beings. UCLA's Dr. Barry Taff began a two-and-a-half month investigation in 1974 that became one of the most controversial and well-known cases in parapsychology. While the physical evidence derived has been debated by many, and Taff admits to having lost two of the four pictures depicting the apparitions, he maintains that what happened was very real.

With De Felitta providing his own adaptation and Hollywood veteran Sidney J. Furie at the helm, cameras rolled on the project, one that delivered seemingly everything a genre fan could desire: convincing special effects, outstanding cast, haunting score (Bernstein also scored the memorable themes for *A Nightmare on Elm Street* and *Cujo*), nudity, and an absolutely chilling premise. In a 2012 interview, Furie told *Rue Morgue* that he prefers to consider the film "supernatural suspense" rather than "horror," going on to reveal that they shot in sequence from beginning to end to build the atmosphere and tension as they went along. Panned by critics upon initial release, its reputation has warmed considerably since, with Martin Scorsese even listing *The Entity* as one of the scariest movies of all time for *The Daily Beast*.

The action begins immediately after the opening credits and gives no quarter. Carla Moran (Barbara Hershey), a single mother of three, returns home one night to be brutally beaten and raped by an unseen force. When she nearly loses control of her vehicle the following day—again at the "hands" of an unexplained presence—she confides in a friend who urges her to see a university psychiatrist, Dr. Sneiderman (Ron Silver). Though the doctor tries to explain that the attacks are merely hallucinations attributable to Carla's troubled past, she returns home unconvinced. Later, she is viciously raped again in the bathtub. (Quentin Tarantino would later appropriate Bernstein's "Bath Attack" track for 2009's *Inglourious Basterds*.) Fearing for her safety, Sneiderman insists that Carla commit herself but she refuses. Deeply troubled and helpless, Carla is finally vindicated when the attacks begin occurring in front of friends and family. At last, she has a circle of allies to validate her story.

While visiting a bookstore to do some research, she overhears two parapsychologists talking and approaches them to discuss her affliction. They express interest, but remain skeptical until they witness examples of paranormal phenomena occurring in her home. The entity continues to torment Carla, leaving her physically and mentally battered, the assaults becoming so violent they result in her hospitalization. Despite these repeated attacks, the trauma of her frenzied past and Sneiderman's stubborn disbelief, Carla's resolve only strengthens. Her endurance and perseverance are the stuff Final Girls are made of; the shocking climax and even more disturbing denouement leave viewers questioning their own beliefs in the paranormal.

In charge of makeup and other practical effects, including the scene where Carla is mauled by unseen hands, was wunderkind Stan Winston. In order to realize this unforgettable image, a prosthetic body was built and laid on top of the bed, with Hershey's real head sticking up through the neck. A special pump was then used to push air in and out, giving the impression of invisible hands on the breasts. Industry pro Joe Lombardi (*The Godfather I* and *II*, *Apocalypse Now*, *Friday the 13th Part VII: The New Blood*) further aided the cause, employing special aircraft engine-like motors to produce the effect of the house shaking.

Furie wanted the scenes of paranormal violence to be as realistic as possible, so he had Hershey and David Labiosa (playing Carla's son Billy) rigged with wires to throw them about to enhance the illusion of their being attacked—a practice previously used by William Friedkin in *The Exorcist*.

A bizarre coincidence came to pass when Labiosa broke his wrist while filming an attack scene—bizarre because although not in the shooting script, Billy's wrist is broken in De Felitta's original novel.

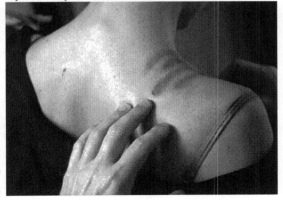

While there are some correlations between the film and what really happened in the house on Braddock Drive, Dr. Taff's final report denies any evidence of spectral rape. In addition, there have been conflicting accounts of recorded events between Taff and Doris Bither's children. What is certain, however, is that *something* unexplained and terrifying occurred in 1974. We are informed during the final credits crawl that the family eventually decided to relocate from California to Texas, and although the attacks decreased in frequency and intensity, they never completely stopped.

Horror is a vehicle of truth. Both visually and conceptually confrontational, the best efforts force audiences to consider what they would do in a character's shoes. Our worst fears made flesh, on screen and unrelenting. There is something inherently frightening about tales of demonic possession or hauntings, as they ask us to imagine things like loss of identity, repression, personal degradation, inexplicable evil, unprovoked torment, corruption of innocence, and insanity...all due to an invasive force that refuses to be contained or controlled. Both in fiction and in fact, the attacks on Carla Moran/Doris Bither continue beyond the observed story, persisting into a kind of doomed fate without end. How can you control or banish something that not everyone believes in? Even then, how can you argue the case when tangible evidence is so elusive? What could be more terrifying than that? How do you know where a person stops and the entity starts? How do you know if there is an entity at all...?

Serena Morrison, a California import, spent her formative years in Europe where she spent many hours staring in abject terror at the local video store's VHS horror boxes. After relocating to America, she broadened her tastes via employment at a comic book store, a movie theater, and as a librarian. Her undying love remains with the horror genre, specifically The Exorcist, *and she is currently writing a book on demonic films and possession cases.*

EVENT HORIZON 1997

BY MONICA S. KUEBLER

"THE SHIP BROUGHT ME BACK. I TOLD YOU SHE WON'T LET ME LEAVE—SHE WON'T LET ANYONE LEAVE."

You never forget those movies that had you clasping the theater-seat armrest—or perhaps your date—in white-knuckled terror. If you're a diehard horror fan, you're likely desensitized to cinematic scares, so these magical moments—which admittedly are as unique to each of us as our tastes in cuisine—may come less frequently than you'd like. Perhaps that's why we fetishize them so much, right alongside the films that gave us that rare, palpable, shuddering reaction.

This is exactly what fuels my love of *Event Horizon*, a horror/sci-fi title with a paltry—and maddening—23 percent on Rotten Tomatoes. (Interestingly and perhaps tellingly, the audience rating is a much more solid and respectable 61% "fresh.") Several reviews decree it "implausible" and "derivative," lambasting it for blatantly ripping off Clive Barker's *Hellraiser*, Stanley Kubrick's *2001: A Space Odyssey*, and Ridley Scott's *Alien*. While no one can deny those influences appear, be it in the flashes of tortures waged in the Hell dimension or the design of the ship itself, none are so bold or widespread to prevent *Event Horizon* from standing on its own. If anything, director Paul W.S. Anderson has taken elements of what has come before and successfully re-combined them into a different sort of science fiction narrative—something filmmakers, regardless of genre, have been doing for decades.

Call me crazy, but I don't come to horror looking for sound science. I come for a scary story. In simplest terms, *Event Horizon* is a haunted house riff set on a derelict spacecraft, the perfect claustrophobic venue since one

can't just leave when the going gets weird and deadly. The things inside the ship may be bordering on lethal, but so too is the cold, harsh vacuum of space. Rock meets hard place. Catch-22.

The *Event Horizon* is a deep-space research vessel launched in 2040 to explore the boundaries of the solar system. In actuality a secret government project

to create a spacecraft capable of faster-than-light travel—opening a dimensional gateway that allows it to jump from one point in space to another—it mysteriously disappears one day off the charts, the official line being that it suffered mechanical failure and exploded. Now, seven years later, the ship has reappeared in a decaying orbit around Neptune. A team is sent out to investigate, with Dr. William Weir (Sam Neill), the scientist who designed it, in tow.

When they arrive, they find the deserted *Event Horizon* full of nonsensical life-form readings. Further inspection leads them to ominous ship logs and a badly mutilated body. Then strange things begin to happen: the craft's gravity drive whirs to life on its own, opening a dimensional portal and sucking a crew member through it, damaging the vessel they arrived on in the process. Other members of the team begin to hallucinate violent and terrible things born from their own minds and memories. It starts to look as if whatever has happened to the ship has no intention of allowing them to leave.

The theories that the crew float, trying to figure out what's going on, are each more spine-chilling than the last. The ship is somehow alive and having an immune reaction to them. Scary. The ship knows their fears and can get inside their heads. Scarier. The ship has been to Hell (or some dimension full of chaos and pure evil) and has brought back a sentient *something* with it. Scariest. What's particularly clever about this final scenario from a

storytelling standpoint is that it manages to invoke Hell and all it may entail without the necessity of religious belief (though if you are a believer, there is equally much you could infer from Dr. Weir's hallucinations of his dead wife, etc.). If anything, it's yet another twist on the vast universal unknown, what may yet await us in space and beyond if we ever become technologically advanced enough to seek it out.

This leads to the final and, to me, possibly greatest thing that *Event Horizon* gets right, and why my love of it prevails to this day: it does not reveal what lies beyond the interdimensional portal. It alludes to the suffering caused by it, utilizing a series of gory, disturbing, and highly effective quick cuts, but never once do we cross over and see it for ourselves. Subscribing to the old adage that what is most frightening is that which is left unseen, Anderson allows us to further creep ourselves out by giving us the opportunity to *imagine* what might have caused the horrifying results we've witnessed—imaginings probably more terrifying than any 1990s special effect.

Event Horizon may be a bit predictable at turns and wear some' of those aforementioned influences on its sleeves, but a lot of great horror stories are and do. It's more about how the pieces of the puzzle are employed; what Anderson has created is a movie that holds up surprisingly well both visually and narratively a decade and a half later. (Read any of those wild multiverse theories coming out of the physics community lately?) Though it uses stock horror tricks we've seen countless times over to build atmosphere and put us ill at ease, it uses them well. The jump scares are there to keep us from dropping our guard, but are not so frequent that they feel cheap and manipulative. Equally well-deployed are the moments of blood, gore, and dead-body set-pieces (the eviscerated corpse in the med bay, for instance), which help create a sense of prolonged dread with sharp bursts of shock.

The solid production design work also deserves attention, particularly the superlative soundscapes (courtesy of designer Campbell Askew, effects editor Ross Adams, and a sound department of more than two dozen), which feature a low, almost perma-rumble in the ship's interior once it's powered up with lots of clangs and bangs and indistinguishable industrial noises throughout. Also notable are the striking stark blue/gray color palette, the cool-looking and more-than-a-little creepy spacecraft, and the roundly solid ensemble performances. I'm simply not ready to dismiss *Event Horizon* as quickly as many other critics.

Paul W.S. Anderson's cinematic legacy may account for much of the criticism leveled against the film over the years. After all, it's difficult to dispute that *Mortal Kombat*, *AVP: Alien vs. Predator*, the 2008 *Death Race* remake and the *Resident Evil* franchise are anything more than pedestrian, blockbuster popcorn fare. But *Event Horizon* was and continues to be something greater than the sum of its borrowed parts, revealing an inkling of what might have been had Anderson chosen to spend less of his career playing in other pre-established sandboxes.

Regardless, sci-fi and horror remain an ever-potent combo, and *Event Horizon*—like *The Fly* and *Scanners* before and *Daybreakers* after—proves that you don't need to employ aliens to pull it off. Perhaps it's time to consider booking a return voyage...*to Hell*.

Monica S. Kuebler is managing editor of Rue Morgue *magazine and the editor-in-chief of the critically acclaimed micro-press Burning Effigy. She is also the author of the* Blood Magic Saga, *a multi-book young adult horror/urban fantasy serial, which can be read free online at http://www.blood-magic.net, and the co-author of the 2002 poetry collection* Some Words Spoken. *For more, visit http://www.monicaskuebler.com.*

EVILSPEAK1981

BY THE DREADFUL DAY OF JUDGEMENT,
BY THE FACE OF THE UNHOLY MAJESTY,
I CONJURE AND COMMAND THEE...
OH PRINCE OF DARKNESS, OH SATAN, OH LUCIFER
APPEAR FORTHWITH AND SHOW YOURSELF TO ME

BY NATHAN HANNEMAN

Over the last ten years writing and working within the world of horror, one of the most frequent requests posed is to name my favorite fright flicks. What titles "make me tick," as it were. I invariably answer with *Jaws*, but beyond that my mind searches for lesser-known juicy gems of gore-drenched goodness. My cinematic aesthetics tend toward the most colorful, schlocky, fun, and satisfying morsels the genre has to offer, such as *Re-Animator*, *The Texas Chainsaw Massacre Part 2*, *Gremlins*, and so on. However, the film that most often elicits the dreaded reply, "I've never heard of that," is the little-known Clint Howard-starring demon vehicle, *Evilspeak*.

> "IT'S A TOUGH WORLD OUT THERE. YOU GOT TO BE ABLE TO KICK AND SCRATCH IF YOU WANT TO SURVIVE."

My discovery of *Evilspeak* was the result of my wholesale devotion to all things Clint, initially ignited by his titular turn in *The Ice Cream Man*. After renting that 1995 schlock-fest slasher a dozen times over (before finally purchasing my own personal copy), I found myself tracking down other titles on the actor's resume; there was something about this odd-looking individual that proved irresistible. A regular cast member of his older producer/director brother Ron's films (including *Apollo 13*, *Cinderella Man*, and *Cocoon*, to name a few), Howard began his career with various TV roles as a child. The actor's distinctive (dare I say *peculiar*) looks have also resulted in his being cast in a number of low-budget horror and grindhouse features over the past 30 years, including *Rock 'n' Roll High School*, *The Wraith*, *Carnosaur*, and *Ticks*. He was even honored with a Lifetime Achievement Award at the 1998 MTV Movie Awards.

In *Evilspeak*, Howard portrays quintessential sad sack Stanley Coopersmith, a young man who has already been subjected to a number of misfortunes by the time we meet him. His parents now deceased, he is forced to live at a military academy populated with what could only be described as the biggest assholes any school could acquire. Couple this with the unfortunate fact that he looks like, well, Clint Howard. Films such as these play upon on the viewer's ability to relate to the main character's personal trials (which may say more about my childhood than I would like), and you'd have to be a cold-hearted bastard to not feel for

this tortured soul. We all cried for Sissy Spacek in *Carrie*, but Coopersmith wins the award for most heartbreaking hapless horror hero.

Following a brief flashback regarding the mysterious Father Esteban (Richard Moll) and his exiled group of satanic followers, we join Coopersmith on menial basement janitorial duty. The beleaguered lad discovers Esteban's codex of cult rituals hidden within the ancient walls of the academy and, using an early-model computer boasting, ahem, *amazing* 2-bit digital renderings (this was 1981, after all), he translates the mystic rituals, an act that results in the poor young fool resurrecting ancient evils that beset his soul. After years of ridicule, pranks, and bullying, the temptation is too great for the cadet; Coopersmith succumbs to the spirits' siren call, harnessing the dark arts in violent retribution against all who have harmed him in a bloody classic climax deserving of multiple viewings.

For the time, what made *Evilspeak*'s story so engaging was its playing upon the mystery of modern technology. In the early '80s, home computers were far from the norm—the word still conjured images of giant rooms filled with boxy machines sporting wheels and punch cards and flashing lights. Likewise, onscreen digital effects were still in their infancy—the *Star Wars* universe still relied on practical effects while Disney's groundbreaking *Tron* was still a year away. Because computers were such an unknown quantity, it was an exciting time to consider the possibilities that this new world could provide. This fear of technology gone awry had been a constant in sci-fi/horror cinema since the 1950s, but the leap of utilizing computers to make contact with Hell itself was screenwriters Eric Weston and Joseph Garofalo's greatest innovation. It is a terrifying premise no more farfetched than killer androids or make-believe worlds we can "visit" within the computer itself, such as in the highly successful franchises-to-come, *The Terminator* and *The Matrix*.

Among the noteworthy cast members, one cannot bring up *Evilspeak* without discussing the amazing Richard Moll who appears (all too briefly) as Father Esteban, the cursed cult leader/demonic entity that entices Coopersmith. The flashback sequence featuring a satanic cult ritual (and a snazzy beheading scene worthy of a highlight reel) boasts one of Moll's most evil onscreen visages (even trumping "Big Ben" in 1986's *House*). Other key actors of interest include Charles Tyner (*The Longest Yard*, *The Outlaw Josey Wales*), R.G. Armstrong (*Children of the Corn*, *Race with the Devil*), and a much younger and dastardly Don Stark (*That '70s Show*). Claude Earl Jones (*Bride of Re-Animator*, *Dark Night of the Scarecrow*) even shows up as Coopersmith's soccer coach (and *man*, is he a dick).

While director Weston and co-screenwriter Garofalo have no significant credits beyond *Evilspeak*, others on the behind-the-scenes roster deserve some attention. Roger Kellaway, composer of the synthy scores for *The Dark*, *Jaws of Satan*, and *Silent Scream* (as well as the 1976 updating of *A Star is Born*), delivers another fine moody collective of notes. Responsible for the film's killer effects were Allan Apone (*Invaders from Mars*, *Faces of Death*), Douglas White (*Return of the Living Dead*, *Neon Maniacs*), and Frank Carriosa (*The Gate*, *Friday the 13th Part III*)—no slouches these three. Apone and Carriosa are still working on some of the biggest films being released to this day, including *The Avengers*, *Iron Man 3*, and *Man of Steel*.

It's worth mentioning that there is a lot of history with the movie's various iterations. The U.S. theatrical release was cut at the last minute by the distributor, a last-minute rush job that resulted in several of the prints going into theaters with the gore scenes still intact. However, most 1983 VHS and cable releases were taken directly from the sloppily edited and neutered version. When Anchor Bay released *Evilspeak* on DVD here in the States, their version reinstated the red stuff, but was still missing a substantial amount of additional footage (some bits containing dialogue, others featuring split-second transition shots). However, Anchor Bay UK's release featured the uncut version with all the gore *and* the extra footage in a two-DVD set.

In the end, *Evilspeak* is an interesting title, appearing both older than it actually is (one could easily mistake it for a mid-'70s effort), yet conceptually years ahead of its time (computers utilized for casting evil spells). The various effects are campy yet effective, with plentiful gore, impressive on-screen kills, and a healthy dose of beheadings. While silly moments (and underwhelming overlay shots) abound and horror clichés are littered all over (man-eating pigs, gratuitous nudity, sword-wielding possessed flying nerds), the film is actually pretty damned good. Older brother Ron may have grown up with Andy Griffith, became pals with Fonzie, and

directed his way to the Oscars, but when it comes to true schlock entertainment, nobody does it better than the iconic Clint Howard!

*Nathan Hanneman began writing for Tomart Publications in 1997, eventually serving as editor for both Tomart publications (*Action Figure Digest *and* Disneyana Update*) and co-writing* Tomart's Guide to Horror Movie Collectibles *in 2003 with Aaron Crowell. In 2005, Nathan helped launch* HorrorHound *magazine, which has become the third most popular horror publication in the world under his stewardship. He is also the co-creator of HorrorHound Weekend, the U.S.'s largest horror convention.*

THE EYE 2002

BY SEAN ROBINSON

"WHAT IF THE REFLECTION YOU SEE IS NOT YOURS?" The old cinema in my hometown of Maryport, England, has been closed now for over forty years, but it was in the dark and dingy confines of that old fleapit that I have my first memory of being scared by a movie, an actual sense of palpable terror. That afternoon's feature was Disney's *Snow White and the Seven Dwarfs* and I actually cowered behind the cinema seats when the Queen turned into the old Witch.

This dalliance with pure fear planted the seeds for my lifelong obsession with horror films. I started to delve deeper into the genre, starting with the black-and-white Universal horrors followed by the discovery of Hammer films. I decorated my bedroom walls with posters of Christopher Lee and Peter Cushing to such an extent that my younger sister was afraid to enter my bedroom. I collected Hammer bubble-gum cards and owned every edition of *The House of Hammer* magazine. I even dragged my 70-year-old grandmother to see *Jaws* on a family holiday to Blackpool when it was playing in a small backstreet cinema on a 24-hour loop. I could have stayed in that cinema all day.

Despite (or because of) this childhood fascination with all things horror, I can never really remember being anywhere near as scared again. In my adult years I became a hardened terror movie buff, seeing thousands of fright films over time...that just didn't scare me anymore. I could appreciate that they were considered "scary" and I experienced tension, anxiety, and even jumped a few times, but I never enjoyed that same sense of genuine sweat-inducing fear...

...until about seven years ago when I first watched *The Eye*. I had been on a big Asian horror kick, watching gems like *Ringu* and *Ju-on*, and had heard very good things about *The Eye*, so expectations were raised. It was a bright summer afternoon when I sat down to watch it, but for the first time since I was a child, that cold chill of genuine fear crept over me. When the film was over, I did something I can only remember doing once before (when *Jaws* was first released on DVD): I immediately watched it again.

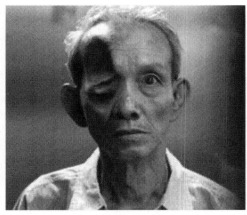

In Hong Kong, eighteen-year-old Wong Kar Mun (the beautiful and talented Malaysian actress Angelica Lee), a classical violinist, has been blind since she was two years old. She agrees to a risky transplant, receiving the cornea of an anonymous donor. At first everything is fine; her vision is restored and Mun gradually adjusts to her new life with sight. However she starts to have troubling visions in the hospital, first with an old lady complaining of bitter cold, followed by a strange silhouetted figure that accompanies the patient in the next bed out of the room. In the morning she finds out the patient died in their sleep during the night.

After several more disturbing visions, including an angry young woman at a calligraphy class who remonstrates Mun for sitting in her seat (one of the best jump scares I've ever experienced) and a strange man in an elevator with half his face missing (a chilling master class in slow, creeping terror), Mun visits a psychologist, Dr. Wah (Lawrence Chou). The two develop a close relationship and soon discover that the reflection Mun is seeing in the mirror...is not her own. They set out to learn who her donor was, a quest that leads to a small village in northern Thailand where mysteries, dark secrets, and skeletons lie waiting, capped by a finale that handily demonstrates Hollywood hasn't solely cornered the market on impressive and explosive spectacles.

Directed by Hong Kong twin brothers Danny and Oxide Pang, *The Eye* (whose original title, *Gin gwai*, literally translates as "Seeing Ghosts") succeeds in terrifying the audience with its impressive visuals. The CGI is easily on par with anything Hollywood was producing at the time—and on a much smaller budget—but it is the excellent sound design that really impresses, raising the gooseflesh and chilling the bones. Thanks to an excellent central performance by Lee (now married to Oxide Pang) and a reliance on atmosphere, style, and substance over shock and gore, the brothers succeeded in creating a ghost story that sits proudly alongside classics like *The Haunting*, *The Innocents*, and *The Uninvited* while surpassing other modern efforts such as *The Others* or *The Sixth Sense*.

The success of the film spawned two sequels, with the first, 2004's *The Eye 2*, well worth seeking out and also featuring another very strong performance by its young female lead, Qi Shu. The following year's *The Eye Infinity* (or rather confusingly, *The Eye 10*), inexplicably went the comedy route; although still entertaining, it's nowhere near the quality of the first two.

The Eye is often included amidst the plethora of post-millennial Japanese horror, despite its directors being from Hong Kong and the film being set in Hong Kong and Thailand. However, this is forgivable as *The Eye* owes much more to moody efforts such as *Ringu* than it does to the traditional Hong Kong action/fantasy horror flicks such as *A Chinese Ghost Story* and the hopping vampires of Tsui Hark with which Westerners may be more familiar.

The Pang brothers (who already had the impressive *Bangkok Haunted* and *Bangkok Dangerous* under their belts) were subsequently courted by Hollywood. They directed 2007's *The Messengers* followed by an ill-advised, ill-fated remake of their own *Bangkok Dangerous* starring Nicholas Cage (which suffered greatly by inexplicably changing a major plot point). *The Eye* also spawned one of the better Hollywood remakes in 2008, although the Pang brothers lost the gig to Frenchman Daniel Moreau, who did a decent job directing Jessica Alba in the lead role. Still, one can't help wondering how the two talented twins might have revisited their original material.

That old cinema changed my world forever. It's not often I get that feeling nowadays, but *The Eye* left me feeling like that small child again. It succeeds where many other films fail, thanks to an excellent central performance and strong supporting cast. It also features at least two of the scariest scenes I have ever seen (yes, even scarier than *Snow White*). It is a masterpiece of Asian cinema that reminds us that beyond the thin veil of normality, a dark and shadowy world may exist, a world that only certain special people can see. It's there standing in the middle of the highway or sitting beside us in class or even standing directly behind us in a lonely elevator.

Sean Robinson lives in Maryport, Cumbria, in England's Lake District with his two horror-loving sons, Curtis and Kenan. He contributed essays on The Exorcist, An American Werewolf in London, *and* The Howling *for HORROR 101. He has written two horror novels,* The Surge *and* Abomination. *He is also the owner of the famous haunted painting* The Anguished Man *recently featured on William Shatner's Weird or What (and potentially the subject of a forthcoming movie—stay tuned...)*

FASCINATION 1979

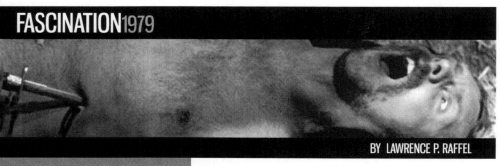

BY LAWRENCE P. RAFFEL

"I'M ONLY TAKEN IF I WANT TO BE. I'M IN CHARGE HERE."

"Some people say I'm a genius, others consider me the greatest moron who ever stepped behind a camera." –Jean Rollin

An extended traveling shot reveals an oil painting and a pair of candles, followed by a pair of gentle female hands gliding slowly across the cover of an aged book. The book cover is unlatched and gracefully opened as the pages are slowly and gently rubbed and caressed before being turned. We cut to a phonograph sitting alone on a stone bridge. There's some light fog and we can sense a damp chill in the air. The camera slowly pans up to reveal two young ladies on the bridge dancing together next to the phonograph. We're barely 3.5 minutes into writer/director Jean Rollin's *Fascination* and already it's a thing of beauty to behold.

By now, you're either thinking to yourself, "This is going to be great!" or "This is pretentious as hell!" I can see both points of view. When it comes to Rollin's work there's a fair share of give and take. To many, he's a master at creating mood though his films are decidedly not for everyone, as evidenced by the above quote from the director himself.

I'm a firm believer that most, if not all, of the French auteur's output falls into the "underrated and overlooked fright flicks" category. To this day I find fellow horror fans confessing their newfound discovery (and respect) of his work, something that somewhat surprises me…that it took them so long. My first encounter with Rollin occurred in the early '90s, dire times indeed with regard to American horror movies. But that period was also a horror fan/tape trader's paradise. Everywhere, folks were swapping relatively obscure horror flicks from around the world by directors with names like Argento, Fulci, and

Bava (to name just a few). We were looking for something different, something fresh, something new, and, preferably, something uncut. These imports offered fresh stories, storytellers, cinematic styles, and an escape from their American counterparts.

Enter Rollin and his canon of erotic French horror films, the director's personal sub-genre of choice (although he often dabbled in hardcore adult fare as well). They were short, many running less than 90 minutes, and often featured little to no dialogue. His simple, stylish productions were put together with minimal money, support, or enthusiasm from his co-producers or hometown audience.

Despite these challenges, Rollin was responsible for a handful of features prior to *Fascination*'s release in 1979. His first full-length offering, 1968's *Le Viol du Vampire* (*The Rape of the Vampire*), was rife with scandal. He went on to direct several additional erotic vampire films including 1970's *La vampire nue* (*The Nude Vampire*), his first to be shot in color, and *Requiem for a Vampire* (aka *Caged Virgins*) later the same year, the latter of which quickly became one of his most financially successful endeavors. 1975's *Levres de sang* (*Lips of Blood*), meanwhile, stands as a polar opposite to *Fascination* in which the sexy vampires serve as a diversion to a young man trying to seek out a long-lost love.

A prime example of Rollin working at his best with the very least, *Fascination* is about as moody and surreal—while still accessible—an erotic horror film as one could hope for. The story follows two beautiful women, Eva (gorgeous

Rollin regular Brigitte Lahaie) and Elisabeth (equally lovely Franca Mai), held up in a *grande chateau* awaiting the remainder of the guests for an annual reunion. In the meantime, having just stolen from his partners, a crafty thief (Jean-Marie Lemaire) hides out in the selfsame castle (well, he *thinks* he's crafty, considering the place is surrounded by water; one way in, one way out). The lovely young ladies tease and taunt the thief, always allowing him to feel he has the upper hand. It isn't long before we discover what's really going on—these women are up to something, and being bad has never looked so good.

While I've always thought of *The Grapes of Death* (1978) and *The Living Dead Girl* (1982) as Rollin's most mainstream efforts (zombies!), *Fascination* (with its quasi-vampire plot) is a shining example of the director at his most straightforward without compromising the elements I love about these films and the virtuoso behind them.

As a filmmaker, Rollin is a visual artist. Silver screen his canvas, camera his brush. He's also a poet, one unlike any the world has ever seen. To watch *Fascination* is to experience it as visual poetry, riding waves of emotions that have nothing to do with conventional narrative drive. His is not a craft of traditional manipulation, but a rather more personal, individual audience relationship.

While undeniably sexy, with lots of nudity and scenes involving rubbing, petting, and light grunting, *Fascination* never descends to prurient jerk-off material, thus transcending the Skinemax curse. Yet the film is erotic before the first dress falls to the floor. (Oh, to switch places with that tenderly caressed book during the opening frames.) But *Fascination* isn't just about lust. Sweeping camera shots, vacation-worthy castle locales, and a nifty little crim-

inal subplot will seduce you long before your first glance at bevies of gorgeous French dames in see-through chiffon finery (and little else).

Speaking of beautiful French women, one would be remiss to not highlight Lahaie. One of the stars (and main draws) of *Fascination*, the actress originally got her start in the adult film industry and, despite dipping her feet into more "legit" fare, never really escaped her past. Rollin provided the leap from hardcore to mainstream for Lahaie with *The Grapes of Death*; after *Fascination*, the two continued to work together in *The Night of the Hunted* (1980) and *La fiancée de Dracula* (2002). Lahaie's other notable genre credits include Jess Franco's *Faceless* (1987) and Fabrice du Welz's *Calvaire* (2004), as well as a small mainstream role in 1990's *Henry & June*.

As Eva, Lahaie exudes sexuality at every turn, yet the viewer always senses that the actress—like most of her lovely female co-stars—is in charge and never feels she's being taken advantage of. Strong female characters are at the heart of nearly every Rollin picture and *Fascination* is no exception. While most genre filmmakers at the time were keen to exploit women, Rollin celebrated their beauty and their power.

No doubt, this was an artist whose love of the horror genre and the female form is evident in nearly his entire body of work. *Fascination* represents a scrappy, sexy, lyrical, and emotional journey that belongs on every self-proclaimed genre fan's must-watch list. Besides, the iconic image of Lahie brandishing a scythe while wearing a black cape and nothing else should be known to horror fans the world over. Period.

Lawrence P. Raffel launched the independent horror review website Monsters at Play in 2001, a small-scale experiment that blossomed into a thriving online horror community. In August of 2006, Lawrence left Monsters at Play to help launch the horror channel FEARnet where he still resides today as FEARnet. com's VP, Digital Content / Editor-In-Chief. A lifelong horror fan, some of Lawrence's favorite horror directors include Dario Argento, Mario Bava, Jean Rollin and David Cronenberg.

FRAILTY 2001

BY FREDDIE YOUNG

The early 2000s were an interesting time for the horror genre. The Nu-Slasher cycle that started with Wes Craven's 1996 classic, *Scream*, was quickly cannibalizing itself while two 1999 mainstream successes, *The Sixth Sense* and *The Blair Witch Project*, had sparked an interest in more adult (i.e. less bloody) "thrillers." When horror fans discuss their favorite efforts from this period, the usual suspects pop up: *Final Destination*, *Ginger Snaps*, *American Psycho* (2000); *The Others*, *Session 9*, *Jeepers Creepers* (2001); and *The Ring*, *Dog Soldiers*, *28 Days Later...*, *Bubba Ho-Tep*, *Cabin Fever* (2002).

"YOU'RE MY SON, AND I LOVE YOU MORE THAN MY OWN LIFE. BUT YOU KNOW WHAT'S FUNNY ABOUT ALL OF THIS, FENTON? I'M AFRAID OF YOU."

But for some reason, until I mention it, *Frailty* never comes to mind. And that's a shame.

A mysterious young Texas man, Fenton Meiks (Matthew McConaughey), reveals to FBI agent Aaron Doyle (Powers Boothe) that he knows the identity of a local serial killer known as "God's Hand." Doyle has his doubts at first, but as Fenton unfolds his childhood story, the lawman starts to wonder....

The tale begins in 1979, with Fenton (Matt O'Leary) and his younger brother Adam (Jeremy Sumpter) living a normal life with their loving and attentive Christian father (Bill Paxton). However, one night Meiks awakens his sons with the news that he has had a vision, one in which God has called on him and his boys to serve as slayers of demons. Of course, these demons, who threaten the existence of the world, are moving amongst us...disguised as human beings. Along the way, Meiks receives three "sacred weapons" for the tasks ahead—an axe, a pair of gloves, and a lead pipe. Adam is excited about being a demon hunter, comparing the act to that of a superhero. But Fenton is understandably concerned, thinking his father has lost his mind.

In addition to essaying the key role of Meiks, Paxton made his directorial debut with *Frailty*, a fact that piqued my interest. Would the reliable character actor prove himself as worthy behind the camera as before it, or should he

stick to thespian work? When *Frailty* entered NYC theaters in 2002, the screening I attended was barely more than a quarter full. I instantly fell in love with the storytelling, visual presentation, and impressive mystery that unveiled itself. I actively recommended it to friends and family, but with other studio-supported features like *Panic Room*, *My Big Fat Greek Wedding*, and *The Scorpion King* released around the same time, *Frailty* made barely a dent at the box office and quickly disappeared. (Even so, the film's $18 million theatrical gross more than covered its modest $11 million budget, making it a moderate success for distributor Lionsgate.)

Though it eventually developed an appreciative following on home video, *Frailty* remains a film few people discuss at any length. It rarely comes up in discussion, nor is it part of any television programming director's regular rotation. How did this gem, so great on so many levels, with a high level of re-watchability, become so forgotten and unappreciated?

The acting by everyone involved is superlative, with Paxton, McConaughey, and Boothe exceptional in their respective roles. (All three leads are native Texans, a casting choice the director felt imperative, and one which I agree brings a level of realism to the film's surreal world.) Subtle, believable, and occasionally creepy, Paxton delivers some of his finest work in *Frailty*, playing a character that the viewer, like his onscreen son, will continue to second-guess. Is he crazy or an authentic servant of God? McConaughey is equally effective as the mysterious narrator who may (or may not be) unreliable. With everything seen through his character's point of view, the rising star's cold delivery makes us wonder if Fenton's trauma-filled past has made him this way...or is there more to the story than he's revealing? As the skeptical government agent, the always-great Boothe serves as the character the audience most connects with, as we collectively try to decipher the truth of Fenton's story. The youngest members of the ensemble, O'Leary and Sumpter, also do very well in their roles.

However, it is Paxton's direction that really makes *Frailty* an interesting and satisfying watch. The rookie helmsman originally intended to show the audience what Meiks sees when touching the "demons" he's about to destroy, but frequent collaborator James Cameron talked him out of this, correctly intuiting it would be more effective to preserve the mystery as long as possible. Instead, Paxton blurs the image of his actors reacting to the "visions," never showing the object of their gaze. Cinematographer Bill Butler's expert framing and composition and Arnold Glassman's precise editing are also key to *Frailty*'s mysterious and effective storytelling. The audience is kept wondering if this is all in Meiks' head—and even when we finally know the answers, we're still unsure whether what we've seen is real or not.

Brent Hanley's subtle yet powerful screenplay was inspired by his Catholic school teachings and a love for the work of Stephen King. According to Hanley, the struggle between Meiks and Fenton is a modern take on the Old Testament "binding of Isaac" story, in which Abraham is instructed to sacrifice his son to show loyalty to God, until Abraham is stopped by an angel of God. The difference is that Meiks refuses to sacrifice Fenton, even when he's "told" that Fenton may be a demon he must destroy. Hanley refers to the film's title as "the frailty of perception, the frailty of morality, and the frailty of right and wrong."

Hanley was also inspired by the story of serial killer Joseph Kallinger, who murdered three people and tortured other families, often bringing his teenage son along to witness and/or help. In court, Kallinger claimed that he was acting under God's instructions, ultimately pleading insanity to get a lesser charge for his crimes. *Frailty*'s power lies in its all-too-believable situation, and the fact that the audience spends so much time relating to these characters, with the answer to whether we should support or condemn their acts constantly in flux.

Though we ultimately learn "the truth" by *Frailty*'s conclusion, we're still left with questions. Is Meiks crazy? Why was he picked by God to be his demon destroyer? Why can Adam see what his father sees but not Fenton? Is Fenton really a demon? Does Meiks fail his test or succeed? Are there other "God's Hands" out there? Hanley and Paxton leave the audience thinking about what they've just seen, and what is "true," what is "right," what is "good."

Maybe that's why *Frailty* isn't talked about as much as other horror movies released around this time. It's a cerebral film, one that is inherently violent without showing much bloodshed. While other flicks rely on gore effects and wacky twist endings whose only point is to shock with one last scare, *Frailty* is subtle and ambiguous, giving its audience the freedom to arrive at their own terrifying conclusions. We are left thinking about how frail we can be when obeying a higher power, be it our parents, the law, or even an all-powerful deity. Would we do what He wishes, or would we try and reason with Him and make Him see that some things Man should not be a part of? I don't know the answer. Like they say, God only knows.

Freddie Young resides in Brooklyn, New York, and is the driving force behind Full Moon Reviews, a horror, action, and fantasy blog he created in 2008. A Film Studies graduate, he's been rotting his brain with both good and bad horror flicks since childhood. Freddie hopes to keep the horror alive through his writing and filmmaking aspirations.

FRANKENSTEIN MEETS THE WOLF MAN 1943

BY DUSTIN JABLONSKI

"YOU THINK I'M INSANE. YOU THINK I DON'T KNOW WHAT I'M TALKING ABOUT. WELL, YOU JUST LOOK IN THAT GRAVE WHERE LAWRENCE TALBOT IS SUPPOSED TO BE BURIED AND SEE IF YOU FIND A BODY IN IT!"

Christmas 1990 was a memorable one for me. I asked for (and received!) a VHS copy of *Frankenstein Meets the Wolf Man* as well as Phil Riley's *Magic Image Filmbook* about the movie. I could not wait to watch the film and to devour Greg Mank's detailed production history. (Up to that point I had only read about it in issue #42 of *Famous Monsters of Filmland* and my beloved Crestwood House Monster Series book.) I was absolutely mesmerized by Lon Chaney Jr.'s performance and the climactic final scenes between the two titular titans of terror.

Frankenstein Meets the Wolf Man holds a special place in Hollywood history as being the first movie to pair up two monsters as a gimmick to draw in audiences. Due to its financial success, other Universal monster rally films followed, including *House of Frankenstein, House of Dracula*, and *Abbott and Costello Meet Frankenstein*. The 1960s featured Japanese *kaiju* stompathons while the 1980s brought classic monster movie lovers *Transylvania 6-5000* and *The Monster Squad*. Its influence even extends to 21st century titles like *Freddy vs. Jason* or *Alien vs. Predator.* This "Death Fight Between Two Beasts!" helped Universal Studios turn a tidy profit in 1943 and launched a horror film subgenre in the process.

Yet, the original double-creature-feature remains woefully underappreciated by classic horror fans, its only critical commentary being of a negative nature directed toward Bela Lugosi's performance as the Frankenstein Monster. Furthermore, in comparison to other classic Universal Monsters movies, *Frankenstein Meets the Wolf Man* never receives the glowing reviews of such highly regarded treasures as the original *Frankenstein* or *Bride of Frankenstein*. However, it's probably fairer to judge the film beside those it inspired to properly evaluate its originality and overall production values.

Universal often lacked continuity in its various classic horror series; locations changed, geography shifted, and time periods became extremely elastic. (Here, to join the two series, the Frankenstein timeline was bumped up to a more contemporary setting.) But thanks to skilled screenwriter Curt Siodmak, a worthy effort was made to maintain story continuity between *The Wolf Man* (1941) and, to a lesser degree, *The Ghost of Frankenstein* (1942).

According to Siodmak's foreword to Riley's *Magic Image Filmbook*, the concept started as a joke at the Universal Studios commissary. The writer told producer George Waggner in jest that "they should do a picture called Frankenstein Wolfs the Meat Man—I mean *Frankenstein Meets the Wolf Man*." Waggner laughed...and promptly commissioned Siodmak to come up with the script; the rest is Hollywood history. It makes sense that the werewolf narrative is more compelling, being that Siodmak conceptualized the original Wolf Man legend

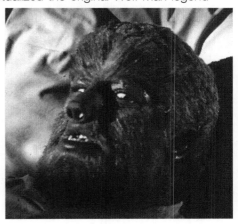

two years prior, but he also does an admirable job of weaving the Frankenstein legend into the mix.

As the film opens, Larry Talbot's (Chaney) grave is robbed, which leads to the accidental resurrection of the lycanthrope. Local authorities pick up Larry and carry him to the hospital to receive care from Dr. Mannering (Patric Knowles). When attempting to identify the patient, Inspector Owens (Dennis Hoey) contacts the police in Cardiff and discovers that Talbot died several years ago. During the next full moon, the werewolf kills a local policeman. Larry

escapes and seeks out the old gypsy woman Maleva (Maria Ouspenskaya), who suggests heading to Vasaria to obtain the medical help of Dr. Frankenstein. En route, Larry transforms again and kills a local woman. Pursued by a village mob, he falls into the icy cave where the Frankenstein Monster is entombed. Larry frees the Monster and searches for the famed scientist's records. The journals do not turn up but they find a photo of Dr. Frankenstein's daughter, Elsa (Ilona Massey). Talbot tracks down Elsa under the pretense of purchasing the old Frankenstein castle. The inevitable battle between the monsters provides a memorable conclusion.

The atmospheric resurrection of Talbot is a great lead-in, and director Roy William Neill (who cut his horror teeth on the 1935 Boris Karloff vehicle *The Black Room* and the lesser known 1932 voodoo chiller *Black Moon*) makes the most of his fog-covered cemetery and crypt. Siodmak also finds dramatic tension by giving Talbot direction in his ongoing search either for a cure from his lycanthropy or eternal peace in death. Clearly the ideal person would be Dr. Frankenstein, the one man who holds the secrets to life and death. Even the method in which Talbot learns of Dr. Frankenstein is fairly reasonable; Maleva, in her travels throughout the European countryside, would surely have heard of the misguided genius.

Siodmak planned on giving the Monster dialogue, since at the end of *Ghost of Frankenstein*, Ygor successfully manipulates Dr. Bohmer into using his brain for the Monster instead Dr. Kettering's. It makes perfect sense that the next entry in the series should use Lugosi as the Monster's voice, as it was at the end of *Ghost of Frankenstein*. When Lugosi agreed to play the part of the Monster, it seemed like a natural progression. But in reviewing the rushes, Universal Studios' production team quickly determined that Lugosi's trademark Hungarian accent sounded comical and ordered all of his dialogue removed from the final

film, as well as any references to the Monster being blind. Is it any wonder that the actor's mute, stumbling performance seems ill at ease and out of place?

This dramatic last-minute executive decision is the key to understanding the picture's perceived flaws. Would it really have been that difficult for audiences to imagine the voice of Ygor coming out of the Monster's mouth? Shouldn't the creative team have been able to expose these problems before filming began, allowing Siodmak to rework the script and Lugosi to alter his interpretation? Instead the production continued as planned, only to have the tables turned at the last second. Yet, in spite of all this, the picture is thoroughly entertaining. One has to wonder where its historical estimation would be had it been allowed a less problematic genesis.

A box office smash, it later became a staple of the Shock Theater package released to television stations in 1957. Since Universal has always treated *Frankenstein Meets the Wolf Man* as a major entry in their horror film catalogue, giving it its first VHS release in 1986 (by comparison, *Ghost of Frankenstein* did not get released until 1993), it's hard to believe a title this popular can still be viewed as a lesser film that rarely appears on any top ten lists. Sure, there are many true classics making the competition fierce, but this particular offering is guaranteed to bring enjoyment to fans of both series. Chaney is electric in his second appearance as Talbot and it's also one of the last times the Frankenstein Monster was more than a simple prop with minimal action sequences.

Frankenstein Meets the Wolf Man represents a true dichotomy: a beloved horror staple denied the respect it richly deserves, written off as the beginning of the end of Universal's noble horror lineage. I prefer to see it as a fun, fast-paced, and slick episodic bit of escapism which—under a bit less scrutiny—still endures as a pleasurable viewing experience 70 years later.

Dustin Jablonski became a Universal Studios Monsters fan after being given his father's Aurora monster models and Famous Monsters *#134 at age four. He has contributed material to* House of Ackerman, The Forrest J. Ackerman Oeuvre, We Belong Dead, *and an upcoming volume on Lon Chaney's lost film* Thunder. *A husband and father, Dustin owns over 2000 reference books, photoplays and other paper material on classic horror/sci-fi films. Facebook/monstermoviebooks*

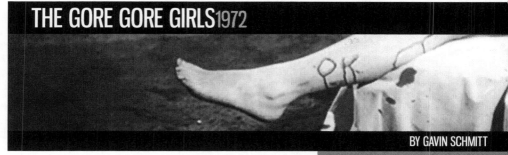

THE GORE GORE GIRLS 1972

BY GAVIN SCHMITT

Herschell Gordon Lewis began directing films in 1951, becoming a pioneer in the "nudie cutie" genre. In the 1960s, he left his mark in the world of horror, creating what many consider his twin masterpieces, *Blood Feast* (1963) and *Two Thousand Maniacs!* (1964), rightfully earning his "Godfather of Gore" moniker. But Lewis saved the best for last, releasing his funniest, goriest picture as a fond farewell to fans: *The Gore Gore Girls*!

> "ONE OF MY FRIENDS SEEMS TO HAVE RUN INTO A BIT OF TROUBLE... AND LOST HER FACE."

(Yes, he did briefly return thirty years later with the seemingly Prince-inspired title *Blood Feast 2: All U Can Eat*, but we'll just pretend that never happened.)

What we have are a series of murders surrounding the city's strip club district. The local newspaper—knowing this is the story of a lifetime—hires legendary private detective Abraham Gentry (Frank Kress) to track down the killer, since the police seem obviously inept at the task. Using his advance payment at the local go-go clubs to observe the patrons and interview the dancers (with such names as Candy Cane and Suzy Creampuff), Gentry begins to compile a list of suspects, including an ex-Vietnam vet who loves to crush produce. But who is the killer and what is his motive?

The Gore Gore Girls is Lewis' best film, full stop. While not one of his "masterpieces" that he will go down in history for, this is the one that really pushes the exploitation genre to its peak: crushed brains, eyeballs pulled out, and lots of stripping. And say what you will about Montag the Magnificent, Mayor Buckman, or Fuad Ramses (all great Lewis characters), Abraham Gentry is just so suave and cocky, he could have appeared in sequel after sequel and

I would devour them like flamingos after shrimp. Yet, despite his self-assured nature, he never does seem too attracted to the women. In fact, he goes out of his way not to touch them. Do they bore the man of refined tastes, is he germophobic, or is there something more? Shockingly, this was Kress' first and last film. Where did he come from? Where did he go? Was he not interested in acting after Lewis retired? His absence is our loss.

What has made the film controversial for many people is not, believe it or not, the excessive gore, but a perceived inherent misogyny. Quite honestly, I do not see it. Sure, Gentry is not particularly kind to the ladies. But he does not seem to like the men any better. Yes, the film flatly exploits women and their bodies (with most of its running time taking place in strip clubs). But it also has a women's liberation movement subplot (shown in what I would call a neutral light). There is really nothing here that cannot be seen in any other horror or exploitation film. Nude women in the late 1960s and early '70s? Are we that shocked by this? I suppose a plotline centering on the murder of women could be seen as misogynous, and the scene where a pair of nipples are cut off and two different flavors of milk come out is pretty out-there, despite obviously being intended as dark humor. But compare this to the straight-faced abuse suffered by the women in Fulci's *New York Ripper* where one victim has her genitals mutilated by a broken bottle while another has her breasts sliced up with a razor blade. The so-called misogyny shown in *Gore Gore Girls* seems quaint and welcome in comparison. There is also never any indication that the violence comes from an actual hatred of women—there is a distinct line between killing to kill and killing for hate; that line is never crossed here.

Less controversial, but far more memorable, is the gore. While perhaps not groundbreaking for mainstream fans weaned on KNB effects, one scene will stand out for those familiar with the work of Herschell Gordon Lewis. Lewis had previously offered grisly torture in *The Wizard of Gore* and some great death traps in *Two Thousand Maniacs!* (The barrel roll, anyone?) But in *The Gore Gore Girls*, he pushes the splatter to eleven on the blood-and-guts scale. Which scene am I referencing? The french-fried face? The sizzling hot iron? The scissors-snipped, milk-squirting nipples? The eyeball-squeezing? No. In one scene, a stripper is actually murdered by having her buttocks tenderized into hamburger with a mallet. No stabbing, no bone-crushing, no poison. Just excessive paddling. For good measure, recall that the killer adds a little bit of seasoning to the carnal creation.

Some interesting things to notice for those paying attention: Ray Sager (aka Montag from *Wizard of Gore*, who also serves as a second unit director) has a cameo, and the bottle of acid in the film is "made in Poland." (I am not really sure what to make of that, but it seems entirely fitting.) The club owner is, yes,

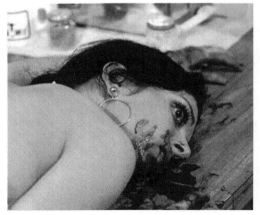

Henny Youngman, the comedian who originated the "Take my wife... please" one-liner. He repeatedly denied appearing in this movie until his death. I have no idea why.

Top it all off with Lewis' most charming actress yet (Amy Farrell as reporter Nancy Weston) and we have a winner. Farrell, sadly, only made one other picture: *Airport 1975*, co-starring Linda Blair, Charlton Heston, and Karen Black. This is also writer Alan J. Dachman's only screenplay—and Lewis only agreed to Dachman's script because his father offered to finance it! In fact, with the exception of Youngman (a friend of Dachman Sr.) and Lewis' assistant Alex Ameri (who both shot and edited the movie), everyone involved with *Gore Gore Girls* had no career in the movie industry before or since!

At one point, Lewis' films were considered lost and not worth finding, so he retired from directing and went into advertising. His absence in the '70s, '80s, and '90s may be the horror community's greatest loss. Yet, while I believe this film's greatness can hardly be overstated, we must be careful not to go overboard. Lewis biographer Randy Miller compares the black-gloved strip club killer with the antagonists of the Italian giallo tradition, which is just wishful thinking. The murderers may have a similar fashion sense, but this is where the similarity ends; the giallo subgenre is art where an HGL flick is gratuitous gore. The artistry lies in the sense of play and fun. Lewis may be many things, but a superb technical director is not one of them. And thank goodness!

Gavin Schmitt has spent over three decades trying to survive in the wilds of Wisconsin. So far, he has succeeded. Aside from his contribution here, he has authored articles for HorrorHound *and* Informer *magazines, and published* Milwaukee Mafia, *the definitive work on organized crime in that city. He writes regularly for northeast Wisconsin newspaper* The Scene. *When not watching horror films, he might be found drinking too much coffee at a local cafe.*

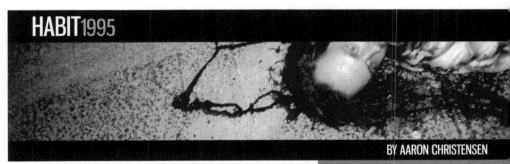

HABIT 1995

BY AARON CHRISTENSEN

Habit: [hab-it] noun, 1) an acquired behavior pattern regularly followed until it has become almost involuntary; 2) a dominant or regular disposition or tendency; prevailing character or quality; 3) addiction, especially to alcohol or narcotics

> "I SUSPECT THAT THE LESS YOU KNOW ABOUT ME, THE LONGER YOU'LL STAY INTERESTED."

The vampire of legend is eternal, and its cinematic brethren are equally durable and widespread. Even before the post-millennial pop culture phenomena of *Twilight* and *True Blood* (among others) but especially in their wake, it's refreshing and rewarding to encounter an undead feature possessing a genuinely grounded and unique interpretation.

As Larry Fessenden's *Habit* (alongside George Romero's *Martin*, Abel Ferrara's *The Addiction*, and Michael Almereyda's *Nadja*) shows, it's not just about bringing the vampire into contemporary settings. Since the 1930s, the silver screen has hosted an array of "modern" bloodsuckers preying upon hip and sensible disbelievers. What's often missing is a true sense of personality, vision, and passion, and it is here that *Habit* delivers with both barrels. No other artist could have made this picture; Fessenden's DNA runs through the sprockets at 24fps and his fierce integrity elevates it above other generic toothy thrillers. Like all great fanged flicks, the fantasy exists as an allegory for something deeper—intelligent and heady material perfectly interwoven with horror trappings such that the subtext eases into our brains unperceived... where it can burrow and grow.

Sam (Fessenden) is introduced recovering from the sudden death of his archeologist father, but it's clear that life has not been going well for some time. His longtime girlfriend Liza (renowned solo artist Heather Woodbury), troubled by his general aimlessness and excessive drinking, has recently moved out. He manages a bar/restaurant, but this is clearly not his passion. In fact, passion is decidedly missing from Sam's world; in its place a yawning disconnectedness into which he pours nightly gallons of booze. He has few interests or friends, and those that he does have, like Rae (Patricia Coleman) and Nick (Aaron

Beall), cluck disapprovingly behind his back. At one point, he refers to himself as "committing suicide on the installment plan."

Into this bleak existence enters Anna (Meredith Snaider, magnetic and sensual in her only screen role), a classy and together mystery gal who sets her unassailable gaze on Sam during a Halloween party. Before long, the two are enjoying public sexual assignations, encounters that end with him alone—bewildered and bleeding—come the morning hours. As their relationship blooms, our hero grows more sickly and wan, leading him to wonder about his paramour's true nature.

What is *Habit* really about? Vampires? Alcoholism? Addiction? Urban disconnectedness? The oppressive, nameless fears of metropolitan life? Sex? Disease? Or is it about Mars, Venus, and the great chasm between the sexes? The answer is yes to all of these and more. Via email, Fessenden explained that he was attempting "a traditional horror story told in a stark, naturalistic way, with heavy life or death themes in the presence of the supernatural. I love looking for new truths in old clichés."

Tweaking of traditions is key to his approach. Repeated references are made to the classic vampires of old: Anna's seeming aversion to garlic, not entering Sam's apartment until invited in, only appearing during sunless hours, etc. Naturally, Stoker's *Dracula* is cribbed from the most, introducing not only a ghost ship sailing into New York's harbor (a la the *Demeter*'s ill-fated voyage from Transylvania), but also a Lucy Westerna character—rocker/waitstaff Lenny (Jesse Hartman), the first of the vampire's unfortunate victims.

Revisiting a long-form video project from Fessenden's NYU undergrad days, *Habit* was shot over the course of three months for a paltry $60,000.

Being that the writer/director/editor was also onscreen for nearly every set-up, a communal responsibility for the project was quickly cultivated, with DP Frank DeMarco and producer Dayton Taylor covering a multitude of roles. Even so, the script is wildly ambitious, with wolves running loose in Central Park, a shattered fire hydrant showering an auto accident's aftermath, late night strolls passing racy photography shoots (a restaging of Nelson Bakerman's "Wall Street Nude" project). There is a desperation sensed on both sides of the camera; Sam the character wondering if he will live through this relationship, the tiny crew wondering if they will complete the film—or even that night's shoot. Watching Fessenden run naked through the midnight streets or hang from a sixth story apart-

ment complex window, we feel the passion of a deeply committed artist inside the skin of a vulnerable character out of his depth. We find ourselves rooting for both, on completely different levels, at exactly the same time.

Fessenden's inherent scruffy likability, highlighted by a missing front tooth, makes for an excellent wounded protagonist. His Sam is clearly intelligent, witty, charismatic, but we instantly recognize him as that friend who could be anything if he would just pull himself together, the one we root for even as we maintain an arm's length to avoid being dragged down if/when he goes under.

The film possesses a certain timelessness (excepting the diner scene's giant mobile phone) and as a writer, Fessenden is much more concerned with character than plot. Some might complain about the leisurely pace, whether we really need to see Sam cleaning out the litter box or pour his two cups of coffee into a saucepan for reheating, but each scene has its rewards, especially upon repeat viewings. If there is a scene that deserves excision, it's the unnecessary third-act confrontation between Sam and Nick, lousy with on-the-nose discussions of whether or not Anna is a vampire (the only time the word is used) and needless exposition about Sam's financial status. It's a rare misstep, but it's a doozy.

As the mystery unfolds in Fessenden's deceptively mundane fashion, several moments rich with possibilities and ambiguity emerge. One shining illustration is when Sam visits his late father's historical society to receive a posthumous award: while Sam is talking to our ostensible Van Helsing character, Mr. Lyons (Lon Waterford), we see Liza enter the frame but in the reverse shot she miraculously becomes Anna. The surprised expression on Lyons' face is open to interpretation: Did he see her transform? Does he know Anna from before? (Likely, since he later calls Sam wanting to talk about her.) What is the strange totem Anna gives to Sam? Why does the assembled group take such an interest in it? Where did she get it? Did she have something to do with Sam's father's sudden demise? Or is Sam imagining all of this?

Inside the head of a potentially unreliable narrator, we often wonder whether what we're seeing is true ("is she or isn't she?") or just Sam's potentially addled perception/fantasy of events. Fessenden tweaks the equation even further, allowing us to eavesdrop on an intimate nighttime conversation between Anna and Rae. This shaded viewpoint continues throughout, right down to the brilliantly ambiguous final shot as Tom Laverack's aching acoustic tune "Mystery" shatters our sensibilities and our hearts break at a struggle lost. Then, in the blink of an eye and a shift of a lens, everything is upside down. Is it true, to paraphrase Joseph Conrad, that we all live—and die—as we dream...alone? That *Habit* ends on a tragic note is undeniable. What remains thrillingly unclear is the nature of the tragedy.

Aaron Christensen is a Chicago-based actor and writer whose blithe and blithering babblings have appeared in numerous printed publications, online destinations and notable lavatories of ill repute around the globe. Aaron served as editor for the Rondo-nominated guidebook, HORROR 101: The A-List of Horror Films and Monster Movies *and is the main scribbler behind the* "HORROR 101/FOOL'S VIEWS with Dr. AC" *blogs.*

HALLOWEEN III: SEASON OF THE WITCH 1982

BY LEE MAROHN

"YOU DON'T REALLY KNOW MUCH ABOUT HALLOWEEN."

"Eight more days to Halloween...Halloween... Halloween. Eight more days to Halloween...Silver Shamrock." Had I heard that jingle as a kid, it would have scared the heck out of me. It would probably creep me out to this day. Unfortunately, many people have deprived themselves of this bit of frightful nostalgia by choosing to ignore the unfairly maligned *Halloween III: Season of the Witch.*

After escaping his pursuers, a man is brought to a hospital, clutching a Halloween mask while whispering, "They're going to kill us...all of us." Moments later, he is gruesomely murdered in his bed. Naturally, his daughter Ellie (Stacey Nelkin) and physician Dan Challis (Tom Atkins) take it upon themselves to investigate, their search bringing them to the small Irish community of Santa Mira which is supported largely by the local Silver Shamrock Halloween mask factory. Conal Cochran (Dan O'Herlihy), the owner of the factory, is actually some kind of Celtic warlock, intent on celebrating Samhain the old-fashioned way: with the blood of millions of children.

For years, everyone told me to avoid this movie like the plague. I was thirteen years old when it was originally released and not yet heavily into horror. I had been suitably terrified by Michael Myers in *Halloween* and *Halloween II*, but as he was not a part of this new movie, I figured seeing it was pointless. After it came out on home video, I vaguely remember talking with a schoolmate who mentioned that it was actually quite good, but the bulk of his argument revolved around the "cool factor" of evil masks. Evil masks? Not interested. Over the next thirty years, it faded further and further from my mind. The only time I ever heard about it was if the whole franchise was being discussed—inevitably, it would be mentioned, but only in a negative way.

As time went on, my intake of horror movies increased, as did my circle of like-minded fans. One day, during a post-movie gabfest, several friends spoke highly of this long-neglected flick and suggested I give it a try. With a "31 Days of Horror" challenge on the horizon coinciding with a bargain-basement DVD find, *Halloween III* soon made my short list of films to watch. It was one of the happiest surprises I've had in years.

In the documentary *Stand Alone: The Making of Halloween III*, writer/director Tommy Lee Wallace and director of photography Dean Cundey both mention that producers John Carpenter and Debra Hill intended for the Halloween franchise (such as it was) to evolve into an anthology series of unrelated Halloween-themed films. Famed UK sci-fi scribe Nigel Kneale was tapped to write the script based on Hill's story concept. According to Wallace in an interview with *Rue Morgue*, Kneale rejected all of Carpenter's editorial suggestions and eventually abandoned the project. Most of Kneale's anti-Irish concepts (he was British, after all) were removed, though Cochran's Irish ancestry remained. Wallace notes that although he ultimately received the sole onscreen writing credit, Carpenter also did a rewrite and more than half of the final screenplay is the product of Kneale's imagination. He also acknowledges the inspiration of 1956's *Invasion of the Body Snatchers* (the fictitious Santa Mira is even the setting for both films), calling *Halloween III* "a pod movie."

Removed from the *Halloween* franchise, *Season of the Witch* could have easily stood on its own. A huge departure from the two slasher installments that came before, it has none of the same characters (although that is an unbilled Jamie Lee Curtis as our Santa Mira curfew announcer and phone operator, so maybe Laurie Strode moved there to escape Haddonfield), and in fact, except for the mention of Samhain—more pronounced but still subtle—there's nothing even remotely similar. Instead, it offers up a terrific plot (the combination of ancient evil Celtic magic with technology is brilliant), great acting, excellent music, and some *outstanding* gore courtesy of f/x expert Tom Burman.

This movie has everything a great horror flick needs: psycho killers, memorable death scenes, intriguing storyline, and a heroic protagonist trying to figure out what the hell is going on. (Granted, we're dealing with Celtic magic, derived from Stonehenge, intended to bring about blood sacrifices in celebration of Samhain here, so Challis' confusion is quite understandable.) There are three Halloween masks spotlighted in the movie that appear to have evil magic powers boosted by computer technology. Mysterious men in identical business suits, never uttering a word, do much of the killing at Silver Shamrock owner Cochran's behest, and while the deaths are not that graphic by today's standards, most are very brutal. In fact, the variety of creative kills is fantastic: crushing, squeezing, burning, power tools...and those aren't even the best ones!

As Challis, the effortlessly badass Atkins is thoroughly in his element and

though Nelkin is a little underused, she still performs well. But it is O'Herlihy, rarely seen without a large, friendly smile, who steals the show with his stellar villainous performance. I particularly enjoy the scene where, after he has captured our hero, he proclaims that the good doctor will have to figure out the plan on his own...and then proceeds to tell him the plan! As he calmly reveals the vicious truth of what's really going on, O'Herlihy *becomes* Cochran while evil just seems to ooze from his pores.

Various supporting characters show up to provide subplot comedy and gore punchlines, in particular a family in town to tour the mask factory, and Mrs. Guttman (Garn Stephens), the owner of a store in San Francisco. In a scene that took me completely by surprise, the obnoxious Mrs. Guttman gives us our first glimpse of the masks' true power while the Kupfer family is ridiculous and lovable right up until their gruesome ends. (I can't be sure, but I think their dated '80s clothing was already dated in the '80s.)

Who knows what might have happened if *Halloween III* had been more successful? Maybe we'd have a series of unconnected (or slightly connected?) films set on and around Halloween. On some level, I'd still love to see an October-inspired anthology series, something along the lines of 2007's similarly underrated *Trick 'r Treat*. I've seen all of the movies in the *Halloween* franchise at this point, and while I love the first two, serving up the same old "stab, stab, toss-through-a-window" action with a bigger body count is not enough to keep me interested.

With all due respect to Michael Myers and the legacy he has carved out, in many ways this is a far more ambitious and superior outing than the series' later outings…which is why it has now earned a place among the select films I watch every October 31. Everyone sing along now:

"Happy Happy Halloween…Halloween…Halloween. Happy Happy Halloween…Sil-ver Shamrock!"

Lee Marohn, a giant self-described Star Wars/LEGO/comic book/movie nerd, has lived nearly his whole life in the Oshkosh, WI, area. His introduction to horror can be traced to midnight showings of old horror & sci-fi flicks on a local TV station, particularly the Universal Monsters. He worked as both cast and crew on the 2012 independent feature Dead Weight and would be happy doing nothing else but producing movies for the rest of his life.

THE HANDS OF ORLAC 1924

BY ASHLEY THORPE

The end of the First World War plunged Germany into a period of intense upheaval that was naturally reflected in the arts. It was a time of artistic unrest, especially amongst the younger generations who, having experienced the horrors of the war, rebelled against old ideas and tired beliefs under the banner of Expressionism.

Subtlety was never a particular aspiration of the Expressionists. Violently emotional and often pessimistic, they sought to restore mankind to the center of things

> "I FEEL LIKE IT COMES FROM YOU…ALONG THE ARMS…UNTIL IT REACHES THE SOUL. COLD, TERRIBLE, RELENTLESS, DAMNED, CURSED…*HANDS!*"

and, through that dark intense subjectivity, render interior psychological states outwardly visible. Although firmly established in art, sculpture, and literature, Expressionism's adaptation to the medium of film was nothing short of a revelation. Cinema was no longer just entertainment; it could be an art form. What's more, it could go some distance in restoring the nation's pride. The medium—easily accessible and classless—was art for the poor. It was a shared experience, a shared longing, a shared grief.

In 1919, Robert Wiene made *The Cabinet of Dr Caligari*. Perhaps Expressionism's greatest celluloid achievement, this startlingly original symphony of light and dark has cast its long shadow over cinema ever since. In a world wherein atrocity was as human as art or prayer, there was solace to be found reflected in the eyes of a madman. Its star, Conrad Veidt, was perhaps Europe's first great horror actor. His greatest asset was his ability to express not just menace but a fractured psyche, one as fractured and broken as Germany and its wounded veterans.

Explicit evaluation of the war, its fallout, and its victims was still very much

taboo but although Germany was reluctant to directly confront these traumas, Veidt enacted the nation's repressed terrors for all on the silver screen. Veidt's characters wage a constant war against the loss of control; outside manipulation, dopplegangers, masks...they are broken men at war with themselves, unable to trust their own actions, their beliefs and, in 1924's *The Hands of Orlac*, their own bodies.

The Hands of Orlac has long stood in the shadow of *Caligari* but in many ways it is the greater, more emotive work. Veidt plays Paul Orlac, a world-famous concert pianist who loses his hands in a train crash. The surgeon replaces them with those of Vasseur, a recently executed criminal. Orlac soon becomes tormented with visions and a sickening, overwhelming paranoia that his grafted hands may have retained his donor's homicidal intent.

The film begins with a tableau of romantic longing as Orlac's wife Yvonne (Alexandra Sorina) lies in a flower-filled bedroom, reading and re-reading her husband's letter expressing his yearning to return and hold her again. The scene instantly makes explicit emphasis on tactile expression of emotion—touch as expression of love, not horror. This is swiftly juxtaposed with a scene depicting the aftermath of the fateful train wreck. Apart from being an important plot MacGuffin, this harrowing scene is a chilling and powerful image of mechanical carnage with powerful echoes of a battlefield. Consumed by a landscape of smoke, flame, and metal splinters, this is the experience of war. This imagery would have especially resonated with audiences of the time. Where war once was a "proud and honorable thing," the audience now knew all too well that technology had finely crafted it into nothing but a mechanical slaughterhouse.

Veidt served in the Great War, fighting on the Eastern front, and perhaps it is this that lends such extraordinary empathy to his character's plight. Once Orlac is robbed of his hands—and by proxy his art—he becomes child-like, shellshocked, and helpless. Yvonne, through necessity, assumes control of their lives whilst Orlac drifts like a satellite on an uncertain orbit around his mute, idle piano. Unable to play, Orlac seems robbed of his masculinity; indeed, after the operation he seems so devoid of any sexual or social potency as to be a ghost.

But beyond the historical significance and use of metaphor to express the anguish and consequences of war and disfigurement, it is Veidt's bravura performance that grips us by the throat. The actor writhes through his scenes as if dancing an Expressionist ballet, simultaneously attracted and repelled by darkness. From the moment that Orlac discovers the origin of his transplanted limbs, Veidt manages to convey without prosthetics or cinematic trickery that his hands are now utterly *alien* to him. Every single gesture gives meaning to each touch; everything he holds or reaches for becomes significant, his body becomes merely a vessel to transport these dreadful hands. You literally can't stop looking at them, as if they are controlled by a foreign intelligence with Veidt merely looking at the strings that are pulling him. In one breathtaking moment, Veidt raises his cursed hands before him and *they physically change*. This is no exaggeration. Veidt's concentration of furies is so great that as he raises his hands, every vein swells, fit to burst, transfiguring his hands as if even his blood is rebelling at his condition. The effect is monstrous and quite frankly extraordinary.

In contrast, when the final revelation comes and redemption is offered, we can almost see Orlac swell, like a shriveled flower restored to life, his masculinity restored, engorged in light rather than withered by shadow, and it is testament to Veidt's skill that we are able to see his hands as truly his own once more. He shrugs off the shadow that has consumed him in a single shot, a moment that is beautiful and profoundly moving.

The Hands of Orlac is also one of the earliest examples of a number of genre staples, including the "possessed hand" trope wherein hands severed from the body continue to act powered by a diabolical will (*The Beast with Five Fingers*, *Dr. Terror's House of Horrors,* or Oliver Stone's *The Hand*) and also what we now call "body horror." Herein resides the cinematic origins of the *body politic* wherein mind and flesh are at war, with soul and sanity in jeopardy. Major surgical procedures carry with them physiological challenges directly contributing to changes in mood and thinking patterns. Orlac, post-transplant, cannot even bear to return his wedding ring to his transplanted finger for fear that the conjunction would wed his love to murder. His mind is at odds with his flesh and Wiene misses no opportunity in reminding us of the chilling consequences of the transplant; witness Orlac's failed attempts to replicate his final love letter or reach for his lover's hair. The "transplant gone wrong" or "flesh haunted by its previous owner" is another staple of the

genre, from *Frankenstein* to *The Eye*, but *The Hands of Orlac* takes genuine neurological disorders such as "alien hand syndrome" and explores the primal fears that organ transplant is fraught with.

A meditation on the traumas of war, the horror of identity, and how we can become monstrous to ourselves, *The Hands of Orlac* is a film that gets under your skin. It's one of those rare beasts in the genre, one that not only speaks directly to our deepest fears, but possesses that immaculate clarity of insight and expression that we call art.

Ashley Thorpe is an award-winning Devon-based animator, writer and illustrator whose work is inspired by the neglected aspects of British folklore. His films are Scayrecrow *(2008),* The Screaming Skull *(2008),* The Hairy Hands *(2010) and* Borley Rectory *(currently in production). He is also the author of "The Demon Huntsman" and "Dead Man's Shoes" for the Glass Eye Pix Radio project* Tales from Beyond the Pale.

THE HILLS HAVE EYES 1977

BY ANDREW HAUBERT

"YOU FOLKS STAY ON THE MAIN ROAD NOW, YOU HEAR? STAY ON THE MAIN ROAD!"

Originally titled "Blood Relations," the core theme of Wes Craven's *The Hills Have Eyes* is family. On the eve on their twenty-fifth wedding anniversary, "Big Bob" Carter (Russ Grieve), a recently retired police detective from Cleveland, his wife Ethel (Virginia Vincent), and their young adult children take a road trip to explore a silver mine they have inherited. The Carters' detour off well-traveled roads leads them through a military testing area occupied by Papa Jupiter (James Whitworth) and his clan, the latter having resorted to cannibalism in order to survive in the rocky terrain and searing heat of the Mojave Desert. The two families clash in a struggle to the death, the "civilized" Carter tribe forced to engage Jupiter's "savage" kin with a level of violence never experienced in Ohio.

Stories set in realistic situations have always been more terrifying to me than those based on the supernatural. Tobe Hooper's 1974 classic, *The Texas Chain Saw Massacre*, scared me to the core with its creative use of sound and set design, and *The Hills Have Eyes* seemed like a natural follow-up after reading its synopsis (and finding out that Craven and producer Peter Locke were so impressed by *The Texas Chain Saw Massacre* they hired art designer Robert A. Burns for their project).

What sets *The Hills Have Eyes* apart from most genre films are the outstanding performances by its dedicated cast, especially Susan Lanier, Robert Houston, Dee Wallace, and Martin Speer as the Carter offspring. During the sequence when Jupiter's clan invades the Carters' camp, the raw emotion exhibited by Lanier when Mars (Lance Gordon) attempts to shoot her—only to be spared because the gun is out of ammunition—is one of the most powerful acting moments I've seen in a film of any genre. Wallace is likewise exceptional, doing everything possible to save her sister and baby from the marauding intruders. The other side of the battle lines features similarly strong turns from Whitworth, Gordon, Janus Blythe as Ruby, and the iconic Michael Berryman as Pluto, preying on those unfortunate enough to venture into their territory. (Berryman's unusual look, used to great effect on screen and in the *Hills* poster artwork, helped launch a thriving career in the horror industry that remains strong 35 years later.)

Craven had already shocked crowds around the world with his depiction of graphic violence and sexual sadism in 1972 with *The Last House on the Left*. The success of *Last House* was a blessing and a curse; it gave the young director a bona fide hit but many of those closest to him were embarrassed by the film's content. (Raised in a strict Baptist household by a domineering single mother, Craven was forbidden to watch anything beyond Disney movies growing up.) Despite  resistance to making another genre effort, he reluctantly agreed to make *The Hills Have Eyes* in order to support his family.

Craven's reputation as a "dangerous" filmmaker kept viewers shaking in their seats—having killed a dog early on in the story, audiences couldn't predict what would happen after Mars and Pluto kidnap Doug and Lynne's infant, intent on making it their feast. (Behind the scenes, some cast and crew would jokingly shout "kill the baby," while other cast members declared they would walk off the picture if the writer/director allowed the child to perish.) Craven's "outlaw" standing also led to significant disputes with the MPAA—not only was *Hills* a violent picture depicting graphic murders and cannibalism, it was coming from the same dark imagination that had yielded *Last House* only a few years prior. As a result, several sequences, most notably Jupiter's rant to a charred corpse, were significantly trimmed with the footage now presumably lost or unrecoverable.

In his terrific book *Shock Value*, Jason Zinoman reports that Craven became inspired to set a film in the Nevada desert after stopping for lunch during a cross-country motorcycle trip, seeking to articulate the insecurity he felt when confronted by locals in an isolated area. He combined this personal experience of being taunted in the desert—where the rules of polite urban society fall to the wayside—with the legend of the Sawney Bean clan, a cannibalistic clan of marauders that terrorized the Scottish countryside in the 16th century. Craven also reveals on the *Hills* DVD commentary that his mother's friends, Bob and Ethel Balmer, were the inspirations for the "civilized" parents Bob and Ethel Carter, and that much of Big Bob's dialogue is based on things the director remembers Balmer saying around the family dinner table.

The Hills Have Eyes spawned a lasting legacy that continues to influence the horror genre to this day. Shot on a modest budget of $230,000, it raked in an estimated $25 million before leaving drive-ins and hardtops. In 1984, with franchise fever in full swing, Craven helmed the universally reviled *The Hills Have Eyes Part II*, infamous for a sequence where one of the dogs has a flashback to the events of the first film. The sequel's poor reception buried the series for over two decades until the reboot-happy 21st century revived the title in 2006, directed by *High Tension*'s Alexandre Aja and produced by Craven, Locke, and Marianne Maddalena. The remake was successful enough to warrant a sequel the following year; as of this writing no further installments are in development.

As his second smash hit, *Hills* paved the way for Craven's long-standing relationship within the horror genre where he is recognized as one of the most successful directors of all time. Craven has since helmed over twenty horror features in a career spanning five decades, a legacy that includes the iconic films *A Nightmare on Elm Street* and *Scream*, both of which changed the face of popular horror for their time and inspired countless imitators.

My initial viewing of *The Hills Have Eyes* hit me like a ton of bricks and I consider it one of the greatest examples of survivalist horror. However, due to admitted similarities to its elder Texas blood relation, it rarely garners the respect deserved. The director's own pedigree may also contribute to the feature's "less-than" standing—having revolutionized the genre three different times in his career, the bar is set pretty high, allowing his other, less-seismic

offerings to slip through the cracks. That said, *The Hills Have Eyes* remains one of my favorite horror films, asking each of us what we would be willing to do to protect ourselves and the ones we love.

> *Andrew Haubert is a 32-year-old resident of Columbus, Ohio. He's a 2004 graduate of Ohio University, majoring in TCOM management with minors in Film and Business. When he's not embracing all things horror he enjoys sports, reading and preparing for the inevitable zombie apocalypse. Remember kiddies, only head shots count!*

THE HITCHER 1986

BY CHRIS AUSTIN

Whilst undertaking the long distance delivery of a car from Chicago to San Diego, Jim Halsey (C. Thomas Howell), a well-meaning but naïve young man, spies a hitchhiker on the side of the road during a particularly stormy night. He opts to do a good turn and pick up

"MY MOTHER TOLD ME NEVER TO DO THIS."

the hitcher, who introduces himself as John Ryder (Rutger Hauer). Little does Halsey realize that this simple act of kindness will have terrifying repercussions.

The Hitcher failed spectacularly during its original theatrical release, as a confused fan base and critics alike railed against it. Roger Ebert awarded it zero stars, describing the movie as "diseased and corrupt." Jay Scott of the *Globe and Mail* notably derided *The Hitcher* as homophobic, a "slasher movie about gay panic," due to various interactions between its two male leads that included the threatening of harm to genitalia, Ryder's almost flirtatious behavior towards Halsey, and a scene in which Halsey spits in Ryder's face. (In truth, these alleged undertones are a very small part of the greater whole.)

Many years later, *The Hitcher* stands not as a piece of homophobia or disgusting trash but as a rebellion against the slasher movie. Throughout the early to mid-'80s, slasher films dominated the horror genre, spurred by the success of franchises like *Halloween*, *Friday the 13th*, and *A Nightmare on Elm Street*. Clichéd and formulaic, the slasher genre, although not wholly without merit or charm, was largely stagnant, producing almost identical films separated only by disparate production values and marketing budgets. In 1996, *Scream* would send up the '80s slasher genre to great box office and critical acclaim, but even as early as 1981 the genre was the subject of parody and teasing in the form of *Student Bodies*.

The Hitcher was different, very different. Unlike the typical slasher film, where killers always had reasoning behind their murderous deeds (no matter how contrived), Ryder has no apparent motivation for his actions. He targets Halsey for no other reason than Halsey's attempt to do a good deed. To be punished for one's sins—or even the sins of one's father or mother—is, in film circles, acceptable. To be killed for a good turn is shocking, even terrifying.

The Hitcher plays heavily on the human fear of the unknown. Traveling through the southwestern plains of the United States, Halsey is placed in unfamiliar, largely barren territory. He knows nobody, he has nobody, and he is repeatedly and unrelentingly victimized for no apparent reason. Howell gives an impressive performance; one truly believes that he is scared beyond comprehension. Furthermore, one can witness the change in his character as a result of Ryder's actions, from a quiet, friendly young man to a mentally scarred, emotionally cold individual.

The anti-slasher methodology is further played up in the film's aesthetic presentation, the largely daytime setting contrasting with most genre efforts. Similarly, although there is an appreciable body count, *The Hitcher* focuses exclusively on the events from the main character's perspective (rather than following minor characters merely to witness them being dismembered). In regards to violence, director Robert Harmon treats *The Hitcher* almost as a throwback to *Black Christmas* and *Halloween*, eschewing gory slayings and presenting only the violent aftermath. The most visceral of Ryder's murders are only suggested, allowing audiences their own interpretation of just how vile and sickening the act was.

Slasher films also historically favor a female protagonist, leading to the "final girl" cliché, but in this case our only female character is Nash (Jennifer Jason Leigh). More than eye candy, Nash is presented as a kind-hearted young woman who takes pity on Halsey, sensing his anguish and torment. While her actions do not always necessarily correlate with rational human behavior, she is a sympathetic character who serves as an emotional focal point, particularly during the finale. And, although hinted at, *The Hitcher* avoids the seemingly requisite (and expedited) romantic entanglements of its main characters.

Possibly the most unique aspect of *The Hitcher*, when compared to similar films of the time, is the filmmakers' empathy for their protagonists. We're never salaciously invited to delight in Ryder's actions or cheer for the latest bloodletting; instead we want Halsey and Nash to overcome their antagonist.

This brings us to the film's centerpiece: Rutger Hauer's absolutely deranged John Ryder, a merciless killer who doesn't even appear to enjoy what he is doing. As the personification of evil, Hauer delivers the role perfectly in word and gesture, using the economy of dialogue in chilling fashion. His entire motivation is limited to the words, "I want you to stop me," without any further elaboration or justification. Ryder is vicious and cruel, but seemingly more

delighted by the chase than its violent outcome. (Those he kills are eliminated because they potentially interfere with his malicious mysterious master plan rather than any inherent thrill.) The pursuit is clearly central to his purpose—he goes to great lengths to draw it out, reveling in having found a

worthy adversary. His victimization of Halsey seems centered around prolonging his victim's agony for as long as possible, a textbook definition of cat and mouse.

Ryder is presented as almost mystical or omnipotent at times, with a knack for improbable escapes and effortlessly tracking Halsey. The heat-haze effect during the scorching desert scenes evokes the aesthetics of a malevolent, possibly supernatural entity. Nothing specifically suggests that he is anything but an extremely cunning and dangerous individual, yet the lack of background and motivation does prompt speculation whether there is more to our mysterious Ryder that anyone expects.

The isolated setting provides a strong atmosphere of horror as well. John Seale's cinematography provides many astonishing glimpses of the morbidly beautiful and barren landscape as Halsey fights for his life without respite. Repeated shots of the sun setting over the scarce vegetation and desert landscape serve as ominous reminders of how lifeless this part of the world is. Halsey's loneliness and desperation are echoed in this radiant photography of desolation.

Eric Red's screenplay also favors a less-is-more approach, with sparse dialogue that only becomes more so as Halsey descends further into psychological trauma, leading some to theorize that Halsey is slowly transitioning into John Ryder. Harmon's direction, on only his second feature film, is superb, utilizing Red's script, Seale's cinematography, and some comparatively high production values and action set-pieces to stunning and memorable effect.

The Hitcher is a true experiment in horror. Cloaked in minimalist dialogue and characterization, it is a terror film that constantly surprises and challenges its target audience. The antagonist's unexplained viciousness, the unwitting protagonist's despair, the avoidance of obvious splatter, the decision to leave much to the viewer's imagination, the anti-cliché sentiment of the storyline, and the outright refusal to tidy things up with some preposterous rationale make this a surprisingly intelligent and subversive piece of cinema. One that will inevitably come to mind the next time you find yourself driving alone late at night with a shadowy figure looming on the horizon.

Chris Austin is from the United Kingdom and has been a fan of cinema, particularly the horror genre, for close to twenty years. He is also a fan of the science-fiction and fantasy genres, currently working on Dawn's Light, *a futuristic science-fiction novel which will hopefully see some form of publication in 2015. For more information, visit www.dawnslight.co.uk or our Twitter feed at @DawnsLightBook.*

THE HORROR OF PARTY BEACH 1964

BY JOHN W. BOWEN

"IT'S THE VOODOO, DR. GAVIN. IT'S THE VOODOO, I TELLS YA!"

In *Danse Macabre*, Stephen King's 1981 treatise on horror in film and literature, he refers to *The Horror of Party Beach* as "an abysmal little wet fart of a picture." I prefer to think King meant this as a compliment, because *Party Beach* isn't just a hilariously bad, el cheapo, rubber-suit monster flick—it's also an endearing and highly evocative little vignette of the era that spawned it.

Beach blanket movies and horror were ruling the teen movie demographic in the early 1960s, and while pop-cultural niche marketing was a long way from being honed to the exact science it is today (didn't think I could write that with a straight face, and...nope, apparently not), the exploitation film industry had long since woken up and smelled the money. A savvy New York theater chain owner (or a couple of equally savvy Connecticut drive-in owners, depending upon which version you believe) staked B-movie producer/director Del Tenney to a measly budget (about $120,000) and invited him to concoct a beach blanket monster movie. Tenney was skeptical about the idea's potential but accepted the job, and was as amazed as anyone when the finished product actually turned a decent profit. Despite that early success, however, it's only in recent years that *Party Beach* has truly begun to be appreciated by the schlock horror cognoscenti.

The first twenty-five minutes of *Party Beach* introduce characters and establish setting (unidentified New England beach resort town), plot, and mood in textbook fashion (and if a B-movie textbook hadn't already been written by the early '60s, it should have). En route to the titular beach, our chiseled hero Hank (John Scott) terminates his relationship with slutty party girl Tina (Marilyn Clarke), who then proceeds to throw herself at every available man on the sand while Hank strikes up a conversation with overdressed, virginal Elaine (the insufferable Alice Lyon, whose delivery was apparently so atrocious that all her dialogue was subsequently dubbed by another actress). A few lines of awkward exposition later, we learn that Elaine's father, local scientist Dr. Gavin (Allan Laurel), is Hank's mentor. Meanwhile, not far offshore, a boat crew is dumping barrels of nuclear waste into the water, transforming some skeletal remains below into a horde of fantastically stupid-looking, googly-eyed, hot-dog-tongued monsters who will soon mount an all-out assault on the town.

Back on shore, New Jersey surf-pop quartet the Del-Aires (more on them later) enthrall the growing crowd of twenty-something-looking teens with

"Joy Ride," "Wigglin' Wobblin'," and the falsetto-driven, Buddy Holly-esque "Elaine." ("Elay-yay-yay-huh-haine/That's my baby's name.") When the party gets crashed by a biker gang, a hilariously choreographed and suspiciously injury-free rumble breaks out for several minutes. (Hey, it's the early '60s, whaddya want?) Once order is restored, the Del-Aires bust out their set highlight, "Zombie Stomp" ("Everybody do the Zombie Stomp/Just slam your foot down with an awful thump/You reach up further/Let's get closer/It's the livin' end"), and the crowd eagerly responds with much twistin' and tuckus-shakin'. Dejected bad girl Tina swims away and finds some rocks to stretch out on and sun herself, only to fall victim to the first of the lurching, grunting monsters to emerge from below.

Early the next day, police arrive (with sirens wailing) at the Gavin residence to deliver a tissue sample found at the murder scene and press the good doctor into service as a consultant before making their exit (with sirens wailing). Dr. Gavin enlists the services of his promising young protégé Hank, who is beginning to hanker for Elaine, insomuch as anyone could hanker for a wan-faced droid who's about as sexy as a pant leg full of recently deceased crawfish.

It's also around this point that the more sensitive among you would be well advised to gird your loins (or whichever body part you prefer to gird) when the Cringe-Inducing Racial Stereotype is introduced into the mix. Sure, such unfortunate caricatures are often par for the course in films of this vintage, but Eulabelle the Superstitious Black Maid (excruciatingly essayed by Eulabelle Moore) would give Spike Lee an aneurism. Eulabelle brings people coffee and spouts folksy advice while stressing about the "zombies" attacking the town, all while sporting some kind of bizarre, early-prototype Jeri-Curl coiffure that looks as if a motorcycle had driven over her head before the hairdresser could finish.

The foregoing proves to be more than poor shrinking violet Elaine can bear, so she begs off attending a slumber party that evening. Good thing, too, as the party—about twenty (!) teenage girls brushing each other's hair and singing third-rate feminist folk songs—gets crashed big-time by several of the monsters, who proceed to waste most of the girls on the spot and carry a couple away into the night. (Hey, at least they put an end to that gawd-awful music.)

More monster mayhem and howl-inducing Eulabelle-isms ensue throughout the remainder of the movie, as well as a monumentally silly climax, but at this point spoiler potential runs too high to allow any further elaboration.

Much has been made of the design lineage between Universal's iconic *Creature from the Black Lagoon* and its latter-day brethren in Roger Corman's

sleaze masterpiece *Humanoids from the Deep*, and rightly so. Hence an equally strong case can be made that *Party Beach's* monsters are the poor, inbred, brain-damaged country cousins the Gill-Man and the 'Noids would have kept chained up in the basement to avoid embarrassment whenever company stopped by.

And what of the Del-Aires? According to North Jersey arts and entertainment weekly *The Aquarian Times*, their story had a rather unfortunate real-life coda. When shooting wrapped early in the fall of 1963, the Paterson, NJ, band went back to gigging regularly in many of the best clubs in their area, including New York's famous Peppermint Lounge, but broke up a year or so later after two police officers were murdered at one of their shows.

My first exposure to *The Horror of Party Beach* came during my single-digit years via *Monster Movie Matinee,* which invaded Kingston, Ontario, every Saturday afternoon from across the border in Syracuse, New York. Even among *MMM*'s hodgepodge of Universal classics, '50s alien invasion cheapies, early *kaiju*, and public domain oddities, *Party Beach* was unlike anything I'd encountered thus far. My critical skills may have been underdeveloped at the time (insert reader heckling here), but I fell for it—hard—because it was loud, cheap, tacky, energetic, violent, and, best of all, completely unashamed. Naturally, I pretty much plotzed when Dark Sky released *Party Beach* on DVD in 2006, paired with *Curse of the Living Corpse*, another Tenney film from 1964, especially since the umpteenth-generation VHS bootleg I'd been clinging to for years was dying a thousand deaths.

The Horror of Party Beach ain't for everybody. Neither are most of the other films you'll find in this book. But hey, ask Stephen King—abysmal little wet farts simply don't get much better than this.

John W. Bowen has been a columnist, reviewer and feature writer for Rue Morgue *magazine since 1999, and has also written sporadically for more (...cough...) "civilized" publications, including the* Kingston Whig-Standard, The Toronto Star *and* Kingston Life Magazine. *Born in Dallas and raised in Kingston, Ontario, John currently divides his time between Toronto and Kingston. He's also a professional musician and recovering strip club DJ.*

THE HOUSE THAT SCREAMED1969

BY DARREN CALLAHAN

In *The House That Screamed*, there is a specific moment where I rose from my sofa and asked aloud, "How have I not heard of this movie before?" Keep in mind: this was not a scene, but an actual moment—one lasting less than three seconds. It's rare to be able to pinpoint such a spark. With that moment, I realized that I had been set up from the first frames and was in the hands of a very special talent.

> "NONE OF THESE GIRLS ARE ANY GOOD. THESE GIRLS ARE POISON. YOU NEED A WOMAN LIKE ME."

To describe said moment requires a bit of context. The house—one which will, yes, lead to screaming—is a French boarding school in the nineteenth century, ruled by a stern headmistress named Senora Fourneau (played by Lilli Palmer, ex-wife of Rex Harrison and the star of many films, including 1936's *Secret Agent* for Hitchcock). As do most classic stories, this one starts with an arrival....

A new girl, Teresa (Cristina Galbó) is enrolled in the school by her mother's wealthy lover. Teresa is beautiful, well-dressed, and intelligent. She betrays little of her feelings as she is shown around the grounds by the headmistress, who dispatches the necessary exposition and geography.

Suddenly, without permission, Teresa pulls the rope against the parlor wall and rings a bell. (Here is where the moment plants its seeds, though I would not realize it for another hour.) The gesture is enough of a disruption that Senora Fourneau must explain that this is not an ordinary boarding school, but one for girls whose character is, "...shall I say...difficult." Damaged goods. Trouble. To crib from *The Great Escape*, someone has put all the rotten eggs in one basket. We soon learn that three girls have recently escaped the locked grounds, there is a Punishment Room where a defiant girl is whipped by fellow students, and the only boy in the school is the headmistress young son Luis, a pubescent voyeur. This school just got a whole lot more interesting.

And, wow, do these girls miss the company of boys; so much that they draw straws each week to roll in the hay with the townie woodcutter. This leads to by far the sexiest scene ever shot about a sewing class, with thread through the eyes of needles, back and forth, in and out, as the girls watch the locked woodshed door.

There is much to admire in the hour since Teresa's bell ringing, but it's really just build up to my moment. Teresa tries to escape (no spoiler—we totally know this is coming). One night, she exits the community bedroom, slinks into the corridor, and tiptoes down the stone steps to the parlor. She feels for the door along the shadowed wall. And what does her hand brush against as she moves? That goddamn rope for the bell. It took one hour to pay that off! It was then that I thought: *This director is in control. This guy knows his audience.* Followed by: *Who the hell is this Narciso Ibáñez Serrador?*

Turns out he's awesome. In 1976, Serrador would make the nearly-as-excellent *Who Can Kill a Child?*, a high-concept horror flick about a pack of murderous children that climaxes with adults mowing down sweet-faced young 'uns

with machine guns—every parent's nightmare or fantasy, depending on the day. You don't often see that kind of story in Hollywood.

The House That Screamed represents the first production made in Spain but filmed in English. Aside from some clunky looping and weak foley, Serrador enlisted great collaborators. The production design rivals any Merchant Ivory production, which leads you to feel safe when you most certainly should not. The cinematography is gorgeous ultra-widescreen with muted colors, long tracking shots, and serves as a real lesson in how to light a fantastic location (and a bunch of hot teenage girls). The music by Waldo de los Rios is a sweeping orchestral score punctuated by the worst-tuned piano I've ever heard (intentionally, I assume, as it underscores the beauty with evil lurking underneath.)

To those in the know, there is also a fine horror pedigree on display. Leads Mary Maude and Cristina Galbó respectively went on to appear in *Crucible of Terror* (1972) and the excellent zombie film *Let Sleeping Corpses Lie* (1974), while secondary player Maribel Martin starred in *The Blood Splattered Bride* (1972). Even within the melodrama, their performances remain compelling.

But what about the flesh and blood? Is this too posh an affair with its ringing bells and sewing needles? Well, for sex, there's a little skin, one community shower scene, some feverish flogging, and that woodshed, but there's also a lot of restraint considering it's a school full of pretty women.

In a similar vein, forty minutes transpire before the first murder, by which point one might have forgotten this is a horror movie, despite creaky doors, dark shadows, and strange faces in foggy windows. Yet it is worth the wait. The sequence is beautiful, shocking, and sad; a young student brutally killed among flowers, in slow motion, in silence, with overlapping multiple exposures. By the end, there's a feeling of, "Did I just see that in such a classy film?"

In a later murder—yes, there are many—Serrador freezes the frame just as a prominent female character is grabbed from behind. (Wait, did my DVD player just crap out? No! Who pulls a freeze frame during a horror murder?!) This device allows the viewer to take in, just for a second, Serrador's twist of the cinematic blade. This girl I've grown to like is surely about to die! No one is really safe, no one is really good or bad, and allegiances shift from character to character in surprising ways.

The school enforcer, young and pretty Irene (Mary Maude), becomes an unexpected focus as she realizes too late that girls aren't escaping the school but being slaughtered instead…and that the killer may or may not be her boss, the headmistress. Rather than face Senora Fourneau, she tries to run away.

Through the parlor…coming closer and closer to that rope on the wall…that bell…until…!

I won't spoil it for you. But it isn't what you expect.

Such is the case with this movie overall — a fun little gem that many middle-aged horror fans have been wearing on their fingers since the '70s when it graced the Sunday morning television matinees (edited, of course). Sadly, at this time it's not available in any special editions, or in any form of quality. (I found my copy on one of those 50-movie compilations for ten bucks.) I don't even dare call it a cult film, as it is still too obscure. I do believe quality endures and that perhaps *The House That Screamed* will be discovered by a larger audience over time. Despite its age, it holds up. Maybe this is because of its nineteenth century setting or its universal themes — girls becoming women, response to authority, random violence. But I also think it holds up because it's damn good. And damn scary.

Darren Callahan has written for many major outlets, including the BBC and the SyFy Channel. Works include the stage plays The White Airplane *and* Horror Academy, *the novels* The Audrey Green Chronicles *and* City of Human Remains, *and the screenplays* Nerves *and* Summer of Ghosts. *Darren is the writer, director, and composer of the films* Under the Table *and* Children of the Invisible Man. *More info at darrencallahan.com.*

HUMANOIDS FROM THE DEEP 1980

BY BRETT A. HARRISON

Ever since the dawn of cinema, movie monsters have lusted after lovely young ladies clearly out of their league. In *Nosferatu* (1922), cadaverous vampire Count Orlok (Max Schreck) tried to sink his teeth into pretty maiden Ellen (Greta Schroeder); in 1933, oversized ape *King Kong* went bananas for beautiful

> "THE SCENE HERE IS ONE OF TOTAL, AND I MEAN *TOTAL*, PANIC."

blonde actress Ann Darrow (Fay Wray); a couple of decades later, the *Creature from the Black Lagoon* (1954) got his gills in a twist over swimsuit sexpot Kay Lawrence (Julie Adams). Of course, none of these classic creatures ever got beyond first base, typically being vanquished before they could get down to any serious inter-species lovin' (particularly good news for Ann Darrow, given the major physical incompatibility issues at hand). This grand tradition continued throughout the '60s and '70s, with frustrated B-movie beasts rarely getting any further than copping a quick feel. But all that changed in 1980 with *Humanoids from the Deep*, a trashy creature feature produced by Roger Corman's New World Pictures in which the monsters finally get their freak on! (The flick was unfortunately cursed with the bland title of *Monster* for the UK market—an act akin to calling an Indiana Jones movie *Archaeologist*.)

The hideous mutant fish-men of *Humanoids*—the result of experimental growth hormones being "accidentally" released into the ocean's food chain by an irresponsible fish canning company—emerge from the surf to mate with women in a bid to speed up their species' evolution. With the horror genre having undergone an evolutionary leap of its own during the '70s, becoming sexier, trashier, and bloodier than ever before, the film is unsurprisingly packed with gratuitous nudity and gore, the slimy sea-monsters raping their way through a collection of buxom bikini babes while tearing apart any men unfortunate enough to be caught between the beasts and their beautiful prizes. Here are 80 minutes of unashamedly misogynistic, splattery nonsense guaranteed to put a smile on the face of any fan of over-the-top '80s horror. However, it was almost not to be.

As directed by Barbara Peeters, one of the few female filmmakers working in the exploitation field at the time, the original version of *Humanoids* was a far less outrageous affair; one that, in producer Corman's opinion, was in desperate need of a man's touch if it were to ever turn a profit. To fulfill the obligatory quota of blood and boobs, Corman brought in another director to film some additional, more extreme footage—some sources cite Jimmy T. Murakami, who helmed *Battle Beyond the Stars* (though he denies any involvement), while others assign the "credit" to second unit director James Sbardellati. Precisely which shots were added to Peeters' original cut is unclear…although it's not too difficult to make an educated guess. Naturally, none of this meddling went down very well with Peeters or female production assistant Gale Anne Hurd (future producer of *The Terminator*), both of whom asked to no avail to have their names removed from the credits. Of course, Corman, an old hand at the exploitation movie game, knew precisely what he was doing. As a result of his timely intervention, *Humanoids from the Deep* proved a modest financial

success and has since become an enduring cult favorite amongst fans of trashy horror.

A traditional monster movie at heart, *Humanoids* is undeniably formulaic stuff with its stereotypical blue-collar hero, fisherman Jim Hill (played by seasoned second-tier hunk Doug McClure), teaming up with pretty ecologist Susan Drake (Ann Turkel) to discover who or what is responsible for a spate of vicious shoreline attacks on animals and humans alike. The clichés come thick and fast: There's a noble Indian, Johnny Eagle (Anthony Pena), protesting against the cannery and coming to blows with the town's local bigot Hank Slattery

(B-movie regular Vic Morrow, who also gave us Jennifer Jason Leigh), a festival turned bloodbath after the libidinous mutations attack, and a gruesome shock finale reminiscent of (i.e. ripped off from) *Alien's* infamous chestburster scene. But don't let the lack of originality and/or an A-list cast keep you from checking this sucker out. The real stars are the grotesque, scaly, sea-dwelling sex-pests, their graphic acts of bloodletting, and the handful of well-developed young "actresses," most of whom probably (and accurately) count this as their career highlight.

Although the frightful fish-men are of the classic "man-in-a-rubber-suit" variety, the unique creature designs—courtesy of make-up FX legend Rob Bottin (*The Thing*, *The Howling*, *Robocop*)—are both extremely memorable and utterly repulsive. Sporting massive craniums, beady eyes, scaly bodies draped with seaweed, freakishly long forearms, razor sharp claws and even sharper jaws, these things are real ugly and extremely savage. A guy frolicking in the surf has half of his face ripped off, a radio announcer gets his torso torn open to expose a glistening ribcage, blood gushes freely from a very nasty throat wound, and so on. The monsters don't get off scot-free either; many are shot, a few have their bulging brains bashed in by plucky townsfolk, and one is stabbed to death by Jim's wife Carol (Cindy Weintraub) with a carving knife. As for the babes...well, they do exactly what is expected of any aspiring starlet in an unashamedly exploitative monster movie: scream a lot and shed their clothes in exchange for a few seconds of precious screen time.

With its vicious sex-crazed creatures, outrageously gruesome splatter (impressive in both quantity and quality), and bevy of busty young beauties, *Humanoids from the Deep* ought to be celebrated as one of the most consistently entertaining horrors of its time. Sadly, this isn't the case. The early '80s are renowned for their steady stream of formulaic slashers, but rarely recognized as the age of the horny killer fish-man. Devoted fans have kept the memory of *Humanoids* alive, but it genuinely deserves to become acquainted with a wider audience...and perhaps the time is finally right. Recent years have seen outrageously over-the-top creature-features enjoying something of a resurgence, with John Gulager's *Feast* trilogy, Alexandre Aja's 3D *Piranha* remake (and its even trashier sequel, *Piranha 3DD*), and even Corman's own *Sharktopus* clearly reveling in their lowbrow status. If you're one of those amazingly insightful people happy to celebrate the schlockier, somewhat less cerebral side of horror, check out this hugely enjoyable "old school" example of the genre. Now available for your enjoyment on DVD and Blu-ray—just don't expect the extras to include a commentary from Peeters or Hurd!

Brett A. Harrison has been a member of IMDb since 2001, where he is one of the regulars on the Horror message board; he has written thousands of reviews for the site, the vast majority of which focus on horror, exploitation, cult and martial arts movies. His taste in film leans towards the trashy, but he's not averse to checking out the artier, more intellectual classics from time to time—especially if they have nudity and blood in them.

THE HUNCHBACK OF THE MORGUE 1973

BY RUBÉN IÑIGUEZ AND ELENA ROMEA

> "TODAY I'VE SEEN YOUR BODY. IT WAS LIKE ILSE'S, AND SOON—VERY SOON— YOU'LL BE LIKE HER. AND GOTHO WILL LOVE YOU FOREVER."

Despite his enormous body of work, the name "Paul Naschy" often fails to generate much recognition outside his home country of Spain (where he is treated as a quaint afterthought) except by the horror faithful. Even with a greater visibility than ever thanks to home video, the late, great Jacinto Molina still struggles for respect. But just try watching titles like *Frankenstein's Bloody Terror, The Werewolf vs. the Vampire Women, Night of the Howling Beast*, or any of the other myriad films featuring Waldemar Daninsky (Naschy's tragic/ heroic lycanthrope creation), and see if you don't find it impossible to stop. See if you don't find yourself hungering to watch and learn as much as possible about where these strange and wonderful stories came from. Such was the power and passion of this former weightlifter who became one of Spain's biggest international exports during the 1970s.

The Hunchback of the Morgue is among Naschy's most original pictures, and as such has not enjoyed the popularity of his hairy-scary Daninsky efforts, sinking into relative obscurity. Even dedicated fans neglect this treasure, only to be reminded upon rediscovery how gifted the man was in creating characters that went beyond horror stereotypes. He presents a sympathetic portrayal of the outsider figure (here, the hunchback Gotho), as well as an intelligent examination of cultural references and class struggles within a simple story.

Naschy was more than just an actor, writer, or director; he was also a horror fan and a well-read one at that. In every one of his films and screenplays, we see evidence of several intertextualities. As he mentions in his DVD introduction, *Hunchback of the Morgue* is a kind of gore reinterpretation of the "Beauty and the Beast" tale with Lovecraftian overtones. The deformed "evil" character Gotho is an outsider bullied by everybody, ultimately finding redemption through love. As in the case of Waldemar Daninsky (the creation of which was inspired by Naschy's love for the Universal monsters), we are not simply dealing with a bloodthirsty animal, but a creature doomed by Fate.

Though he spends his days at the morgue, preparing corpses and/or cutting them into pieces, Gotho is full of emotion, able to feel the purest love towards an ill woman, Ilse (María Elena Arpón), who shows him kindness. Utterly devoted to his ailing companion, he attempts to save her from the hands of death, putting his trust in a mad scientist, Dr. Orla (Alberto Dalbés). Based on his reading of the Necronomicon, Orla (whose name pays tribute to Maupassant's "The Horla") is bent on re-creating a Great Old One, utilizing a single-celled proto-Old One in his subterranean laboratory which is then fed living creatures, its voracious appetite increasing in accordance with its size.

With no qualms about killing his own mates, lying to the police, or putting the lives of others at risk in the name of science, Orla sees in Gotho the perfect opportunity to satisfy the monster's bloodlust, commanding him to unearth corpses (as well as commit murders when the occasion calls for it). In return, the duplicitous doc offers the false promise of restoring Ilse to life. Gotho worships at Orla's altar, doing everything asked, waiting resolutely for the resurrection of his beloved one. (Our misshapen hero's love is so strong he can't even see the real corpse before him, only the beautiful illusion of his sleeping girlfriend to whom he brings a daily bouquet of flowers.)

Unfortunately, Gotho's delusions do not extend to Orla's other assistants; complaining of the smell, two scoundrels toss Ilse's decomposing, rat-nibbled corpse into an acid bath. With his dreams of true love destroyed, Gotho murders the dastardly duo in a rage—one meeting a grisly fate in the same acid bath—then heads through the catacombs in search of Orla. The doctor promises to create a new mate for the hunchback, thereby retaining Gotho's loyalty for the time being.

Surprisingly, love does come to Gotho in the form of a beautiful doctor, Elke (Rosanna Yanni). Able to see beyond his appearance and discovering a heart full of tenderness, warmth, and good feelings, she falls in love with him, resulting in a singularly bizarre onscreen event: a scene in which a hunchback makes love to a hot sexy blonde! This romantic twist serves as the trigger of Gotho's redemption; when Elke finds herself on the menu for the Great Young Old One's nightly feeding, the slave rebels against his master, putting an

end to the nightmare. No longer the freak outsider, Gotho becomes a true hero in this epic battle against evil.

In addition to playing the lead character, Naschy was responsible for the story and co-writing the screenplay (as he had already done several times at this point in his career). *Hunchback* represented one of three films made with director Javier Aguirre in 1973 (alongside *Count Dracula's Great Love* and the lesser-known thriller *The Killer Is One of Thirteen*), and while he undoubtedly had a great deal of influence, it would not be until *Inquisition* (1976) before Naschy—as Jacinto Molina—began directing his own movies. Due to the political and social changes in Spain, i.e. the end of Franco's dictatorship and the beginnings of a democracy, audiences were demanding other types of films and many Spanish directors turned their backs on the horror genre. Naschy continued writing horror scripts and, frustrated by the inability to find

directors, found himself working not only in front of but behind the camera in order to continue making the movies he wanted.

Longtime Naschy fans will likely recognize various cast members: Yanni appears in *Frankenstein's Bloody Terror* (1968) and 1979's non-horror *Naked Madrid*, Víctor Alcázar in *Horror Rises from the Tomb* and *Vengeance of the Zombies* (both 1973), and the pair reunited with their friend for *Count's Dracula Great Love*. In a recent conversation, Naschy's son Sergio Molina revealed his father preferred to work with the same cast and crew any time he could, enjoying the sense of community.

Gotho was one of Naschy's favorite characters, and remained so throughout his career. The actor always displayed great affection for the role whenever speaking about it, even including the tragic hunchback among other mythic characters in *Alaric de Marnac*, a novel he wrote (with illustrations by Javier Trujillo) before his death in 2009. Years after *Hunchback*, Naschy played Quasimodo in 1987's *Howl of the Devil*, and one cannot help but view it as another conspiratorial wink to his original handicapped hero.

According to Naschy biographer Ángel Agudo, the actor was inspired to write *Hunchback* based on his experiences at Zaragoza Morgue, but behind the scenes, there were also a number of interesting elements. Naschy claimed that a real cadaver was used onscreen, and it's undeniable that numerous unsuspecting rats met with tragic ends during filming, either set ablaze or thrown across rooms (or both). Thanks to this visceral environment, some impressive gore effects, and a memorable final-reel rubber-suit monster, *Hunchback* stands as a must-see for both new and experienced fans of Spanish horror. It is a movie that endures through the ages because of its moving love story...as well as the horror that lives inside it.

Rubén Íñiguez is a scholar of Spanish literature who, together with Elena Romea, created the Spanish site Un Fan de Paul Naschy. He has written several articles about cinema in different publications and is now organizing short movie festivals. Rubén is now working on a new film and also on the publication of a fanzine.

Elena Romea is a researcher and teacher of linguistics and literature. She has a podcast called Horror Rises from Spain about classic and new European and world wide horror and cinema that contains interviews, reviews and news.

ICHI THE KILLER 2001

BY AARON CROWELL

"DAMN...NOBODY LEFT TO KILL ME."

Anyone encountering the horror films of Japanese director Takashi Miike for the first time is in for a real treat...if they enjoy sadistic torture, extreme gore, and graphic violence, that is. Miike was instrumental in creating the new millennium "Asian Extreme" genre by crafting a string of shocking and awe-inducing titles that included *Audition* (1999), *Visitor Q* (2001), *Gozu* (2003), his "Box" segment in *Three... Extremes* (2004), as well as earlier shock titles *Full Metal Yakuza* (1997) and the over-the-top shoot 'em up *Dead or Alive* trilogy. In 2006, Miike's episode for Showtime's *Masters of Horror*, "Imprint," was deemed so shocking and disturbing that it could not even be edited down for airing. Cranking out an average of two features per year over the past decade, the full resume of this legendary film-maker is mind-bogglingly diverse, but it is his distinctive flair for the erotic and grotesque that has earned him a loyal international following.

The perfect Miike gateway flick is the 2001 splatterfest *Ichi the Killer,* possibly his most ambitious and widely beloved cult classic. *Ichi* premiered at a packed-house midnight screening at the Toronto International Film Festival, where attendees were handed promotional barf-bags as they entered, a precursor to the grotesque wonders that awaited them inside.

This genre-bending title—incorporating themes of yakuza gangsters, horrific torture, misogynistic violence, a bizarre love story, and a very mixed up hero—took root when producer Dai Miyazaki first became aware of the eponymous *Ichi the Killer* manga in *Weekly Young Sunday* magazine. At the time, Excellent Films was primarily concerned with straight-to-video films, and when Miyazaki showed the manga to the collection of directors and producers on hand, Miike showed immediate interest. *Ichi* creator Hideo Yamamoto's storyline had not yet run its full course, so it fell to screenwriter Sakichi Sato to work out a narrative throughline for the feature, one that met with Miike's enthusiastic approval.

The story follows Kakihara's search for boss Anjo who is believed dead or to have run off with a girl and a large sum of the gang's money (3 million yen). Kakihara (Tadanobu Asano), a blonde, sadomasochistic thug with unique facial scars, believes a rival gang is behind Anjo's disappearance and that his superior is still alive. It turns out Kakihara's obsession with finding Anjo lies in the fact that his boss is the only person sadistic enough to punish our fair-haired S&M-loving maniac to full satisfaction. (Miyazaki believes this to be the key element that attracted the director to this project.)

Meanwhile, we are introduced to our titular "hero," played by the innocent-looking Nao Ômori. Bullied from a young age, Ichi (Japanese for "one") remains reserved until his inner anger boils over, after which he becomes a sobbing juggernaut of violent rage, erupting in a frenzy of flying kicks and leaving a sea of entrails, blood, and body parts in his wake. Brainwashed into becoming the ultimate killing machine, Ichi serves the interest of Jijii (Shinya Tsukamoto) and his two-man crew, who plan to overthrow the organized crime syndicate by turning the gangs against each other, using Ichi as their personal one-man hit squad. Outfitted in a padded black leather outfit with a huge yellow #1 on the back and retractable blade-heeled boots, Ichi continues to kill the "bullies" placed in his path. (Our crying killer has also developed an odd side effect from the brainwashing process—he becomes sexually excited by watching and/or participating in violence.) Having witnessed the aftermath of Ichi's bloody deeds, Kakihara becomes obsessed with finding the reluctant assassin for his own masochistic needs.

But lest it be written off as a mindless parade of dismembered limbs and arterial spray, it should be noted that a great deal of attention was given to every role by Miike and Sato, with overlapping subplots and memorable peripheral characters. Truth be told, the visual and mental onslaught can be a little overwhelming for first-time viewers, but the fast-paced story so captivates with geysers of gore, severed tongues, and devastating fight sequences that one is eager to hit the "replay" button once the credits finally roll. (Fear not, lazy caption complainers: there is a dubbed version available, but I strongly urge you to experience the film in its native Japanese.) A special "hats off" to actor Susumu Terajima (playing Suzuki) who endured the ghastly "tempura torture" sequence, requiring twelve hours of set-up and another twelve hours of filming.

From costume designer Michiko Kitamura's selection of Kakihara's shimmering jacket and the twins' rubber toy-adorned hats to Hideo Yamamoto's

swirling camerawork, every detail in this strangely beautiful and artistic comic book film is the result of a culmination of a large group of talented people. Actor Shun Sugata (Takayama) went on to appear in Quentin Tarantino's *Kill Bill Vol. 1* and *Vol. 2*, while another *Kill Bill* alumnus, Jun Kunimura (Funaki), can be seen in *Audition* and *Godzilla: Final Wars*. A celebrated cult director in his own right (*Tetsuo: The Iron Man*, *Hiruko the*

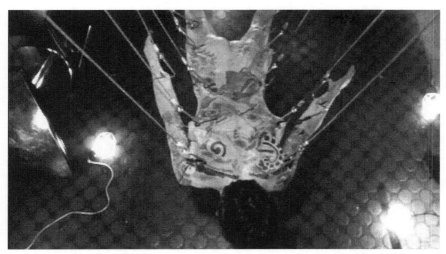

Goblin), Tsukamoto also is reported to have personally contributed to the pool of real semen that slowly reveals the *Ichi the Killer* title logo. (Gross, right?)

Miike's comedic grue-infused sensibility has cast a long shadow over the next generation of Japanese filmmakers. With notable titles like *Machine Girl*, *RoboGeisha*, and *Mutant Girls Squad*, Noboru Iguchi is known for his no-holds-barred approach. Make-up effects artist-turned-director Yoshihiro Nishimura demonstrates a flair for gory effects sequences in *Tokyo Gore Police* and *Vampire Girl vs. Frankenstein Girl*, while Yudai Yamaguchi displays an affinity for Miike's legendary over-the-top style with *Battlefield Baseball*, *Meatball Machine*, and *Dead Ball*. While these rising auteurs could be considered heirs to the Asia Extreme cinematic throne, it is Miike's ability to perfectly juggle gore, violence, and comedy that continues to make him a force to be reckoned with.

His influence crosses international lines as well. The case could be made that Heath Ledger's Joker in *The Dark Knight* boasts a few memorable traits first seen in *Ichi* (Kakihara's telltale scars, a unique flare for flashy fashion). Eli Roth is another unabashed Miike fan—the Hollywood director even tapped his elder Asian blood brother for a brief cameo in the 2005 smash *Hostel*, as well as sitting his cast and crew down to watch *Ichi* before shooting began.

I hope *Ichi* inspires further exploration into the vast world of Asian extreme cinema. (If you can't get enough, the character's original high school ordeal can be seen in the 2003 prequel *1-Ichi*, directed by Masato Tanno—who served as second assistant director on *Ichi*—and again starring Nao Ômori.) There is nothing like experiencing a Miike film for the first time. I envy you, Faithful Reader—you have no idea what horrific wonders, shocks, and delights lie ahead!

Aaron Crowell is a lifelong cinephile, collector and pop culture junkie. With horror movies and cult sleaze his tainted bread and butter growing up through the '80s, Aaron co-authored the book Tomart's Price Guide to Horror Movie Collectibles, *and is currently the managing editor of* HorrorHound *Magazine.*

IN A GLASS CAGE 1987

BY JORGE DIDACO

"THE MACHINE MAKES ME NERVOUS. IT'S LIKE BEING AT THE CINEMA."

An opening sequence prepares us for the disturbances of mind and body that follow: in a squalid, dimly lit, abandoned place, a young, barely conscious boy hangs naked from his wrists, his body severely bruised. An ex-Nazi doctor, now hiding in a Spanish villa, calmly takes photographs of the boy's perishing body, embracing, smelling him, before brutally killing him with a piece of wood. A third person—whom we don't see—observes the dreadful actions. An eye, a camera; a victim, a perpetrator, a witness; these are the elements that constitute the filmic discourse of domination, control, and dependency distilled from one of the most controversial, extraordinary, and genuinely disturbing horror films of the '80s, Agustí Villaronga's *Tras el cristal* (*In a Glass Cage*).

These initial moments point to the director's themes and concerns: the horrors of history (Nazi atrocities) re-contextualized into the present (Franco's Spain); evil and its assimilation/transmission; the complex relations of power established between victims and oppressors; the sensual, even erotic, fascination with death and fear; and, as Villaronga often says in interviews, the lethal attractiveness of the "tenderness of wolves." These issues are also evident in the opening credit sequence juxtaposing scenes of concentration camps and frail, bruised, cadaveric Holocaust victims with homoerotic images of Nazi soldiers and the film's key narrative mystery—a photo of Klaus, the Nazi criminal, and a young boy—all pointing to a phrase that is repeated twice in the film and becomes its own leitmotif: "Horror, like sin, can become fascinating."

The narrative continues: Klaus (Günter Meisner)—living in exile with his wife Griselda (Marisa Paredes) and their young daughter Rena (Gisèle Echevarría)—has become tetraplegic and confined to a mechanical iron lung after a failed suicide. A mysterious young man, Angelo (David Sust), arrives and quickly insinuates himself into their house, proposing to care for and nurse Klaus. Soon Angelo reveals the real intentions of his appearance: he is the unseen witness of Klaus' crime in the prologue, and it was he who hid the body after Klaus' attempted self-slaughter. Angelo becomes progressively obsessed by Klaus' criminal activities and engages in reenactments of some of them, whilst dominating both the doctor's wife and daughter until the devastating final revelations.

When Villaronga filmed *In a Glass Cage*, the '80s were still being culturally dominated by "La Movida Madrileña" (The Madrilenian Scene) and its hedonistic, colorful times after years of Franco's repression and censorship, a

period commonly associated with Pedro Almodóvar's cinema of bright colors, humor, and feisty sexuality. Villaronga resides in the Movida's aesthetic opposition, bathing imagery in steely blues and clinical grays, finding visual inspiration in the paintings of Belgian surrealist Paul Delvaux, whose images not only recall a museum of medical curiosities—the idea of the "glass cage" (the breathing iron lung) seems lifted directly from the artist—but also in his restricted use of color and nearly morbid fascination with the cadaveric and disincarnated. Angelo sitting next to the iron lung, reading excerpts from Klaus' Nazi diary, becomes visually akin to one of Delvaux's Venuses attracted to a skeletal figure, thus achieving seductive and disturbing contrasts between desire and lust, horror and menace.

Villaronga will reserve color—a bleeding red—for two startling sequences which are amongst the film's most beautiful and thematically resonant. One follows a shocking murder sequence halfway through the film: a corpse hangs down from a rope and, as Angelo pushes a large red curtain to cover the body, the carnation tone of the fabric splashes through the screen in a gesture that recalls the red cape of a matador dancing on air as he applies the final killing stroke. Angelo's ritual of passage from victim to victimizer is now complete; he has transformed himself into an Angel of Vengeance/Death. Later, he slits a young choirboy's throat, a cascade of blood covering the pale white skin, another instance where red violently intrudes upon the oppressive, cool atmosphere Villaronga sustains throughout. Likewise, the villa in the woods, where Klaus and his family have isolated themselves after the war, is a breathing, living corpus from which the camera rarely sets foot—a circular architectural structure with labyrinthine corridors, deadly stairs, doorways to secretive rooms. It becomes Angelo's own private concentration camp, where he will resume Klaus' experiments as a form of expiation through suffering and horror.

In Glass' DVD interview, Villaronga states that among his initial inspirations were the crimes committed by fifteenth-century French nobleman (and Jeanne d'Arc's lieutenant) Gilles de Rais, who raped, mutilated, and killed several children, mostly young boys. Klaus' Nazi experiments and fascination with death and horror in the eyes of young men make him a descendant of de Rais, with the slow dissipation of these boys' lives enhancing his sexual arousal. It is through the release of sperm, serving as a consecration for the fecundity of crime, that the monstrous is finally led to surge, like a golem, in the final sequences, when the reenactment of Angelo's past violation makes explicit the cyclical transfer of guilt and crime. Characters become both victims and agents, trapped in a never-ending cycle of ritualistic violence, murder, and shame.

The film descends progressively into a more symbolic and allegorical territory, not only during the last astonishing fifteen minutes, but in several other intriguing touches. (Angelo redesigns the house to fit his own obsessions, notably the set of fishing nets used to catch pigeons in the house's open atrium, a visual metaphor for his own twisted mind.) This allegorical nature is certainly indebted to the Barcelona Film School tradition, whose '60s/'70s output represented some of the most formally daring, risky, fatalistic, and increasingly nightmarish horror-related films Spanish cinema ever produced. These young Catalonian visual anarchists—Vicente Aranda, Gonzalo Suárez, Pere Portabella, Joaquim Jordà, José María Nunes, and Jacinto Esteva—all eager to challenge Franco's heavy censorship limitations, often chose the horror genre to produce some powerful anti-naturalist allegories. *In a Glass Cage*, Villaronga's feature debut, is a film conscious of this tradition, one to which it often pays tribute.

The director, consistently adept at directing children and unseasoned actors, elicits exceptional performances from his cast. Especially notable is young David Sust as Angelo, whose terrifying ambiguity and expressive

dark eyes become striking forbidden portals to the darkest areas of a damaged soul hidden behind his angelic handsomeness. The film also boasts an extremely inventive production design, a score by Javier Navarrete that crawls under our skin, and remarkably stylish cinematography by Jaume Peracaula, notable in his Munchian images of bodies distorted—the absolutely unforgettable stretched body/neck of a young boy expiring after receiving a lethal injection. (Peracaula would continue to collaboarate with Villaronga, notably in 2000's companion piece, *The Sea*.)

In a Glass Cage was invisible for many years, often cited and talked about, but rarely seen. Its explosive melting pot—Nazism, pedophilia, torture—makes it sometimes difficult to grasp and assimilate, but in recent years, books, articles, and retrospectives of Villaronga's work have accessed the film's torturous beauty and profoundly disturbing nature. It is still not as well known as it should be amongst horror fans, but, like sin, it is cinema that fascinates and disturbs, one that affects and leaves no one safe and sound.

Jorge Didaco, a Brazil-based teacher of theater and film, has been under the spell of horror ever since the tender age of four. When the evil Maleficent (from Disney's Sleeping Beauty) *cried out in fury, "Now shall you deal with me, and all the powers of hell," it was love at first sight.*

IN THE MOUTH OF MADNESS 1994

BY KENNETH NELSON

John Carpenter is one of the most celebrated horror film directors of all time. As such, citing anything from his resume as "underrated" may raise a few eyebrows. However, greatness breeds expectations and fans

"I THINK, THEREFORE YOU ARE."

have certainly been justified in their disappointment at times; anyone sampling the former USC prodigy's cinematic canon can attest to more than a few clunkers populating the landscape. Yet I can't help but ponder whether unrealistic expectations are often and unfairly awarded to Carpenter, likely in reaction to the director's legendary early track record.

Criminally underappreciated upon release (during one of the greatest lulls of horror genre popularity in history), *In the Mouth of Madness* is a mind-bending delight that many fright fans have never given its proper due. Carpenter's final entry in his "Apocalypse Trilogy" alongside *The Thing* and *Prince of Darkness*, *Madness* follows insurance investigator John Trent (Sam Neill) as he explores the potentially fraudulent disappearance of bestselling horror novelist Sutter Cane (Jürgen Prochnow). Piecing together the puzzle of what he deems an extravagant publicity stunt, Trent embarks upon a bizarre journey where the line between reality and fiction becomes more blurred with every passing moment.

Scripted in the late '80s by future powerhouse Hollywood exec Michael De Luca, the story went through many fine tunings (and *Pet Sematary* director Mary Lambert) before Carpenter finally agreed to take the helm in 1993. Combining his fascination with the homeless population of New York City with the mythos of H.P. Lovecraft, De Luca infused an element of rabid fandom verging on religious fervor to create the world of his fictional author. In the completed product, De Luca's object of inspiration is blatantly obvious; aside from sharing book cover art fonts and a phonetic similarity, Charlton Heston's publisher character even takes a playful jab by stating that Sutter Cane is "more popular than Stephen King."

I first discovered the movie on cable back in the late '90s. Just entering my teenage years and long before the advent of the IMDb, my youthful mind recognized "Dr. Grant" from *Jurassic Park* while flipping through the channels. With modern day accoutrements like digital cable and an info button still years away, I paused to determine whether this seemingly innocent, dialogue-heavy, in-progress feature was deserving of my Saturday afternoon or not. Needless to say, when an axe-wielding maniac crashed through the glass window of a diner to accost John Trent (spouting the memorable line, "Do you read Sutter Cane?"), my attention had been earned. The next scene further piqued my interest, learning that said maniac was Cane's literary agent.

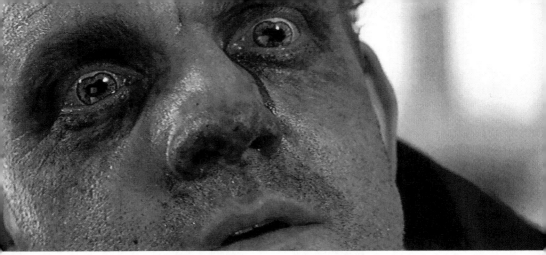

Despite being an avid reader in my youth, I had somehow overlooked the brilliant work of H.P. Lovecraft. Cane's writings are presented as modern day Lovecraftian lore (a monstrous genre of its own). As the plot develops, various creatures begin to inhabit the storyline. Fabricated by effects heavyweights KNB, these slimy, tentacled "miscreations" are the stuff of fever dreams, perhaps none more so than the "Wall of Monsters" that pursues Trent during the hair-raising climax. As mesmerized as I was revolted by the incendiary onscreen images, victim to one cinematic sucker punch after another, I also found my head spinning as I attempted to diagnose the sanity of our protagonist.

Carpenter and De Luca masterfully ally forces such that the viewer is never quite sure where the line is drawn between truth or make believe, fact or fiction. The film expertly changes tone from noir-ish to nightmarish, requiring anyone watching to make their own personal interpretations regarding the on-screen events' reality-bending nature. Over numerous repeat viewings of this little gem, I'm always left with an internal debate when the final credits roll as to what actually happened and who was pulling the strings. This open-endedness has created some discontent among audiences, but I commend any filmmaker whose garish tale I can revisit over and over again, discovering something new every time.

However, to solely credit the director and writer for *In the Mouth of Madness*' success would be a disservice to the excellent cast assembled. As John Trent, Sam Neill is brilliant, his snarky sense of humor and inherent charisma instantly establishing a kinship with the viewer. In many ways, his wonderful performance is the key that allows this outlandish story to even approach believability. Alongside Trent throughout his horrid journey as we are, Neill's authentic portrayal is essential to our emotional investment regarding his descent into madness. He is ably supported by a wealth of veteran character actors—including Heston, Julie Carmen, John Glover, and David Warner—who lend welcome gravity to the fanciful events. And as brief as his appearance may be, Prochnow eerily endows Sutter Cane with a god-like authority.

Ultimately the success of any artwork lies in the eye of the beholder. Over the years, more than a few critics have accused *In the Mouth of Madness* of having an identity crisis, stating that it takes itself too seriously while bludgeoning the viewer with utterly fantastic elements, that it's too cerebral to be a monster movie yet too saturated with ghastly ghouls to be considered a thinking fan's horror film. Yet I argue these are the same elements that make the picture such a rousing success. Rather than choose a mold and follow it, *Madness* breaks several and glues them all together so that we don't quite know what we're looking at...and can't prevent ourselves from trying to figure it out.

In many ways, *Madness* is a victim of its creator's success. With bona fide genre classics like *Halloween*, *The Fog*, and *Escape from New York* in his rear-view mirror, not many would place Carpenter's cinematic love letter to Lovecraft among his top five. To this day, cinephiles remain divisive over the director's admittedly inconsistent output following his decade of prominence. Even so, a less-than-perfect Carpenter flick stands head and shoulders above many other scary tales and a cult appreciation has developed for *In the Mouth of Madness* since its release. It may never garner the respect it truly deserves, but I implore you to give this oft-overlooked item a whirl. If all goes well, you'll be infected by Sutter Cane just the way I was.

Kenneth Nelson is a staff writer for HorrorHound *magazine and resides in New Jersey. Their very first subscriber, Kenneth began writing for the publication with issue #6 and has been a regular contributor ever since. He also works on the staff of HorrorHound Weekend, a semi-annual horror convention held in various locales throughout the Midwest.*

ISLE OF THE DEAD 1945

BY MIKE MAYO

I first encountered *Isle of the Dead* in the summer of 1997, when I was in the middle of writing *VideoHound's Horror Show*, a collection of about 1,000 short reviews. I was trying to watch and re-watch films in some kind of chronological order, but that was the heyday of the VHS rental business and so I picked up odd titles wherever I could.

I remember being a little surprised when I saw the name "Karloff" on the box in my local video store and realized that I was unfamiliar with the title. I thought I knew all of his important films from *Frankenstein* to *Targets*, but since he averaged 3-4 a year throughout the 1930s and '40s, some of them are easy to miss. More important, though, I remember how delighted I was sitting down to watch it. After weeks and months of monsters, psycho killers, and *X-Files* imitators, here was a short, quiet picture with a thoroughly sympathetic and effective performance from the star.

> "GO ON WITH YOUR NONSENSE, OLD WOMAN. THESE ARE NEW DAYS FOR GREECE. WE DON'T BELIEVE THE OLD FOOLISH TALES ANYMORE."

Karloff plays General Pherides, in command of a unit of Greek soldiers during the first Balkan War in 1912. He's known as "the Watchdog" because he is so thoroughly dedicated to the safety of his men. The first scene establishes how single-minded he is in pursuit of that goal with the severe punishment of another officer. Oliver Davis (Marc Cramer), a wet-behind-the-ears newspaper correspondent, doesn't understand the older man and thinks him needlessly harsh. In response, the General invites the kid to accompany him to a nearby island that's been turned into a cemetery. He explains that his wife is buried there.

They arrive to find that the place is inhabited. The garrulous Albrecht (Jason Robards Sr.) plays host to a British couple, Mr. St. Aubyn (Alan Napier) and his sickly wife (Katherine Emery) who's being looked after by Thea (Ellen Drew), a

Greek girl. Kyra (Helene Thimig), a suspicious, ill-tempered old biddy, and a Cockney salesman (Skelton Knaggs) round out the lot. Before long, one of them has succumbed to Septicemic plague. Pherides summons Dr. Drassos (Ernst Dorian), a fellow soldier, and they quarantine the island. If any of them were to return to the mainland, the troops would be exposed to the disease.

Initially, the conflict seems to be between rationality and superstition. The military men are skeptical of all things magical and horrific. Kyra believes that Thea is a "vorvolaka," a vampiric creature that drains life from her victims. It's true that Mrs. St. Aubryn is in poor health, but Kyra's ideas about Thea might just be one bitter woman's reaction to another who's younger, prettier, sweet-tempered, and stacked.

At the beginning of the third act, the action takes a sharp turn into Edgar Allan Poe territory.

Throughout, *Isle of the Dead* is a modest production. It's short (only 71 minutes), with a small cast and shot entirely on simple sets, with the exception of a couple of establishing shots. Lighting and camerawork come straight from *film noir.* Like much of producer Val Lewton's best work, scenes tend to be heavily shadowed with angular tree branches and blinds carving ominous patterns across the characters' faces. Those atmospherics replace conventional scares, and even a fan has to admit that things get a little silly toward the end. (A fan also has to admit that there is one major mistake. Hint: keep an eye on the lantern.)

As a producer, Lewton seems always to have been a bit embarrassed to be associated with horror. He avoids most of the clichés that come with cheap theatrics. At the same time, he opts out of big genuine scares. He does come up with one good moment, but it's aural not visual. He was always a great proponent of the idea that the unseen can be more frightening than the visible, and that's true enough if special effects cannot create a believably frightening figure. But would *Frankenstein* be the masterpiece that it is if Jack Pierce's monster make-up had been kept in heavy shadow? Or *King Kong*, without Willis O'Brien's astounding stop-motion magic?

Good taste is not necessarily beneficial to horror. Director Mark Robson, who would go on to make his career with such high-profile studio productions as *Peyton Place, Earthquake*, and *Valley of the Dolls*, isn't completely comfortable with the scary stuff either. For my money, excessive restraint isn't frightening. Neither is excessive violence, but I digress.

Flaws notwithstanding, the film still rates an unequivocal recommendation for Karloff's performance. He's playing another man who is viewed as a monster. All of the other characters, save Dr. Drassos, consider Pherides to be, at best, an uncaring martinet, or at worst a murderer who slaughtered his countrymen for no good reason. Karloff, writer Ardel Wray, and Robson refuse to do anything to soften the General. He's a cold man, but he is not selfish or mean. His only consideration is the safety of his troops. Note the importance of the opening shot of Pherides washing his hands. In the course of the film, the image is revealed to be literal in a medical sense, not metaphoric or Biblical. In fact, it is precisely the opposite of Pilate's washing his hands to deny responsibility. Pherides understands that his job is to accept responsibility, to bear the weight of it without complaint.

The first audiences must have understood that attitude. When the film was first released in September 1945, World War II had been over for less than a month. Concern for the guys who had done the fighting was still on everyone's mind. By the time I saw the film in 1997, that aspect of the story did not make the proper impression. I saw Pherides simply as a hard case but Karloff made him a fascinating, subtly powerful hard case. That's what drew me in then and it's still the reason to watch the film. The role marked the second of Karloff's three excellent collaborations with Lewton (between *The Body Snatcher* and *Bedlam*), arguably the best films he made after the original *Frankenstein* series.

During the filming, Karloff suffered from back problems. In fact, the production was halted for a time while he had surgery. His limited mobility and stiff gait are absolutely right for an aging warrior approaching the end of a long, hard-fought campaign. This is a man who has been wounded but refuses, as much as he can, to let anyone know it.

As David Thomson says in his *New Biographical Dictionary of Film*, Boris Karloff "carried with him an honorable record of insisting on human values within one of cinema's most exploited forms. Karloff has always shown us monsters and mad magicians who had been isolated by the unthinking cruelty of the 'wholesome' world." That was never truer than it is in *Isle of the Dead*.

As it happened, I revisited the film when I was finishing work on *The Horror Show Guide*, another collection of short reviews. Looking at the horror efforts made between 1997 and 2012, I'd experienced new levels of graphic "photo-realistic" violence and torture porn that made the 1990s look timid. But I saw few performances equal to Karloff at his best.

> *Mike Mayo is the author of* American Murder, VideoHound's Horror Show *and its (sort of) sequel,* The Horror Show Guide. *His most recent book is a novel,* Jimmy the Stick.

ISOLATION 2005

BY JON KITLEY

"JOHN, WE'VE GOT TO SHUT IT ALL DOWN. IT'S GONE WRONG."

I first heard about *Isolation* in 2007 via a genre mag's monthly video spotlight giving it high praise. Hoping to avoid spoilers, I didn't read many details—only that it had something to do with a few people being quarantined on a farm. Upon watching, I was blown away by how effective and well-done the film was; I immediately wanted to know more about it and the man responsible, writer/director Billy O'Brien. Going online, I was dismayed at how little info was available. But through tenacity and a sheer twist of luck, I was finally able to get in contact with O'Brien to learn more about his absorbing and dark tale.

If you have not yet seen the film, go find it and watch it. Then come back and read the rest of this essay. Not because I will be giving away spoilers, but because I think you'll enjoy it more. Going in completely blind, like the characters themselves, you will discover the real horror as organically as they do. So go ahead...we'll wait for you.

Are you back? Great. Let's get on with this.

What makes *Isolation* so unique and different from most modern horror efforts is that first and foremost, it has a good story. The action takes place on a small farm in Ireland, where the owner Dan (John Lynch) has agreed to let some doctors/scientists perform some tests/experiments with his cows. While

he suspects that things might not be on the "up and up," he really needs the money and so doesn't ask questions. Things start to go awry while the staff veterinarian Orla (Essie Davis) is giving a pregnant cow an exam. With her arm inside the animal, checking on the unborn calf, she suddenly jerks and winces in pain, pulling out her arm to reveal that she has been cut or bitten by…something. That night, the calf is born in a sequence that is traumatic, sad, and terrifying all at the same time. Once the scientist in charge of the experiment (Marcel Iures) shows up, we start to realize that something was wrong with the newborn calf. Or more accurately, something is wrong *inside* of it. Matters only get worse when a young couple (Sean Harris and Ruth Negga), on the run from their families, camp outside of the farm and get sucked into the bizarre goings-on.

As Dan, Lynch does an incredible job, earning our empathy every tragic step of the way. O'Brien says Lynch got the job thanks to his "incredible soulful eyes; I thought I could really hang the film on him." While she doesn't appear on screen as long, Australian actress Davis dives head first (actually arm first) into her role as the rural vet; we grow to care deeply about her character, especially as seen through Dan's eyes. Iures, a highly rated star of Romania's stage and screen who has even appeared in a few Hollywood films like *Mission: Impossible* and *Pirates of the Caribbean: At World's End*, does a stellar job as the misguided scientist. When things go wrong, he is the "villain" responsible despite his best intentions in the grand scheme of things. The intense Harris and Negga are invaluable additions to the small ensemble—what lies in store for their characters is much, much worse than any parental disapproval.

Growing up on a farm, O'Brien recalled being woken up in the early morning many times by his father with just the words, "Cow calving," to start his day. Referencing these real-life experiences, he does an excellent job of making us care about these everyday characters just trying to get through life, and then cranks up the tension and suspense by putting them in peril. Thrown together by twisted circumstances to battle an unsightly flawed-science creation, we helplessly watch in shock and panic as they struggle for survival.

The real beauty here is the dreary atmosphere. Everything is cold, bleak, dark, and rainy; we feel a chill watching the characters' breath and steam rising from warm water. Even in the daytime, the sun is covered by clouds with no sense of warmth. The soundtrack is almost non-existent, with only a rare series of chords or long screeching sounds breaking up the organic noises of the onscreen action. Adrian Johnston's score offers no melodies or tunes, nothing to give any comfort. Many of the camera angles, shot behind fences or through narrow openings, convey a feeling of being trapped, of confinement. All these

elements conspire together to give a feeling of…isolation.

Sure, we've seen horror films that take place in remote locations before, but rarely do they feel this genuine. A mud-soaked farm isn't one of your typical genre settings, which lends a sense of realism to the story. We relate to these human characters, which in turn causes more terror for us when their lives are threatened. Mindless killing of a cast means nothing if we don't care for them. The sense of dread we feel for Dan, who genuinely seems like a decent man, really makes our hearts ache for the guy, especially as his already cold and tedious world slowly gets worse and worse.

It might be hard to believe, but half of the $1 million+ special effects budget was dedicated exclusively to creating fake cows. (Speaking of which, the original title, *The Calf*, was changed midway through because O'Brien's producers didn't think it would translate well.) This is one of those special effects movies where the skilled labor behind the scenes is virtually undetectable, about the highest compliment one can pay. One of the artists responsible was Bob Keen, known for his superb work on the first two *Hellraiser* films. Keen also had the troublesome task of bringing the feature's main creature, based on designs by Stephen Brown and O'Brien's future wife Philippa Wright, to life. Another good chunk of the production budget went to creating the slurry pit (where a farm's bovine waste is stored over wintertime) which figures greatly into one of the most suspenseful scenes. Because actors were going to be submerged in this pit, it had to be completely sanitary and safe. Suffice to say, O'Brien's production team did their jobs perfectly, creating a visceral set-piece that will undoubtedly provoke groans of disgust and apprehension.

The film won multiple accolades during its festival run, such as Grand Prize at the Gérardmer Film Festival and top awards at Screamfest in L.A. and Austin's Fantastic Fest. (Predictably, O'Brien subsequently received several offers to direct "Hollywood horror films of teenagers in a van in the desert," but he elected to concentrate on writing his own material.) Unfortunately, in 2007 Lionsgate decided to release *Isolation* with little fanfare direct to DVD where it has lain relatively undiscovered ever since. I say unfortunate because this is the kind of film you won't soon forget after watching, with images that will haunt your consciousness for days. The kind of film that provokes enough chills to make you reach for a sweater or jacket even in the middle of summer. The kind of film that we, as horror fans, desperately need.

Jon Kitley is the head corpse behind Kitley's Krypt, which he's been running since 1998, making it one of the oldest horror sites on the web. There, he strives to encourage other horror fans to "Discover the Horror" by delving into the genre's rich history and seeing as much as they can. Jon also is a staff writer at HorrorHound *magazine, using his "They Came from the Krypt" column to bring some much-needed attention to obscure and overlooked films.*

I SPIT ON YOUR GRAVE 1978

BY BJ COLANGELO

A BFCC Video Nasty, named one of *TIME* magazine's "Top 10 Most Ridiculously Violent Films of All Time," awarded "zero stars" by Roger Ebert, and still banned in many countries around the globe, *I Spit on Your Grave* remains to most horror fans a disgusting piece of exploitation cinema better swept under the rug.

"TOTAL SUBMISSION. THAT'S WHAT I LIKE IN A WOMAN —TOTAL SUBMISSION."

Infamous for its nearly 45-minute onscreen rape, the movie is often discredited as shamelessly vulgar, excessively violent, sexually degrading to women, and an immature theater of cruelty. The unfortunate truth is that many audiences, turned away by these unflattering presumptions, completely miss out on one of history's most misunderstood and underappreciated horror films.

I Spit on Your Grave (originally titled *Day of the Woman*) is a story about an aspiring writer, Jennifer Hills (Camille Keaton), who is gang-raped by a group of men and then takes it upon herself to hunt down, manipulate, and slaughter each of them. On paper, it's easy to see why most conventional moviegoers are repelled, but *I Spit on Your Grave* is at once an honest look at the dangers of humanity, an overlooked examination of the power of rape victims, and an inspiring film to female audiences everywhere. In failing to look past the red flag-waving "45-minute rape," they also fail to observe *I Spit on Your Grave*'s significant contributions to cinema as a whole. This is an *important* film, misperceived (and unfortunately marketed) as exploitative trash.

I'm obliged to reveal that I am a survivor of rape myself. I am thankful my experience was nowhere near as grotesque as Jennifer Hills', but without divulging the gritty details, rape is rape. The first time I ever got my hands on *I Spit on Your Grave*, it was only a few months after my own rape. I had my reservations at first, but thought it might be therapeutic to see the grand-mother of all rape/revenge films. Simply put, it changed my life. For the first time, I saw a rape victim represented onscreen as something more than *just* a victim. I saw a strong woman, one who had endured, survived, and accepted the horrific acts forced upon her, resolved not to allow her rapists any power over her. (I don't know who decided that anyone who has ever been raped must now be some fragile creature. I'm sure *Law & Order*'s Dick Wolf had something to do with it, but I digress.)

As heartbreaking as it was to watch this poor woman suffer for over an hour, her ultimate acts of revenge—fantasy or no—were downright inspiring. Not that I was immediately filled with visions of reprisal against my own attacker, but for the first time I realized that I didn't have to let this incident ruin my life. I may have been without control in that specific situation, but how I responded to it was something *totally* within my control. *I Spit on Your Grave* taught me that.

Now, I understand the criticism. I do. I get it. Rape isn't easy subject matter for people to swallow, but writer/director Meir Zarchi does something that no other film had ever dared before: he never cuts away from the act. Ever. Audiences are forced to see every last dastardly and brutal moment. Some, maybe even most, people would call this exploitation. I call it reality. Rape victims aren't allowed to look or pull away; similarly, Zarchi doesn't allow his audience that luxury. Over 30 years since the film premiered, we still live in a culture that doesn't talk about rape, where politicians genuinely believe that any female's anatomy can shut down if she's raped to prevent a pregnancy. We are encouraged to cheer if we defeat cancer, but asked not to mention surviving rape at the dinner table. We choose to avoid the subject altogether, finding it too unpleasant, preferring to imagine such a thing doesn't exist.

I Spit on Your Grave holds our heads in place, imposing some virtual Ludovico Treament from *A Clockwork Orange* upon us, screaming, "*Look at what happens.*" We see the plotting, the scheming, the deed, and the heartbreaking aftermath. It's disgusting, and audience members *should* be disgusted. If they are not, there are far deeper issues to be addressed.

Working through his own personal anger towards the unnecessary violence he had witnessed firsthand towards women, Zarchi has repeatedly stated that he always intended for his film to serve as social commentary. The graphic presentation was a deliberate artistic decision, an attempt to convey just how terrible such instances could be in the hopes that judicial systems would take rape crimes more seriously. As a dramatist, he wanted his heroine to experience cathartic justice, to make her attackers pay for their actions, for her revenge to be as horrific as the actions they had forced upon her. He also challenges his viewers to ask themselves whether the punishment fits the crime, providing a healthy dose of moral ambiguity that rises above any claims of mere escapism.

I Spit on Your Grave is also one of the most uniquely crafted horror films, born of a perfect marriage of financial limitations and keen cinematic instinct. The entire movie appears to be shot with a single camera, one capable of capturing prolonged shots of bucolic beauty and frenetic scenes of violence and pain. Zarchi's script is composed of minimal dialogue, with absolutely no soundtrack other than Jennifer's screams and the men's "bat-

tle cries." There is a rawness here, the action captured almost documentary-style; it is this realistic approach that imbues the film with its ferocity and power. One senses this is exactly the way events would really play out. By eliminating all of the typical cinematic aesthetics (artfully composed camera angles, musical score, jump scares), the audience—male and female—is disposed to focus all of their attention and empathy on Jennifer, connecting to her character on a primal and unconscious level.

Casting was not easy. Zarchi insisted on Keaton after seeing a black-and-white photograph of the actress, saying she was the only one he could imagine playing Jennifer Hill. With no fear of hyperbole, her gutsy performance is a masterstroke, fearlessly revealing layer after layer both physical and emotional. Interestingly, the director didn't prepare his actors for the infamous scenes of assault, preferring to just let them play out naturally as they would. This unconventional and terrifying approach—all but Keaton were making their feature film debuts—worked as these sequences feel disturbingly realistic. (Zarchi later admitted that he specifically cast less-appealing actors to play the attackers so audience members would have a difficult time identifying with these monsters.)

Women are bred to believe that we should be ashamed of our sexuality and, in turn, remain silent about any sort of sexual trauma. Wrongfully condemned as a reprehensible exercise in exploitation, *I Spit on Your Grave* will likely forever exist in the shadows, denied its status as a daring and courageous attempt to examine the rape act in an honest and unflinching manner, as well as satisfying the revenge fantasy so often denied its victims. I say it again: This is an *important* film, one of the earliest and most powerful examples of female empowerment in the face of sexual trauma.

BJ Colangelo is special. Not in a "please don't give her chocolate or knives" kinda special, but close. She is a graduate of Western Illinois University with a B.A. in Theatre; Acting. Conquering beauty pageants, musical theatre, and baton twirling, BJ Colangelo writes about horror from the female and millennial perspective. Currently residing in Elyria, OH, you can find her award-winning commentary over at her blog, Day of the Woman.

KAIRO 2001

BY J.T. McROBERTS

"DEATH WAS... ETERNAL LONELINESS."

It was a muggy Carolina Saturday afternoon in the convention hall when that familiar urge to discover something new and unusual led me to a movie vendor's corner booth. It was here, shoulder to shoulder with my fellow film geeks, that I encountered the J-horror phenomenon firsthand. I asked the sweat-stained Yoda behind the table for a recommendation, adding, "Something scary."

As my fellow collectors know, the bootlegger is seasoned in discovering the latest gems from across the globe. He/she is the first and best guide one can find at any given gathering. This particular grimy guru reached past the stack of bootleg *Star Wars Holiday Special* DVDs and *Within the Woods* fifteenth generation transfers to a special rack carrying region-free imports from around the world. His hand returned with a DVD of *Whispering Corridors* which he handed to me along with the admonition that it was "pretty good."

Without hesitation, I replied that I didn't want pretty good but was instead looking for "the best." With that, he placed a second DVD in my hands.

"This one will creep you the fuck out," he said with a sly grin on his face. I stared down at a cover comprised of a computer monitor with a ghostly image beating against the screen—ostensibly trying to escape. The case was covered in Japanese kanji so I was at first skeptical of being able to play the disc on my player and equally so that the entire film would be in Japanese without benefit of subtitles. He reassured me that the disc was indeed region-free and subtitled throughout. I bought the two imports and as I walked away, I focused intently on the only word on the case that appeared to be in English, with no idea what horrors lay within: "*Kairo.*"

After the obligatory studio credits and logos, the movie opens to darkness and silence...quickly broken by the old familiar electronic buzz, beep and tone of a modem dialing into the internet. (At the time of its release, modem connections were quite prominent but would soon be made obsolete by the rapid advance of internet ubiquity.) We fade in from the darkness upon the somber setting of a gray freighter adrift somewhere upon a cloud-covered sea. It is here that we meet our narrator Michi (Kumiko Asô), whose memories will be our guide through the events to follow. Said events involve a group of loosely connected university students investigating a bizarre website, one that may be instrumental in a strange spate of suicides overtaking their circle of friends and ultimately the world at large.

There is not a lot of character development in *Kairo* (or *Pulse*, as it was retitled for U.S. audiences), but we are shown enough of each of our main protagonists at work and play to get a handle on the kind of person they might be. The cinematography is gray and bleak, even for its time when desaturated films were poised to saturate the market, so to speak. The performances throughout are quite believable and nothing feels forced or false. We alternately stare in shock and horror at the peculiarities that our heroes witness: from Harue (Koyuki) witnessing a woman frantically sealing the edges of her door frame with red tape to Kawashima (Haruhiko Katô) stumbling to his backside as one of the apparitions from the internet advances, we are held just as captive as the protagonists.

Director Kiyoshi Kurosawa was responsible for *Kairo*'s script as well as its novelization and his familiarity with his subject translates into a mastery of the medium, keeping viewers just as puzzled and terrified as his characters. During "The Making of *Pulse*" featurette on the 2005 Magnolia DVD, Kurosawa states, "I don't put too much deep thought into it, but it's simply impossible to show everything that's happening on the screen, in the frame. There are some things you just can't see. The audience is presented with the illusion that the entire world is contained in what's onscreen but there's an entire world off-screen too." He continues, "What you can show on-screen is finite but there's an infinite world right outside of it, and when someone moves off-screen I think the audience will recognize that. I think that's something that's hard to achieve in comics and probably in animation as well."

Kurosawa's lens captures just enough of a world falling into quiet chaos to allow the viewer to imagine an apocalypse of worldwide proportions. The website discovered by Kawashima asks him, "Would you like to meet a ghost?" and the rest of the film purports to show us what happens when ghosts utilize the internet as a gateway into our world. Kurosawa muses, "I think that ghosts are beings that lack human emotion and personality. They're human-like but all of the emotional elements of a normal person are missing. They're empty shells. That's what scares me when it comes to ghosts."

Although there is a lot of talk of ghosts throughout, it is never made explicit what these apparitions are seeking or how they are using the internet to cross into our world. This dark, murky ambiguity is what gives the movie its power. It is a truly bleak, nihilistic vision, a dark portrait of society collapsing under

the weight of its own apathy. After being exposed to the creatures from the cyberworld beyond, our human characters dissolve to ash and scatter in the wind. With its use of the internet as a gateway between worlds, *Kairo* becomes a doomsayer of technology not unlike the message of *Videodrome* twenty years prior.

Kurosawa's film prompts an alarmingly prescient allegory, one that presages the rise of online social media and its dehumanizing effect on many who have disconnected from reality to live in the safety of chat rooms, forums, and web cams. Years before the proliferation of the internet in our daily lives, Kurosawa painted a cautionary tale reminding us not to discard emotions and human interaction in favor of the ephemeral world proffered by the computer keyboard and monitor.

Kairo remains a truly terrifying picture, rich in subtext and subtleties. It's a shame that it was essentially buried in the J-horror deluge of the early 2000s, being every bit as praiseworthy as classic contemporaries like *Ringu* and *Ju-on*. Kurosawa magically captures the cinematic spirit of the apocalypse; during its two-hour run time, we believe that we are watching the world come to a quiet, disturbing end...

...one that comes not with a bang but with the buzz, beep, and lonely drone of a modem calling out in the darkness.

J.T. McRoberts is a founding member of Mutantville Productions, a group of no-budget filmmakers based out of Charlotte, North Carolina, responsible for the paranormalist feature G.H.O.S.T., Tales from Mutantville, an anthology horror collection hosted by Muticia the Movie Goddess, and Muticia's Movie Morgue featuring George A. Romero's Night of the Living Dead! Visit MVP at www. Mutantville.com, MVP Mutant Radio on iTunes, and @MVPlayers on Twitter.

KILL, BABY... KILL! 1966

BY CHARLEY SHERMAN

How many times have you woken up from a dream, and then reveled in the process of piecing together the fragments in order to make some sense of it? The pleasure I derive watching *Operazione paura* over and over again is a bit like that, thanks to the imagination of its Italian director, Mario Bava. In the

"NOBODY EVER MAKES IT BACK FROM THE VILLA GRAPS."

2004 documentary *Mario Bava: Operazione Paura*, Tim Burton said, "[His movies] stayed with you, because they were so different. They were so emotional...and they were so much truly like bringing dreams to life."

Bava originally wanted to be a painter, but after many years working as a cinematographer and special effects designer, he eventually became one of Italian cinema's most audacious and imaginative directors, one whose influence was never truly heralded until after his death in 1980. (His visual artistry is still underrated when considered alongside other more lauded greats of the cinema.) *Operazione paura* shows Bava at the height of his ingenuity, creating one of the most fully realized explorations of dream logic on celluloid. Its influence can be clearly seen in the masterful works of Federico Fellini, Martin Scorsese, and David Lynch, yet it has never acquired the reputation of a movie that *must be seen*.

One reason lies in its unfortunate fate of being saddled with one of the most misleading American titles in the history of cinema, the bizarrely inappropriate *Kill, Baby...Kill!* The Italian title is not considerably more enticing, translating as *Operation Fear*. In England it was known by the blandly generic *Curse of the Dead*. I firmly believe that these titles have deterred people from seeking it out—just as I was. But once seen, like any great artist's work, I guarantee that the film will demand and reward frequent viewings.

The plot is as follows: a doctor (Giacomo Rossi-Stuart) is summoned to perform an autopsy on a young woman who has been impaled to death. He discovers that the inhabitants of the remote European village are living in a state of constant fear and that the source of their terror is the ghost of a seven-year-old girl and a house called The Villa Graps. As the practical-thinking doctor investigates the nature of their superstition, he plunges into a nightmare world where magic and psychic possession wield more power than medicine or science.

What I love first and foremost is the world that Bava creates: reminiscent in parts of other horror tales, but, taken as a whole, unlike anything else in cinema. As most of the action takes place at night in a village under supernatural influences, Bava's passion for stylistic lighting, baroque set design, splashes of vivid color, shadows, fog, and special camera effects is unleashed to full effect. This style is prevalent in the way that segments of the walls, streets and corridors are textured with hues of green, yellow, and blue. Where are these colors emanating from? While making no literal sense, they are simply sumptuous to look at. (If you ever wondered where Dario Argento got his inspiration for *Suspiria*'s color schemes, look no further.) Bava's inspired use of windows and mirrors demonstrates how simply and brilliantly glass can be utilized to create chilling and disorienting effects. Then there is the production design: from a spiral staircase to a cobwebbed painting to medieval corridors, the décor provides Bava and cinematographer Antonio Rinaldi with a perfect palette to work their magic. All this is accompanied by Carlo Rustichelli's bewitching melodies, a genuinely haunting score well ahead of its time.

The narrative follows Dr. Eswai's investigation and the plight of the strange people he meets. These include a heroic witch called Ruth (Fabienne Dali), the Burgomaster (Luciano Catenacci), a female medical student called Monica

(Erika Blanc) who has a wonderfully bizarre nightmare involving a doll, and the spirit-channeling Baroness Graps (Giovanna Galletti). But the most unforgettable character is the ghost of the seven-year-old Mellissa Graps. (A role actually played by a boy, Valero Valeri, the son of someone working in the production office who Bava thought was perfect for the part!) Mellissa appears outside windows, sometimes gliding towards the misty glass, hands outstretched, eyes demonically glaring...visuals which surely influenced the best moments of Tobe Hooper's *Salem's Lot* (1979). In another scene, she giggles as she goes up and down on a swing in the graveyard, with the swing as the camera's POV, showing off Bava's bravura cinematography. In the most famous sequence, she is seen playing with a white ball in a corridor, an unforgettable image which Federico Fellini would imitate for his "Toby Dammit" segment in the anthology *Spirits of the Dead* (1968). Another film influenced by this character is Martin Scorsese's *The Last Temptation of Christ* (1988), revealing the devil in the guise of a young girl. (Scorsese has often acknowledged his appreciation of Bava's work.)

Without diminishing the acting of the fine cast, the film's other main character is really the house itself—The Villa Graps. This is a very special haunted house—a fusion of Jean Cocteau, M.C. Escher, and Terence Fisher. What takes place inside this residence, or in the minds of the characters

inside of it, comes close to capturing the essence of dreams. David Lynch was surely influenced by a chase scene in the Villa Graps for the finale of his TV series *Twin Peaks*. When I first saw this scene in *Operazione paura*, I found myself saying, "Did that really just happen—what the f***?" When I revisited it years later, I had the same response—the mark of a very special piece of work.

Referring to *Operazione paura* years after its making, Bava said: "I once made a film in twelve days as a bet with some Americans [...] improvised from a thirty-page script that was written on the spot." (By most accounts, filming actually took about twenty days, working in a remote village in Tuscany.) Halfway through shooting, the production ran out of money, but the cast and crew worked on, without pay, apparently due to their admiration for Bava and the project. Imagine what could have been done with time and a proper budget.

But then, perhaps the very lack of funding enabled a collective creative energy which makes *Operazione paura* a masterpiece of visual imagination, provoking Luchino Visconti to give a standing ovation at the film's Italian premiere. It is a shame that such applause and appreciation was not as forthcoming until after Bava's death. I have personally spent an untold amount of time persuading even the most knowledgeable of horror buffs to watch it, and then watch it again. Rest assured this film will linger in the memory longer than most, just like your favorite nightmare.

Charley Sherman grew up in Nottingham, England. He is the founder of Wild-Claw Theatre, dedicated to producing works of horror for the Chicago stage, and was its artistic director from 2007-2011. He has adapted works by Clive Barker, Arthur Machen, H.P. Lovecraft and William Peter Blatty for the theatre, and also contributed to HORROR 101 *with essays on* The Black Cat *(1934) and* Dracula *(1958).*

THE LEGEND OF HELL HOUSE 1973

BY J. NELSON SMITH

> ## "THE HOUSE TRIED TO KILL ME. IT ALMOST SUCCEEDED."

Movies come into my life in many ways: recommendations from friends, critics' reviews, studio marketing, or just plain dumb luck. *The Legend of Hell House* came to my attention in the form of audio samples on Skinny Puppy's 1985 album *Bites*. Their music often deals with the darker side of humanity and sound bites like, "Church in Hell," and "Touch me or I'll find somebody who will," piqued my interest in this underrated gem. Several years passed before a friend acquired a tattered VHS copy from the local Goodwill. In the middle of a cold Indiana winter, a group of us sat on the cold floor of his unheated house and watched as the secrets of the Belasco house unfolded before our eyes.

The plot is simple enough: Mr. Deutsch (Roland Culver) has purchased the Belasco house, the "Mount Everest of haunted houses," believed to be haunted by the deceased Emeric Belasco. In life, Belasco boarded up the house's windows to keep anyone from seeing in (or out), then invited his guests to partake in everything from deviant sexual acts to cannibalism. Deutsch is willing to pay £100,000 apiece to the quartet of individuals he has charged with providing proof (or disproof) of life after death after a one-week stay in Hell House.

Two previous attempts to investigate the house have resulted in death or madness. The only person to make it out alive (and relatively sane) is a physical medium by the name of Benjamin Fischer (Roddy McDowall), who has agreed to revisit the house 20 years later. This time he's joined by mental medium Florence Tanner (Pamela Franklin), physicist Dr. Barrett (Clive Revill), and Barrett's wife, Ann (Gayle Hunnicutt).

In movies of this ilk, the skeptical scientist usually ignores the obvious supernatural elements, dismissing them to his peril. However, Dr. Barrett doesn't reject the paranormal; he just feels there is a practical explanation for these unexplained events. This gives his character depth while keeping the audience guessing as to whose theories are the most sound. While Miss Tanner is open to suggestion (as long as it fits her preconceived notions), Ann is truly open and gets more than she bargains for. The only one who really knows what they're up against, Fischer keeps his mental guard up and with good reason.

John Hough is one of the few directors to have both Hammer horror (*Twins of Evil*) and Disney family fare (*Escape to Witch Mountain*) on his resume. While much of his 1980s output wasn't as well received—think *Howling IV: The Original Nightmare* (or better yet, don't)—there's no denying his contributions to the previous decade.

Franklin had been a horror staple since she first appeared in *The Innocents* at the tender age of 11. A dozen years later, her youthful good looks made her the ideal candidate to portray the naïve yet willful Tanner. Hunnicutt's mature beauty adds to her appeal as the wife who's just tagging along; not particularly fearful of the paranormal, but she's never encountered anything like Hell House. Revill's extensive experience both on the stage and screen make him a great fit for Barrett, bringing conviction to his role of the stubborn, overconfident pragmatist. McDowall—best known to horror fans as Peter Vincent in the 1985 horror classic *Fright Night*—shines as the reluctant physical medium who knows that the Belasco house doesn't mind a few visitors, as long as no one tries attacking it.

Oddly enough, both McDowall and Revill's most famous mainstream roles were in sci-fi movies that kept their mugs out of sight. McDowall portrayed Cornelius (and later Caesar) in the *Planet of the Apes* films while Revill lent his voice to the Emperor in 1980's *The Empire Strikes Back*.

Lauded for his classic apocalyptic novel *I Am Legend*, a number of classic *Twilight Zone* episodes, and several Roger Corman 1960s AIPoe gothic thrillers, Richard Matheson penned *The Legend of Hell House* screenplay based on his original 1971 novel, *Hell House*. While a fan of Shirley Jackson's *The Haunting of Hill House* (1959), Matheson didn't like the idea that the reader was left unresolved whether the ghosts were in the main character's imagination or not. He wanted a haunted house that was truly haunted and therefore based much of his book on recorded paranormal events. There are clear similarities

to Jackson's work (two men and two women investigating the house, one is skeptic, another is either crazy or a medium, etc.), with a much darker and more sexual approach taken.

Toning down the book's liberal carnality for the big screen awarded the film a PG rating, but one has to wonder if it hurt more than it helped (witness the success of *The Exorcist* a few months later). Even with its libido throttled back, *The Legend of Hell House* remains more provocative than most haunted house films, with Hough ably hinting at more than actually meets the eye. This mix of sexuality and horror is part of what makes the film unique, and Matheson smoothly blends these elements like cream and honey. The Belasco house doesn't just want to kill you; it wants to touch a moral nerve by blurring the boundaries of appropriate behavior.

Cinematographer Alan Hume, who would shoot *Return of the Jedi* and a string of James Bond flicks in the 1980s, lurks around corners and shoots from low angles, giving the Belasco house a distinct personality. Hume isn't afraid to linger, letting the action occur within the frame. Delia Derbyshire and Brian Hodgson, who also worked in the sound and music departments on *Dr. Who*, provide a haunting ambient score that adds a layer of mystery and horror. This, combined with Robert Jones' flawless set design, adds the perfect finishing touches.

Despite its underrated status, *The Legend of Hell House* was parodied in 2001's *Scary Movie 2*. (Sadly, the possessed cat scene is nearly as laughable in its original form.) However, Hough and his associates were wise to rely on practical effects in most situations, making this folly the exception and not the rule.

The secrets of the Belasco House are many (I doubt anyone has ever guessed the film's divisive ending), but after my initial viewing on that cold winter day I knew I had just witnessed something special. Yet, like the mystery of Emeric Belasco, *The Legend of Hell House* has managed to stay hidden in the shadows for far too long. Explore it now—if you dare.

J. Nelson Smith grew up amid the cornfields of Indiana, so watching horror films seemed a logical choice. The only film that ever gave him nightmares was The Elephant Man *which, oddly enough, was forced on him by his parents. Justin's writing can be found online at HalfGleason and Flickfeast, as well as in the printed pages of* New Empress *magazine.*

LEMORA: A CHILD'S TALE OF THE SUPERNATURAL 1973

BY STEVE GRIFFES

> "SHE RAN AWAY, JUST LIKE A LOT OF PEOPLE WHO DON'T WANT TO ACCEPT WHAT THEY TRULY ARE. AND SO SHE KEPT RUNNING... RUNNING...FROM WHAT SHE KNEW SHE WAS. UNTIL SHE COULDN'T RUN ANYMORE."

The lesbian vampire is a familiar archetype to horror fans. Early examples of Sapphic suckers include *Blood and Roses* (1960), *Terror in the Crypt* (1964), and *The Vampire Lovers* (1970). These movies are all loose adaptations of Sheridan Le Fanu's 1872 story "Carmilla," a subtly homoerotic tale in which an undead countess seeks a female companion. *The Vampire Lovers'* success paved the way for more overtly erotic European lesbian vampire movies, from the stylish and sleazy entries by Jess Franco to the disorienting nightmare worlds of Jean Rollin to Harry Kümel's masterpiece *Daughters of Darkness* (1971). The subgenre eventually lost its steam; other than the occasional Erzsébet Báthory offering, the lesbian

vampire has mostly been relegated to a nostalgic genre relic.

Lemora: A Child's Tale of the Supernatural follows an angelic girl (Cheryl "Rainbeaux" Smith) as she journeys from her small town to find and forgive her father for murdering her adulterous mother. Her travels take her to the mysterious town of Astaroth, where she is ensnared by a monstrous woman (Leslie Gilb). Though obviously influenced by "Carmilla," *Lemora* is shamefully over-looked in the discourse of vampire films in general, and is likewise absent from chronicles of queer cinema. This could be because neither the "V-word" nor the "L-word" are uttered, or because more attention has been devoted to the titillating Euro-vamps of the era. It also doesn't help that the film has had limited availability over the years. Produced for approximately $200,000, *Lemora* was released in 1973 to little fanfare, and then re-released in 1975 as *The Rape of the Vampires*, undoubtedly an attempt to capitalize on other salacious vampire titles.

The narrative is like a familiar fairytale that unfolds like a nightmare, with an unnatural cerulean tint enhancing the dreamlike atmosphere. When Lila sneaks into the backseat of a car and escapes to the nearby decrepit town, it's as if this horrible place is literally up the road from the pure sanctuary of her home with her guardian, the local Reverend (played by director Richard Blackburn). Lila's dangerous after-hours travels lead to unsettling encounters with a series of lecherous and leering adults. While these grotesque scenes possess dark humor (when the bus station attendant offers her candy, he asks if she likes "soft or hard centers," with a repulsively wet, flicking tongue), the tone during Lila's bus trip is total terror. As the disturbing driver (played with delightful dementedness by the late Hy Pike) ferries his sole passenger to her destination, he ominously reveals the history of Astaroth, whose inhab-itants were victims of a horrible epidemic. Lila peers out the window, and the viewer sees from her point of view (achieved with a slightly shaky handheld camera) the terror that is lurking in the woods.

Of course, Lila's journey into horror does not end when she arrives at Lemora's gothic manor. She is tormented by a witchy crone chanting a morbid song and androgynous diseased children (with almost inhuman-sounding cackling voices) in dress-up clothes who mock her prayers. When she finally meets Lemora, she is a stark contrast to Lila's blonde pigtails and Sunday dress. She has more in common with a fairytale evil queen: tall and imposing with hair in a matronly bun, piercing black eyes, sunken, emotion-less face, and adorned in an ornate, proto-goth gown that covers her arms and neck. As Lila experiences what it is like to be a guest in Lemora's home (e.g., instinctively and hungrily gnawing up raw meat chunks, partaking in awkward bathtub-time with the hostess, nonconsensual dancing in circles with the impish children), the viewer becomes aware of Lemora's true intentions. There is also an incredibly long chase scene (again using handheld camera to show Lila's disoriented point of view), winding through the woods and abandoned buildings in the night. It's all very circular, much like the taunting songs and dances. Whether she's escaping from men's sexual advances, her father, the infected kids, the minions, or any of the other monsters, there is one constant: she is always getting closer to Lemora.

Lila's "tale of the supernatural" is really the hellish misadventure that is adolescence. The male characters in *Lemora*—the trusted Reverend, her monster father, every man she encounters in her travels—all subconsciously or blatantly want a piece of Lila. Even the church sign says "Community Church—Lila Lee—Our Singin' Angel," as if she belongs to the (exclusively female) congregation. Lila's adventure through town symbolizes the path she is expected to take into adulthood, to become the object of male desire.

On the surface, Lemora is another manipulative, selfish monster. But as she shares with Lila the story of her past, and the possibilities of their future, Lila reflects on the meaning of her journey. The alternative that Lemora presents is one of empowerment, sexual and otherwise, as well as embracement of true self: "You've been drawn to me from the beginning. Come to me and find peace." It is ambiguous whether Lila's fate is predetermined or if it's directed by Lemora. Unlike other lesbian vampire films where the monster is attempting to lure her victims away from their male lovers, Lemora wants to remove Lila from male oppression and religious repression, to teach her to turn the tables on a predatory world. When she asks Lila, "Wouldn't you rather I do it out of love than have one of those wood-things do it out of their own animal hunger?", Lemora is referring to monsters, but also to the Reverends, Ticket Men, Fathers, Abusive Boyfriends, and anyone else who wants to corrupt her innocence to satisfy his own needs.

Blackburn states that he chose the vampirism backdrop simply because he thought it would be the most affordable way to make his first movie. All of the trademarks (neck-biting, lack of reflection, the gothic estate) are present; however, *Lemora* is more Lovecraft than Stoker, more *Night of the Hunter* than *The Vampire Lovers,* and more unapologetically queer than *Vampyros Lesbos.* While its influence can be seen in later coming-of-age horror films, such as Neil Jordan's *The Company of Wolves* and Philip Ridley's *The Reflecting Skin*, *Lemora* remains in a class of its own. Blackburn never directed another film. Gilb left acting, and passed away in a car accident in 2009. Smith, who left

us too soon in 2002, went on to gain cult classic status for her B-movie roles, but never found another role as juicy as Lila Lee to sink her teeth into.

Just as it seems predetermined that Lila is drawn to Lemora, it almost seems like destiny that these three novices came together to create such a unique cinematic treasure. *Lemora* is a frightening film, but it's also incredibly thoughtful. I find something new to appreciate in every viewing and it allows me to tap into my inner misfit in a way no other horror film has. I appreciate how difficult it is to successfully create a monster that is both scary and sympathetic—anyone who has felt marginalized can identify with Lemora's plight. But the story is really Lila's, and how her journey culminates in self-realization of otherness. It's horror's greatest coming-out tale.

Steve Griffes enjoys horror films from any country and time period, but has a penchant for offbeat indies, Vincent Price, Aussie horror, Grand Dame Guignol, and anything featuring Karen Black. In his spare time, he helps throw retro dance parties, enjoys microbrew "tasting," and eats too many nachos. He resides in Ann Arbor, MI, where he works for the University of Michigan Library as an Information Resources Supervisor.

LET'S SCARE JESSICA TO DEATH 1971

BY ELAINE LAMKIN

When I was growing up, every day after school I would rush home in time to watch either *Dark Shadows* or the local 4 o'clock movie, which usually presented some schlocky horror film like *The House That Wouldn't Die*.

"DON'T TELL THEM. ACT NORMAL."

Among the drivel, though, there were the occasional gems like Alfred Hitchcock's *The Birds* (AGH!! The plucked-out eyeballs!!) that would put me in a state of sleep-with-the-lights-on, check-twice-under-the-bed fear.

One *very* memorable mid-afternoon discovery was the eerie, dream-like, and ultimately horrific 1971 feature *Let's Scare Jessica to Death*, directed by John Hancock. The film stars New York stage actress Zohra Lampert as the fragile titular former mental patient who, along with her husband Duncan (Barton Heyman) and their friend Woody (Kevin O'Connor), moves into an old farmhouse in the Connecticut countryside with a creepy cove behind the property.

Opening with what turns out to be the final scene, we find Jessica sitting alone in a rowboat, bobbing in a body of water, with Lampert's voice-over both setting the stage and summing up the film: "I sit here and I can't believe that it happened. And yet I have to believe it. Dreams or nightmares. Madness or sanity. I don't know which is which."

What follows is a haunting flashback, one that includes a haunted house, a vampire bride (Mariclare Costello), an enigmatic Woman in White (Gretchen Corbett), graveyards, tombstone rubbings, a séance, infidelity, murder, a town full of inhospitable and inexplicably bandaged locals, whispering voices, and *something* hidden beneath the cove's surface. What *did* prompt Jessica to take refuge in that boat, doubting her mental stability?

Our introduction to Jessica, Duncan, and Woody begins with the unexpected shot of a large black object being loaded into a hearse, a vehicle which is then seen cruising through the gloomy, autumnal Connecticut countryside. These are not your typical early '70s hippies, although Woody has the funky hair and clothes one associates with that era and the trio use a hearse emblazoned with the word "Love" to get around. The former NYC residents have escaped to the countryside to farm apples and get away from it all. (We also get clues about Jessica being in recovery from a breakdown of sorts; no small thing as we'll see.) These are slightly older, anti-establishment types with Duncan being a classically

trained bass player (the afore-mentioned large black object being his instrument's case) and Woody the seemingly footloose and fancy-free type.

When they discover the mysterious Emily (Costello) squatting in their new home, instead of calling the police, they ask her to stay with them. Their obviously trusting behavior and period clothing may put some viewers off as dated, but the characters themselves are innately interesting, particularly Jessica and Emily. The first night Emily joins the group, Jessica is instantly on her guard, watching how both her husband and Woody are attracted to the redhead's ethereal beauty. Her fears are well-founded as Emily proceeds to seduce both men, furthering Jessica's instability.

TV screenwriter Lee Kalcheim's original *Jessica* script was comedic, a parody of scary movies with a larger cast and a legitimate monster instead of the vampiric Emily. But Hancock began afresh, trying to make the story as scary as possible by using elements from his own childhood, including his parents' apple orchard, their hobby of gravestone rubbing, and his father's huge coffin-like bass case. He also hit upon giving the story a *Turn of the Screw* aspect where the audience never knows whether what is happening onscreen is in Jessica's mind or not. In speaking to Hancock recently, he said, "This was risky at the time, not to answer that question, and it confused people in 1971. But now people like that [aspect]. Go figure." However, following a disagreement with the producers over the use of the Woman in White, Hancock chose to be credited as "Ralph Rose" for his screenwriting efforts. (Kalcheim, ironically enough, also elected for a pseudonymous credit, that of "Norman Jonas.")

Filmed in 25 days from October to November 1970 with a budget of only $250,000, the picture was a modest success when it was released in August 1971, bringing in a box office of around $20 million before being relegated to late night (and after school) TV where it developed a cult following.

Hancock recalls the filming of *Jessica* as being very tight but hardly horrific, other than the death of one of the story's key players: the mole "sleeping" in the production office that turned out to be most assuredly deceased. (A mouse was reluctantly used as a replacement although it is still referred to as a "mole" in the film.) There were also fish in the cove that would nibble on cast and crew as they froze in the frigid water…acting as though it was warm and comfortable swimming weather. (Line producer Bill Badalato remembers *snow* falling shortly before shooting the swimming scenes.) For his part, Hancock was none too thrilled to be filming in a chicken coop where any number of chickens would peck at his legs.

The director also commented on the importance of music to his films. With Orville Stoeber's mournful opening credits piano solo, Walter Sear's electronic score that produces quite a few "zingers," the impromptu dinner concert, and Joe Ryan's percussion-filled sound design (which rivals *The Texas Chain Saw Massacre* in its ability to unnerve), *Jessica*'s aural elements are among its most memorable. Even ordinary sounds such as a screaming seagull or a far-off tractor motor are used to enormously unsettling effect. Then there is the *wind*— sinister, rustling Jessica's wall-mounted gravestone rubbings, filling the attic as she discovers Emily's secret. Within the wind are the whispers—disembodied voices and evil chuckling that get under our skin since we, like Jessica, don't know if these sounds are real or not.

Despite its strong word-of-mouth reputation, *Jessica* languished in out-of-print VHS limbo for decades before finally being released on DVD (a regrettably no-frills, but still welcome issue) by Paramount in 2006. (Hancock says Paramount never asked him to contribute a commentary track, though he'd very much like to participate in one accompanied by Lampert and Costello.)

The talented cast went on to make many other film, stage, and television appearances. Genre fans might recognize Lampert from her turn opposite George C. Scott in *The Exorcist III*, or from scores of roles in soap operas and crime dramas over her six-decade career. Heyman also enjoyed an extensive career as a character actor before his death in 1996 at age 59, notably appearing as Dr. Klein in *The Exorcist*.

Jessica, so disturbing and creepy, has haunted me ever since I was a small child. I believe that intangible creepiness is why Hancock's gem remains underrated and/or overlooked today. The uncertainty of whether what we're seeing is real or part of Jessica's insanity meshes perfectly with Ryan's unforgettable sound design and Stoeber & Sear's haunting melodies. *Jessica* is most definitely a slow burn and lacks the gore modern horror fans seem to consider a requirement. But given a chance, she will get under your skin... and probably never leave.

Elaine Lamkin, who has loved the scary and spooky ever since she can remember, got her start writing about the horror genre back in 2005 after seeing the Civil War creepfest, Dead Birds. *She has since contributed to many horror sites including Bloody-Disgusting as well as* Rue Morgue *magazine before settling in with Dread Central. She has also been a publicist for several indie horror films. Elaine resides in the Deep, Dark Gothic South and wishes everyday was Halloween.*

THE LIVING AND THE DEAD 2006

BY DAVE CANFIELD

> ### "I'M GOING TO PROVE TO BOTH OF YOU THAT YOU CAN TRUST ME. WHEN DADDY GETS BACK, YOU'RE GOING TO BE BETTER..."

Horror is a term that, unlike any other, describes not only a genre of cinema but an affect, a feeling that can be germane to part of any narrative. Is *The Living and the Dead* truly a horror film? It is clearly a horrific one, but it also transcends such reductive labeling. Writer/director Simon Rumley avoids peopling his tale with simplified good guys and bad guys, the end result all the more disturbing precisely because the locus of evil eludes us. Within the physical locale of our story—a decrepit family mansion—madness and sickness and death are in ample evidence, but they seem strongly linked to a desire for independence, fatherly recognition, and the urgency to leave a legacy behind. In Rumley's world, the human condition is at war with everything, destroying community, family, and finally the individual.

Aging patriarch Donald Brocklebank (Roger Lloyd Pack) has had to declare bankruptcy, leaving his vast estate in ruinous disrepair while he scrambles to provide for his sick wife Nancy (Kate Fahy) and their mentally ill adult son James (Leo Bill). After his father is called away to deal with financial matters, James— anxious to make daddy and mommy proud—dismisses his mother's nurse and assumes the role of head of the household. Ditching his own much-needed medications and forcing his own questionable treatments on Nancy, it's a disastrous journey worthy of Dante with James descending level by level into Hell.

Of course, nothing really prepares you for a film like this. All the shit, piss, pain, suffering, and violence inherent to the above scenario are present and accounted for, but every disturbing moment the audience sits through feels earned. It's a draining experience but an empowering one. Ever dealt with a loved one suffering from mental illness? Family members who've made bad decisions about money or made poor parenting decisions? *The Living and the Dead* is a stark reminder of how badly people need one another, how much responsibility being human and alive entails. Rumley doesn't have a lot of answers, but he knows where the starting point lies; with love and mercy, the only chains that keep us tethered to one another or our own sanity.

Rumley divides his all-important timelines and points of view in the film via subtle lighting techniques that also serve tonal functions, signaling connections between the landscape, the people who inhabit it, and their shared fate. The director employs a frenetically undercranked shooting style to evoke James' increasingly manic state of mind. He knows how to effectively incorporate the grotesque gore and body imagery he employs to serve his story. He is, in short, a master storyteller.

James' gawky frame is stuffed into a suit he's clearly not comfortable in. His entire relationship with his father is based on an etiquette meant to serve someone far beyond his mental years. Yet Donald is not an unloving father. He is confused by James' emotional needs, overwhelmed by his loss of social station and the imminent loss of his beloved wife. Called Longleigh House, he pronounces his family home "lonely" and it isn't hard to see why, yet he clings to it as he thinks it contains all he is.

Moved from place to place by the men, ultimately at the mercy of the social order she has followed and nurtured, Nancy has come to the end of her days without any real assurance of safety inside the one place that should be her

refuge: her family. As a mature woman so physically and emotionally naked on-screen, Fahy's performance is a thing of bravery, utterly in the moment no matter what is required. She is at once a mother, a wife, a victim, and a determined individual doing what she can to match the chaos brought down upon her.

In virtually every scene, Bill creates a fully realized individual out of what could have been a one-note characterization and won the Best Actor award at Fantastic Fest 2006 for his efforts. Pack, best known as the star of any number of 1970s Britcoms, has since moved on to solid character parts in bigger budget films. But he gives a heartbreaking performance in this little indie as a man swallowed by life. It's a level of artistry one never would have expected from merely encountering his TV work.

In speaking with Rumley for this essay, he explained, "The owner of the manor we shot in was a man named Lord Cardigan. He and his family had owned the property for more than four hundred years. But he lived in a house about half a mile down the road because he couldn't afford the upkeep. There are massive old manors like those all over the UK. If they aren't owned by the state or a few extremely wealthy families, they just crumble."

All that history gone, just like the people who lived in those homes. But Rumley's macro/micro approach to apocalypse is more than just a nifty way of reminding a viewing audience of the thematic breadth of his work. "My films are first and foremost character studies. *The Living and the Dead* details the Armageddon of one family. That's the apocalypse I find most interesting."

During the above conversation, he alluded to the filming of *The Living and the Dead* as a sort of exorcism. (Shortly after Rumley's father had passed away from a heart attack, his mother was diagnosed with cancer and died three months later.) All the more impressive that he managed to take that personal tragedy and infuse it with a complex and telling social commentary on the decayed idea of nobility, one that held an older generation in thrall even as it dissipated. Despite the edifice of society, we each inexorably devolve into ourselves,

only to discover that our bodies decay. Where refuge? Rumley hints at a spiritual void exacerbated by emotional remove and reliance on national identity, but he's too smart to lay all that weight down upon one cause.

The Living and the Dead suggests a keen insight into the character of nations in decline and the sense of anger, helplessness, and despair that individuals must confront to escape, however momentarily, the early grave awaiting those that barricade themselves inside crumbling facades. Is there an escape from the madhouse, the poorhouse and grave? Perhaps the most important step is a willingness to risk the madness of love and family devotion even if it means letting go of the past and moving on towards something that is not yet visible. Rumley's film is full of panacea, unfaithful oasis, and visions of false rescue that double back on the viewer. One can envision the tragic Brocklebank family joining hands and simply walking out the front door, down that impossible lawn towards the land of the real if only Donald's haunted eyes would blink, leading him back from the abyss. If only his other relatives were not so bound by tradition and appearances. And if the society around them were willing to invest in something other than ambulances and strait-jackets to carry away the casualties of history.

Dave Canfield is a founding member of Twitch Film, the largest world cinema website. A longtime lover of all things spooky, he's also a staff member of Videohound's Magill's Cinema Annual, a member of the Chicago Film Critics Association and can be found hosting screenings and leading discussions on a near-constant basis in the Chicago area and abroad.

THE LIVING DEAD AT MANCHESTER MORGUE 1974

BY DODD ALLEY

When watching a zombie movie or TV show, modern horror audiences have certain expectations. We wish to tap into that unspoken fear of a fate worse than death — being surrounded by carnivorous corpses eager to tear us apart with their bare hands and teeth. The odds of suffering such an unsettling, grisly demise are considerably low (attacked and eaten by reanimated stiffs?) yet this now-established

> **"I WISH THE DEAD *COULD* COME BACK TO LIFE, YOU BASTARD, BECAUSE THEN I COULD KILL YOU AGAIN!"**

horror scenario leaves fans cringing and begging for more. Who do we have to thank for this flesh-eating craze? The obvious answer is George A. Romero who, after unveiling *Night of the Living Dead*, forever cemented the expectation that zombies, once defined as reanimated Haitian corpses condemned to slavery, are now on a mission to eat the living.

However, the not-so-obvious answer as to who helped perpetuate this cinematic convention is Spanish filmmaker Jorge Grau, who directed 1974's *The Living Dead at Manchester Morgue* (also known as *Let Sleeping Corpses Lie*, amongst many other alternate titles). Romero deserves credit for creating the cannibalistic zombie, but *Manchester Morgue* went to even greater lengths, depicting victims torn limb from limb by ravenous living dead...and in color! While Romero's 1978 sequel *Dawn of the Dead* is an established classic, highly regarded for its groundbreaking and gruesome effects, *Manchester Morgue* had already introduced many of its shocking visuals to the genre four years prior. Effectively frightening and unsettling, Grau's overlooked treasure trove of chills and vibrant bloodiness remains undiscovered by many horror fans to this day.

The story revolves around a London antiques dealer named George (Ray Lovelock) and his unlikely travel companion Edna (Cristina Galbó). They venture into the quaint English countryside together after Edna backs over George's motorcycle at a filling station, leaving him without transportation. However, things are not as serene in the rural community of Windmere as the duo expect. Edna is attacked by the town drunk, who supposedly drowned a few days prior. The newborns at the local hospital are behaving with mysterious aggression. Not so coincidentally, these odd occurrences happen in unison with the government's testing of a new form of ultrasonic pest control which causes bugs to furiously murder each other.

George, represented as a radical thinker and anti-bureaucrat, quickly assesses what is causing the dead in the area to come back to life. His theories are shot down by the simple country folk, particularly the head Irish inspector (Arthur Kennedy) who dismisses George because of his "long hair and faggot clothes." In fact, the inspector suspects this liberal outsider is the culprit guilty of splattering the pastoral countryside with blood. With primed-for-reanimation corpses piling up, George and Edna must put a stop to the zombie infestation before it spirals out of control.

In a 2000 interview on the Blue Underground DVD, Grau reveals that when given the script by the Italian producers, it was described as "like the *Night of the Living Dead*—but in color!" No doubt, the film definitely owes a debt of gratitude to Romero's landmark offering. The parallels are certainly there and, as with the 1968 classic, there is social commentary at its undead heart, much of it laid out before the action even begins.

During the opening credits, the audience is treated to a montage of pollution as George leaves his urban surroundings for the countryside. Smoke stacks and car exhaust pipes are viewed in close-up as gases spill into the atmosphere. It comes as no surprise that these images foreshadow things to come when George discovers the government-owned pest control machine shortly after his arrival in the countryside. "Just another machine to pollute the Earth," George laments to the lackeys operating the machine. "Till now at least, this part of the country's been left alone!" The dead coming back to life is not left to the imagination as a fantastical phenomenon; it is emphatically due to a corrupt government

ignorantly releasing hazardous material into Earth's ecosystem. With his leftist idealism and willingness to protest, George is an ideal protagonist to fight such a villain. Unfortunately, coming from the city, he is also considered an outsider, comparable to *Night of the Living Dead*'s African American hero being shanghaied in white, rural America.

However, Grau does not merely mimic Romero, making minor changes to setting and characters. Despite the aforementioned similarities (and a climactic moment that strikes a familiar chord), *Manchester Morgue* manages to set itself apart from its inspiration. The film's most impressive aspects are, of course, the undead themselves. The director relied on photographs of real cadavers for inspiration, and his keen eye for detail is uncanny. Since Grau's zombies are recently deceased, there is not a lot of decomposition detail; instead these creatures look as if they came straight from their own funerals. The faces and bodies are physically intact, but there remains an eerie vacancy in their expressions.

The suspense factor of these creatures' appearance is multiplied when accompanied by composer Giuliano Sorgini's music. Undoubtedly one of the movie's more memorable attributes, Sorgini's haunting melodies are effectively accented by the sound of the zombies breathing. This effect lends a spine-tingling resonance throughout, a recurring cue as to when our heroes are in the presence of the living dead. According to Grau, the notion behind this unsettling aural motif is rooted in the director's experience of hearing his own father gasping on his deathbed. This, Grau decided, is what the living dead probably sound like.

The overall creepiness is perfectly complemented by just the right quantity of impressive practical effects, culminating in a vibrant bloody extravaganza. Having shown considerable restraint throughout, Grau unleashes an unexpected grand gut-spilling finale that remains rather shocking even by contemporary gore-desensitized standards. In particular, the carnage depicted during the hospital raid scene, where the recently reanimated sate their appetites on unfortunate staff members, is pretty mind-blowing. (One casualty that ranks particularly high on the gore score is the nurse getting her chest torn apart by the zombie horde.) The wise decision to save such gruesomeness for the end keeps the film balanced, positioning the splatter as a disturbing surprise rather than a kitschy spectacle.

The Living Dead at Manchester Morgue is a gem hidden among many other lower-budget and less-memorable flesh-eating flicks. Grau slowly builds a sense of dread, holding his audience in suspense, saving the shocking moments of jaw-dropping gore until all undead hell breaks loose. Originally conceived as a rip-off of a classic, *Manchester Morgue* stands proudly on its own merits, a must-see for zombie connoisseurs and appreciative horror fans alike.

Dodd Alley resides in Columbus, OH, with his wife and twin boys. He graduated from Ohio University with an M.A. in Film Studies, where he taught courses on Cult Cinema and Hollywood Reflexive films. His publications include Gamers *and* Gorehounds: The Influence of Video Games on the Contemporary American Horror Film. *He also contributed a chapter introduction about the presence of Dracula within video games in the reference book* Dracula in Visual Media.

MANIAC 1980

BY STEVE DE ROOVER

We now live in an age where information is instantly accessible in a couple of computer mouse clicks. But before the modern heyday of cyberspace, fans of the seventh art—especially horror buffs—got the same craving for movie trivia as fans do today. We did it "old-school" by reading film magazines, visiting movie

> "PEOPLE DIE...BUT IN A PICTURE OR PAINTING, THEY'RE YOURS FOREVER."

theaters and by constantly bugging the local video store owners for various printed memorabilia. Of course, I also spent hours gazing upon glorious VHS box covers that I couldn't rent due to my boyish age. One of those mysterious titles was William Lustig's *Maniac*. The beautifully painted image of the sleazy guy holding the bloody scalp fueled a lot of horrifying dreams, with the infamous tagline, "I warned you not to go out tonight," seemingly directed explicitly to me. But by the time I had reached the age where I could rent the film myself, it had vanished from the video shelves. Finally, an opportunity ultimately arose via this strange new technology called "The Internet." Since *Maniac* was still unavailable in 2002 (and even as of this writing) on DVD in Belgium, I took out a credit card and ordered the Region 1 disc from overseas. After all those years of anticipation, I was finally going to encounter the disturbed psychopath portrayed by talented character actor Joe Spinell (*The Godfather*, *Rocky*) firsthand. And boy, I wasn't disappointed.

But let's first start with a little history. The genesis for *Maniac* dates back to an NYC revival house showing of the obscure exploitation film *The Hollywood Hillside Strangler* (1973). Self-trained actor Spinell and aspiring young filmmaker Lustig attended the screening together, and were convinced that they could do better than what they had just seen. The creative triumvirate of Spinell (who co-wrote the *Maniac* script with C.A. Rosenberg), Lustig, and producer Andrew Garroni raised $48,000 by themselves, sure that the rest of the budget would be found during pre-production. They conceived a film about a deranged killer, Frank Zito, leaving a trail of blood throughout New York City. But when Zito strikes up a tentative relationship with spunky photographer Anna D'Antoni, will he be able to restrain his murderous impulses?

Production schedules were soon created and talent locked down, including Daria Nicolodi in the key role of Anna. Unfortunately, the Italian star of *Deep Red* and co-writer of *Suspiria* had to back out at the last minute due to schedule conflicts with Dario Argento's *Inferno*. Luckily, at a Fangoria Weekend of Horrors convention, Lustig, Spinell, and make-up wizard Tom Savini (*Martin, Dawn of the Dead*) crossed paths with famed B-starlet Caroline Munro (*The Spy Who Loved Me, Starcrash*). They immediately offered her the role, which she accepted only a couple days before principal photography commenced. Thanks to this last-minute stroke of casting genius, the rest of the budget came into play, as Munro's then-husband, producer/actor Judd Hamilton, coughed up more money.

Even to this day, the disturbing atmosphere and grim, almost documentary look of the finished film is so pervasive that you'll probably want a shower immediately after watching. This is in no small part attributable to the fact that Lustig and his crew filmed *Maniac* all-out guerrilla-style, stealing shots all over Manhattan and the surrounding areas without proper permits. This led to more than a few "creative solutions" in getting what the team was after. For instance, because

it is forbidden to shoot a live gun in NYC, a car was stationed with a production assistant at the wheel waiting to drive the weapon off the set following Savini's infamous "shotgun to the head" scene. Amazingly, nobody ever got into trouble. This remains *Maniac*'s main selling point: it looks and feels real yet surreal at the same time. The streets and subways of New York

have never been more threatening, almost characters on their own.

Then there is the one-man show that is Joe Spinell. While some see *Maniac* merely as a misogynistic torture flick, there is more going on besides insanely bloody kills. While delivering on its promise of sheer terror, it is first and foremost a dark and emotional descent in the mind of a serial killer. *Maniac* was—even in all its sleazy glory—ahead of its time, voyeuristically documenting a couple days in the life of a serial killer (years prior to John McNaughton's celebrated *Henry: Portrait of a Serial Killer*). Spinell's Frank Zito is not just another Michael Myers or Jason Voorhees, but rather a realistic reflection of how messed-up human beings can be. While his scenes of beastlike psychosis are far showier, the actor shines even brighter in his grounded dialogue scenes opposite love interest Munro. Herein lies the power of *Maniac*. Zito may be vicious, he may be scary, but throughout he is simply a very tragic, emotionally damaged human being that wants a normal life. You may never be truly rooting for him, but you are also not against him. Quite a feat really, especially given the gruesome scenes detailing how Frank handles innocent women (who are, by the way, not the typical meatheads one sees in most slashers).

While time has been relatively kind, *Maniac* does show its age on occasion. Lustig definitely knows how to stage a tense horror moment and every stalking sequence still brings me to the edge of my seat, but during a recent viewing I noticed that some of the slower scenes feel, well, *slow*. Some of Savini's makeup effects are likewise a bit dated. But gorehounds can rest easy—most of the gloriously bloody effects are quite unnerving to watch even by today's standards.

Now considered a sleaze classic, the original film has never reached the same level of recognition as blood brothers *Halloween, Friday the 13th, Dawn of the Dead*, or the aforementioned *Henry*. Released unrated without ever attempting to cross paths with the dreaded MPAA, *Maniac* generated a healthy profit in its day, but wasn't a huge money-maker. Its scenes of gory violence towards women courted a lot of controversy. In fact, it was one of the films that fueled discussions about senseless violence in motion pictures, with feminist groups protesting outside movie theaters showing the flick. In England, *Maniac* was instantly banned by the British Board of Film Classification. (The 2002 UK Anchor Bay DVD is still cut.)

Maniac is without a doubt a true 42nd Street grindhouse experience, but a lot of the PG-13 youngsters of today don't know Frank Zito and that's a shame. *Maniac* is how real horror supposed to be: dirty, disturbing, crossing boundaries every step of the way. It is a pity that fans will never experience the full gory glory of the proposed sequel, *Maniac II: Mr Robbie*. (Just before his tragic passing in 1986, Spinell shot a promo short under the direction of *Combat Shock*'s Buddy Giovinazzo.) But with the luxury of worthy home video releases, the one and only real *Maniac* lives on to slash and stalk innocent women in the seedy streets of '80s New York forever and ever.

Steve De Roover made his bones as a critic writing for MovieGids.be and Publicity. In 2010 he began working on movies, including Amsterdam Heavy *starring Michael Madsen and* The Fifth Estate *directed by Bill Condon. In 2012, Steve directed the first part of* Innocent Belgium *which, after positive notices, was optioned by Flemish production company Studio A. His short* Un Homme Bien *was selected for the 31st BIFFF and the 5th Artisan Festival International.*

THE MAN WHO LAUGHS 1928

BY KRISTIN WICKS

> "WHAT A LUCKY CLOWN YOU ARE—YOU DON'T HAVE TO RUB OFF *YOUR* LAUGH."

Following the smash successes of his two previous collaborations with Lon Chaney, *The Hunchback of Notre Dame* (1923) and *The Phantom of the Opera* (1925), Universal Studios founder and producer Carl Laemmle was eager to find similar literary source material that would appeal to a wide audience. His eye ultimately landed on Victor Hugo's 1869 novel, *L'Homme Qui Rit*, which he hoped would strike the same chord of empathy for its tragic titular character as the Chaney films. German Expressionist filmmaker Paul Leni (*Waxworks*, 1924) was selected to helm the project, a logical choice following the popular reception of the director's previous Universal effort, 1927's classic "old dark house" chiller *The Cat and the Canary*.

Despite similar production values and a tried 'n' true "Beauty and the Beast" formula, *The Man Who Laughs* did not connect with general audiences. The heroic main character, Gwynplaine, failed to win over viewers in the same fashion as Quasimodo, in spite of Conrad Veidt's superbly crafted and sympathetic performance. Critics decried its extreme morbidity (despite having a less bleak outcome than Hugo's novel) and Leni's German-styled production, seemingly at odds with the 17th century England setting. Over time, however, the film's reputation has grown—Gwynplaine's facial features having reportedly inspired Bob Kane's "Joker" character in the original *Batman* comics—though it still languishes in the long shadows cast by Universal's 1930s/40s horror classics.

The story begins in 1690, with English nobleman Lord Clancharlie (also played by Veidt) refusing to kiss the hand of the despotic King James II and being promptly sentenced to die via the Iron Maiden, a brutal torture-chamber method. Before his demise, Clancharlie asks about his son Gwynplaine, to which the King chillingly replies, "A Comprachico surgeon carved a grin upon his face so he might laugh forever at his fool of a father." (These Comprachicos—a term coined by Hugo for his novel—are presented as amoral freakmakers, practicing unorthodox surgical experiments on children to sell them as human curiosities; in this case, the young man is irrevocably marked by a permanent jester-like grimace.)

Gwynplaine moves along with the strange travelers, who later abandon him in a snowstorm. Struggling against the elements and looking for shelter, he comes across a baby wrapped within its deceased mother's arms. He and his little companion, Dea, are eventually taken in by the mountebank Ursus (Cesare Gravina), and it is discovered that the girl is blind. As time goes by, the three eke out a living in a sideshow community, exploiting Gwynplaine's ghoulish visage for money. Because Dea (now played by Mary Philbin) cannot see his disfigured, frozen smile, she is able to love him for who he is, though he is reluctant to marry her due to feeling unworthy. "Hear how they laugh—nothing but a clown!"

Unbeknownst to him, Gwynplaine's father's estate is now owned by the Duchess Josiana (Olga Baclanova, showing a surprising amount of skin for the era). After her cunning servant Barkilphedro (Brandon Hurst) finds paperwork on Gwynplaine's lineage, Josiana's sister, Queen Anne, insists the two wed to legitimize the estate. Upon their meeting, the Duchess displays dishonest and perverse intentions toward Gwynplaine, who responds to her attentions but continues to struggle for personal freedom.

For almost two full hours, the film's gloomy eye candy captivates, beginning with disturbing imagery of hanging corpses swaying in the wind, slowly haunting the viewer into cinematic seduction. Universal dropped $1 million into the project, resulting in impressive production values displaying deep shadows of Expressionist-styled chiaroscuro, detailed costumes, elaborate sets, and a commanding musical score. Veidt, a German actor known for strange, standout roles

in *The Cabinet of Dr. Caligari, The Hands of Orlac, Waxworks,* and *Rasputin, Demon with Women* (though most viewers will recognize him as Major Heinrich Strasser in *Casablanca*), is nothing short of brilliant as Gwynplaine. Considering he spoke no English while on the American set, his effective and conflicted performance is amazing, managing to silently convey grief, joy, passion, fear, and even lust with his eyes alone.

Veidt is ably supported by a venerable ensemble, many of whom have lasting genre credentials. Philbin is probably best known as the woman who unmasks Lon Chaney in *The Phantom of the Opera*, while the Russian-born Baclanova would go on to play the cunning trapeze artist Cleopatra in Tod Browning's infamous 1932 classic *Freaks*. Though a less familiar face for casual fans, Hurst sports the most distinguished horror pedigree, having appeared in *The Hunchback of Notre Dame* (1923), *White Zombie* and *Murders in the Rue Morgue* (1932), and both the 1920 and 1941 versions of *Dr. Jekyll and Mr. Hyde*! Behind the scenes, history was also being made. Years before he would famously create the Frankenstein's Monster makeup worn by Boris Karloff in *Frankenstein*, the legendary Jack Pierce lent his estimable skills to realizing Veidt's unforgettable rictus, the first of his many iconic creations for Universal.

It bears mentioning that Laemmle was never a huge fan of the horror genre—it was his son, Carl Jr., who took the Universal reins in 1928 (the same year *The Man Who Laughs* was released) and eventually molded the company into the classic monster factory that horror fans so fondly treasure. But personally and professionally, Laemmle did an incredible amount of good. Periodically visiting his homeland of Germany, he witnessed the encroaching Nazi threat; paying both immigration and emigration fees, he helped over 300 families avoid the Holocaust.

I first heard about *The Man Who Laughs* via a silent film thread on an online horror forum. As someone who has always been drawn to characters who are victims of circumstance—as well as a soft spot for the grotesque—the briefly outlined plot instantly resonated with me. I sympathize with Gwynplaine's freakishly rare physical problems; a titanium cage spine implant replacing several lower vertebrae has left me often feeling less "normal" than my peers. As a result, a tortured, good-hearted protagonist attempting to survive against the odds is a formula sure to turn me into a melodrama-lovin' fool.

Accepting the hand Fate has dealt us—with all its limitations—is something everyone has to battle at some point. The movie carries a grand message of personal acceptance and true love conquering obstacles. The phrase, *"This above all: to thine own self be true"* is quite a relevant theme here. Despite its tragic nature, *The Man Who Laughs* is an incredibly romantic love story and an important piece of the German Expressionism movement in Hollywood.

Kristin Wicks is a writer, photographer and dark artist, breathing all things macabre. AKA "Kreepylady," she founded Chicago Creepster in 2006 and runs the horror events blog on ChicagoNow.com, aptly titled The Chicago Creepout. Body horror flicks intrigue her, being genuinely biomechanical herself. Kristin contributes to several online outlets, works with many film festivals programming/ volunteering, and refuses to live in a world without macaroni and cheese.

MATANGO1963

BY DAN FULLER

My love affair with Japanese horror cinema began in the summer of 2008 when I watched Kaneto Shindô's *Onibaba* (1964), a visually stunning morality tale that captured my imagination from the opening frames. Struck by the austere black-and-white imagery, I launched into a feeding frenzy of 1960s Japanese horror; some of my favorite discoveries from that fruitful time include *Blind Beast*, *Kuroneko* (aka *The Black Cat*), *Female Demon Ohyaku*, and *Matango*.

> **"UNDER TRYING CONDITIONS, MAN BECOMES SELFISH AND CRUEL."**

This last title is one that I picked up with very low expectations. Based on its alternate title, *Attack of the Mushroom People*, I assumed it to be a typical, low-budget, cheesy monster flick of the late 1950s/early 1960s. That suspicion was further reinforced when I noted it was directed by Ishirô Honda, godfather of the Japanese giant monster genre known as *kaiju*. Although I am a huge fan of Honda's 1954 anti-nuclear masterpiece, *Gojira*, I have found his other *kaiju* films lacking in substance. But *Matango* is far from frivolous guys-tussling-in-suits kiddie fare—to my surprise, I found it to be a mature and thoughtful meditation on the human condition. It's now my favorite Honda movie.

Based on William Hope Hodgson's story "The Voice in the Night," the film begins and ends in a Tokyo insane asylum, a wraparound flashback structure reminiscent of the 1956 horror/sci-fi classic, *Invasion of the Body Snatchers*.

A raving young man, Kenji (Akira Kubo), recounts the story of a recent yacht trip with friends which culminated in a freak storm shipwrecking the group on a deserted island. Exploring the foreign terrain for food and shelter, they discover an abandoned research vessel covered with a bizarre fungus. As they delve further, they learn that the research facility was set up to examine the effects of radiation on plant and animal life.

The days slowly pass and it becomes apparent that the strange fungal growth is the only source of food on the island. Unfortunately, it not only has the effect of driving those that consume it mad, it turns them into hideous creatures. With delirium setting in, each of the castaways must eventually decide whether to die of starvation or eat the mushrooms; those that choose the latter path transform into grotesque freaks, mutant aberrations of hu-

manity that subsequently lure the others to join their strange new world order.

From the outset, we are immersed in an aura of dread and foreboding. Once stranded, the passengers have no chance; there is no hope for escape or rescue. Trapped alongside them, we come to know and sympathize with the victims, bearing witness to the internal drama between these discordant individuals. The skipper Naoyuki (Hiroshi Koizumi) is a great leader, but removed from his ship the other castaways rebel against his authority. Masafumi (Yoshio Tsuchiya), the rich businessman, no longer has influence because his money is useless within this "uncivilized" setting. The intelligent and well-meaning professor Kenji (Kubo) tries to persuade the others to listen to logic and reason, but his warnings go unheeded. The lovely singer Mami (Kumi Mizuno), with her well-honed feminine wiles, still uses her sexuality to get what she wants...ultimately proving to be the most terrifying monster of all.

Honda permeates his picture with an incredible sense of bleakness and despair, proving a master of creating eerie atmosphere with the early scenes of discovering and exploring the fungus-covered craft. In addition to all the mirrors aboard being broken, the radiation-exposed animal specimens—the results of the former residents' experiments—reveal the ship's ghastly true nature. It is later revealed that not even the birds will fly over the island, a fact that only heightens the mystery.

With an emphasis on atmosphere and relationships over action (the first mushroom monster doesn't appear until 43 minutes in), many modern horror fans may protest *Matango*'s deliberate unfolding. But in truth, it is this dreamy pacing that makes the film. A none-too-subtle allegory for societal breakdown, we observe this microcosm as they partake of "forbidden fruit." Like Adam and Eve, their eyes are now opened to a blissful new existence...but at what price?

As a symbol of Man's experiments gone awry, the mushroom people are also more subtle beasts than the era's typical Toho *kaiju*. Similar to zombies, these slow and clumsy creatures were once human, and now exist only to spread their "dis-

eased" condition. While certainly alluded to, screenwriters Shinichi Hoshi and Masami Fukushima stop short of explicitly laying the blame at atomic energy's feet. Even so, the film was almost banned in Japan before its release—the government feeling the mushroom people too closely resembled the radiation-afflicted survivors of Hiroshima and Nagasaki.

Another highlight is the giant mushroom field. Production designer Shigekazu Ikuno and special effects art director Akira Watanabe teamed with Toho's resident f/x genius Eiji Tsuburaya to create giant multicolored mushroom shapes out of foam while using rice pastry to create the larger edible fungi. (A nearby pastry shop baked these odd creations, adding sugar and other flavorings to make them palatable for the actors.) While the mushroom costumes might look a little cheesy to a contemporary eye, they add immeasurably to the hallucinogenic-drug-trip mood. Honda and his team concoct a visual nightmare, the ever-giggling man-sized mushrooms intimating that people under the influence of *Matango* are on a constant LSD high.

Sadly, the film never got a mainstream release in the United States—at least not in its original form. In 1965, American International Pictures (AIP) oversaw a hacked, poorly dubbed version under the hokey *Attack of the Mushroom People* title in an attempt to attract indiscriminating drive-in audiences. Then, to further add insult to injury, it was never released to theaters but only shown on late-night television. This TV cut eventually slipped into the public domain and was later "rescued" by Something Weird on home video. While it has its campy charms, this bastardized version should be avoided in favor of the out-of-print Media Blasters DVD. Subtitled and in anamorphic widescreen, this is the best way to experience this haunting masterpiece at home, with excellent DVD extras including a commentary by Akira Kubo and an interview with special effects guru Teruyoshi Nakano.

I highly recommend this surreal, undiscovered gem. As a huge fan of apocalyptic films, I enjoy seeing the image of the twisted, surreal fungus field full of mushroom people each time more than the last. The final line nicely sums up the overriding theme: "Is it really any different in Tokyo? They're becoming inhuman. Just like there."

Dan Fuller is the corporate tax director of a major business-to-business Internet company located in Irving, Texas. He graduated Magna Cum Laude with a bachelor's degree in Accounting from the University of Texas at Arlington in 1992. In his spare time, he is an avid runner (25 miles per week), watches vintage horror movies from the 1930s - 1950s and is the author of the children's book, The Adventures of Polly Panda. *Boris Karloff is his favorite actor.*

MAY 2002

BY KRISTY JETT

"IF YOU CAN'T FIND A FRIEND, MAKE ONE."

In our formative adolescent years, most of us hit a groove where we begin to show interest in dating. We have our ungainly fumblings that land us in embarrassing situations, and even the most outwardly beautiful aren't born smooth operators. The naturally shy and awkward May Canady, with the additional handicap of a lazy eye covered by a patch, is quickly branded an outcast when she enters grade school. In the age-old nature vs. nurture argument, it's apparent that May's social ineptitude is a by-product of both: in addition to the ridicule of her classmates, her overbearing mother makes it clear that she is different...and different is not good.

Those who have encountered writer/director Lucky McKee's feature debut find a unique kinship to this tortured soul—we have all felt like outsiders at some point in our lives. An instant festival favorite, *May* premiered in 2002, but was overlooked by genre fans in favor of heavy hitters like *28 Days Later...* and *Cabin Fever* as well as mediocre entries in two of the largest horror franchises, *Halloween: Resurrection* and *Jason X*. It was only later, on home video, that she developed her small but passionate following.

May eventually grows into a young woman (Angela Bettis), but there isn't much deviation from the insecure child of her past. She makes her own clothing (most erring close to rag doll wear) and works at an animal hospital with her wild-child co-worker Polly (charmingly played by Anna Faris). Though still inexperienced in the ways of romance, a local mechanic, Adam (Jeremy Sisto), has recently come to her attention; she soon finds herself obsessing over him. She elaborates in a voiceover, "You know how when you meet someone...and you think you like them? And then, the more you talk to them, you see parts that you don't like. And sometimes, you end up not liking any parts at all. But this boy is different. I like every part of him. Especially his hands, they're beautiful."

It is during these painfully awkward "courtship" moments, as she tries to make herself known to Adam, that May completely gains our affection and empathy. We watch and cringe along as she follows him to a coffee shop and silently eyes him from across the outdoor patio as he falls asleep in a book. When she approaches him, we hold our breath; when she touches his sleeping face, we tense; when he awakens startled and confused, we wince in embarrassment as she stumbles gracelessly to the ground before scurrying away. It is clear that May has no real basis for romantic human interaction, or even the etiquette that leads up to it. What is unclear is whether her obsession with his hands is part of some fetish or rooted in a deeper psychological problem.

Surprisingly, the hunky young gent responds to our heroine's quirky charms and the two begin a tenuous relationship. With the consideration lavished on her, May absolutely blooms. It's clear that no one has ever shown this much attention and/or kindness to her. The viewer roots for their innocent love to survive, for May to be happy, but we worry that her naiveté and "weirdness" might prove to be too much for the conventionally minded Adam.

As a socially awkward child born with a lazy eye, McKee wrote the script for *May* based partly on his own life. When Bettis came in to audition, she was so drawn to the beautifully fractured lead character that the first question she asked was, "Who wrote this?" Within their first meeting, the director and his star had forged a friendship that has endured through numerous collaborations—McKee has been quoted as saying, "As a director she's my great love; we're soul mates in what we do. We were made to work together." McKee added a lot of himself into all the characters—during a recent chat, he revealed that the scene of Adam parting from May to attend Dario Argento's *Trauma* was based on a real experience. "In film school they told me to write what you know."

After charming us for the first half of the film with a winning portrait of a lonesome loser who finally experiences childlike glee in a "normal" relationship, the scenes following Adam's rejection are where Bettis truly shines. Angry, embarrassed,

and hurt, May sulks back to her apartment, her misfit status crashing back in. After a grateful reprieve, she is again reminded of just how different she is, a realization she can no longer overlook. Bettis' fearless turn conjures images of a wounded, cowed animal that morphs into a ferocious wildebeast when provoked; the transition is so subtle you don't know it until it's upon you. There are many stellar performances in *May*, but make no mistake, Angela Bettis *is* May—not just the character, the entire film.

Heartbroken after her calamitous night with Adam, May seeks out solace from Polly, who has exuded an intense, almost carnal fervor from the beginning. Her sexuality awakened by her recent but limited experience, May finds herself responding to her friend and co-worker's flirtatious energy (and to be honest, Faris could seduce anyone in this role, and all who come in contact with her fall under her spell). Following a somber, sensual evening of lovemaking, May sees Polly as her new salvation, but we have a sneaking suspicion that this relationship too cannot last. We are firmly on May's side, even as the darkness falls.

Not your typical gore-soaked parable relying on the "rules" of horror movies, *May*'s final act is a series of tumultuous incidents, all of which further our lead character's emotional upheaval. We follow her through a black comic montage of realizing her perfect companion—not a lover or a mate, but the friend she has always needed to "see her" and love her unconditionally. There is pain. Deception. Anger. Bloodshed. In other films, we might find ourselves on the side of the victims, but May has earned our love. Rather than judge her, we want to comfort her, to hold her, to love her. A sweet and tender lost soul who inexorably descends into madness, she's as sympathetic as Frankenstein's Monster imbued with the heart of Carrie White. (It should be no surprise that Bettis went on to portray *Carrie* in the 2002 TV-movie.) In the last moments she and Adam spend together, Sisto's performance is sublime. We feel sympathy for him, and even though this is the man who broke May's (and our) heart, we want to see him survive this crazy episode in his life.

But ultimately, we're happy when May is happy. The end of *May* delivers real resolution, something that most movies—let alone one from the horror genre—have trouble achieving. We've gone on an incredible journey with Ms. Canady and in the end, both of us get more than we bargained for in the most positive of ways. Roger Ebert characterized McKee's bold conclusion as "a final shot that would get laughs in another kind of film, but *May* earns the right to it, and it works, and we understand it."

This is a film that could change your life, if only you let it.

Kristy Jett is a staff writer at HorrorHound *magazine. She is currently writing* The Ultimate Guide to Shockumentaries & Mondo Films, *as well as producing a retrospective documentary for the Blu-ray release of the 1991 horror film* Popcorn. *Kristy spends most of her days as the Executive Director of Service & Sass at Fright Rags (www.fright-rags.com). She also works for Glen Echo Entertainment helping to resurrect Leslie Vernon. She wears headbands and drinks juiceboxes and is Thom Mathews' biggest fan.*

THE MOTHMAN PROPHECIES 2002

BY CORY COLOCK

"...the entities now began to tell me about a terrible forthcoming disaster on the Ohio River." So wrote John A. Keel in his 1975 book *The Mothman Prophecies*, an investigative compendium of first-hand accounts and his own personal experiences while researching anomalous phenomena in West Virginia during the late 1960s. The book is steeped with sightings of strange lights in the sky, disturbing phone calls, mysterious visitors, and, of course, some winged, red-eyed being called the Mothman, culminating in the all-too-real Silver Bridge tragedy of 1967. The victims of the aforementioned occurrences would swear they were all too real as well.

> "I HAVE SEEN YOU AFRAID. YOU'RE AFRAID RIGHT NOW, AREN'T YOU?"

Such a story was ripe for film treatment. In 2002, the horror genre had moved on from *Scream*-inspired slashers, Asian horror was on the rise, and the remake craze was only starting to catch on. It was a brief period in time when the genre was between trends, yielding a welcome variety of efforts such as *28 Days Later...*, *Cabin Fever*, and *May*. *The Mothman Prophecies* arrived under the radar in January (a month known for the unloading of disregarded pictures) to mixed reviews and modest box office, barely earning back its budget. As a Hollywood-produced, PG-13-rated "supernatural thriller," it was quite easy to overlook. Over time, however, the film has slowly gained traction in the eyes of horror devotees, and for good reason. This sleeper is as compelling as it is creepy, hitting eerie notes that linger in the mind long after watching it. This is a film that haunts.

We are introduced to John Klein (Richard Gere), a reporter for *The Washington Post*, whose life takes a turn for the worse when his wife, Mary (Debra Messing), inexplicably wrecks their car and, during treatment at the hospital, is unexpectedly diagnosed with a fatal brain tumor. John manages to move on with his profession, but not his life. When a co-worker offers to set him up with an acquaintance one evening, John opts instead for a late-night drive to Virginia, where he is scheduled to interview the governor the following day. On the way, his car dies suddenly and he has no choice but to walk to the nearest house to use a phone. A solemn man, Gordon Smallwood (Will Patton), answers the door, and then forces John inside at gunpoint, demanding to know why he has come knocking at his house three nights in a row. John is understandably confused, only becoming more so when he discovers he is actually in Point Pleasant, West Virginia, far off course from his intended destination. He now finds himself part of a terrifying equation that he will struggle, up to the edge of madness, to understand.

Director Mark Pellington had previously shown his acumen for making suspenseful, psychological cinema with his terrorist thriller *Arlington Road* (1999). He also had a background in music videos, from which he brings the best elements to *The Mothman Prophecies*, with the help of cinematographer Fred Murphy and editor Brian Berdan. The film possesses a certain aesthetic flow, drawing the viewer in while adding mysterious, often surreal layers that enhance the story without being forceful or obtrusive. Scene transitions are sometimes accompanied by a mild electrical interference that hints at being monitored, or through an odd Y-shaped motif that indicates some sinister imprint. The camera repeatedly and effectively uses POV perspectives, always gazing from tree branches, drifting above cars, or flying over the town itself. In one particularly chilling scene, when Mary wakes up in the hospital after her accident, she knowingly searches the room with terrified, bloodshot eyes to no avail, as the camera takes on a hidden presence, peeking at her through the partition. The film presents a dreary, colorless world, with the exception of red, which subtly infiltrates most scenes in

some manner, be it a close-up of lipstick or a pair of caution lights in the distance. Finally, the soundtrack, provided by the duo known as tomandandy, envelops the film with a darkly ethereal aura. These elements might make for an overwhelming or heavy-handed experience if not for the filmmakers' careful, organic application. The film is, in fact, designed to go beyond the already intriguing story and unnerve on a subliminal level, a level that saturates the viewer's psyche, essentially obscuring the line between fiction and reality. Every viewing of it leads to new discoveries.

"If your friend thinks he's talking to God, he's off by more than a few degrees." This is what Alexander Leek (Alan Bates), an author and authority on unexplained phenomena, tells John in regards to a recent conversation with one Indrid Cold over the phone. Cold is an enigmatic, ominous character who gives a name and voice, as it were, to the peculiar happenings plaguing the community of Point Pleasant. In his few scenes, his otherworldly voice and oblique profile are the stuff of nightmares. He also possesses an uncanny knowledge of things past, present, and future. He tells Gordon of a plane crash that hasn't happened yet. He knows what John is holding in his hand during the phone call. He displays upsetting insight of John's obsession over Mary's death. And eventually, he reveals to John a final, cryptic prophecy: "Great tragedy on the River Ohio." John

futilely attempts to connect all these dots. His life, like the film itself, is being divided by the rational and irrational, the known and unknown. This state of duality is alluded to numerous times through John's reflections in glass or mirrors, and attentive viewers will notice that the image doesn't always match his actions. His closest lifeline is Connie Mills (Laura Linney), a local police officer. She remains grounded, despite all that is going on in her small town, and she realizes the destructive path John is on. Without some sort of profound reckoning — on the loss of Mary, on the Mothman, whatever it may be — John will lose himself.

The Mothman Prophecies is a film that appeals to those with an appreciation of the secret and strange world around us, those who both shiver at and relish the possibility of the unknown. Like many of the best horror pictures, it succeeds here by offering precious few answers, leaving the questions to revolve in our minds, along with our perceptions. In the film, Leek emphatically states, "We're not allowed to know." Perhaps he was right, yet still we ask. The fact that it was based on real experiences and events, as documented in Keel's fascinating account, certainly enhances the effect. The movie does differ from the book in several ways, but as Keel himself reported, the "basic truths" are there. The talented filmmakers and professional cast took this original and frightening tale and delivered something special. Regardless, the movie remains hidden from too many genre fans who may mistake it for being too mainstream, or perhaps it is simply lost to them in the vast sea of mediocrity that is contemporary Hollywood horror. It is indeed a feature begging for, and quite worthy of, (re)discovery. Watch *The Mothman Prophecies*. And watch the skies...which I'm certain you will.

Cory Colock has always had an interest in the macabre, even as a child, before he was allowed to watch horror movies. He contributed the essay on The Blair Witch Project *for 2007's* HORROR 101. *Cory currently resides in Western Pennsylvania, which, coincidentally, is the location of one of the more recent Mothman sightings. He sincerely hopes the Mothman finds his essay to be...agreeable.*

A NIGHT TO DISMEMBER 1983

BY JASON COFFMAN

There is a school of thought regarding Ed Wood in general and *Plan 9 from Outer Space* in particular that they are, respectively, the worst director and movie of all time. However, a quick dip into more treacherous celluloid waters proves that *Plan 9* and its ilk may be a little weird, but ultimately they are enjoyable and entertaining on some level. There is, however, another type of cinema related to these—but much, much stranger. Films so spectacularly weird, so utterly perplexing, that they seem less like they were made by incompetents and more as if they were made by *aliens*. Moving images that so profoundly defy audience expectations of what a film is and does that they become unsettling in their own unique way. Doris Wishman's *A Night to Dismember* is a prime example of this kind of "outsider cinema." This is its own class of horror movie—giving the audience a taste of what it must be like to go insane.

Wishman was never particularly interested in learning about the technical side of filmmaking—her techniques remained largely the same from her first feature to her last. She worked with extremely low budgets and her apartment was frequently put to use as a set which appeared in virtually everything she made from the mid-1960s through the 1980s. She often used insert shots of random background objects to indicate passage of time, and a good chunk of each of her films' running time is comprised of shots of people's feet. Wishman never used live sound until she shot on video during the last part of her career, so it's rare to see anyone facing the camera and speaking at the same time. Her stories often feature difficult family relations, inexplicable plot twists and character behavior, and usually end with a downbeat finale. In short, Doris Wishman made movies her own way, and her (anti-?) style is immediately identifiable. It also virtually guarantees that only the most dedicated fans of the bizarre will be able to sit through anything she ever made.

Dismember was Wishman's first attempt at making a horror movie, having mostly avoided genre cinema other than the sci-fi trappings of *Nude on the Moon* (1961). Wishman explains on the Image DVD commentary track that her producers were interested in making a horror film following the slasher boom of the early 1980s. The DVD also features a promotional trailer that portrays *Dismember* as a sort of combination knock-off of *Carrie* and *The Amityville Horror* in which a teenage girl with telekinetic powers and her family move into a house haunted by the ghosts of a family who was savagely murdered there years earlier. This trailer also features quite a bit of footage not seen in the final cut. Wishman claimed that after she completed shooting, the majority of the footage was lost in a fire at the film processing lab. Between writing the project off or trying to salvage it via the footage that remained, the ever-resourceful Wishman, unwilling and/or unable to take the loss, chose the latter option.

The resulting feature is quite different from anything suggested by the promotional trailer. Detective Tim O'Malley narrates the events that befell the Kent family on the night of October 15th, 1986. (Yep, we're in the future, folks.) The families of Phineas and Broderick Kent are all murdered or other-wise dispatched ("Susan had accidentally fallen on an axe. She was dead.") and their stories are out of the way in the first five minutes. Then O'Malley tells the story of what happened to Adam Kent (Saul Meth) and his family after they brought daughter Vicki (porn star Samantha Fox) home from the sanitarium, where she had been sent after killing two neighborhood boys in 1981. Vicki's sister Mary (Diane Cummins) and brother Billy (William Szarka) don't want Vicki around, so they hatch a plot to drive her back to the sanitar-ium. While Vicki has to deal with her hateful parents and even worse siblings, someone is killing people in the periphery of the Kent family; by the time O'Malley is called to the Kent house, most of them have met violent deaths as well. Has Vicki gone insane once again, or is someone else getting away with murder?

The actual experience of watching *Dismember* is considerably more puzzling than the above plot summary suggests. Wishman cut the original footage she shot for this project with stray sequences from her other films, and often repur-posed the footage in ways that blatantly disregard rules of cinematic space and structure. The Kents' apartment becomes a black void lined with wood paneling, a stairwell stretch-es endlessly, and Vicki flees a monster against an impossibly long blank stretch of wall. Vicki's old flame Frankie (Frankie Sabat) has a seriously disorienting love scene with another woman inter-cut with footage of a completely different couple. O'Malley's nar-ration extends beyond explaining the circumstances of the case to 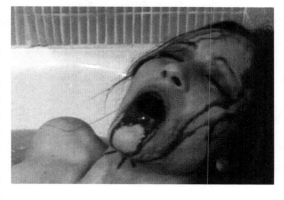 describing exactly what is happening on the screen: "Vicki felt as though some-one faceless was making love to her in bright, flashing colors that were changing from one second to the next!" A woman is decapitated, after which a patently fake *bald* wax head is placed in a fireplace. Mary has a nightmare in which her family murders her while she moans orgasmically. Wildly inappropriate Muzak and what sounds like the theme from a 1970s cop show play endlessly over scenes of murder and shots of bloody corpses. O'Malley keeps talking over the end credits, asking the audience to contact him if they have any in-formation on the whereabouts of the Kent family killer. In short, hardly a minute goes by without the viewer asking themselves: "What the *hell* is going on here?"

Another important question has no doubt sprung to the reader's mind: "Why the *hell* should I watch this?" Simply put, films like this have the power to tear down everything a viewer thinks they know about movies and demand they build anew their entire concept of cinema. One walks away from *Plan 9* laughing and shaking one's head at the cheap sets and bad acting; one retreats from *Dismember* (or *Manos: The Hands of Fate* [1966] or *Boardinghouse* [1982] or *Things* [1989], etc.) with their basic understanding of cinema in shambles. These movies don't just break the rules; they show the viewer in the most direct way possible that *there are no rules*. Wishman repeatedly insists in her DVD commentary that the story makes perfect sense to her. To be fair, it is possible to tease out an idea of what is happening after careful repeated viewings, but the form and structure of the film refuse any traditional idea of "sense" and create their own impenetrable "non-sense." The viewer must accept it as it is or dismiss it outright. Ultimately, *A Night to Dismember* is an unforgettable experience, and perhaps the purest kind of horror movie: one that unsettles in ways the viewer might have never known they could be unsettled.

Jason Coffman is an unrepentant cinephile and filmmaker living in Chicago. He is a regular contributor to FilmMonthly.com and Fine Print Magazine, and his writing has appeared in HorrorHound *and* Cashiers du Cinemart. *Coffman is also a film programmer for the Chicago Cinema Society and proud owner of a 35mm print of Andy Milligan's* Guru, the Mad Monk.

NIGHT WARNING 1982

BY BRIAN KIRST

"COLLEGE IS FOR RICH KIDS AND PEOPLE WITH BRAINS. *YOU* DON'T BELONG THERE!"

Childhood ends at 17 for Billy Lynch in the 1982 cult classic *Night Warning*. Filmed as *Butcher, Baker, Nightmare Maker* several years prior to its actual release, this bloodily over-the-top celluloid morsel reeks with incestuous longing, gleeful hag horror antics, and a well-rounded political slant that is decades ahead of its time.

At the core of this ambitious undertaking is wild-eyed Cheryl, played with Shakespearian prowess by the oddly magnificent Susan Tyrrell. Cheryl is a domesticity-bound yet secretly frenzied aunt, determined to hold onto her maturing, frequently shirtless nephew at all costs. Her creative method for doing this, you ask? She tarts her preserve-packing self up and makes a move on the television repair man. He rejects her. But just as young Billy walks

in the door (to celebrate his birthday, no less,) she hysterically stabs the non-consenting blue collar worker in the chest, claiming that he tried to rape her. Cheryl now believes Billy will stay at his distressed relative's side forever.

Unfortunately for her, Joe Carlson, the bigoted detective assigned to the case, smells a rat. When he discovers that the murder victim was actually the longtime companion of Billy's male mentor, Coach Landers, he assumes that Billy killed the man as part of a lover's quarrel. As Carlson begins harassing close friends, including Billy's girlfriend Julia, Cheryl further loses her grip on reality. Soon, cooking utensils become vicious weapons, neighbors are gutted, and Billy's world explodes in a bloody mess.

In a seeming anomaly, this horrifically fun mash-up—whose off kilter elements earned it a place on the BBFC Video Nasties list—was directed by broadcast television wunderkind William Asher. Married to actress Elizabeth Montgomery, Asher was best known for producing such iconic comedies as *I Love Lucy* and *Bewitched*. A more personal glance at Asher, though, reveals a past possessing more correlation to this dark gem than his other lighthearted works. After his parent's divorce, Asher was sent to live with his alcoholic mother at the age of 11. His father's death two years later led him to a life of vaguely criminal activity, a painful past he escaped by working his way into the Hollywood fantasy factory.

Such tragic circumstances anchor Asher's solid direction of *Night Warning* and help bring out the best in his Billy, Jimmy McNichol. The teen idol offers up a tenderly confused performance, one only occasionally marred by a pouty awkwardness. Asher's background in '60s beach flicks, including *How to Stuff a Wild Bikini*, puts him in good stead with McNichol as well. Years spent surrounded by barely clad male pop sensations allow the director to film his frequently exposed hero with nonchalance. The focus on McNichol's smooth handsomeness feels natural to the tone of the picture, only coming off as strange in comparison to traditional slasher fare and their flesh-baring female ingénues.

One might assume that the trio of credited screenwriters, Steve Briemer, Alan Jay Glueckman, and Boon Collins, were attempting to offer up a different take on the traditional holiday-themed stalk 'n' slash efforts glutting the market in the early '80s. But a recent conversation with esteemed actor Steve Eastin, whose focused portrayal of Coach Landers is an unqualified highlight, confirmed that the film was completed in 1978 or 1979 and later shelved due to battles between its various producers. This means that only the original *Halloween* could have been in theaters during *Night Warning*'s conception, proving the creators were walking to their own monster's beat from the very beginning. (Unfortunately, these ownership disputes continue today, contributing to the film's obscurity.)

Briemer, Glueckman, and Collins imbue their primary antagonist, the vile Carlson, played with offhanded ease by character actor Bo Svenson, with menacing subtleties. Not only is Carlson homophobic, with an intense agenda against Billy and Landers, but an uncompromising racist as well. The scene where he shakes down a trembling Mexican immigrant during an interrogation attempt is chilling and masterfully conceived by all involved.

The writers and Asher also give Billy an evolved sensibility at least twenty-five years ahead of its time. The character's reaction upon finding out about his mentor's homosexuality is the non-reaction of a contemporary child who has been reared on episodes of *Glee* and *Will & Grace*. It simply makes no difference to him and he continues to treat Landers as his most trusted confidante.

Then again, many rainbow-colored threads decorate this film: from Asher's involvement in gay favorite *Bewitched* to Tyrrell's perfection of the '60s Gothic hag horror antics begun by Bette Davis to McNichol's generous nude shower scene. Even Broadway stalwart Marcia Lewis, best known as Big Mama Thornton in the 1996 revival of *Chicago*, shows up as Tyrrell's boisterous neighbor and eventual nosey nemesis!

But it is Easton's coach character who has received a lion's share of acknowledgement by queer fans for being perhaps the first non-stereotypical gay character in a modern horror film. The straight, but incredibly gay-friendly Eastin recalls, "I just had the feelings that the guy would have. I found it interesting that he was in a gym, in a locker room with a lot of naked boys, but he wasn't a pervert of any kind. He was a gay man who was in a relationship who just loved coaching kid's basketball."

In a script so overloaded with sensory pleasures and social subtleties, some things do go awry. The introductory head-crunching car crash, rumored to be the work of an uncredited Jan de Bont (*Speed*) and the object of considerable praise from such gorehounds as Chas. Bulan, seems to belong in another picture. It also feels odd that no arrests occur after the initial murder. While it would have changed the movie's structure, Cheryl's defense seems flimsy at best.

Additionally, Landers has no emotional onscreen reaction to the death of his partner. "It just wasn't on the page," Eastin maintains. "I think that the

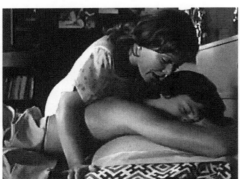

justification was that immediately after the murder, the guy is outed and is the primary suspect in the murder. If it had been on the page, I would have been glad to play it."

Another flaw may lie with Tyrrell herself. For all her magnificence, she is too quirky a presence to be believable as the happy, perfect, jelly-canning aunt. It is only as she tears down the walls of Cheryl's composure and emerges in all her ferocious splendor that her character is 100% believable. In a truly fair world, the image of Tyrrell—sloe-eyed with madness, heaving breasts covered in blood—would be iconic among horror fans everywhere instead of just the few, the proud, the lucky....

Yes, childhood may end with violent suddenness. But *Night Warning*, a wildly careening but always enjoyable beast, proves that the wild and wicked things that emerge from that loss are definitely worth exploring.

Brian Kirst broke out of the straight-laced confines of Amish country in Western New York to unleash Big Gay Horror Fan (www.biggayhorrorfan.com) upon an unsuspecting world. He has written about cult films for Chicago Free Press *and his interviews with horror personalities have decorated the* Fangoria *and* Rue Morgue *websites.*

THE OLD DARK HOUSE 1932

BY DAN KIGGINS

During my decades-long quest to encounter all the Universal horror classics firsthand, I became aware of one of the studio's least-known gems, *The Old Dark House*. That a film from the golden age of horror, with a cast and crew comprising a "Who's who" of horror legends both before and behind the camera, could fall by the wayside—and even be considered "lost" for a

> "WE'RE ALL TOUCHED WITH IT A LITTLE, YOU SEE, EXCEPT ME. WELL, AT LEAST I DON'T THINK I AM."

time—is utterly shocking. Based on a book by J.B. Priestley, directed by James Whale, and produced by the legendary Carl Laemmle Jr., the film's cast includes such rising Hollywood notables as Charles Laughton, Melvyn Douglas, Gloria Stuart, Raymond Massey, and Ernest Thesiger. Even make-up effects master Jack Pierce is on hand with the putty and greasepaint. But it is the presence of Boris Karloff, in his first horror role since his star-making turn in *Frankenstein* the year before, which makes this overlooked milestone a must-see.

The story opens with three lost travelers driving along a rural English country road through a torrential storm: bickering wedded couple Philip and Margaret Waverton (Massey, Stuart) and Mr. Penderel (Douglas), a back-seat singing cad with cheerful indifference to their dire situation. The road washed out and unable to travel further, they decide to seek refuge in the ominous mansion nearby. They are greeted at the door by Morgan (Karloff), a deeply scarred and menacing mute manservant. Pleading their case, they are admitted into the shadowy abode.

They are greeted by the gaunt fey figure of Horace Femm (Thesiger) and his foreboding, selectively deaf sister, Rebecca (Eva Moore), who is much less hospitable. Rebecca proceeds to regale the newcomers with a blasphemous history of both the house ("a place of laughter and sin") and her family, including her bedridden 102-year-old father upstairs, Sir Roderick Femm (actress Elspeth Dudgeon, billed under the pseudonym "John Dudgeon"). The group is joined by two more soaked, wayward travelers: cheerful showgirl Gladys Perkins (Lillian Bond) and wisecracking Sir William Porterhouse (Laughton). With their arrival, the stage is set for a grand night of power outages, drunken butlers, dark family secrets, and fledgling romances, climaxed by the show-stopping appearance of Horace and Rebecca's crazed pyromaniac brother Saul (Brember Wills, whose ability to go from sheepish cowering victim to a raving lunatic is a wonder to behold).

With its familiar classic feel, this grand adventure envelops the viewer in the dark and atmospheric essence of gothic filmmaking. The entire production is

surprisingly effective through extremely minimalistic means; one of its most memorable scares utilizes an early camera trick reminiscent of funhouse mirrors. Excluding the title sequences, the soundtrack is devoid of music, replaced instead by a symphonic storm—relentless howling winds and rain spatter punctuated by the constant crash of thunder. Shadows prevail throughout, with illumination springing solely from flickering fireplaces and sporadic candles. (Stuart later reminisced how Whale had her switch from her rain-soaked garb into a flowing white gown so that she would appear like a white flame as Karloff chased her about.)

Though many might consider it an early example of horror comedy, in actuality it's no more comedic than Whale's other work. Though it does contain the director's trademark dry wit (mainly delivered by Thesiger, who would come to full flower as Dr. Pretorius in 1935's *Bride of Frankenstein*), its tangled subplots involving multiple characters set it apart from many of its classic contemporaries. Here, it's not just a single monster our heroes have to contend with, but rather a litany of foes including a raging storm, two psychopaths, a mad family, and the Old Dark House itself.

Even more significant, the film spawned an entire subgenre of horror more or less on its own. How many times have we watched onscreen young travelers (in groups or alone), beset by either bad weather or car trouble, decide to approach and enter a foreboding house? *The Old Dark House* is the granddaddy of classics like *Psycho*, *Tourist Trap*, *House of 1000 Corpses*, and many, many more. Likewise, it plays on the basic discomfort and disorientation of being away from home and our familiar surroundings.

Universal certainly knew what they had and, evidenced by the opening title screen, it's apparent they were determined to capitalize on Karloff's newfound fame:

PRODUCER'S NOTE: Karloff, the mad butler in this production, is the same Karloff who created the part of the mechanical monster in Frankenstein. We explain this to settle all disputes in advance, even though such disputes are a tribute to his great versatility.

However, this strategy may very well have worked against them. Though Karloff delivered an emotionally stirring performance, he was overshadowed by Laughton's enjoyably blustery portrayal and Thesiger's nimble delivery ("Have a potato."). It seemed that audiences were disappointed that the story did not revolve around their new favorite monster star; the film did not perform well at the box office and was pulled early in its New York run. (By contrast, it was hugely successful in England, especially in London where it broke house records.) It was re-released only once, in 1939, and subsequently shelved where it sat literally gathering dust for decades.

Then, in 1957, Universal's rights to Priestley's novel *Benighted*—upon which Benn W. Levy and R.C. Sherriff's screenplay was based—lapsed and were promptly acquired by William Castle. (Castle's version, produced in 1963 by England's Hammer Films, is a much hokier version and is similar in title only). This would have lasting results, as it meant Universal could not include their 1932 version in Screen Gems' original Shock Theater package. These 52 classic fright flicks, including such horror staples as *Dracula*, *Frankenstein*, *The Wolf Man*, *The Invisible Man*, and *The Mummy*, were released for use on television. Without the youth of America being exposed to its gothic glory by their local late night horror hosts, *The Old Dark House* was denied its rightful place within the psyche of Monster Kids everywhere.

Time passed and this neglected classic was eventually considered lost by the mid-1960s. Thankfully, through due diligence, the negative was discovered in one of Universal's vaults by filmmaker and close personal Whale friend Curtis Harrington (*Queen of Blood*, *Ruby*) in 1968. (It would eventually be restored and released to home video by Kino, to be rediscovered by cinema enthusiasts young and old.)

To all dedicated fans out there seeking to explore the vintage black-and-white cornerstones of the horror genre: Your quest is incomplete without a trip into *The Old Dark House*.

Dan Kiggins was spawned on Chicago's north shore, his most vivid childhood memories being his family huddled around the TV, wearing 3-D glasses to watch Revenge of the Creature. *Graduating with a degree in Business Management, Dan started a career at the Mercantile Exchange, but never forgot his passion for cinema, especially horror. With networking (and a bit of luck), he has produced several independent genre efforts, including* The Landlord *and* Dead Weight.

THE OTHER SIDE 2006

BY JOEL WARREN

> "REAPERS ARE OUT THERE RIGHT NOW HUNTING FOR US. THEY DON'T FEEL PAIN. VERY HARD TO KILL. YOU SEE ONE OF THOSE BASTARDS, YOU BLOW THEM AWAY."

Did you ever have a really bad day? You know, the kind of day, when nothing seems to go right and everything seems to go straight to hell? Sam North (Nathan Mobley) heads home to his small town to visit his girlfriend Hanna (Jaimie Alexander) before his college graduation. Sam lays out a romantic dinner at "their spot"—a lovely waterfall on a river—and waits for Hanna, but instead gets knocked into the water by a white van, dies, ends up in Hell, and is subsequently liberated in a mass escape of other damned souls. He spends the remainder of the film trying to figure out what happened, all while evading a trio of Reapers (underworld bounty hunters) ordered to return him to the pit.

So, barring exceptional circumstances, Sam has had a much worse day than yours.

Writer/director Gregg Bishop offers a story that contains a mystery and a chase, all with a supernatural twist. In many ways, it's not that different from *The Fugitive* or *North by Northwest*, films in which an innocent man is pursued by the authorities and must somehow clear his good name before he's caught. (Except of course, anyone in Hell is by definition guilty of something.) The other major difference is, while U.S. Federal Marshals or secret agents are bad enough, Reapers from the abyss with unfathomable powers are a lot worse.

The Reapers are memorable antagonists, generating considerable menace without uttering a single word. The two "switchers" move from host to host (all recent émigrés inhabit fresh corpses) while carrying an object that gives them a sort of continuity—swords for the female, fedora for the male—that they pick up from their former meat suits. The lead Reaper is a "changeling" with the power to manifest its actual Hell-form on Earth, although its human form—played by Daniel Massey Tovell, resembling an ancient pagan idol made flesh—is imposing enough, able to both take and dish out a tremendous amount of punishment.

Speaking of which, how odd is it that our hero—not an antihero, mind you—has been condemned to Hell? Sam appears to be a really nice guy, a golden boy whose teeth practically glint in the sunlight. Yet, despite his Columbia University education, being true to his best girl back home, loving his brother David (Shale Nelson), and being on good terms with the local lawman (Stephen Caudill), Sam is still some kind of terrible sinner. Even after falling in with fellow escapees—the whiny, womanizing jerk Mally (Cory Rouse) and criminal-with-a-heart-of-gold Oz (Poncho Hodges)—he refuses to reveal what his mortal sins are/were. It's a mystery that keeps viewers emotionally invested throughout.

Yes, this is a tale of sin and redemption, albeit one more optimistic than those that fix any last chance for salvation as coincident with the end of a person's life. There are other religious elements as well, most notably the names and a discussion of a coming battle between good and evil.

Despite Bishop's assertions on the DVD commentary that he was careful to avoid the look of *The Matrix*, *The Other Side* contains numerous elements that recall the Wachowski siblings' 1999 blockbuster. The Reapers, in particular, share more than a passing resemblance to the three "Agents," except that they're not allowed to inflict collateral damage. Tovell's changeling Reaper also sparks memories of a certain T-1000 from *Terminator 2: Judgment Day*, especially during the chase scene involving a truck and a shotgun.

However, the fact that any comparisons can be drawn between these groundbreaking Hollywood titans and Bishop's $15,000 effort at all is pretty astonishing. Yes, you read that figure correctly. Bishop made his debut feature in his hometown with help from friends, acquaintances, family, local businesses, and the nearby film school. Since the shoot was essentially guerrilla filmmaking, everyone did everything; the result being that different scenes have different looks, making the picture appear much more costly than its meager budget would imply. The cheapest (yet most fundamental) part of a low-budget film is its screenplay—Bishop took the time to find out what people were willing to do, what locations could be had, etc., and wrote his script to take advantage, effectively nullifying the restrictions placed on many microbudget projects.

For instance, rather than a river of fire, Bishop's vision of Hell is a bunch of naked people in a dark culvert. The lighting is kept low enough that some faces can be seen, but everything remains dim and cold. Upon arriving in the netherworld, the membrane-like caul that Sam tears through is clearly a plastic garbage bag, but it works. (Do you know what is avoided? Cheesy CGI bullets and gore. Man, that never looks good.)

The Other Side does have its issues. Some of the lighting and other technical aspects are a bit shoddy, but not so offensive as to ruin anything except maybe for film students or lighting enthusiasts. Minus the occasional clunky line reading or stiff performance, most of the principal actors do a fine job, with Mobley and Rouse the standouts. (Some of the blame has to be laid at Bishop's feet since he

wrote the script and/or allowed the actors to improvise on set.) The complex plot is ambitious even for a veteran filmmaker working with a large budget and crew, but Bishop and his mad band managed to hold it together, although sometimes there is so much going on that it can feel like you've taken a sip from the river Styx.

Even so, this is a professional effort by creative artists making a lot out of a little; true independent filmmaking. It also served as a hint of what was to come: Bishop's next feature, 2008's *Dance of the Dead*, was impressive enough that Sam Raimi—who knows a thing or two about humble beginnings—released it through his Ghost House Underground label. Quite a step for a guy who started by making a neat little film with his friends, $15,000, and a hell of a lot of ambition.

Joel Warren continues to induct young minds into the beautiful world of mathematics, sometimes forcibly. He's also an occasional contributor and co-founder of cultreviews.com, where more of his erudite, brilliant and very modest opinions can be found. Otherwise, he's not very interesting and vigorously asserts that he's not a bitter shell of a human being.

THE PENALTY 1920

BY DAVID LEE WHITE

"LAUGHTER BURNS A CRIPPLE LIKE ACID."

Having kids is hell for your hobbies. After adopting my son, Nicholas, I returned home to discover my father-in-law had boxed up all my DVDs and stored them in the garage to make room for a crib, mobiles, and large, brightly-colored pieces of plastic that light up and buzz. It was just as well. Having a kid is like waking up outside The Matrix—it takes awhile to clean the muck out of your eyes and adjust to the new reality. My horror-fan gore-hound friends warned me that watching violent horror films would be much more difficult, that I'd become more hypersensitive to onscreen violence now that I was more in tune with the fragility of life. *Oh, please.* I had been watching Dario Argento films for so long, geysers of arterial blood were nothing more to me than part of a rococo color scheme. I once watched *Cannibal Holocaust* while eating a plate of bacon.

Of course, my friends were right. As a new parent, it's nearly impossible to watch onscreen suffering without thinking of the victim as someone's child. And if young children are the victims? Forget about it. I was reassured that my skin would someday build back up to its appropriate thickness and I'd be able to indulge in bloodthirsty cinematic voyeurism once again. But until that happened,

I needed some other kind of fix—something to keep my hobby alive. I started watching silent films, largely because when holding a sleeping infant, the last thing you want are the sounds of bloodcurdling screams. Plus, I was unlikely to see anything too upsetting. Silent films were objects of nostalgia—they were *safe*...right?

Right. Here's how *The Penalty*, starring Lon Chaney, begins: After a young boy is crippled in a car accident, an incompetent doctor needlessly amputates both of his legs, driving him to grow up and become a murderous criminal.

Everything that drew you to the cinema has been there since the beginning. Even horror. *Especially* horror. There's no escaping it. Oh, sure you might not see the Gish sisters drowning in pools of blood and entrails, but dismemberment, metaphysical suffering, torture, even child endangerment...it's all there. Thankfully I was able to choke back my anxiety attack and push through, because *The Penalty* is a crackerjack, pulpy, sinister little thriller as potent today as it was in 1920, in spite of a cop-out ending that I'll talk more about in a bit.

The Penalty began life as a novel by Gouverneur Morris, the great-grandson of the same Gouverneur Morris who became one of America's founding fathers. Morris' novel is like a cracked mirror version of something by Horatio Alger—the famous boys' adventure author that encouraged young men everywhere to "struggle upwards" with optimism and pluck. Morris is more concerned with how tragic acts of fate mold and shape lives. The young protagonist of *The Penalty* struggles upwards, all right...right to the top of San Francisco's criminal underworld.

After its opening interlude of psychological child scarring, limb mutilation, and negligent parenting, *The Penalty* picks up twenty-seven years later as our unnamed protagonist has become a criminal mastermind and taken on the sobriquet "Blizzard." Chaney famously put his knees in buckets and strapped his legs behind his back during filming, which makes him tougher than Gary Sinise who had his legs digitally erased for *Forrest Gump*. Chaney hobbles through the streets of the Barbary Coast with freakish dexterity, even leaping onto a table to threaten a room full of starved and abused hat makers. His performance is so electric and savage that very few performances from the silent era can compare. Only Rene Navarre in Louis Feuillade's *Fantomas* even comes close.

Now that Blizzard has successfully established his network of crime, he is ready to embark on his master plan to loot the entire city of San Francisco through the brilliant use of hats.

Look...just *go with it*.

What's important is that Blizzard gets distracted from his master plan when he sees the opportunity to take revenge on the doctors that crippled him.

It comes in the form of the following newspaper advertisement: "WANTED— Model to pose for statue of 'Satan after the Fall.' If you think you look like Satan, apply at studio of Barbara Ferris, 32 Institute Place." Turns out, Barbara Ferris is the daughter of the doctor who crippled Blizzard twenty-seven years ago. This realization leads to one of my favorite moments in the film, in which Blizzard suffers a burst of melancholy and asks two of his agents "Do I look like Satan?" to which they shrug and nod as if to say, "Sure, I guess. I guess you look like Satan."

While Blizzard is busy posing for sculptures and plotting to crash San Francisco's economy with hats, the police have sent their best agent, Rose (Ethel Grey Terry), to infiltrate his gang. Her superior hopes that she'll turn down the assignment—this is no place for a woman, after all—but only a woman will be able to blend in with all the other female hat makers. Naturally, Blizzard is immediately attracted to Rose and invites her into his study to help him play the piano. He can't reach the pedals, you see. Rose dutifully bends down and works the pedals while Blizzard bangs away at an anguished concerto. The two make beautiful music together; before long, Rose is too captivated by the madman to turn him in to the authorities.

It would be bad form to reveal any more of the plot, but if you've been mentally tabulating the pile-up of absurdities (mistaken amputations, coincidental Satan sculpture, mischievous hats), you may safely add "leg grafts" to the list.

The Penalty is a hell of a great little film. *Until the ending*. Without giving anything away, everything you don't want to happen, winds up happening. A last-second plot device almost makes things right, but not quite. Still, if you can stomach a climax that feels like a bit of a cheat, the rest makes the ride worth the trouble. This was Lon Chaney's first starring role and he plays it like he knows he'll never get another chance to make an impression. Even beyond his

shocking physical contortions, he commands our attention in every single frame he's in.

Chaney would later join forces with Tod Browning, and while that partnership yielded some great films, *The Penalty* benefits from not having an auteur at the helm. Director Wallace Worsely had no intention of creating an atmosphere of weirdness the way Browning did. Instead, Chaney was allowed to create the character...then dropped into the real world—our world. The images of Blizzard plodding along the streets of San Francisco are jarring and indelible. Worsely and Chaney later collaborated on *Ace of Hearts*

(1921) and the classic *The Hunchback of Notre Dame* (1923).

While Kino's DVD release is probably the preferred means of watching *The Penalty* today (despite its jarring electronic score), there are also perfectly legal, watchable versions on the internet. My most recent viewing was via YouTube on my iPhone, lying down in my son's darkened room, waiting for him to drift off...reminding myself of the horrible things that can happen when children play in traffic.

David Lee White currently resides in New Jersey. He is the author of the novel Fantomas in America *(available from Black Coat Press) and the plays* Blood: A Comedy, Slippery as Sin, White Baby, Random Horrible Thoughts About Love *and* If I Could in My Hood I Would. *He has written articles for* Video Watchdog, Geceyarisi Sinemasi, Belphegor *and is a contributor to the Turkey edition of the* Directory of World Cinema. *www.davidleewhite.net*

PHANTOM OF THE PARADISE 1974

BY ANNA McKIBBEN

Phantom of the Paradise is a rock and roll musical fantasy with its roots firmly grounded in classic terror literature. Lifting its story primarily from *The Phantom of the Opera* and *Faust*, writer/director Brian De Palma's film may have been a commercial and critical failure on release but is now considered a cult classic. The usual De Palma flourishes and references—as well as a brilliant cast and an ear-catching, Oscar-nominated soundtrack—ensure that *Phantom* has more than earned its place in horror cinema history.

"IT'S ALL HERE. READ IT CAREFULLY, AND THEN SIGN AT THE BOTTOM IN BLOOD. MESSY, I KNOW, BUT IT'S THE ONLY WAY I CAN BIND IT. TRADITION."

Released in the United States on Halloween in 1974, *Phantom*'s plot resembles that of Gaston LeRoux's famous novel if that particular Phantom was hopped up on sex, drugs, rock music, and then covered in glitter. It's the story of a talented songwriter, Winslow Leach (William Finley), whose *Faust*-based rock opera is stolen by record producer mogul Swan (Paul Williams) and given to a mediocre Sha-Na-Na rip-off band, The Juicy Fruits. When Leach attempts to retrieve his music from Swan's mansion, he meets and quickly falls for Phoenix (Jessica Harper), a young starlet auditioning for a part in the *Faust* chorus. Arrested for trespassing, Leach is sent to Sing Sing where his teeth are forcibly removed and replaced with metal ones. When he finds out that Swan and The Juicy Fruits are about to release their recording of *Faust*, Leach launches into a murderous rage—he kills a prison guard, escapes in a crate of tiddly-winks games, and heads to Swan's record plant. While vandalizing the new records, he is caught by the police, only to slip and fall headlong into a record press. His face and vocal cords now crushed and disfigured, and crazed beyond saving, Leach makes his way to Swan's new music hall, The Paradise, to exact his revenge.

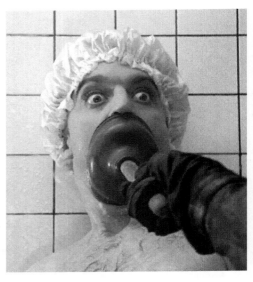

My introduction to *Phantom of the Paradise* came via the Internet Movie Database's horror message boards. At the time, I was interested in seeing other De Palma films aside from *Carrie* (1976), and other little-known genre gems that had flown under my radar. From the opening narration (delivered by an uncredited Rod Serling or a *really* good impersonator of same), I was completely enamored. *Phantom* kicks off with The Juicy Fruits singing a rather-awful-but-still-somehow-catchy song called "Goodbye, Eddie, Goodbye" that calls to mind every absurd doo-wop ballad ever written about dying in car crashes or losing your girlfriend in a knife fight. On top of that, *Phantom* is a grand satire of glam rock, exemplified by Gerrit Graham's portrayal of Beef, an over-drugged, over-glittered singer who is built entirely of pure macho buffoonery. It was like someone had made this just for me, a *Rocky Horror Picture Show* fan who had grown tired of that particular groove.

Interestingly enough, *Phantom* came out almost exactly a year before *Rocky Horror*, but never enjoyed the same level of success (except in Winnipeg, Canada, of all places, where it played for 18 consecutive weeks). There is no real explanation for its failure to connect with paying audiences or critics, but really, when it comes to cult films—especially cross-genre ones like this—some just have better legs, touch a particular nerve, or have that elusive "it factor." The *Rocky Horror* comparison is particularly noteworthy since on the surface, the two share many similarities. Both have soundtracks that recall 1950s and '60s rock and roll as well as '70s glam rock, both have characters that fall outside of the hetero range of sexuality, and both borrow liberally from existing horror stories. Looking back on the film, it's relatively tame in comparison to something like *RHPS*, which carried an R-rating. The drug use in the film—from Beef rifling through a collection of pills and powders prior to his opening night performance to the Juicy Fruits smoking an obnoxiously enormous joint—is largely played for comedic value. The sex scenes amount to a bunch of women (and Finley, in drag) writhing around in lingerie and the sight of Paul Williams' nipple, which is undeniably shocking on its own, but nothing quite like the shadowplay sex scenes in *Rocky Horror*. For a film set in the wild world of glam rock, it's awfully mild. Perhaps audiences weren't in tune with someone like Finley (he of the frizzy hair and buggy eyes) as a leading man, despite his being masked for the majority of the running time. That's all speculation, though, and seeking the bedrock reason for *Phantom*'s flopping at this point is both moot and futile.

It's much more fun to discuss all the things that make the film worth watching. As unconventional a choice as he might have been, Finley's work as Winslow Leach is probably his best and best-known, though seasoned fans might recognize him from two other De Palma teamings, *Sisters* (1973) and *The Fury* (1978), or Tobe Hooper's *Eaten Alive* (1977) and *The Funhouse* (1981). He manages to be sympathetic and villainous at once, but not in a typical antihero kind of way. Then again, these aren't exactly clear-cut villains and heroes; we bounce back and forth between Swan and The Phantom as to who to root for—even by the end we're not exactly sure. It's a slick move by De Palma, who handily feeds us a steady stream of ever-evolving references and homage. He also gives us one of the best visual representations of Hitchcock's "bomb under the table" explanation of suspense in the scene where The Phantom plants a bundle of TNT in a prop car about to be wheeled into a Juicy Fruits (now called The Beach Bums) dress rehearsal. De Palma then shifts into split-screen—another trademark—and we follow the car as it's moved onto the stage while simultaneously watching the band sing and dance to a horrible surf rock ditty. The scene remains effective, even after multiple views.

For those used to slashers or ghosts or buckets of blood, *Phantom of the Paradise* might not be a traditional horror film. It isn't even a traditional musical, where people break into song for no apparent reason to the accompaniment of invisible orchestras—almost all of the songs and music are completely diegetic, the musicians and singers creating the music onscreen before our eyes and ears. However, De Palma so deftly modernizes (well, for

the 1970s) *The Phantom of the Opera* and *Faust* while weaving in nods to other horror classics, his brainchild becomes a whole new beast of terror. Its cult following grows every day, encouraged by folks like Paul Williams, who seems to take great pride in his roles both as co-star and composer of the musical score. Williams, who De Palma initially approached to play the Phantom (despite writing the role for Finley), is as responsible for the film's appeal as anyone, contributing a memorable soundtrack *and* an insidiously sympathetic villain. You'll likely find yourself singing along (or at least keeping time) with the songs, smiling and nodding all the while at the various allusions contained therein. So find yourself a copy for the hell of it and meet the devil who is so special to me—The Phantom of the Paradise.

Anna McKibben hardly ever speaks of herself in the third person but she's willing to try. She writes a lot of nonsense online at Bemused and Nonplussed, occasional horror reviews for Dreams in the Bitch House, and says whatever is on her mind on Twitter as whynotanna. She likes weird movies, weird people, taking naps and piña coladas.

PIECES 1982

BY JOHN PATA

> **"IMAGINE. THEY STILL HAVEN'T FOUND A HEAD. I WONDER WHAT THE MURDERER WANTED WITH IT."**

"You Don't Have to Go to Texas for a Chainsaw Massacre!" How's that for a tagline?! If you're anything like me (and since you're reading this, I'll assume you are), any film with the balls to make such a statement instantly becomes required viewing.

It would be quite easy to pass off *Pieces*, or *Mil Gritos Tiene la Noche* ("A Thousand Screams Has the Night"), as a train wreck of deficient characters spewing brainless dialogue in a wretched execution of filmmaking chock full of horrendous acting, atrocious dubbing, arbitrary situations, excessive nudity, and sexual overtones topped off with gratuitous bloodshed with the most painfully obvious red herring in cinematic history...and you'd be right! But that's the charm of this flick, and what makes it so goddamn fun! This is a prime piece of grindhouse celluloid we're talking about here.

Writer/director Juan Piquer Simón, no stranger to horror fans with such titles as *The Pod People* (1983), *Slugs* (1988), and *The Rift* (1990) to his credit, was originally approached by producers Dick Randall and Steve Minasiam to helm *Last House on the Left Part Two*. Simón ultimately (and shall we say thankfully) wasn't fond of the follow-up's script, but showed interest in a fifteen-page synopsis for another project the producers had. This new script, cranked out in just fifteen days "based on what would be fun for me to do," as Simón puts it, became what we now know as *Pieces*.

In the *Pieces of Juan* interview on the (superb) Grindhouse DVD, the director describes the story as "the childhood trauma of a boy whose mother hates his father. She undervalues the boy, attributing to him all the defects that she encountered in the father. The boy reacts violently and afterwards, throughout his life, he intends to recover the mother he killed." Based on this synopsis, one might actually anticipate a fairly intelligent and thought-provoking narrative. But let's face it, folks, *Pieces* is anything but intelligent and thought-provoking. In fact, I'd go as far to say it's one of the most bizarre, nonsensical, and random offerings the genre encompasses. There's no delicate way to put it: *Pieces* is insanely fucked up and all over the place. It's unlike anything you have seen or ever will.

The film opens in Boston in 1942 (shot in Spain, mind you), with a young boy, Timmy, working on a puzzle. As he fumbles over putting the right *pieces* in their place, his mother enters the room and discovers that her son's assembled puzzle features the unclothed figure of a woman. Mom freaks out and starts chastising the boy, spewing insults about him and his father. Timmy, reacting the way any ordinary kid would in this situation, hacks up his mother with an axe, finishes the puzzle, and retreats, drenched in blood, into the closet. Enter the nanny with the utterly confused police, and we skip ahead forty years.

Set in present day (circa 1982) Boston on a college campus, we are immediately introduced to a figure donning black leather gloves, a box containing shoes, a bloody dress, a photo of the mom from earlier with a big ol' red 'X' over her face, and the nudie puzzle... Hey, wait a minute. This must be Timmy! Ah, yes, it all comes together now. To expedite matters, we also learn that Timmy is running around campus sawing females up with a chainsaw. Only question is: who is "Timmy" now?

The crack crime-fighting duo of Lt. Bracken and Sgt. Holden (Christopher George and Frank Braña) start quizzing the Dean (Edmund Purdom) and Prof. Brown (Jack Taylor) to narrow down a list of suspects. They ultimately decide to send in undercover female officer/professional tennis player Mary Riggs (Lynda Day George, billed as Linda Day) to pose as the campus tennis coach. Mary better watch out, as the resident campus Casanova, Kendall (Ian Sera), has the hots for her. Meanwhile, Willard (Paul Smith), the bearded, larger-than-life groundskeeper who enjoys keeping his chainsaw suspiciously spotless, lurks around every corner....

Now, we don't want to get bogged down trying to decipher the plot (especially since there are a wealth of unnecessary, undeveloped, and irrelevant subplots throughout) because that's not what makes this film exceptional. This puppy excels in absurdity and more than delivers in fun. Once our storyline is (somewhat) established, randomness is the status quo. Simón even admits, "The truth is that the script was very short. I was so preoccupied with getting the necessary coverage to even consider it a feature that I would come up with stuff as events presented themselves." He continues, "We even did a few pick-up shoots to finish some of the scenes and to pad out the movie."

A prime example of such "padding out" can be experienced during the sequence where a mysterious martial arts-wielding Asian man, dressed in a full-body track suit, literally jumps out of the bushes, kicking and punching at Mary. Suddenly the unidentified male drops face first to the ground. Kendall comes along on his motorbike, recognizes the assailant as his kung-fu professor (???) and shakes his hand. The prof explains, "I am out jogging, next thing I know I am on ground. Must be something I eat. Bad chop suey. So rong!" and runs off into the night...never to be seen again.

Considering this is indeed a slasher flick from 1982, rest

assured there's plenty of college coed red stuff flying all over the place, and you don't have to be a pathologist to figure out that a chainsaw is the weapon of choice. Unlike most of the subpar technical attributes, Basilio Cortijo's practical effects are quite impressive and innovative. The memorable deaths are frequent, but the pinnacle gore scene features a topless (and "healthy") female being chased through the women's locker room, only to be corned in a shower stall. It doesn't take long before the chainsaw slices through the door...and her torso. (A pig's carcass was used for the close up.) But the real payoff is when the aftermath is revealed: the upper half of the female's body resting on the floor, intestines spilling out while blood covers everything.

There is no possible way to adequately put this picture into words. A film like *Pieces* could only exist in our beloved genre and be celebrated by bastards...bastards...BASTARDS like us. Be it intentional or freak happenstance, *Pieces* reminds us that sometimes being entertained by erratic fun is all you need, just as "the most beautiful thing in the world is smoking pot and fucking on a waterbed at the same time." From the endlessly quotable one-liners, constant plot twists and turns, ruthless chainsaw play, to a final scene you'd be nuts to see coming, all the pieces come together to make this an experience unlike any other, one best viewed amongst your closest fiends. After all, "It's Exactly What You Think It Is!" And yet so much more.

John Pata hails from Oshkosh, WI. He's the main dude behind Head Trauma Productions and co-wrote/directed Dead Weight, *the Rondo-nominated, award-winning survival horror/post-apocalyptic love story. HTP's latest short film,* Pity, *will begin hitting the festival circuit in early 2014. In between film projects, John is the president of a non-profit movie theater, rides his bike too much, listens to records while reading comics, and never gets his fill of veggie burritos.*

PIN 1988

BY TERENCE GALLAGHER

In a classic scene from 1967's *The Graduate*, Benjamin Braddock (Dustin Hoffman) is being counseled by one of his father's rich friends as to his future employment:

Mr. McGuire: I just want to say one word to you. Just one word.

Benjamin: Yes, sir.

Mr. McGuire: Are you listening?

Benjamin: Yes, I am.

Mr. McGuire: Plastics.

Benjamin: Exactly how do you mean?

> **"OH, LEON, YOU FRIGHTENED ME. I THOUGHT YOU WERE PIN."**

Great question, Benjamin, how *did* he mean? Looking back at *The Graduate* 40-odd years later, I know exactly what Mr. McGuire meant...plastics are the future, and he was completely right. Everything is plastic today. Everything!!! Our cars, bracelets, celebrities...even our politicians are plastic.

The Canadian feature *Pin* (subtitled *A Plastic Nightmare*) extends the idea of everything, and everyone, becoming plastic to macabre levels. Now, even your nanny can be plastic. Pin, a medical doll, is a training tool that Doctor Linden (the always great Terry O'Quinn) uses in his practice. Remember those Invisible Body models that used to freak us out in our school science classrooms? Through clear, thick plastic, we see all of the organs, veins, arteries, etc. of the human body in striking clarity. Pin is the Invisible Body model, only life-sized. Pin is also anatomically correct, as we observe in an early scene in which Dr. Linden's nurse, with help from Pin, gives herself a gynecological exam in the doctor's office.

Looking at a life-sized, see-through human is unsettling on its own, but when the doctor uses ventriloquism to make Pin speak, the effect is downright unnerving. Pin's most compelling feature, though the aforementioned nurse might claim otherwise, is his startlingly clear, piercingly blue eyes. Director Sandor Stern often employs a close-up of Pin's face as a reaction shot, where we can read into Pin's eyes—the plastic windows of his plastic soul—anything we conjure, whether it be the serene gaze of a saint or a madman's scrutiny of the abyss.

Dr. Linden lives with his perfectly plastic family—a perfectly plastic wife and two perfectly plastic children, Leon and Ursula—in their perfectly plastic suburbia. The consummate symbol of the family is their living room, the furniture encased and enshrined in polyethylene coverings. The parents are as repressed as their furniture, opting to instruct their kids by using Pin as a transparent Mary Poppins, with help from Dr Linden's ventriloquism. To say that the children are ill-served by this child-rearing manner is an understatement. Leon, a repressed, psychologically troubled boy, becomes dependent on Pin as his constant companion, and Ursula, though she recognizes Pin as an extension of her father, is also affected by her strange upbringing. Pin eventually even delivers a graphic lesson in sex ed to the children, a conversation that appears to delight Ursula and further depress Leon.

By high school, Leon is more angry and repressed than ever, and Ursula has become the school's good-time girl. Leon is now completely invested in the reality of Pin and will not tolerate the truth about the true plastic nature of his only friend, shoulder to cry on, father confessor. Cracks appear in the family structure when Ursula gets in the family way and has to be treated by her father. Further cracks develop when Dr Linden discovers just how close Leon is to Pin. The doctor tries to get rid of the medical doll, with decidedly disastrous results. Leon and Pin's personalities intertwine more and more, with the latter's advice to Leon darkening every day. As Leon's world spins out of control, those threatening Leon and Ursula develop bad cases of death. Is Pin behind the mysterious attacks? Is Leon around the bend and killing people? Is the Pope plastic???

Actually, there is no great mystery here. Rather, the movie works on a different level than its '80s slasher movie brethren, flirting with darker subject matters such as incest, schizophrenia, fear, etc. There are no bloody gashes or big knives (until the end, of course). As adapted and directed by Stern (screenwriter for the original *Amityville Horror*), *Pin*'s horror is of the mind and of the soul, which just happens to be my favorite style of horror. We watch as Leon vainly strives to hold together some sort of family unity while the simple act of living life pulls those he loves away. David Hewlett is wonderful as Leon, pathetically vulnerable in one moment, frighteningly deranged the next. As he reads his poetry about sister rape to Ursula's new boyfriend, we watch slackjawed at Leon's cluelessness about human relationships and his desperation for love, any sort of love, even a love from a plastic dummy. Cyndy Preston is sweet as Ursula, torn between her compassion for a broken brother and her desire to live as normal a life as she can find. When Ursula and Leon finally part, we truly feel the pain and loss for both of these sad, shattered children.

Many might wonder about Pin's name and how it relates thematically. In an early scene, Ursula explains that Pin is short for Pinocchio, the puppet who desperately wished to become a real boy and whose nose grew when he told a lie. Ursula states that Pin would never tell a lie to her or to Leon. While Pin never dreams of becoming a real boy, the film inverts Pinocchio's wish; Leon

comes to terms with his true connection with Pin.

As an obsessive horror nerd, I've spent untold hours sifting through obscure web sites, libraries, and close-out bins for quality horror that has slipped through the cracks in the celluloid frame. Sick of re-makes, "contemporary nods to the classic '80s slasher flicks," and the latest "found-footage" debacle, I've had to go far afield of my local cineplex to mine quality horror. That's why finding *Pin* was such a joy for me. It's a film that celebrates real people; real crazy people, but real people nonetheless. I truly feel for Leon and Ursula and the forces that are pulling them apart. Over the last couple decades, horror movies and horror fans have lost an integral part of what makes the medium work: *empathy*, an emotional investment in what happens in the film and to its inhabitants. Most horror offerings today are little more than videogame checklists, where we watch a group of uninteresting, unlikable characters get offed in (hopefully) creative ways. These films don't really care about their characters, and, in turn, neither do we. If the movie pulls us away from our iWhatevers for a moment, it's considered a success. *Pin* offers horror fans that rare opportunity to connect to the onscreen characters so we actually feel with them and through them. In a society where ever-increasing technology is intended to bring us together, true emotional connection is more precious than ever. That's why *Pin* works so well. The horror of connecting...perhaps that's most frightening of all.

He's got a plastic wife who wears a plastic mac,
And his children wanna be plastic like their dad,
He's got a phony smile that makes you think he understands,
But no one ever gets the truth from Plastic Man.
   --"Plastic Man" by The Kinks

Terence Gallagher's descent into madness began at seven after hearing horror gems from radio's phenomenal Lights Out. *He never looked back (except in fear); countless novels, stories, TV/radio shows, and movies have been grist for his terror mill. His favorite film is* Videodrome, *favorite TV show is* The Dick Van Dyke Show's *"Haunted Cabin" episode, favorite novel is Theodore Roszak's* Flicker, *and favorite short-horror series is* The Pan Book of Horror Stories. *Spread the love...*

POSSESSION1981

BY NILE ARENA

Polish expatriate and provocateur Andrzej Zulawski's apocalyptic feature *Possession* is all about destruction. It opens where most stories would find their middle, within the disintegration of a young couple's marriage, then quickly moves to the destruction of their sanity, their lives, and finally of society at large. After a year in

"WELL, THAT'S WHY I AM WITH YOU. BECAUSE YOU SAY 'I' FOR ME."

clandestine employ, Mark (Sam Neill) returns home to his wife Anna (Isabelle Adjani) and their young son, Bob (Michael Hogben). Anna leaves, informing her spouse that their marriage is finished, whereupon Mark learns of her affair with another man, a New Age pseudo-intellectual named Heinrich (Heinz Bennent). Things only get stranger when Mark hires a detective (Shaun Lawton) to follow his wife; Anna's affair with Heinrich is effectively over, replaced by something far more bizarre. Living in a garret apartment, Anna has become romantically involved with…something. What it is, exactly, that Anna has left her old bourgeois life for is where the film truly fascinates, frustrates, and astounds.

As an unabashed fan, I was surprised to discover *Possession* more reviled than revered in critical circles. Thomas Gianvito makes mention of it in his essay "An Inconsolable Darkness," charting the rise of European films depicting civilization's decay and/or complete annihilation. Zulawski's movie certainly fits the described "directionless society, adrift in a fever dream from which there is no waking," yet a few lines later Gianvito criticizes the film's "over-the-top histrionics," simultaneously dismissing the fine performances and Bruno Nuytten's sublime camerawork by saying "the very filmmaking itself seems as possessed as anyone, and everyone, on screen." Meanwhile, *Eyeball* magazine's Daniel Bird's assertion that Zulawski "…through a mixture of almost sarcastic naiveté and downright stubbornness, has pursued a cinematic career producing indigestible work which has consistently annoyed, infuriated and occasionally humiliated film critics," speaks greater volumes about the writer's personal biases than the any insight into *Possession*'s bleak, enigmatic style.

It may be losing the forest for the trees to dissect *Possession* as belonging to one particular genre or movement. Some dozen viewings later—on screens large and small—it is still a confounding, fevered piece of cinema. But struggling with whether it is horror or domestic drama seems misguided. I submit it should be treated as a different beast altogether, for there is no other film like it,

even among Zulawski's canon. The astounding cinematography, with its long tracking shots of winding, decaying, depopulated streets surveying a near-abandoned West Berlin, gives the impression something horrible has happened even *before* the onscreen events unfold. As Andrzej Korzynski's eerie electronic score plays, the opening credits arrive over rolling images of blighted urban landscape. Are we seeing Mark's journey home through his perspective? Is it Anna's return from the harrowing "subway scene?"

Possession may in part be so difficult to analyze because of how successfully it operates on an unconscious level. In "An Introduction to the American Horror Film," Robin Wood describes the connection between the unconsciousness of the moviegoer and that of the dreamer, defining both experiences as "a losing of oneself in a fantasy-experience" and "a kind of partial sleep of consciousness." Seen this way, *Possession* is far less problematic—a married man away on business might well have a nightmare that his wife has sought comfort in the arms of some monstrously superior Other. Indeed, it is only the men that react

so profoundly towards the creature's appearance—the implication perhaps that it is sexually superior and, worst of all, preferred by the beautiful Anna over them. In particular, Heinrich's panic seems to stem not from being placed in mortal danger, but rather of the creature *re*placing him as Anna's supreme lover.

The ever-evolving creature—realized by effects master Carlo Rambaldi—that Anna leaves Mark and Heinrich for is undoubtedly the film's most infuriating element as well as its most uncanny. It deliberately refuses to remain classified as any one thing for very long, slipping from captive lover to child (if we are to read Anna's terrifying fit in the subway as its birth) to its ultimate haunting metamorphosis.

"He's very tired. He made love to me all night," Anna affectionately tells the doomed private detective as he watches the wet pile of tentacles breathe laboredly in bed. Anna's sexuality and affection toward this otherworldly *thing* seem more horrific than any carnage the creature could commit. Indeed, it is a completely submissive monstrosity (albeit profoundly sexualized) until its final transformation.

The other character that inhabits the uncanny is Bob's school teacher, Helen, who becomes a redemptive force in Mark's life as his marriage disintegrates. Adjani turns in a remarkably subtle, sensual performance in sharp contrast to her electrified turn as Anna; more daringly, the doppelganger is never explained. Mark is initially as perplexed as the audience, convinced Helen is his wife playing at some disguise, but Helen assures Mark, "There is nothing in common among women except menstruation." (A comment which seems to contrast sharply with certain critics' estimation of the film as a misogynist indictment of women at large.) Her appearances hint at a stability and a stay against madness for Mark, as well as a chance to start over, to possess and love again. Yet Helen never assumes the object of desire she seems poised to become. Perhaps thanks to her efficiency, her cool dismissal of Mark's diatribe against the evils of women, or her ability to care for Bob while his parents are falling apart, she is spared the grisly fate that love brings to the other characters. Spared, at least, for a while.

Possession may be read as a perfect illustration of Wood's definition of the horror film: "...when the repressed wish is, from the point of view of the consciousness, so terrible it must be repudiated as loathsome." Anna's meticulous shedding of the stock roles (wife, mother, even bourgeois mistress to the "enlightened" Heinrich) is banally familiar, but even through a twisted lens of monsters, gore, and murder, the suggestion is that Anna is right to shed these suffocating and unpleasant roles. What could have been a love triangle's drama of hysterics becomes truly horrific as Zulawski explores forbidden sexuality and defiance of social conventions.

Rather than some meticulously crafted riddle filmed for the sole purpose of upsetting critics and audiences, it seems Zulawski is operating on a level of unconsciousness rarely carried off with such zeal. *Possession*'s critical dismissal and frustrated reception can be set aside if the text is read within the parameters of a nightmare. Not necessarily a feminist nightmare, for it seems as much Mark's as Anna's, but one painfully aware of the impossibility of existing as another's object of possession and desire. This haunting narrative owes as much to the viewer's unconsciousness as the troubled consciousness that created it. As Zulawski himself says on the Anchor Bay DVD's audio commentary track: "This is the most difficult word in this whole discourse of mine—what is true?" Perhaps the answer lies within a less conscious interpretation of *Possession*, or, in the words of Hassan i Sabbah, "Nothing is true, everything is permitted."

Nile Arena developed an appreciation for the grindhouse and the arthouse working as a video store clerk. He continues that proud, vanishing trade to this day, watching as many films as possible to advance his knowledge of the horror movie, creature feature, slasher flick, and video nasty. He lives in the Midwest.

PRETTY POISON 1968

BY ANTHONY TIMPONE

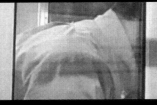

"YOU KNOW, WHEN GROWN-UPS DO IT, IT'S KIND OF DIRTY. THAT'S BECAUSE THERE'S NO ONE TO PUNISH THEM."

Produced eight years after the landmark *Psycho*, the opening moments of *Pretty Poison* almost play like a dry run for star Anthony Perkins' later work in 1983's *Psycho II*. A disturbed young man, fresh from a long stint in a mental hospital, meets with his parole officer to discuss his reentry into society after serving time for some unspeakable crime. However, this isn't Norman Bates, but rather one Dennis Pitt, a "reformed" arsonist who, we ultimately learn, "accidentally" set his aunt on fire years ago. A child trapped in a man's body, Pitt has an active imagination and lives in a fantasy world of his own making. He may be able to con his parole officer and the people in the quiet Massachusetts town that he relocates to, but he will soon meet his match in the form of a gorgeous teenage cheerleader (Tuesday Weld, never better), who catches his eye.

That's the basic set-up for a potent black comedy whose reputation continues to grow despite being a "hidden horror" in more ways than one. As a fan, I'm a prime example; being a traditionalist who seeks out films (old and new) on the big screen as much as humanly possible (living in a repertory-friendly city like New York sure helps), it wasn't until 2012 that I finally caught up with *Pretty Poison* (in a luscious new 35mm print) during a one-week revival engagement at the Big Apple's Film Forum. The movie had been on my bucket list ever since I read about it in an early '80s issue of *Fangoria*.

Buried upon its release by antsy distributor 20th Century Fox, *Pretty Poison* has continued to garner a cult sheen ever since. Perkins is wonderful as the awkward but likable Dennis, who tries to make a go of it by toiling in a paint manufacturing plant. Then he becomes smitten with the "innocent" Sue Ann Stepanek (Weld). He seduces her into his imaginary world of espionage (this was the era of prime Sean Connery-as-James Bond and TV's popular *The Man from U.N.C.L.E.*, where even President Kennedy professed his literary love for Ian Fleming). Perkins comes across as quite charming and funny in the scenes of his unusual courtship with the young high-school beauty, displaying none of Norman's trademark nervous tics and stammers. Dennis drafts Sue Ann into accompanying him on his latest secret mission: to sabotage the factory where he has just been fired, accusing the company of poisoning the local river (shades of the water-fluoridation conspiracy espoused by General Jack D. Ripper in 1964's *Dr. Strangelove*).

A quick study, Sue Ann seemingly buys Dennis' spiel hook, line, and sinker. But the girl has her own duplicitous agenda. Her mother (former B-movie starlet Beverly Garland of *It Conquered the World* and *Not of this Earth*) won't let her run around at night, so after Sue Ann shockingly murders a night watchman at the plant during an after-hours "assignment," she hatches a bloody plan to do away with Mom and run away with her older beau. See, all is not what it seems when it comes to Sue Ann, especially when we notice how cool and collected she appears bashing in the guard's head with a big pair of cable cutters while Dennis cowers in the shadows.

Adapting Stephen Geller's blandly titled novel *She Let Him Continue*, screenwriter Lorenzo Semple Jr., best known for his camp efforts (TV's *Batman* and such infamous feature films as 1976's *King Kong* and 1980's *Flash Gordon*), exhibits a subtlety and jet-black humor with *Pretty Poison* missing from his broad fantasy work. His dialogue crackles here, as in this amusing exchange between the two lovers:

Dennis: Boy. What a week. I met you on Monday, fell in love with you on Tuesday, Wednesday I was unfaithful, Thursday we killed a guy together. How about that for a crazy week, Sue Ann?

Sue Ann: Unfaithful Wednesday?

Dennis: I was just joking, Sue Ann. That was in another country. Forget it. I do, no kidding, love you. I love you.

(Funny how our antihero fell in love with Tuesday on Tuesday! Nice work, Mr. Semple.)

And, of course, there's Dennis' revelation to his dogged parole officer Azenauer (*Seconds'* John Randolph) regarding the harmless Sue Ann's true nature, which also explains the film's contradictory title: "There was some poison once, but no one recognized it. In fact, that poison was even quite... pretty-looking. So, the problem was, what to do about it? It took me some time to realize that what to do about it was very simple: nothing."

Despite its sunny summer setting, the film plays like classic film noir, as we witness the machinations of our erotically charged femme fatale and her ensnared chump. The only misstep *Pretty Poison* makes is its ultimate break from that James M. Cain tradition in the closing moments. (SPOILER ALERT) Without spelling out every detail, the now-incarcerated Dennis has convinced Azenauer in a roundabout way that Sue Ann is the real murderer (by now, she has also committed matricide and pinned that crime on poor Dennis as well). So the pseudo-Columbo returns to Sue Ann's town and almost immediately overhears the seductress hatching a new scheme with another love-struck dupe. In most film noir, things aren't wrapped up so tidily, and the villainess gets off scot-free. *Pretty Poison's* denouement reminds me of 1956's *The Bad Seed*, which trots out an outrageous *deus ex machina* lightning bolt to set things right in the moral universe.

Sadly, the cinematic career of neophyte director Noel Black never blossomed. The fact he frequently clashed with Weld on his debut feature (as well as studio Fox, which did not embrace his leisurely shooting schedule) probably did him no favors. Important critics like Pauline Kael and *Cult Movies'* Danny Peary ultimately championed *Pretty Poison*, but Black got shunted to TV for the decades that followed.

Paid a meager $75,000 for his work, Perkins delivers one of his best performances (funny, sympathetic, and finally tragic), though the actor report-edly found the film a slow-moving (it's not) affair. Garland, on the other hand, told *Fangoria* (#50, Jan. 1996) that she ranked *Pretty Poison*'s suspicious mom as her favorite screen role. Commenting on why the picture never caught on during its initial release, the actress replied, "*Pretty Poison* came out a few years ahead of its time. People were really not ready for that sort of movie. It was one of the first of its kind, and it's been copied many times since."

Well said, Bev. Who can argue with that?

Anthony Timpone served as Fangoria*'s editor-in-chief from 1987-2010 before moving on to manage the company's VOD/DVD divisions. In the 1990s, he helped guide the first three Fangoria feature films to the screen:* Mindwarp, Children of the Night *and* Severed Ties. *He served as associate producer to Bravo's* 100 Scariest Movie Moments *and has appeared on over 100 TV/radio shows, DVD features and documentaries. Tony produced/co-hosted Sirius XM's* Fangoria Radio *and is the author of* Men, Makeup and Monsters.

PSYCHO II 1983

BY JOHN SQUIRES

In 1982, over 20 years after Alfred Hitchcock turned his novel *Psycho* into a terrifying motion picture, Robert Bloch re-opened the doors to the infamous Bates Motel, once again unleashing its heir unto the world. In many ways ahead of its time, Bloch's se-quel took a meta approach to Norman Bates and his crazy cross-dressing ways—in the book, Norman

> "OH NORMAN, YOU'RE MAD, DON'T YOU KNOW THAT? YOU'RE MAD AS A HATTER."

breaks out of the mental hospital where he's been incarcerated and treks his way to Hollywood where a movie about the murders he committed is being made. Cue the satire of the Tinseltown movie-making machine, specifically the slasher films that came in *Psycho*'s wake, long before Wes Craven ever got around to doing it.

Not surprisingly, Universal's executives were hardly fans of Bloch's vision. They did, however, begin production on their own sequel to Hitchcock's classic the very same year, written by Tom Holland (who would go on to write and direct fan favorites such as *Fright Night* and *Child's Play*) and directed by Australian filmmaker and Hitchcock protégé Richard Franklin. Holland's script sees Norman released (much to the chagrin of Lila Loomis, sister to the murdered Marion Crane) from the mental institution after 22 years and returning to his old homestead. Though his doctors feel that he has shaken the evil that once resided within, bodies begin piling up almost as soon as

he is set free. Is "Mother" responsible for the bloodshed? Or are somebody else's fingerprints on the knife handle, with the intention of framing Norman?

Making any sequel is hard enough, but following up a masterpiece is a downright Herculean task that one would have to be a little foolish to even attempt. The greater the esteem given a classic film, the longer the shadow cast over its sequels; the original 1960 *Psycho* commands such massive respect that until very recently, I had written off its direct successor sight unseen, thinking there was no way it could possibly deserve its legacy. I figured here was just another waste-of-time, cash-grab horror sequel, and since nobody ever bothered to tell me otherwise, I stuck with that thought process for many years.

But then one day, the completist in me finally decided to dedicate an entire week to watching horror sequels I'd always passed over, with *Psycho II* topping the list. I was pleasantly surprised, nay, *shocked* at how worthwhile it was—and equally disappointed that nobody had ever pressed it upon me sooner! *Psycho II* is one of the most overlooked horror sequels of all time, which is a damn shame because it's also one of the best. In fact, it may very well be *the* best.

What makes Hitchcock's *Psycho* so effective is that not only is the viewer unaware of who the killer is until the very end, *the killer doesn't even know he's the killer. Psycho II* impressively utilizes these same two factors throughout, even though we, and Norman himself, are completely cognizant of what he did 22 years ago. Holland and Franklin brilliantly push the reset button, reintroducing us to Norman Bates and even inviting us to root for him. Having worked diligently to put "Mother" behind him, Norman spends the majority of the movie wondering if he has in fact truly been reformed, as his doctors seem to believe, or if he's the one responsible for the new batch of murders. His guess is as good as ours, and *Psycho II* doesn't make the guessing easy.

In one of my favorite scenes, Norman is preparing a late-night snack for Mary Samuels (Meg Tilly), a cute young girl working at the local diner who becomes a houseguest at the Bates residence. Always the gracious host, Norman makes her a sandwich; as he opens the kitchen drawer and sees a large knife staring back at him, we see in his face the fear of what he might end up doing if he were to pick up the blade. He closes the drawer, but when Mary finds the kitchen knife herself, she places it directly into Norman's hands. This act encapsulates the theme of *Psycho II*: every character and situation seems to be encouraging Norman to revert back to his old ways, with him fighting that temptation tooth and nail. It is this inner struggle—and wondering if our "hero" is about to plunge a knife into someone or simply go about a daily task—that makes *Psycho II* so compelling. Norman himself isn't sure either, a mind game that adds another brilliant layer of complexity.

Rather than going the easy route of writing a simple "horror icon set free" slasher flick, screenwriter Holland digs deep inside the mind of Norman Bates, a real treat for any fan of Hitchcock's classic. Best of all, as Holland himself states in an interview on Robert Galluzzo's must-see 2010 documentary *The Psycho Legacy*, "There's not a logic point in the sequel that doesn't come off the original, or that violates anything in the original." (If

only the same care and smarts were put into every horror sequel.) Holland's smart and respectful script is a veritable roller coaster of twists and turns, playing with audience expectations while keeping us on our toes and the edges of our seats.

In fact, it was Holland's care and attention to character that lured star Anthony Perkins back to the Bates Motel, and the role haunted him for the better part of his career. Perkins felt that a sequel to any film should be made only if there was an interesting story to tell about the characters from the original, rather than for financial reasons, and he found that story worth telling in Holland's script. (Before Perkins signed on, the project had been originally conceived as a made-for-TV movie, with Christopher Walken on the short list to play Norman. Can't help but wonder how *that* would've turned out.)

With a higher bar to match than perhaps any horror sequel ever made, before or since, it's doubly impressive that the results go down as satisfyingly tasty as one of Norman's famous toasted cheese sandwiches. Thanks to Franklin's tight direction, stunning cinematography (by frequent John Carpenter collaborator Dean Cundey) that would've made Hitchcock proud, a fresh new score by Jerry Goldsmith that's as layered as Perkins' exceptional performance, and a shocking finale that hits like a shovel to the head, the completed film fires on all cylinders from start to finish. Here is a sequel clearly made by people with an immense love and appreciation for the original; it had some large shoes to fill, yes, but *Psycho II* has some pretty damn big feet. Chock full of Hitchcockian suspense (and some terrific '80s-style gore gags that would've had The Master squirming in his seat with pudgy hands over his eyes), it actually feels like a follow-up to the 1960 original. Perhaps most impressively of all, *Psycho II* emerges from its predecessor's shadow as its own movie, a seemingly impossible feat that demands respect. If nobody has ever urged you to drop everything and give this one a watch, I hope I've just become that person for you. I only wish I had been turned on to it sooner myself.

John Squires was born and raised in Hampton Bays, New York, to parents who were cool enough to feed him a steady diet of Nightmare on Elm Street *sequels,* Goosebumps *books, and monster toys, ushering in a lifelong love of the macabre. Married and a whole lot hairier, he still spends the majority of his time playing with toys, watching horror movies, and writing about all of the above on his blog* Freddy In Space *as well as on FEARnet.*

Q 1982

BY PATRICK MATHEWES

> "WITH A WINGSPAN LIKE YOU'RE TALKING ABOUT HERE, THAT THING COULD FLY MILES INTO NEW YORK CITY EVERY DAY. AND IT WOULD DO THAT, OF COURSE, YOU KNOW, BECAUSE NEW YORK IS FAMOUS FOR GOOD EATING."

Thanks to Larry Cohen's career retrospective interview in V. Vale and Andrea Juno's *Re: Search #10: Incredibly Strange Films*, I had wanted to see *Q: The Winged Serpent* for a long time before I got the chance. *Q* was not exactly the sort of blockbuster title that most videocassette rental stores stocked in the late '80s; complicating matters further, I owned a Betamax. When I eventually found a tape of it, it was as outlandish as I expected while the actors' performances had a spontaneous feel, as if they had somehow been filmed in their real lives just as this giant monster began terrorizing New York City. A few months later, I saw my first John Cassavetes movie and felt much the same way…except I missed the blood and guts of the flying serpent's rampage. Subsequent viewings of *It's Alive* (1974) and *God Told Me To* (1976) sealed the deal—I'll always be a Cohen fan. I admire his guerilla approach, improvisational feel, and radical subtexts, but what keeps me watching is his ability to thrill while soliciting unexpected mirth.

As *Q* opens, Jimmy Quinn (Michael Moriarty) is having a really bad day. After failing to get a piano-playing gig at a Greenwich Village bar, he is coerced into joining a jewelry store robbery. While escaping from the botched heist, he is struck by a cab and loses the loot. Seeking sanctuary in the Chrysler Building, he impulsively climbs to the top of the tower where he discovers what may become the catalyst for changing his fortune: an enormous egg. Meanwhile, Detective Shepard (David Carradine) is not having any better luck with his murder investigations. His superior completely rejects Shepard's theory linking a flayed corpse and a headless window washer to the ancient Aztec worship of plumed serpent god Quetzalcoatl. Rumors persist that a giant bird is snatching victims from city rooftops, but no one has actually seen the feathered creature, turning Quinn's discovery of its lair into a potential nest egg for him if he can just figure out the best way to exploit it.

As Quinn, Moriarty gives one of the quirkiest, freewheeling performances of his career, very much like the scatting he does for his audition in the bar. In the commentary on the Blue Underground DVD, Cohen praises Moriarty's concentration, claiming, "He's in complete control of what's going on." The actor proved to be the perfect instrument for the frequently improvising Cohen who often rewrote scenes on the set just to keep from getting bored and frequently shouted new lines at Moriarty mid-scene. They collaborated on three more features—*The Stuff* (1985), *It's Alive III: Island of the Alive*, and *A Return to Salem's Lot* (both 1987)—although both regard *Q* as their best work together. In an interview with Tony Williams, Moriarty talks about how much the role means to him: "Some part of my soul immediately answered to Jimmy Quinn…a bigger-than-life symbol of a certain street creature. And, ironically, I still get street people in this city stop me and tell me how much they love *Q* and Jimmy Quinn." He goes on to describe seeing it in a 42nd Street cinema where the audience screamed and cheered, treating the film more like a stage play than a movie.

Supplementing Cohen's repertory group of excellent New York actors are Richard Roundtree and Candy Clark who both do fine work. But Moriarty aside, it is David Carradine who really shines, having signed on without a script as a favor when the director needed some fast star power to attract investors. The B-movie icon began filming his first scene just an hour or two after

flying into New York from the Cannes Film Festival. When he arrived on set, Cohen parked him on a barstool at Moriarty's jazz audition, fed him a couple lines of dialogue, and told him to react to whatever happened. Carradine seems bewildered and vulnerable, which perfectly suits his character at that point in the picture. He also seems very relaxed despite later confessing that this style of filmmaking so unnerved him that he walked outside and vomited the moment the cameras stopped rolling.

Even with the focus on character, *Q* is still a giant monster on a rampage flick. Inspired by the way *King Kong* immortalized the Empire State Building, Cohen wanted to do the same thing for the Chrysler Building. After six attempts, he finally gained permission to film inside the building, but only as

high as the observation deck. Of course, Cohen's guerilla sensibility led him and his crew to climb beyond that to the very tip of the tower for the explosive climax. The thunder of machine gun fire almost got the production kicked out of the city when the *New York Daily News* decried the disturbance. (Although Cohen stationed a camera crew on the streets below to catch crowd reactions, the pedestrians were so blasé about the loud gunfire that he had to reuse footage of a panicking crowd from *God Told Me To*.)

Except for the scenes at the nest (constructed in an abandoned police tower) and a couple of scenes which utilized miniatures and blue screens (shot at the director's California home), all the other footage set in the Chrysler Building was actually filmed on location. This realism helps keep the flying monster more believable as the small-scale rubber model constructed by Randy Cook and David Allen interacts with several New York landmarks. There was also a giant claw designed by Aiko that appears in two rooftop scenes where Q grabs victims. Other "actual-size" models were built but Cohen decided not to use them because he didn't want to fall into the fake-looking prop trap that plagued Dino De Laurentiis' 1976 *Kong* remake.

The budget ($1.1 million) and Cohen's own sensibilities kept the effects simple but effective. Rather than repeatedly showing the monster, the director frequently relied upon point-of-view shots from Q's perspective (filmed by Cohen with a daredevil helicopter pilot who zipped through the canyons of skyscrapers duplicating the creature's flight). My favorite of the serpent's appearances is even simpler: its shadow is shown sliding across the cityscape, winging through the sky in search of prey. Although I suspect cel animation was utilized, I'm not really sure how this effect was achieved. As Cohen says on the DVD commentary, "I just always have to do something completely ridiculous when I have no money."

Ironically, since *Q: The Winged Serpent* was quickly launched as an independent project after Cohen was fired as a director from his adaptation of *I, The Jury*, both ended up opening the same day. Four times as many people flocked to see *Q*, and it's not hard to understand why. Even non-genre fans appreciate its outré take on a big monster flick, with a focus on character as well as special effects and monster thrills. Cohen definitely succeeded in his quest to immortalize the Chrysler Building. As he told Amy Wallace in an interview for *The New Yorker*: "Every time I look up at that building, I feel it belongs to me."

Patrick Mathewes contributed essays on The Incredible Shrinking Man *and* Plan 9 from Outer Space *for* HORROR 101. *Although he enjoys managing a library, his all-time favorite job was projecting and introducing films in a small repertory cinema in Seattle. He lives in Oregon with his wife, ten geese, two dogs, three cats and twenty-something chickens. When not running trails, he can be found as psychotronicbeatnik on the Horror Boards at IMDb.*

QUATERMASS AND THE PIT 1967

BY DAVID SCHMIDT

In those dark ages before home video, a dedicated fan of the frightful and fantastic had to comb *TV Guide* looking for genre titles, frequently staying up for "The Late, Late, Late Show" to partake of a rare showing. In this case, it was well after midnight, I was deeply aware of the dark house...and the fact that I was the sole creature awake in it. I know I watched another movie afterward, probably a Jerry Lewis comedy or a Godzilla rampage, but I don't remember it. I was fourteen, I had just watched *Five Million Years to Earth*, and I was totally spooked.

> "WHAT'S BEEN UNCOVERED IS EVIL. AS ANCIENT AND DIABOLIC AS ANYTHING ON RECORD."

I'll never forget the chill I had that night.

Though I didn't know it then, *Five Million Years to Earth* was the U.S. release title for 1967's *Quatermass and the Pit*. It proved to be my introduction to Hammer Films, the writings of Nigel Kneale, and a whole lot of cosmic horror thrills to come.

The Quatermass stories are well-known in the UK. (The original TV broadcast of *Quatermass and the Pit* is estimated to have been seen by over 30% of the country's viewing audience and also appeared on the list of the British Film Institute's "100 Greatest British Television Programs.") Despite these honors, they haven't gained the same recognition in the States and many other countries.

Under various company names, Hammer Films had been scraping along since the '30s, making low-budget programs with mixed success. In 1955, Hammer had a surprise hit with the first big-screen adventure of rocket scientist Dr. Bernard Quatermass in *The Quatermass Xperiment*, based on Kneale's TV serial. They quickly followed with an adaptation of the sequel, *Quatermass II* (1957). The success of these films gave them the financial stability and marketplace visibility to make *The Curse of Frankenstein* later that year, a groundbreaking Gothic horror epic that would define the company's signature style for a generation. Kneale's third installment, *Quatermass and the Pit*, aired on TV in 1957, but ten years would pass before Hammer brought it to the the cinema, with Roy Ward Baker (*The Vampire Lovers, Asylum*) in the director's chair.

The story tells of a London Tube construction crew that unearths ancient fossils of early ape-men. The resulting archeological dig is further disrupted by the discovery of what is initially thought to be an unexploded bomb from the war, but turns out to be significantly larger. Enter the rebellious Quatermass (Andrew Keir), accompanied by Col. Breen (Julian Glover), the military advisor whom the government has foisted on his peaceful civilian aeronautics group.

Quatermass theorizes that the mysterious object is an alien spacecraft that has lain buried in the earth for five million years. While Breen dismisses his theory, Quatermass continues to investigate, aided by archeologist Prof. Roney (James Donald) and his assistant Barbara (Barbara Shelley). But when members of the bomb squad and digging crew begin to experience mysterious events, the trio realizes that the craft is alive and growing more active with its own sinister purpose.

Quatermass and the Pit is a great piece of sci-fi/horror, full of intriguing ideas, unnerving atmosphere, brisk action, and sinister implications. The script includes a dark thread of superstition and the occult when a "pentangle" is found inscribed in the ship's hull. Quatermass learns that the local area has long been considered haunted, plagued by poltergeist attacks and

ghostly apparitions of a hideous, horned dwarf. Further investigation traces its "evil" reputation back to the 13th century, with each incident tied to digging in the earth. The psychological and physical effects the enigmatic buried object exerts on the people around it start subtly, eventually escalating into mind-numbing assaults and violent psychokinetic displays. Ultimately, the ship's malevolent influence awakens primal memories in the London population, leading them to riot through the city, blindly obeying the "hive mind" and killing any outsiders to the alien order.

Within a year or two, I would stumble over the works of H.P. Lovecraft in my school library and be drawn in by the similarities. Kneale told writer Andy Murray that he had never read any of Lovecraft's work, but many elements of the author's "cosmic horror" are clearly present: an ancient eldritch object, the awakening of a distant sleeping intelligence, folklore and legend mixed with science, local residents subjected to invisible influence/corruption, alien forces unconcerned with our existence, and towering manifestations of evil.

This was also my entry drug for the horrors of Hammer. The feisty little British studio produced an impressive run of groundbreaking genre features, including a number that are considered absolute classics. Their rich performance style and scrappy resourcefulness seem drawn as much from the British theater tradition as the mainstream cinema industry. Once I started studying to be a filmmaker, I came to love and admire Hammer—I've found as much inspiration from the people behind the pictures as from the films themselves.

Quatermass and the Pit is worthy of attention, not only because it's a creepy, cracking good yarn, but because of its thematic richness. The digging of the pit seems a metaphor for exploring the cultural unconscious. In an article for *Sight and Sound*, Kneale says: "I was trying to give those stories some relevance to what is round us all today," calling *Quatermass and the Pit* "a race-hate fable" inspired by the then-current tensions and race-riots in Notting Hill. This fear of

the Other is strong and poignant, especially considering that it is Prof. Roney's "mutant outsider" who ultimately sacrifices himself to save the world.

Additionally, Kneale touches on other issues in a surprisingly prescient way, such as political paranoia and the creeping rise of the military-industrial complex (Quatermass seeing his rocket group being taken over by military concerns). The desire to create a base on the moon from which to wage nuclear war also sounds remarkably like the "Star Wars" programs of the '80s. In the longer BBC script, when given Col. Breen's explanation for the alien ship, a government official declines to look at the evidence because Breen's theory "feels right," sounding eerily like our modern political "truthiness." However, it's nice to see both spiritual and scientific sources providing not only clues to the truth, but solutions in the end.

The Quatermass films have been influential on a number of other films and TV programs, including the long-running *Doctor Who*, with its adventurer/scientist defending mankind. The idea of an unearthed alien object and extraterrestrial intelligences shaping our early development, evolution, and expanded intelligence reoccurs in *2001: A Space Odyssey* and other movies to this day.

However, Kneale's view of that alien influence is much darker than Kubrick's. Mankind is not significant to these aliens—we are the "insects" to them, nothing more than primitive creatures altered to be used as tools. We are the carriers of their legacy, their memories, and ultimately their xenophobia and hatred. Our civilization—as well as our warfare, contention, and violence—is the result of an unconscious attempt to reconstruct their past glories. *Quatermass and the Pit* ends on a dark note: Mankind may have survived, but we continue to carry within us the seeds of our own destruction.

David Schmidt grew up in the '70s watching movies & TV his parents didn't want him watching. As a result, he's the writer/director of two feature films, including the critically acclaimed Lovecraftian ghost story House of Black Wings, *and a Deathscribe audio drama winner for "The Change in Bucket County." Check him out at swordandcloak.com, or on YouTube where he posts short films and plays with puppets.*

RAZORBACK 1984

BY THOMAS T. SUEYRES

> "I DUNNO, THERE'S SOMETHING ABOUT BLASTING THE SHIT OUT OF A RAZORBACK THAT JUST BRIGHTENS UP MY WHOLE DAY."

In the cinematically liberated days of the '70s, British cinema always had a place in American theaters, as did Italian, French, Hong Kong and even Australian. While most Aussie cinema that got nice press in the States tended to be of the art-house and serious-drama variety, 1979 saw a little Australian indie film called *Mad Max* drive a white-line nightmare through cinema turnstiles around the world. In the much less open-minded '80s, *Mad Max 2* bludgeoned American box offices in 1982 under the title *The Road Warrior* with a $2.5 million opening weekend followed by week after week of multi-million dollar sales and a buzz that came on stronger than a supercharged V8. Hell, even my grandparents knew about *The Road Warrior*. Suddenly Aussie films became acceptable imports.

Like many, my introduction to Down Under cinema started off with George Miller and Peter Weir, but it grew well beyond that, to a point where I would be hunting down movies with actors and directors who I had cross-referenced from the indexes of trade-paperback movie guides (this was over 15 years before the invention of the IMDb in 1990). *Razorback* was a no-brainer, bagged and tagged in a Melbourne minute from my local mom-and-pop video store. Even with a low-def, pan-and-scan transfer, there was nothing on the horror shelves that even came close to matching *Razorback*'s atmospheric hybrid of giant animal and backwoods horror.

Starting life as a 1981 novel by what I suspect is a pseudonymed author, Peter Brennan, *Razorback* in print form is set against the backdrop of corporate empires, their lack of scruples, and the plight of the workers. A crusading American journalist, Beth, after seeing a news blurb about the hunting of kangaroos for the Petpak dog food company, plunges into the Aussie outback with her righteous fury and a few statistics. Once there, she singles out Jake Cullen, a professional kangaroo hunter with a limp caused by a run-in with giant boar that smashed into his house and stole his grandson from his crib. Left with bitter memories of a monkey trial (after which even his family rejects him), Jake is actually a conscientious hunter who knows that an uncontrolled kangaroo population leads to famine and economic disaster for humans in Australia. Oh, and that razorback that stole his baby? It's out there.

The novel mixes plot elements such as Petpak's illegal diamond smuggling operation with the then-hot-button issue of kangaroo hunting. As chapter heads, Brennan gives us large chunks of prose describing the giant boar hunting down its prey and surviving in the blistering heat, searching for water and smelling the blood of his next dinner. These interstitial bits are really the only point in which the razorback itself is actually in the story in present tense until the very end. Brennan's book is essentially a beach novel. Its 378 pages contain a huge amount of long-winded descriptive passages that exist to fill space between the covers and kill time while contracting melanoma.

The 1984 film adaptation is a completely different animal. Directed by Melbourne native Russell Mulcahy and adapted by American ex-pat Everett De Roche, the novel is stripped down and rebuilt like a Ford Falcon on a King's Cross lawn. De Roche, responsible for a stunning amount of certified Aussie classics including *Patrick* and *Long Weekend* (both 1978), *Road Games* (1981), and *Frog Dreaming* (1986), wisely chucks out most of the superfluous characters and political subplots about corporate greed and the plight of the kangaroo, refocusing the plotline upon the bloodthirsty beast.

Mulcahy cut his teeth in the entertainment industry directing a staggering 91 music videos, many of which are considered to be the most influential in the history of the medium, including The Buggles' landmark "Video Killed the Radio Star." His first entry into the film world was the very uncharacteristic, highly inflammatory docu-comedy *Derek and Clive Get the Horn* (1979). It wasn't until five years later that Mulcahy would start creating films that would redefine pop culture cinema.

Crusading journalist Beth Winters (Judy Morris) heads into the outback to expose the kangaroo hunting that goes into making dog food; her incandescent fury, a large part of the novel, is a little more under control here and makes for a more tolerable character. Jake Cullen (Bill Kerr) is now a boar hunter, so we can say good-bye to long, dry discussions about the ethics of hunting. With Beth in pursuit of her cause and Cullen in pursuit of his giant boar, both find themselves dodging the Baker brothers, Benny (Chris Haywood) and Dicko (David Argue), who run the Petpak plant. After a victim is literally torn out of a car by the boar, Jake gets fired up to finally bring the beast down, all the while avoiding the Baker brothers who are afraid that Jake might try to pin the crime on them. Meanwhile, Beth's husband Carl (an underachieving Gregory Harrison) arrives to find his wife gone missing and himself running afoul of both man and beast.

As bland as Beth and Carl are (Morris and Harrison's performances represent the film's only major stumbling blocks), Jake, Benny, and Dicko more than make up for it. Kerr plays Jake like a sort of guilt-ridden Richard Farnsworth of the outback, drawing the viewer in with his gritty determination. Like the book, Mulcahy uses the boar as a cut-away from the human action, but still wisely integrates it into the current timeline—sometimes just as a glimpsed silhouette on the horizon and sometimes dragging off the entire corner of some hick's house as he is watching TV (probably the film's most iconic sequence). Also, the Petpak plant is a nightmarish, ramshackle outfit that looks like something run by Leatherface after opening the Lament Configuration. Littered with bones, spattered with blood, and driven by steam, chains with hooks hang from the tin ceiling with chunks of meat dripping on the dirt floor. Backlit with fog crawling around its periphery, the slaughterhouse almost becomes a character of its own.

Director and screenwriter are perfectly paired, with Mulcahy's strong use of chiaroscuro and diegetic sound aligning perfectly with De Roche's grim outsider's view of outback hillbillies (which I remember finding terrifying as a teenager). It's a real shame they didn't go on to make more films together. Freed from the plastic pop culture of his music video past, Mulcahy creates an intensely atmospheric landscape with its roots steeped in Mario Bava's gothic horrors. Carl's near-death experience after being left to die in the outback by the Baker brothers is an intensely painted hallucination that evokes the likes of Alejandro Jodorowsky with a color palette that Richard Stanley would adopt years later for *Hardware* (1990). As it stands, *Razorback* is not only the best of breed, standing head and shoulders above its own imitators and knock-offs (such as the forgettable 2009 Korean horror-comedy *Chawz*), but also emerges as one of the finest entries in the genre.

Thomas T. Sueyres has been annoying people with his writing for almost 30 years. Starting with a high school 'zine, he went on to create the short-lived Video Junkie Magazine *which has been reincarnated in blog form. Mr. Sueyres studied Film and Journalism before obtaining a degree in Culinary Arts from JWU. Formerly known as Thomas T. Simmons, Mr. Sueyres has been to 20 of the 48 contingent states, and is absolutely not in a witness relocation program.*

THE REFLECTING SKIN 1990

BY DAVE ALEXANDER

The prairie is a paradox: a place of bounty and scarcity, virility and decay, the sublime and the surreal. You can see this in the juxtaposition of lush landscape paintings depicting thick wheat fields, warm sunsets and quaint farmhouses, with black-and-white photos of massive dust storms, crops decimated by grasshoppers and hollow-eyed farmers. For every grain elevator that rises stoically into the sky, there are a hundred abandoned farmhouses sinking into the soil. Nature, as indifferent as it is, can seem both nurturing and cruel. And therein sprouts the kernel of madness.

> "IT'S ALL SO HORRIBLE, ISN'T IT? THE NIGHTMARE OF CHILDHOOD. AND IT ONLY GETS WORSE."

Having grown up on the prairies of Alberta (in and around the northern city of Edmonton), I've always felt that schizophrenic relationship to the landscape. Once you get out to where dirt roads are lined with rusted barbed wire and the wind-whipped barns start their death-lean, there's mystery, danger, and the sense that anything can erode here, particularly your sanity.

No film has so fully explored the horrific possibilities of this place as *The Reflecting Skin* by Philip Ridley. The obscure 1990 feature takes the prairie gothic aesthetic made famous in paintings by the likes of Edward Hopper (*House by the Railroad*, 1925) and Andrew Wyeth (*Christina's World*, 1948) and renders it into a surreal world where delirium is the inevitable harvest of a place sowed with predators, cruelty, and the grotesque.

Wide-eyed Jeremy Cooper stars as Seth Dove, an eight-year-old growing up in post-WWII Idaho. The film opens with him cutting through a golden wheat field as he brings a huge toad to his friends, Kim and Eben. The Norman Rockwell tableau turns hideous when Seth sticks a reed in the creature's anus and inflates it, leaving it on its back in the middle of a dirt path. The boys hide and wait for a woman in black to walk by and look at the toad. Seth uses his slingshot to explode it all over her. Blood drips from her horrified face as the boys escape.

Seth returns home to a weather-beaten house, a yard full of decaying farm equipment and cars, and a ramshackle garage with gas pumps. The building's signage has partially collapsed, so what once read "Dove Garage" now reads "Dove rage"—a hint of things to come. Dove patriarch Luke (Duncan Fraser) lounges on a broken couch, reading pulp fiction about a prairie vampire. The bloodsucker on the cover—a pale, blonde woman in black—resembles the bloodied prank victim, Dolphin Blue (Lindsay Duncan).

When Seth's hysterical mother, Ruth (Sheila Moore), finds out about what happened, she sends the boy over to Dolphin's house to apologize. In one of the movie's most bizarre scenes, Seth sits in a room full of shark jaws, whale bones, and mounted fish, cradling a harpoon as the widow explains how her husband, who came from a family of whalers, hung himself in the barn a week after they were married. She opens a box of keepsakes that includes the dead man's glasses, a lock of his hair, and a tooth—all while bemoaning her fate and terrifying Seth with proclamations such as, "Sometimes terrible things happen quite naturally." He runs away, convinced that she's a vampire. From here, the boy's innocence isn't so much lost as torn out of him by the human monsters and monstrosity that surround him.

Soon, Seth discovers Eben's body floating in their well (water, drinking, bursting, and being drained are reoccurring motifs throughout). The police suspect Luke, who years earlier was caught kissing a seventeen-year-old boy. The real killers, however, appear to be four greasers who cruise the back roads in a giant black Cadillac that glides with the predatory menace of a steel shark (one that drinks gas at the Dove Garage).

The Reflecting Skin is layered with symbolic imagery that runs the gamut from arresting to absolutely shocking. For example, one character douses himself with gas and immolates himself in front of Seth. Later, the boy finds a maggoty dead baby that "smells like fish" in a barn and believes that it's Eben in angel form, so he hides it under his bed, taking it out at night to talk to it. Innocence is stillborn—the movie makes death and decay downright Shakespearian. (Ridley, also a celebrated playwright and visual artist, won awards for his literary film when it played the Cannes Film Festival.)

Even the one ray of hope in Seth's life is already dimming before it arrives. Seemingly normal older Dove brother Cameron (Viggo Mortensen) comes home from being stationed in Japan to tell stories of witnessing beautiful explosions. Before long, his hair starts to fall out, he loses weight and his gums bleed. Seth mistakes the radiation poisoning for the effects of vampirism (during scenes of Cameron's physical decline, Ridley added subtle bat noises to the soundtrack) due to his burgeoning relationship with Dolphin. Meanwhile,

another boy goes missing, Ruth slips further into hysteria, and that black Cadillac continues to circle ever closer....

There's certainly an established tradition of prairie gothic horror (notably in the novels and short stories of Flannery O'Connor), but nothing that approaches the hyperbolic trauma and morbid ick of *The Reflecting Skin*. The title is taken from a scene which perfectly encapsulates Ridley's sensibility: Cameron shows Seth a photo of a Japanese baby whose skin has turned silver due to the effects of the bomb, so that "you can see your face in it." Of course, here, "reflecting skin" also refers to the pale countenance of the vampire, that shiny metal Cadillac

and, of course, Seth himself, who reflects the real-life horrors around him as supernatural fancy (monsters, angels, etc.). In much the way our protagonist processes his world through the eyes of a child, Ridley approaches the prairie through the eyes of an outsider, reworking it into something new entirely.

For me, however, the movie is pure Canadiana, as the Alberta landscape is unmistakable. But what hews closer to the bone is a sense of something darker stirring beneath the black prairie soil. In the 1990s, I participated in a search for a friend's missing father who had disappeared and was believed murdered, the body dumped in rural Alberta. We looked into murky culverts, by the remains of rusted-out cars with trees growing through them, and into long-abandoned farmhouses. A few hours of this and the mind would play tricks; what looked through a grimy window like a body was just a pair of shoes and some clothes left behind decades earlier. The experience lowered a spooky shroud over that idyllic rural landscape that never fully lifted.

Other filmmakers have used this setting to explore their own brand of prairie gothic; Terence Malick's *Days of Heaven* (1978, also shot in Alberta) romanticizes it, while Terry Gilliam's *Tideland* (2005, shot in neighboring Saskatchewan) gave it a magical realism makeover. But the *Reflecting Skin* is the only work that explores the horrific implications of prairie gothic horror with such depth and flair for the surreal.

Beyond monsters real and imagined, beyond childhood trauma, and beyond the pale is a prairie that lives in the dark imagination. It's alive in the frames of *The Reflecting Skin*, where sometimes bad things happen quite naturally.

Dave Alexander is the editor-in-chief of Toronto's Rue Morgue *magazine. He moved to the city from Edmonton in 2005, after getting a degree in Film and Media Studies from the University of Alberta. He also programs films, hosts panels at the annual Festival of Fear, is a published fiction writer, and an award-winning filmmaker.*

THE SADIST 1963

BY ROBERT C. RING

> "YOU CAN'T REASON WITH THAT KID. HE WANTS BLOOD...AND NOBODY'S GONNA TALK HIM OUT OF IT."

I first saw *The Sadist* on Turner Classic Movies' *TCM Underground*, which I had gotten into the habit of staying up until the wee hours of Saturday morning to watch. Unfortunately, my body did not have the energy to match my cinephile desire that night, so despite being captivated by the methodic pace and camerawork of the opening, I was unable to remain fully alert throughout the rest of the feature. As a result, my mind perceived things on screen that could be explained only by the fact that I was passing in and out of a dream state. The bizarre mixed with both the horrific and the ordinary in such a way that I knew my rising subconscious must have filled in some of the blanks, but I couldn't say precisely where.

Eager to discover the true film beneath, I ordered a copy of *The Sadist* the next day. When it arrived, I put it in my DVD player to discover something amazing: it was the exact movie I remembered watching.

Three teachers (Richard Alden, Don Russell, and Helen Hovey) are on their way to a baseball game when their car breaks down. They pull into a deserted wrecking yard and wander the property, wondering whether they'll make it to the game on time. Enter Charlie Tibbs (Arch Hall Jr.), one of the most unique villains to set foot in the horror genre. Charlie's overblown hairstyle, childlike facial features, and oafish voice reveal a dementedness and limited mental capacity that make him both intimidating and indecipherable. He quickly proves himself effective at instilling terror in his victims, beginning with intimidation and petty theft. He then tears up their game tickets—a subtle but powerful gesture indicating he's not looking to gain anything from a practical standpoint; he simply wants to make them miserable. He eventually moves on to pistol-whipping one of them and briefly molesting another, taunting them while they sit bloody, disheveled, and helpless in the desert sun between moments of abuse. He orders them to fix his car, not with the promise of mercy but with the explanation that if they do so, they'll at least live until the car is fixed. All the while, Charlie laughs and drinks Coke, purposely fizzing it up before each sip.

As the sweltering day wears on and Charlie's actions become progressively malicious, the protagonists become more and more desperate in their attempts to escape. Initially, they try reasoning with him. Then they try begging. One teacher challenges Charlie to a fight. When none of these ideas have any effect, the characters make elaborate plans to distract him and run away, despite understanding the dangers of such an attempt. It is this aspect of the story that elevates *The Sadist* from boldness to brilliance. When the main characters devise their plans, our hopes rise. Precisely when our guard is down, Charlie heightens his malevolence. This pattern is repeated throughout the movie, with our dismay increasing each time.

Charlie threatens his victims, watching them cower in fear, but he also follows through with his threats and delights in their pain. He teases them to build their anger and then crushes their rebellion. In the film's most distressing scene, Charlie uses his Coke as a countdown to one teacher's execution, informing the unfortunate instructor that he will be shot when the drink is finished. He giggles throughout all of these events, but it's unclear whether his doing so is a sign of joy or an attempt to further antagonize his victims. Is he a true sadist, as the title and introduction suggest, or is he bent on revenge against a society that has wronged him?

As if the film itself weren't enough of an anomaly, the story behind its creation makes its well-executed nature even more surprising. The father-son duo of Arch Hall Sr. (proxy producer and owner of the production company, Fairway International Pictures) and Jr. made a number of flicks in their time, but none besides *The Sadist* approach any semblance of "good." One of them, the previous year's *Eegah*, was so ill-conceived that it has entered the ranks of *Mystery Science Theater 3000* immortality. As Hall Jr. tells film historian Tom Weaver in the latter's book of interviews, *Earth vs. the Sci-Fi Filmmakers*, the goal of the Hall films was nothing more than to provide "entertaining cannon fodder for the drive-in audiences." They never had enough money to make and market a film properly—they just made something that resembled a movie and hoped people happened to catch it at the drive-in.

Aside from being a difficult way to make a living, this dirt-budget approach proved dangerous to the well-being of the actors. Live bullets were used in most gunshot scenes, and gunpowder from one of the rare blanks used burned one actor's face so badly that he required first aid. In the set's closest call, Hall Jr. was thrown into a pit of poisonous snakes with their mouths sewn shut for a scene near the end of the film. After agitating the snakes so they would strike at the actor, the crew realized they had thrown him in with the wrong snakes—ones with nothing holding their mouths shut. The pit was too deep for Hall to escape from without assistance, and the entrance was blocked by a camera rig. Fortunately the crew was able to pull him out before he was bitten.

The Sadist had no business turning out to be a good film. Luckily, Hall Sr. happened to hire writer/director James Landis who was able to draft a great script, execute the surrounding elements with equal skill, and effectively coach the largely inexperienced actors through their paces. Future Oscar-winning cinematographer Vilmos Zsigmond also delivers a virtuosic performance, with eerie camera angles that squeeze as much horror as possible out of every scene.

Despite its quality, *The Sadist* suffered the fate of all other Fairway films and was not a widespread commercial success. This is partly because it was released during a bad time for independent filmmakers, and partly because Hall Sr. just wasn't a strong businessman. Hall Jr. tells Weaver that back then, the world of independent film distribution was one of "thieves and charlatans," while his dad was "of the mindset that people are just basically good at heart." He says his father did at one point receive an offer to work as a producer for Warner Bros., a job which likely would have pulled the family out of debt, but he declined, preferring to work for himself.

The Sadist serves as a textbook horror film, not because it follows convention, but because it balances a willingness to do anything with a discipline to do only that which works best to further the viewer's despair. Perhaps as amateur filmmakers, the Halls didn't feel tied to providing occasional relief for audiences or allowing characters to escape harm through virtue. This is where true horror comes from: knowing that a traumatizing event can occur to anyone at any time.

Robert C. Ring started writing horror film reviews in 2006 for Classic-Horror. com and eventually moved on to start The Sci-Fi Block, a film review site for the genre he loves equally. He is a fan of virtually every geek culture medium, a former writer in the competitive gaming community, and the author of Sci-Fi Movie Freak *and* The Year in StarCraft II: 2011. *His weaknesses include* The Venture Bros., Invincible, *and single-malt scotch.*

SANTA SANGRE 1989

BY SVEN SOETEMANS

"SHE'S A DEAF-MUTE, SO YOU CAN DO WHATEVER YOU WANT WITH HER AND NO ONE WILL HEAR HER."

More than just a movie...*Santa Sangre* is avant-garde cult cinema perfection! A bold opening statement, to be sure, but from start to finish, visionary writer/director Alejandro Jodorowsky cultivates one brilliant sequence after another, employing a staggering use of color shades, sensational aural cues, disturbing themes, and some of the most original onscreen imagery ever unfurled. As I drank it all in during my initial viewing—with eyes and mouth wide open—I kept thinking how I never wanted this movie to end. Hypnotizing and enticing, repugnant and crude, *Santa Sangre* is a thoroughly absorbing and unforgettable experience. While most horror/fantasy movies are straightforward efforts, Jodorowsky effortlessly incorporates various genres here. A genuine character-based drama and psychological thriller, it's equally a unique type of musical featuring ominous nonstop trance-inducing tunes and spellbinding ballads. If that isn't enough, it's also an experimental artistic display filled with uniquely bizarre visions and daring symbolism.

The story is divided between two separate timelines, both revolving around our main protagonist Fenix. Before flashing back to his childhood (where he is played by Jodorowsky's own son, Adan), the young man is shown residing in a mental institution, sitting naked in a tree with a large bird tattooed on his chest, clearly traumatized beyond repair. As the camera slowly zooms in on his phlegmatic features, we fade into the first (and most dazzling) part of the film: a 40-minute retrospective of Fenix's unpleasant upbringing. The son of traveling circus artists, and a promising young magician himself, the boy and his parents don't exactly form a model family unit. His obese, alcoholic, and aggressively dominant father Orgo (Guy Stockwell), the circus' director, engages in a barely concealed affair with the troupe's newest member, an obscene Tattooed Woman (Thelma Tixou). Meanwhile, his aerialist mother Concha (Blanca Guerra) is the leader of a dangerously fanatical cult—one whose glorification of an armless Goddess named Lirio antagonizes the local religious leaders to no end.

A series of traumatizing events soon follow, including the destruction of Concha's life's work, the death and subsequent funeral of a loyal circus animal, and a devastating "I-will-make-you-a-man" ritual executed upon Fenix by his brutal patriarch. However, the cherubic deaf-mute mime artist Alma (played in her younger incarnation by Faviola Elenka Tapia) always brings a slight bit of comfort and human warmth into the boy's sad life. His parents' final argument results in real tragedy, saddling young Fenix with the mother of all mental and emotional traumas.

This brilliantly choreographed opening act, filled with surreal colors and extraordinary occurrences, is indescribably unsettling and nightmarish, yet doesn't contain an overload of graphic imagery or violence. Like Tod Browning's classic film *Freaks*, Jodorowsky effectively uses the circus' unconventional setting, introducing a wide variety of eerie characters (midgets, clowns, white-faced acrobats, magicians) and unique horror/fantasy scenarios.

The second and larger chapter is less overwhelming in terms of spectacle and visuals as Jodorowsky gradually moves toward more familiar territory, uncovering darker, more grounded themes even within his fanciful plot contrivances. As a form of reintegration therapy, the institutionalized Fenix (now played by the director's older child, Axel) joins a group of Down syndrome patients (played by same—talk about controversial) during a field trip to the city. But instead of going to the movie theater as planned, the party accidentally ends up in the sinister red-light district of town. The adolescent Fenix spots the lewd Tattooed Woman in her new habitat; recognizing her, his blood begins to boil. Under the influence of his mother, who suddenly returns after many years absence, Fenix escapes the mental clinic and returns to show business with a totally new act. Concha remains dominant, though, employing her son as an instrument of vengeance. Only the reunion with his long-lost love Alma (Sabrina Dennison) can finally bring some peace and quiet into Fenix's unbalanced life.

Filmed with enough fascinating camera angles and color shades to make the head swim, this latter section is far bloodier than the first, with the uncanny circus setting replaced with grim, big-city ghettos rife with drug abuse and prostitution. The references to Freud's infamous Oedipus complex are genius and, like approximately ten thousand other great horror movies, *Santa Sangre* gives a big nod to Alfred Hitchcock's landmark *Psycho*. However, most of the supporting characters now evoke authentic sentiments of compassion and admiration, like the beautifully grown-up Alma and Fenix's amiable dwarf sidekick Aladin (Jesús Juárez).

During the opening credits, the very first name that appears onscreen, one that should have attentive genre fans sitting up to take notice, is that of Claudio Argento. Indeed, the younger brother of (and frequent producer for) multi-talented and versatile Italian director Dario made a side trip to Mexico in the late '80s, where he also co-wrote the *Santa Sangre* screenplay with

Jodorowsky and Roberto Leoni. Considering his impressive filmography, which includes George A. Romero's *Dawn of the Dead, Deep Red, Suspiria,* and many other motion pictures directed by his brother, it's no small thing to say that *Santa Sangre* stands as one of the high water marks on Argento's production resume.

Speaking of glory days, no one could have predicted that the film would prove to be Jodorowsky's greatest and most accessible masterwork. The

Chilean-born actor, writer, director, composer, producer, etc. already had two legendary early '70s "midnight movie" achievements to his legacy with *El Topo* (1970) and *The Holy Mountain* (1973), but had been absent from the director's chair for nearly a decade following the helming of the rarely seen 1980 elephant drama, *Tusk*. The iconoclast's decision to cast his own offspring in the lead roles also proves to have been a fortuitous one, as both Axel and young Adan tender brilliant portrayals. The rest of the terrific cast might not be familiar to viewers, the possible exceptions being Dean Stockwell's older brother Guy as the repulsive Orgo, and Blanca Guerra, a staple of Mexican film and television, who has also appeared in occasional English-language efforts like *Clear and Present Danger* and Alex Cox's *Walker*.

Special praise must be given to legendary horror composer Simon Boswell's soundtrack, a mixture of traditional Mexican folklore classics ("Besame Mucho," "Dejame Llorar") and original musical creations. Boswell, who collaborated on several Italian genre soundtracks like *Phenomena* and *Stagefright*, has also lent his estimable talents to slightly larger international horror productions like *Dust Devil, Lord of Illusions*, and 2012's ambitious omnibus project *The ABCs of Death*. To this day, the second song on the *Santa Sangre* soundtrack disc, entitled simply "Alma" in honor of Fenix's unforgettable silent sweetheart, can often bring tears to my eyes.

One of *Santa Sangre*'s promotional taglines states, "Forget everything you have ever seen." While this is a tall order to ask of any audience, I personally guarantee you have never witnessed anything like it before...and you will leave Jodorowsky's film a different person than when you began.

Sven Soetemans used to write an average of 10 horror/cult reviews per week on the IMDb website under the pseudonym Coventry. New career opportunities and a flourishing family life have marked a tremendous decrease in watching and reviewing films, but he doesn't really mind since it means more time spent with his adorable wife and son.

SEASON OF THE WITCH 1972

BY JUSTIN McKINNEY

> ### "THE LEAST-QUALIFIED PERSON TO UNDERSTAND A DREAM IS THE DREAMER."

There comes a time in each of our lives, particularly as we start getting a little older, when we take a long, hard look at what's going on. Are we where we want to be? Are we with the person we want to be with? Are we doing what we want to be doing? Are our needs being fulfilled? Are we *happy*? Despite having what many would consider a respectable and comfortable life, 40-something upper-middle-class Catholic housewife Joan Mitchell (Jan White) is at such a crossroads. Her grown daughter Nikki (Joedda McClain) no longer really needs a mother, and her neglectful, oft-absent, casually abusive, workaholic hubby Jack (Bill Thunhurst) offers her next to no physical affection or companionship and is completely oblivious to his wife's feelings and needs. Joan's very existence has deteriorated into running everyday errands, voicing unease to her shrink about what her life has become, and attending the occasional society party where she listens to fellow bored housewives gossip and complain. At one such party, Joan learns about Marion (Virginia Greenwald), a local woman who claims to be a witch. Later, she decides to accompany an equally jaded older friend (Ann Muffly) to the witch's home for a tarot card reading. Intrigued by this mysterious new lifestyle, the wheels are now set in motion for Joan to start reclaiming her life.

Falling between writer/director George A. Romero's trendsetting, rightfully famous, and much more commercially viable zombie films *Night of the Living Dead* and *Dawn of the Dead*, *Season* has long been considered an also-ran for the director. It came at a time when Romero and his colleagues at the Pittsburgh-based The Latent Image, Inc. were attempting to branch out and experiment with new things, which also resulted in the barely released 1971 romantic comedy *There's Always Vanilla*, 1973's reasonably successful *The Crazies* (a realistic grounding of Romero's "living dead" films), and even the TV sports documentary *O.J. Simpson: Juice on the Loose*. *Season* is certainly more low-key than most of Romero's other genre efforts, but it also shares a kinship with them in that it refuses to wallow in stereotypes. Instead, it utilizes horror elements to enhance what it has to say. Of all of Romero's films, the undervalued *Season* perhaps requires the most patience. It may take multiple viewings to fully appreciate, but many rewards lie in its meticulous structure. Nearly every single scene has purpose and meaning and nearly every character ties into its theme. Despite any rough edges, this is intelligent and mature adult horror with the kind of depth seldom seen in today's genre offerings.

Season is frequently written off as lesser Romero, and with that come criticisms leveled at the photography, acting, and editing. However, a case can be made for each of these. Filmed on grainy 16mm for a paltry $90,000 budget, everything looks quite muddy and drab, but this is a case where budget limitations are actually beneficial. The earthy, even ugly, look helps to perfectly capture the mundane suburban lifestyle. Several long dialogue scenes (one lasting nearly 15 minutes!) have a Cassavetes-like realism to them, with naturalistic acting and an almost improvisational air that make them feel like actual conversations instead of scripted dialogue. The sometimes jagged editing cuts, when applied to the various dream sequences, give them a chaotic, unpredictable punch just like real nightmares. Ironically, the movie's harshest critic is Romero himself. In a 2010 interview with movieweb.com, the director stated that *Season* was the only film that he "always felt was a real failure," and goes on to say that it's the only one he'd like to remake. Romero's feelings may have something to do with what was lost during the distribution process.

A talky, low-budget, non-exploitative, women's lib witchcraft flick is a difficult sell to begin with, but *Season* has been done a disservice over the years. Conceived and filmed as *Jack's Wife*, with a director-approved running time of 130 minutes, the film's distributor, Jack H. Harris, hacked out nearly *50 minutes* and released it as *Hungry Wives* instead, playing up the scant nude scenes in the trailer and trying to pass it off as a soft-porn flick. ("Caviar in the kitchen…Nothing in the bedroom!" read the poster taglines.) As a result, it failed to gain an appreciative audience in its day, bombed in theaters and then quickly sank into obscurity. (To this day, only a small portion of the omitted footage has been restored; the "extended cut" released by Anchor Bay in 2005 runs 104 minutes.) It wouldn't be until Romero's cult reputation increased that it was reissued as *Season of the Witch* with the director's name above the title. This new moniker not only recalls the eponymous Donovan song used during a montage sequence, but also the subtle use of seasons paralleling Joan's inner changes as the story progresses. After a rough winter of uncertainty and death, the lead character will be rejuvenated and reborn by the following spring.

One certainly doesn't need to be a feminist, a menopausal housewife, or a relic of the 1970s to relate to this material. Anyone who's ever done a little soul

searching, felt alienated by their surroundings or been unsatisfied by the compromises they've made should find something to grasp onto. The journey of self-discovery isn't an easy one for our protagonist. It's a battle with both external and internal forces that constantly threaten to tempt her back to the relative safety of her "normal" life. After many years of conservative complacency as wife and mother, dreams and desires left unfulfilled in the process, Joan is uptight, resentful, scared and apprehensive. Her reservations about life and the drastic changes she's contemplating are reflected in a series of skillfully directed, sometimes strikingly surreal nightmare sequences. Many of these involve a masked intruder, representative of Joan's anxieties as she fights through fears and insecurities to get where she wants to be. She later finds herself drawn to Gregg (Raymond Laine), an arrogant, perceptive student teacher who represents the "free love" hippie counterculture of the day. Carrying through on an affair with him not only gives the repressed housewife an alternative to her stuffy, empty existence and loveless marriage, but also reignites her passion for life by introducing elements of risk and danger into it, enabling her to finally take the plunge into witchcraft and walk on the dark side.

Joan's final words in the film are deceptively simple. As the camera closes in on her face right before the fade-out, she states, "I'm a witch." This is not a mere confession said with reservations, but a character revelation said with triumph, perfectly delivered by the lead actress with a knowing twinkle in her eyes. No longer "Jack's wife," a woman defined almost entirely by her husband, Joan now has freedom, a purpose, a place in this world and, perhaps most importantly of all, an identity.

Justin McKinney resides in Ohio. A lifelong horror fan, his love for the genre stems from a childhood viewing of Night of the Living Dead, *which traumatized him so much he refused to be left alone at night for years afterward. Away from his 9 to 5, he enjoys writing, acting, tennis and working in various capacities on film projects. He also runs The Bloody Pit of Horror blog, focusing on horror films made between 1950 and 1990.*

THE SENDER 1982

BY WILLIAM SEAN WILSON

"YOU CAN'T CONTROL IT; THAT'S WHAT REALLY SCARES YOU."

In mid-1981, my older sister and I achieved the impossible. We convinced our mother that allowing us to see R-rated movies in the theater was in our best interest. Fueled in equal parts by *Famous Monsters of Filmland* and *Fangoria*, our desires could not, would not be deprived and our powers of persuasion were mighty. Either that or the idea of living overseas in a foreign land with not much to do and two hyperactive kids convinced our mother that the realm of "Restricted" was okay for us. We soon found ourselves awash in a world of the forbidden.

Just over a year into our journey, we encountered *The Sender* at a half-empty military base cinema. I was familiar with the title thanks to an article in *Fangoria* #24, my interest piqued by a series of bloody stills, most notably the cover image of a severed head lying on the floor (amusingly, a shot that

didn't make it into the final product). What I wasn't prepared for was the film's eerie and spooky qualities, nor its focus on the theme of death (both matricide and suicide). It turned out to be the scariest movie I'd ever seen up to that point.

A young man (Zeljko Ivanek) wakes up alone in the forest. Dusting himself off, he begins walking down the road before he comes to a small public beach. He enters the area and slowly starts filling his clothing with large rocks before walking out into the water. This apparent suicide attempt results in his being placed in a state-run mental hospital where, because he appears to be suffering from amnesia, he is given the moniker John Doe #83. His assigned psychiatrist is Dr. Gail Farmer (Kathryn Harrold), an overworked single woman who is constantly coming into conflict with her colleague, Dr. Joseph Denman (Paul Freeman), over methods of rehabilitation. Dr. Farmer takes an almost motherly interest in her mysterious patient, but soon finds she is suffering from hallucinations. Things get even odder when Jerolyn (Shirley Knight), a woman professing to be John's mother, shows up wanting to reclaim her son, whom she refers to as "evil." Following a bit of electroshock therapy gone wrong, the doctors soon begin to suspect that John Doe #83 is a "sender," a telepathic person who can transfer his thoughts and nightmares to other people.

The most successful horror movies are obviously the ones that affect us. *The Sender* scared the hell out of me by introducing my 8-year-old self to a concept my formative brain had not encountered before. Death was no stranger, but I had never entertained the suggestion of suicide. The wordless opening five minutes proved to be the most terrifying thing I had ever witnessed as John Doe calmly stepped onto that tiny public beach to begin his death march. As he wades out into the water (masterfully handled with a crane shot that begins high above and slowly lowers to meet the protagonist in the face and then follows him under the surface) and tries to drown himself, my brain slowly processed this information. He wanted to kill himself and, even worse, was using rocks as leverage against his instinctive reflex to live. As if *Jaws* (1975) and *Piranha* (1978) hadn't scared me out of the water already. For weeks afterward, I was haunted by the image of this man filling his jacket with rocks (they got bigger and bigger in my mind) so that he might sink down to the bottom of a lake and end his life.

The creator of my nightmares was English filmmaker Roger Christian. It is incredibly rare for a neophyte to already have an Academy Award when making his feature-length debut; Christian had one win and one nomination for his art direction on *Star Wars* (1977) and *Alien* (1979), respectively. Yet his maiden voyage is unlike anything one would expect from someone known for their artistic contributions to big-budget sci-fi cinema; his work is never showy outside of a couple of hallucination sequences, opting instead for stark realism. The entire affair is low-key, harking back to an earlier era of horror. Perhaps regrettably, the film seems to be constantly overlooked due to a blemish on the director's filmography nearly two decades later—the lambasted L. Ron Hubbard adaptation *Battlefield Earth* (2000).

Christian applies this realistic approach to his casting as well, opting for mostly unknowns. The classically trained Ivanek, making his big-screen debut, eschews the eye popping and vein bulging seen in earlier telepathy pictures like *Carrie* (1976) and *Scanners* (1981), resulting in a much more subtle and relatable performance. Female lead Harrold is potentially recognizable to dedicated horror fans from her work in *Nightwing* and *Vampire* (both 1979). A clever bit of casting comes with Freeman, seen the previous summer as the villainous Belloq in *Raiders of the Lost Ark*, as her adversarial colleague.

Unfortunately, this kind of understated, psychological horror was completely the opposite of the market's then-current demands. I didn't realize at the time

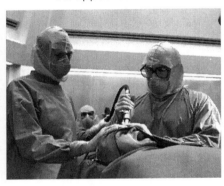

how lucky I was to have caught a theatrical showing. Paramount released *The Sender* on only 300 screens on October 22, 1982, where it opened in ninth place. It disappeared from theaters within a few weeks with a gross of just over $1 million dollars. By contrast, *Friday the 13th Part III*—Paramount's biggest horror release that year—made 34 times that amount at the box office. I wanted to talk about it, but none of my friends had seen it. It is here that I learned an early lesson that not all horror efforts are created (or received) equal.

Thankfully, the years have been kind to *The Sender*, as it has maintained a cult following and earned several prominent champions along the way. In 1988, Roger Ebert highlighted the film on an episode of *Siskel & Ebert* titled "Hidden Horror" (focusing on unheralded horror pics). More recently, director Quentin Tarantino named it his favorite horror of 1982 while *Fangoria* honored it with a 2012 retrospective. That a three-decades-old box office flop is still being discussed today is a testament to its quality.

Personally, a return to *The Sender* every few years is always welcome as it displays a certain growth within me. True, as a child I was drawn in by the visceral aspects and I'll never forget how it initially shocked me. Each subsequent viewing, however, reveals a new layer. In my mid-20s, I was mesmerized by Christian's understated direction, smooth camerawork and brilliant building of tension. Having survived into my mid-30s, I'm now taken in by the psychological aspects of Thomas Baum's screenplay dealing with everything from interpersonal politics to the unspoken relationship between mother and son. What more can you request of a horror flick than something that scares you to the core, but also makes you think? These frequent rewards are what keep me constantly recommending the film to anyone with an open mind.

William Sean Wilson is a film fanatic of the highest (and lowest) order. He graduated from The College of William & Mary in Williamsburg, Virginia, with a degree in Literary and Cultural Studies and his written work has appeared in several magazines including Fangoria *and on many websites. He is a co-contributor at* Video Junkie *and loves looking up information on horror films that never got made. When not watching good movies, he is usually watching really bad ones.*

THE SEVENTH VICTIM 1943

BY LEE PRICE

Produced in 1943, *The Seventh Victim* was the fourth horror gem to emerge from Val Lewton's "B" unit at RKO Pictures. Lewton promoted his trusted editor Mark Robson to the director's chair and populated the cast with familiar faces from the previous films. Critically panned at release, *The Seventh Victim* broke

> "ONE CAN TAKE EITHER STAIRCASE. I PREFER THE LEFT: THE SINISTER SIDE."

Lewton's string of commercial successes, considerably underperforming when compared with *Cat People* (1942), *I Walked with a Zombie*, and *The Leopard Man* (both 1943). In the years that followed, it was largely forgotten.

The Seventh Victim's theme of loneliness intensely resonates with me. While classic art house directors like Fellini, Bergman, Antonioni, and Tarkovsky have often explored the loneliness of the human condition, I've always appreciated discovering these themes in more unexpected places. I'm constantly on the lookout for the rare great comedies of loneliness—movies like Chaplin's *City Lights* or Billy Wilder's *The Apartment*. Best of all is to find loneliness beating at the heart of a fine horror story, such as *Peeping Tom* (1960), *May* (2002), or *Let the Right One In* (2008).

The Seventh Victim reminds me of an Edward Hopper painting come to life. Hopper gained fame for his haunting images of people alone in impersonal contemporary settings. In 1942, as Lewton launched his RKO horror unit, the artist created his most famous painting, *Nighthawks*, depicting a street corner at night, with four characters visible through the plate glass window of an ordinary-looking diner. As always with Hopper, each person appears to be utterly alone. It strongly resembles the world of *The Seventh Victim*. Looking at *Nighthawks*, one can imagine the man at the counter as a failed poet; the other male customer as tubercular, slowly wasting away. It's frighteningly easy to envision the woman leaving without a word, returning home to hang herself in an unfurnished apartment.

Val Lewton didn't take credit for *The Seventh Victim*'s screenplay, but he could have. He was responsible for the Greenwich Village setting, a great deal of the story, much of the dialogue, and the erudite references that deepen the narrative. He bookended the movie with two lines from 17th century poet John Donne's "Holy Sonnets," placing the verses on a stained glass window for the opening shot and then closing with the words spoken on the soundtrack:

"I runne to death, and death meets me as fast,
And all my pleasures are like yesterday."

Unusual for a Hollywood professional, Lewton deeply loved great literature. His choice of these lines was astute. Viewed within the context of the entire sonnet, the verses become even more chilling. Consider the lines that follow:

"I dare not move my dimme eyes any way,
Despair behind, and death before doth cast
Such terrour, and my feebled flesh doth waste
By sinne in it, which it t'wards hell doth weigh…"

This is the world of *The Seventh Victim*, too—a world where people live in despair, feel terror at the approach of death, and are helplessly pulled down by their pasts.

The story depicts a young woman's journey into darkness, as Mary Gibson (Kim Hunter) leaves a sheltered convent for New York City to find her missing older sister Jacqueline (Jean Brooks). For most of its length, the movie follows Mary on her quest, but viewer identification begins to shift when Jacqueline enters the film.

It's a "Once upon a time…" story. Once upon a time, a young lady became involved with a group of devil worshippers in New York City… Sound familiar? This could be the opening of a dark fairy tale about a young married woman named Rosemary or a successful entrepreneur named Jacqueline. But while *Rosemary's Baby* (1968) remains tightly focused on its devil worship plot, *The Seventh Victim* spreads a much wider net. Its Satanists are merely the bait to lure horror fans in—to borrow from Alfred Hitchcock, the black masses are the MacGuffin. The demons that rush Jacqueline toward death are far scarier than the evil toyed with by the devil cult—hers are much more effective at making the kill.

Even though *The Seventh Victim* failed to find a wide audience, its influence ran deep. Returning to work with the Lewton unit for the first time since *Cat People*, cinematographer Nicholas Musuraca continued to develop the emerg-

ing black-and-white palette of film noir, a style of filmmaking that was about to blossom (in a nightshade kind of way) the following year with films like *Phantom Lady* and *Double Indemnity*. The main characters' night walks through darkened Manhattan streets in both *Cat People* and *The Seventh Victim* are a virtual catalog of budding film noir imagery, with their deep shadows, single-source lighting, and expressionist touches.

In an interview published in the 1969 book *The Celluloid Muse*, Mark Robson reported that a group of English filmmakers—including director Carol Reed— were smitten with *The Seventh Victim* in the immediate post-war years. That's easy to believe since Reed's classic film noir *The Third Man* echoes it in several places. One of its greatest scenes merges two memorable moments from *The Seventh Victim*: The audience first sees Orson Welles' iconic Harry Lime

when his face is suddenly illuminated in the shadows of a city doorway. A car drives by and Harry has vanished. During *The Seventh Victim's* climactic nighttime walk through the city, the face of Jacqueline's knife-wielding pursuer is revealed in the shadows of a city doorway. Now recall the film's introduction of Jacqueline: Mary opens a door and is startled to find her missing sister standing there. The door closes and Mary immediately reopens it...only to find that Jacqueline has vanished. As with Harry Lime, Jacqueline has the advantage in this urban cat-and-mouse game because she knows how to maneuver through the dark city. I suspect that one of *The Third Man* principals—Carol Reed or perhaps Graham Greene or Orson Welles—was watching these scenes closely, taking notes.

General critical consensus suggests that yet another filmmaking genius was taking notes. There's the case of the shower scene. As Mary showers, the shadow of the mysterious Mrs. Redi (Mary Newton) appears against the shower curtain. Sound familiar? Hitchcock always playfully shied away from acknowledging his influences but it's well known that he kept an eye on his competition. The shadow of Mrs. Bates in *Psycho* is practically interchangeable with that of Mrs. Redi in *The Seventh Victim*. If Hitchcock indeed cribbed this, he borrowed from the best.

Through the work of Polanski, Reed, Hitchcock and a whole pack of film noir masters, key ideas and imagery from *The Seventh Victim* ripple outward in many directions. Somehow, this minor film from 1943 subtly managed to exert an enormous influence on the direction of cinema in the second half of the 20th century. (Can you imagine today's film culture without a shower scene?) *The Seventh Victim* is the hidden horror source, still capable of sending a shiver down the spine as it poetically rushes its characters toward death—and death meets them as fast.

Lee Price is a grantwriter specializing in arts and cultural organizations. He manages two blogs: one on tourism/history, Tour America's Treasures, and one devoted to cultural history, 21 Essays. He's published in-depth examinations of classic horror films on the latter, such as Der Golem, King Kong, The Beast from 20,000 Fathoms, *and* Creature from the Black Lagoon. *Lee lives in New Jersey with his wife, two children, and the family dog, Riley.*

SHOCK WAVES 1977

BY MICHAEL KLUG

"THERE IS DANGER HERE— DANGER IN THE WATER."

Once, they were almost human!

My older brother got me started down the "dark path" to my horror film obsession. Among the many classics he weaned me on as a kid, the titles that really stuck were the zombie flicks. *Shock Waves* (also known as *Death Corps*) was introduced to me in the midst of my blossoming love for the Romero flesh-eating variety of the undead.

Courtesy of some *Texas Chain Saw Massacre*-styled narration over a photographic still of a group of Nazis (the same ones we'll see later?), viewers are given a tantalizing, unsettling opening setup...while also becoming vividly aware they're about to watch a gritty, low-budget '70s horror flick. The meager $200K budget elevates the realistic atmosphere, with that grainy snapshot setting the stage for the scary goodness soon to be unveiled.

After a strange, eclipse-type situation on the open sea—as well as a debilitating run-in with an apparent ghost ship—the passengers and crew of the shipwrecked island-hopper *Bonaventure* find themselves stranded on a "deserted" island. Among the group, we find Brooke Adams (who would later fight the pod peeps of 1978's *Invasion of the Body Snatchers*), horror icon John Carradine, and yes, Flipper's best buddy Sandy (a now grown-up hottie Luke Halpin—complete with '70s porn-stache and feathered hair). Once on shore, they discover a run-down hotel (a giant salute to the production's location scout, who scored an *actual* abandoned Biltmore hotel in Florida for $250) and an equally run-down SS Commander, played by the legendary Peter Cushing.

As it turns out, the Commander was in charge of a group of Nazi super soldier experiments that culminated in "...a perfect weapon. A soldier capable of fighting under any conditions, adapting to any environment or climate, equally at home in the Russian winter or the African desert." However, the resulting monstrosities were too uncontrollable and horrific (even for the Nazi regime) to keep on the payroll. Thus, Cushing's character took them to sea, sank the ship, drowned the creatures and placed himself in "voluntary exile" in this lavish, but deserted hotel. (Was it deserted when he got there 30+ years ago? Hmmm...) This rambling exposition is all revealed in a lengthy monologue by the brilliant Cushing (both he and Carradine worked about four days for $5,000 each), and who doesn't love that camera shot through the lamp glass?

As fate and the movie's screenwriters would have it, the zombie soldiers have come back for revenge, and our mismatched group of sea-goers happens to have arrived just in time for the big show. We've got the usual band of characters here: the drunken cook (Don Stout), the annoying naysayer (Jack Davidson) who insists on carrying his luggage even in the most ridiculous of situations, his long-suffering wife (D.J. Sidney), the surly old sea captain (Carradine), the inexperienced shipmate (Halpin), the bikini-clad young beauty (Adams), and the seemingly cool, almost hippie-attitude loner (Fred Buch). The pleasure lies in watching these disparate personalities interact during a crisis, specifically when they find themselves hiding out in a huge refrigerator deep within the hotel (one of the film's best and creepiest sequences). If ever there were a moment to scream at the characters in a horror flick, this would be it. "Open the goddamned door!"

The performances are all serviceable. They're pros, but not given much to do other than scream, run through the mud, and look scared. Even before the you-know-what really hits the fan, we're treated to the usual in-fighting and disagreements. Kudos must be given to Adams' delivery of my favorite line: As our group settles in for their first night in the hotel, unaware of what is about to come looking for them, our hippie (Buch) is fast asleep as the rest of the

group is still trying to figure out what to do. Beverly (Sidney): "How can he just fall asleep like that?" Rose (Adams): "He played very hard today."

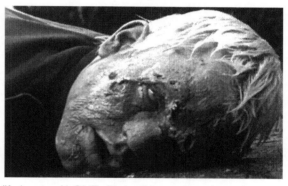

Multiple escape attempts, zombie attacks, and lots of wandering around the swamps later, the group's numbers dwindle as they encounter untimely and gruesome ends. This isn't a spoiler—the film starts out with Adams adrift in a life boat—ALONE. ("I don't know how long that dinghy floated around with me lying in it.") The opening sequence is revisited in the final moments—a nice little epilogue to balance out the nice little prologue... but there's a twist; nothing monumental, but effective and oh-so-depressing.

Then there are the zombies. Before anyone gets their panties in a bunch because these ghouls aren't hungry for flesh or brains, rest assured that they are *truly* scary. The recurring shots of these dudes rising from the depths (individual close-ups or panoramic views of the group—doesn't matter) are powerful enough to elicit shudders each and every time. They've got their darkened aviator goggles, their tattered SS uniforms and their rotten, fish-nibbled faces complete with oozing sores. They're strong, fast, stealthy, and identical—with the exception of one conspicuously corpulent soldier—making their numbers unclear. (There were actually only eight actors portraying this army of creatures.) Effective on dry land or at the ocean's bottom, they've got lots of advantages over our sad, unprepared little group.

Shock Waves benefits greatly from its disquietingly remote feel (despite being shot around the hopping Coral Gables area), Richard Einhorn's quirky and jarring synthesizer score, splendid underwater photography by Irving Pare and some sterling shoestring direction by co-writer Ken Wiederhorn, who conjures genuine tension, dread and that endearing '70s-era atmosphere. (Wiederhorn would go on to direct 1981's *Eyes of a Stranger* and the equally underrated *Return of the Living Dead Part 2* [1988].)

Despite its cult status, the film never found a huge audience, perhaps because of its low-budget pedigree with questionable subject matter (as opposed to how Nazis are *so* the rage right now). Or perhaps because the original negative apparently went missing 20 years ago. Or perhaps no one wanted a zombie flick without flesh-eaters. (They don't eat flesh? They don't bombard farmhouses or have voodoo connections? And they're *Nazis*? Who would make such a picture?) I personally recommend the 2003 Blue Underground DVD release, sourced from Wiederhorn's personal vault print with lots of fun extras.

While *Shock Waves* won't necessarily satisfy avid gorehounds (although the minimal and creative makeup effects by Alan Ormsby—a man with industry writing credits ranging from *Mulan* to *Cat People* to *Porky's II*—work well), it does have tense atmosphere in spades, horror film legends rounding out the cast, tremendously icky locations, Nazi zombies, and some really good "boo" moments. Plus, you've probably never seen it. Maybe you should.

> Michael Klug is a screenwriter, actor, and director born in South Dakota and currently living in Hollywood, California. Obsessed with zombies since his youth, most of his writing efforts (including "House of the Dead" at age 10) have revolved around flesh-eaters. His script, ME & SIMON BAKER, was a finalist in the 2012 Beverly Hills Film Festival screenwriting competition. For everything "klugula"-related, check out www.notmymess.com.

THE SIGNAL 2007

BY AARON GILLOTT

"DO YOU HAVE THE CRAZY?" Expectations, when great, are seldom met and tend to leave an impression of disappointment. I often find the opposite to also be true; the fewer expectations, the more gratifying when something turns out to be a jewel amidst detritus. With this in mind, it fills me with quiet dread that by cresting hopes right at the beginning, I could be setting *The Signal* up for a fall. However, to properly crow about one of the most interesting, smart, and creepy films that the horror genre has had to offer since the calendar struck 2000, superlatives are required.

Jacob Gentry, one of the movie's directors (yes, *one* of the directors), admits he and his cohorts wanted to do more than just pay lip service to genre conventions; instead they wanted to deliver "...a fresh and original

hyphenate that totally subverts expectations." He and fellow directors Dan Bush and David Bruckner had met in Atlanta (where the movie was shot) and had become friends though prior collaborations. According to Gentry (in an interview with indiewire.com), some of the more esoteric and challenging ideas forming the backbone of *The Signal* resulted from the trio's previous short film, *Exquisite Corpse*, where one of them would begin the story and the others would pick it up and take it in another direction.

It's in this hotbed of experimentation that *The Signal* was born, not only in their desire to make its content unconventional but also in terms of *how* the movie was made. To call it "risky" is an understatement. Shot over the course of thirteen days on a microbudget of $50,000, the apocalyptic setup is worthy of a Hollywood blockbuster: Due to a mysterious broadcast that causes madness and murderous behavior, a trinity of connected characters' lives (and minds) begin to unravel amidst a total societal breakdown. Further complicating matters, the creators' intentions from the outset were to have each director be in charge of how their plot segment would develop—deliberately using their idiosyncratic directorial styles—*and* to tell the story from the viewpoint of a different character. Bruckner's musings on this collaborative process suggest that at times reaching a compromise could verge on the surreal: "We began to make little deals: 'Okay, Dave, you can kill Jerry with the baseball bat, but Rod's gonna need to find something else to duct tape knives to because Lewis has the baseball bat at that point in *my* movie!'"

It should have proven a celluloid car crash, but through a combination of talent, creativity, and cinematic alchemy, it's a joy, with much of its strength coming from this unconventional structure and sensibility. The narrative is divided into three distinct "Transmissions," with Bruckner's strong opening, "Crazy in Love," an example of unadulterated horror; taut and stylish while creating the requisite suspense needed to drive the action. It barrels through plot exposition, although in a manner familiar to any consummate genre fan. It's a feint, and in hindsight a masterstroke by the filmmakers, using expectations against the viewer just before pulling the rug out from under us.

Gentry's segment, "The Jealousy Monster," is where the slap-in-the-face realization comes of just how *different* this film is going to be, doing exactly what the directors wanted—meeting expectations only to then subvert them. This middle entry is a total change of gear, a pitch black comedy with a dash of farce (though before "pure" horror lovers balk, note that this Transmission is punctuated with moments of brutally visceral, flinch-inducing violence, hitting with full force in relief to the comedy). It evokes the sheer lunacy of the Hatter's tea party, adds a pinch of *Monty Python* and throws in the terror of dining with Grandpa in *The Texas Chain Saw Massacre*.

"Escape from Terminus," as directed by Bush, is different yet again, taking time to acknowledge the science fiction angle of the story's premise, combined with some memorably mind-bending moments. Whilst managing to deftly bring together all the assembled threads, it also delivers an emotionally satisfying resolution that still remains rewardingly ambiguous. By this, I don't mean a cheap trick, twist or shock finale—the denouement is simply one that is open to interpretation, giving viewers food for thought as the credits roll.

Not content to go the usual "zombie apocalypse" route (where the narrative follows a band of survivors coping with hordes of crazies), the creative triptych have broached larger, more philosophical ideas.

Where their unique approach truly bears fruit is in the way it allows us inside the terrifying depiction of insanity that the signal causes. We bear witness to the infinitely more unsettling notion that these "mad" people, their perceptions altered by the signal, are completely unaware of their actions, believing them- selves to be acting in a perfectly logical fashion. It's chilling because there are no simple "heroes and villains" on these terms, not even "Us vs. Them." If psychosis and paranoia were communicable in this manner, "Them" could be "Us," and we would have absolutely no way of knowing—we might think we are acting reasonably by clubbing that old lady to death, convinced she is one of "Them," when we are really the insane ones, attacking someone without cause.

It's a concept that forces us to consider the essentially solipsist nature of our existence and reconsider how we define the boundaries of reality. We are slaves to perception and ego, our "objective reality" formed by consensus. If something were to change those perceptions on a grand scale, there no longer remains any ability to ascertain what is real and what is merely in our heads. It can be seen as commentary on an increasingly isolationist society, one ever more dependent on technology to mediate our interactions. It's also a stinging critique on how media can warp events and interpretations of same for the masses. With each segment viewed from a different character's perspective, the fragility of our definitions regarding sane/crazy or real/fantasy is brought into sharp focus; we could easily lose control of ourselves and yet remain perfectly oblivious. Moreover, this approach justifies and unites the three differing styles of the directors, emphasizing the individuality of each character and their perception of events as they unfold.

For such a modest movie, it's filled with big ideas done well. Though we can always wonder what might have been accomplished with a larger budget, the constraints seem to have been fertile ground for breeding solutions, proving the old maxim, "Necessity is the father of invention." *The Signal* is creative, intelligent, and one of the few movies that truly immerses the viewer in the terror of madness. Any fan of horror should seek it out. But then, that's just my perspective.

Aaron Gillott lives in Mexico with his ghoulfiend Angelia (to whom he is eternally indebted and indeed contractually obliged to mention her awesome taste in films) and their two teenage frankenbeasts (all proud horror lovers). He divides his time between teaching, cursing the utility companies with every dark art in the book, and writing when the moods are upon him. He also occasionally contributes movie reviews to www.gorepress.com.

SILENT SCREAM 1979

BY ROBERT FREESE

Four college students rent rooms in a Gothic manse where a deadly secret lurks behind the locked attic door. Within this simple premise, director Denny Harris crafted one of the most underrated thrillers released in the midst of the late '70s/early '80s slasher craze.

Suspense builds immediately as Lt. McGiver (Cameron Mitchell) and Sgt. Ruggin (Avery Schreiber) arrive at the Engels house after a grisly multiple slaying. We see blood and lifeless bodies, but little else is revealed. We are then introduced (via flashback) to our

> "I DON'T KNOW WHY YOU HAD TO BRING PEOPLE INTO THIS HOUSE. I TOLD YOU IT WAS GOING TO BE TOO DANGEROUS AND NOW LOOK WHAT SHE'S DONE!"

fresh-faced and attractive heroine, Scotty Parker (Rebecca Balding), a college student in dire need of housing. Her search leads her to the Engels house, a sprawling structure perched on a hill overlooking the Pacific Ocean. (The house used for the exteriors, the Smith Estate in Highland Park, California, served as the Merrye Mansion a dozen years before in Jack Hill's *Spider Baby, or The Maddest Story Ever Told*.) Scotty secures a room from young Mason Engels (Brad Rearden) and soon meets her other housemates, Doris (Juli Andelman), Jack (Steve Doubet) and Peter (John Widelock).

After unpacking her bags, Scotty lugs her empty luggage to the attic for storage. On her way she meets Mrs. Engels (Yvonne De Carlo), who seems to be keeping vigil on the upper floor. Unknown to Scotty, the eyes of Victoria

Engels (Barbara Steele) watch her from cracks in a nearby wall that hides a secret room.

Silent Scream (or *The Silent Scream*, as the title card reads) was a troubled production practically from its inception. Commercial director Harris was eager to break into features and felt the horror genre would be the most viable route. Using his own money, Harris began production in 1977. Unable to afford an agented text, he read every horror script he could lay hands on until settling on Wallace C. Bennett's screenplay. (Bennett had previously written 1974's chilling and underappreciated *Welcome to Arrow Beach*.) But, after a few weeks of shooting, the results were disappointing; the characters all fell flat, with no real suspense generated.

As Harris vainly attempted to edit his existing scenes into a coherent shocker, John Carpenter's *Halloween* opened to stunning reviews and revenue in the fall of 1978. Suddenly, every producer in Hollywood was scrounging for hack-and-whack scripts that could be made cheaply and turn a profit quickly. Harris sensed his moment had arrived.

Writers Jim and Ken Wheat were brought in to help rework Bennett's script, whereupon they also assumed the roles of producers. (The two would go on to pen a number of horror films, including *The Fly II* and the terror anthology

After Midnight—both 1989—as well as 2000's sci-fi/monster flick *Pitch Black*.) All but 12 minutes of footage from the original shoot were scrapped, along with several cast members, and a full re-shoot was soon underway. (At one point, Mason is shown watching a horror film on TV—actually excised scenes from the 1977 footage.) Mitchell, Schreiber, De Carlo, and Steele were brought in to lend some much-needed marquee value, while original cast members Balding, Andelman, Doubet, and Widelock returned for the massive overhaul. Interestingly, the character of Mason, with Rearden now in the role, was originally portrayed by Murray Langston aka "The Unknown Comic."

Sean Cunningham's cut-and-slash potboiler *Friday the 13th*, bloodier and more graphic than *Halloween*, made a fortune when it opened in May of 1980. As teen-kill movies blazed across screens nationwide, Harris, along with the brothers Wheat, finely tuned their shocker for market with editor Edward Salier. American Cinema Releasing officially opened the film wide in late summer 1980. While *Silent Scream* no doubt benefited from riding the wave of Cunningham's surprise hit, it was quickly capsized in the tsunami of exploitative babes-and-blades flicks. After an unremarkable theatrical release, it was unceremoniously dumped onto the home video market via the Media label where it became lost and mostly forgotten.

Many factors contributed to this unfortunate fate, not least of which being its failure to conform to the quickly established clichés of teen-chum cinema.

It offers no iconic killer, none of the subgenre's "creative" slayings and wasn't centered on a specific holiday or youthful rite of passage (i.e. *My Bloody Valentine*, *Prom Night*, etc.). Its setting was a far cry from the summer camps and college campuses in which most of the stab-and-die canon were set. Additionally, *Silent Scream* is a "slow-burn" style thriller, building upon its premise until the finale. Roger Kellaway's moody score works beautifully, but possesses no signature, easily identifiable melody (i.e. *Halloween*'s opening theme or *Friday the 13th*'s "Ki-ki-ki, Ma-ma-ma"). Finally, though it makes perfect sense, the title itself is shockingly generic, and the tepid and uninspiring ad campaigns didn't help the cause.

I didn't discover the film until the early '90s, finding a VHS copy in a record store cut-out bin. (Media had recently gone out of business and factory-sealed copies of their titles were showing up everywhere cheap.) From the handful of reviews I'd read, I knew only that it was of the early '80s stalk-and-kill vintage and that it starred Rebecca Balding from the 1981 creature feature *The Boogens*. I fell in love with it immediately. Because it was never made to cash in on the body count fad, it did not follow the "rules" of the subgenre, and the characters seemed like real people while the coastal locale gave it a fresh look.

Silent Scream is no *Halloween* clone, but what it shares with Carpenter's film is a reverence toward its true influence, Alfred Hitchcock's *Psycho*. It's an homage in the manner of William Castle's *Homicidal* and *Strait-Jacket* or Hammer's *Nightmare* and *Paranoiac*. Harris revealed in his final interview that *Psycho* was his favorite horror film. He refers to it as "character based," in which the characters are so well-drawn the audience is physically shocked when something horrible happens to them. The Hitchcock influence on Harris' film is evident, from its slow-burn approach, attention to character, and preoccupation with mental illness; the Mason character is very much in the Norman Bates mold while Mrs. Engels is a living Mrs. Bates.

Harris also delivers a number of visual flourishes, among the best being a scene where we spy Victoria staring into a mirror. As the camera advances, we see that the mirror is actually a portrait of a young Victoria. When the zoom suddenly stops, an aged, broken Victoria is revealed. The effect is jarring.

Thanks to Balding's innate "girl next door" charms, her Scotty is instantly likable and relatable. Andelman delivers an equally memorable, if somewhat sullen, performance, and Doubet plays well against the cliché of "heroic jock." Rearden deserves mention, too, for his fantastically layered and calculated portrayal of off-kilter voyeur Mason. It is Steele, though, who steals the show

as the enigmatic Victoria. Her incredibly expressive eyes reveal volumes of unspoken history and depth; it is a haunting performance that burrows under your skin.

All these wonderful disturbing bits add up to an entertaining edge-of-your-seat thriller that's well worth your 87 minutes.

Some thirty-plus years later, *Silent Scream* is ripe for rediscovery, standing high above the pack of generic slasher titles that have found their way into the cracks and crevices of time.

> *Robert Freese has been a horror fan ever since a late night viewing of* The Blob *on Shock Theater at age six. He currently contributes to* Scary Monsters \Magazine, The Phantom of the Movies' VideoScope *and* Drive-in of the Damned. *He also wrote the novel* Bijou of the Dead, *the sci-fi/horror novella* The Santa Thing *and the horror collection* 13 Frights.

SOCIETY 1989

BY SCOTT LeBRUN

> ### "WE'RE JUST ONE BIG HAPPY FAMILY...EXCEPT FOR A LITTLE INCEST AND PSYCHOSIS."

Every once in a while, horror movie fans are treated to that something special, a film that's marvelously quirky, not easily classifiable, genuinely twisted, and rather intelligent. An amalgam of ideas that coalesces into a striking whole. Such is the case with Brian Yuzna's outstanding directing debut, *Society*. Part of the appeal lies in the supposedly semi-autobiographical yet highly accessible screenplay by fellow first-timers Woody Keith and Rick Fry. If viewers have ever believed that they *must* have been adopted, they'll strongly identify with Billy Warlock's bewildered and increasingly apprehensive teen.

I was led to the wonders of this warped bit of cinema via the DVD revolution. Unlike many horror fanatics, mine was not a childhood highlighted by rampant video rentals. But once I realized just how much was out there for the taking, I purchased, either online or in brick-and-mortar stores, any terror flick that looked even remotely interesting. When I happened upon *Society*, I really knew nothing about it, which proved to be a bonus as this particular movie works best on unsuspecting minds.

Yuzna had already enjoyed a fair deal of success, developing projects for Charles Band's nascent Empire Pictures before serving as producer for Stuart Gordon's first few directorial efforts: *Re-Animator*, *Dolls*, and *From Beyond*. Fry brought the *Society* script to Yuzna, who instantly recognized the material's political nature and commercial potential. They coined the term "psycho fiction," enjoying the idea of a yarn where one person's paranoia would turn out to be justified. They also saw the possibility for a great deal of fun with the incestuous subject matter, knowing full well its taboo content.

In Beverly Hills, the handsome and popular Bill (Warlock) is starting to have his suspicions about the upper-crust family to which he belongs. His paranoia, fueled by bizarre dreams, is only amplified when his sister Jenny's (Patrice Jennings) ex-boyfriend (Tim Bartell) plays a freaky audio recording of a family get-together involving Jenny and Bill's parents (Charles Lucia, Connie Danese).

The opening scene introduces Bill's hallucinatory, ill-at-ease world nicely, first with little incidents such as maggots and worms crawling out of a just-bitten apple. (Yuzna shoots all of this in as straightforward a manner as possible—no need to embellish what is already promising to be insane.) These events turn out to all be just a nightmare, but a very prophetic one. Later, Bill glimpses Jenny in the shower, but his sister's nubile body appears to be twisted in some unnatural position. Slowly but surely, he comes to believe that his sis' ex might have been onto something....

Bill's worldview is soon shattered, as other adults and high school acquaintances reveal themselves to be more than your typical human beings, culminating in the you'll-have-to-see-it-to-believe-it "shunting" finale where the rich make mincemeat out of the lower class. There is a disarming parallel drawn between the shunting and dog breeding, as the blue-bloods need to keep up the quality of their flesh by introducing a few "mongrels" into their DNA on a regular basis. This mind-blowing climactic half hour doesn't involve blood or gore (perhaps hoping to dodge the increasingly sensitive MPAA's scissors), but it does dole out bucketloads of slime and eye-popping "surrealistic make-up effects" by the great Screaming Mad George. It's not often one can say a horror film is truly shocking, but *Society* admirably fills the bill. (The original final-act revelation was to have been more mundane—that of a cult making blood sacrifices—so genre fans should appreciate the filmmakers' opting for the crazier route.)

Society is part urban thriller, part social satire, and eventually, full-out outré horror. Yuzna nicely peoples the Keith/Fry script with offbeat characters and

delicious details, while the actors all do a super job at selling the demented material. Warlock, later a TV staple on *Baywatch* and *General Hospital*, has a likable presence as the lead and has some horror cred going for him—he's the eldest son of veteran stuntman Dick Warlock and had a small part in *Halloween II* in which his dad played Michael Myers. Evan Richards (*Down and Out in Beverly Hills*) is likewise endearing as his good friend Milo. Ravishing brunette Devin DeVasquez is extremely easy to watch as Clarissa, a society member deeply ambivalent about her position within it. Ben Meyerson is reasonably amusing as Bill's nemesis, a stereotypically smarmy jerk. Other familiar genre faces include Heidi Kozak (*Slumber Party Massacre II*), Brian Bremer (*Pumpkinhead*), and David Wiley (*Friday the 13th Part III*). Lucia (*Hospital Massacre*) is particularly funny as Billy's proud adoptive papa, whose face is integral to one of the film's most memorable images. Finally, hats off to the uncredited but extremely enthusiastic extras who ended up giving Yuzna more than he could have dreamed for the big finale.

Filmed in 1988, legal problems forced distributors to initially shelve *Society*, giving it a limited U.S. release in 1992. Unfortunately, American moviegoers just didn't know what to make of it at the time; it took the burgeoning home video market to turn the movie into a cult favorite. Meanwhile, European audiences were quicker to embrace it (despite its being dubbed "sodomy gore" at Cannes), the classist theme perhaps possessing greater resonance within their cultures.

Though it may garner recognition from diehard genre aficionados, *Society* remains undervalued by a larger audience. Part of the problem may be its limited availability—only a handful of out-of-print VHS and DVD versions (abetted by the occasional YouTube scofflaw) rescue it from complete obscurity. Strictly speaking, it's not attempting to be "scary" and only the shunting sequence really tips into horror waters. But Yuzna and Co. concentrate first and foremost on being original, a task at which they succeed wholeheartedly. I honestly haven't seen anything quite like it before or since. *Society* takes full advantage of a premise ripe with political and social relevance to push boundaries, visit strange places, and ultimately...blow our minds.

Scott LeBrun, otherwise known as Hey_Sweden at IMDb, considers himself a proud horror fan with a love of the genre lasting over a quarter century. By day a diligent employee for the Manitoba provincial government, by night a dedicated cinephile, nothing makes him happier than watching as many movies as he can get his hands on, writing about them every chance he gets, and discussing overlooked and underappreciated gems with like-minded individuals.

SPIDER BABY 1964

BY ERIKA INSTEAD

"NOW, CHILDREN, WE'VE GOT TO KEEP SOME SECRETS TODAY."

A dingy, dilapidated room. Tattered curtains. Dust and cobwebs. A joyful shriek, and then a dark-haired, petite young girl scurries arachnid-like into the room. "I caught you!" she proudly screeches, "I caught you!" Her posture is bent low towards the ground, eyes gleaming wild with excitement, an eager smile upon her lips. Her playfulness is betrayed by the menacingly poised chef's knives, one in each hand.

"I caught a big fat bug right in my spider web," she delightedly announces.

Her eyes never blink as she stares intensely, drawing nearer by the moment. The girl casts her tangled web of twine at her freshly caught prey. "And now the spider gets to give the bug a big sting." She menacingly smacks her blades together, hungrily licks her lips.

"Sting! Sting! Sting!"

And just like that, transfixed, trapped, the viewer becomes the big fat bug caught in the web that is the 1964 black-and-white horror/comedy, *Spider Baby, or the Maddest Story Ever Told*. This quirky film has stolen (and cannibalized) my heart, as I'm sure it has done to legions of fans in the decades since it began playing its deadly game of "spider."

From the moment horror legend Lon Chaney Jr.'s sinister cackling and crooning appears over *Spider Baby*'s opening credits, we realize we are about to experience a rare treat. Sweetly strange illustrations of the eclectic cast of characters and a spooky, kooky theme song serve to set the tone for this charmingly dark tale. Lyrics like, "Sit 'round the fire with this cup of brew / A fiend and a werewolf on each side of you / This cannibal orgy is strange to behold and the maddest story ever told!" convey its morbid, albeit lighthearted, tongue-in-cheek attitude. Even the film's title is a play on the 1965 biblical epic, *The Greatest Story Ever Told*.

We are then introduced to the wonderfully bizarre Merryes, a family cursed with a hereditary disease so rare that the only known sufferers are descendents of the Merrye bloodline. This ailment, thought to have been brought on by years of inbreeding, causes those afflicted to begin—around the age of ten—to regress to "a pre-human condition of savagery and cannibalism." The clan consists of three children: bug-eyed, slack-jawed Ralph (cult actor Sid Haig), the eldest, is a combination of childlike innocence and animal instinct; strait-laced blonde Elizabeth (former child actress Beverly Washburn) takes her role as big sister quite seriously; and impulsive brunette Virginia (Jill Banner in her film debut), the youngest, prefers playing her forbidden game of "spider" to following household rules.

After the death of their father, the Merrye children have been left in the care of their faithful and trusted chauffeur, Bruno, played lovingly by Chaney. The plot focuses on the fateful day that the family receives word that some distant relatives (Carol Ohmart and Quinn K. Redeker), the only known surviving heirs of the Merrye estate, are seeking to become the children's legal guardians. This has a chaotic impact upon the delicate balance Bruno has striven to maintain at their unusual household.

Spider Baby's set-up provides an ample mix of ominousness and humor as the audience becomes acquainted with the bizarre family through the eyes of the interlopers. Horror fans will especially enjoy the liberal seasoning of in-jokes as characters make references to Universal's monster pictures. Some citations are in straightforward conversations about horror films, others in referential dialogue such as when Chaney dramatically intones, "There's going to be a full moon tonight," a nod to his classic role in 1941's *The Wolf Man*.

Despite the plot ostensibly revolving around the Merrye clan's doomed fate, *Spider Baby* is truly Bruno's story and Chaney plays the role of the tortured, gentle giant so believably, with genuine tears in his eyes as he struggles to protect the children from the cruel outside world. A stark contrast to the gold-digging Ohmart and her conniving lawyer, seeking only to profit from the Merrye estate, it's heartbreaking to watch Bruno's mental and emotional decline that leads to his final act of loving desperation.

So why has this charming and unique piece of 1960s cinema taken so long to find its audience? *Spider Baby*'s success was impeded right from the start. When the film's original producers went bankrupt, their assets, which included *Spider Baby*, were held up in litigation. Writer/director Jack Hill was certain his project would forever be lost in legal limbo. As he explains in the documentary *The Hatching of Spider Baby*, "As far as I knew, nothing would ever happen with the movie. It was dead." Luckily for audiences he was wrong as it was briefly resurrected in 1968 for theatrical release. But whether fans just weren't prepared for its quirky strangeness or it was simply overlooked as one of the last of the dying breed of black-and-white features, we'll never know.

Despite its initial box office failure, the film must have made an impact on those fortunate enough to see it in theaters and drive-ins; by the time home video hit the market in the '80s, pirated videocassettes began making the rounds. A curious Hill obtained a copy, only to discover the heartbreakingly bad quality. Determined to see a proper release, he tracked down the negatives and, after

forging a purchase order, was able to obtain a video transfer from the negative. Hill then teamed up with trash film historian and enthusiast Johnny Legend to bring his true vision of *Spider Baby* to the public via videocassette. The fanbase of "Spider Baby-ites" (as Haig lovingly refers to them) continued to grow. Its popularity has led to festival and independent cinema screenings, DVD releases (Image Entertainment and Dark Sky Films), stage adaptations and even covers of the movie's theme song.

At one point in the film, Bruno tells the girls, "How many times do I have to tell you, just because something isn't good doesn't mean it's bad." Although that line specifically references the letter announcing their distant relatives' imminent arrival, the loyal chauffeur is also effectively voicing his love and devotion for this family. Despite their terrible deeds, Bruno will never be able to think of these children as "bad." Compassionate and sympathetic to their malady, he has become a true father figure in their lives. Beneath its monster-movie references, macabre atmosphere, tragic storyline, and twisted sense of humor, *Spider Baby* is at its heart an endearing tale of unconditional love. It is this universal and timeless theme that guarantees *Spider Baby* will continue to trap fans in its web for years to come.

> *Erika Instead hates being awake before noon and writing mini-bios. She enjoys bad photography, sleazy films from the '70s, cheezy flicks from the '80s and tacky tourist attractions. She is allowed to eat anything she catches and enjoys playing spider in her spare time.*

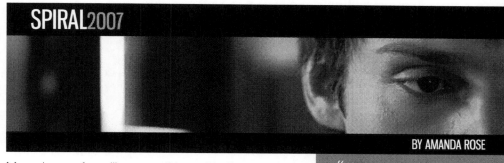

SPIRAL2007

BY AMANDA ROSE

Many horror fans like something with "in your face" gore, splatter, the works. Others enjoy a monster, demon, or werewolf. Lots more seek the thrills of the ghostly, relishing goosebumps crawling about on their skin. But for me, the best horror is discovered hiding insidiously in the mundane. The happy family moving into a new home. The friendly motel clerk checking you in.

> "TO ACCENTUATE SOME PARTS, YOU HAVE TO HIDE OTHERS."

However boring and routine your life, however quiet and *normal* your family and co-workers, the truth is it can all go horribly wrong, because we all go a little mad sometimes. In 1960, Alfred Hitchcock turned the mirror to face us, and had Norman Bates ask the question that we all occasionally ask... even to this day. A probing little splinter that lodges in our minds and gets us thinking — we *do* all go a little mad, sometimes, don't we?

Star Joel David Moore, well-versed in playing geeky and nerdy in films like *Hatchet*, *Dodgeball*, and *Avatar*, explores this idea with his intelligent feature *Spiral*, which he co-wrote (with Jeremy Danial Boreing) and co-directed (with Adam Green). Taking his lead from The Master of Suspense, Moore poses the questions: Does antisocial mean psychopathic? Where is the line drawn between real and imagined, between lonely and loony?

With its mere $600,000 budget, *Spiral* was never going to have a massive PR machine chugging away. It didn't have supremely controversial subject matter, and unlike Green's first feature, *Hatchet*, it wasn't considered too hardcore for the critics and didn't make horror headlines by pushing for an "R" rating.

Recognizing this, Green informed me the decision was made to release *Spiral* to just four theaters, for one weekend only, in order to attract mainstream reviews; despite a marketing budget of zero, it sold out every showing. It was later embraced on the festival circuit, winning The Gold Vision Award presented to the "most innovative and unique film with an inspiring and groundbreaking vision" at the 2007 Santa Barbara International Film Festival—an award not only of recognition but of financial distribution backing to the tune of $30,000. When I saw it during its European premiere at Frightfest in London, its quiet, creeping, rain-swept unfolding unsettled me in ways that anything more graphic or obvious could not have. Its growing, passionate following eventually led to a successful home video distribution deal with Anchor Bay. *Spiral* is the little independent film that *could*.

Some may feel *Spiral* doesn't deserve a place in the underrated "horror" rankings, but stick with me here. In the days that followed my initial viewing, I found myself looking askance at the people in my life who were quiet or withdrawn. I even found myself reevaluating my own behavior; what could be more horrific than planting doubt in a viewer's own mind? Jumps and screams are fun, but they don't keep us up at night thinking.

Mason (Moore) is, well, *different*. Reclusive, he avoids contact with all but a single childhood friend, now his supervisor at work, Berkeley (Zachary Levi). Berkeley tolerates Mason's unusual late-night telephone calls yet displays a level of co-dependence and genuine affection.

As an artist, Mason is immersed in his compositions and muses to a startling degree. There is a rigid structure to his life; there are *rules* to be followed. His models that he persuades to sit for him must adhere to these instructions—

specifically, there must not be any deviation from the poses he wishes to capture. He obsessively produces each piece, working toward the final pose, which ends as it must always end: the woman must be disposed of violently, in the bathroom, behind a closed door. In the days that follow, Mason is tortured by nightmares and visitations from his victim, and by the nameless fear of what lurks behind the bathroom door. He cannot find solace until the ritual starts again.

Enter Amber (Amber Tamblyn) as our next damsel in danger. She joins the company Mason works for and seems to like him despite his reticence at engaging with her. It's interesting to note that during their initial meeting, the two are physically very similar with identical hair color, sitting on the bench with in-turned feet, yet are polar opposites personality-wise; Amber's smiles and laughs contrasting Mason's expressionless monotone, her inquisitiveness to his indifference, her reaching out to his withdrawal.

Therein we see a reoccurring theme: contrast. Smooth shots of the city and bland everyday working life interspersed with jarring shots of mental instability. "Normal" Berkeley standing in the light, "abnormal" Mason waiting in the shadows. An original jazz soundtrack denotes breaks in reality while a contemporary recording ("Sometimes" by Alex Lloyd) reveals truths. By the time the credits roll, we are left with the ultimate contrast — what we think we know versus what is real. As their relationship unfolds, as Amber sits for Mason, as she challenges and then *breaks* the rules, it's no longer clear that we know what we know.

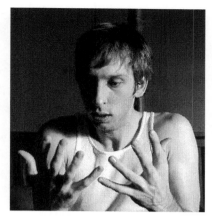

When I asked how it was bringing two directors to the process, Green said, "Since Joel was going to have his hands full acting, we did months of pre-production work to have everything on the same page creatively before rolling cameras, in an effort to not have to be figuring out what the vision was on the day." Putting in the hours beforehand paid off in spades. Moore gives an impressive, immersive performance as our troubled protagonist and Green's long-term director of photography, Will Barratt, offers a stylish, sometimes oppressive approach — his camera becomes a third character in what is often a two-hander between Moore and Tamblyn. Happily, Green also asserts that "Joel and I got along famously and never had any problems creatively or otherwise," a claim borne out by the clear intention of each scene.

As the final frames play out, there is a rapid reevaluation of what we have witnessed. While there is the expected desire to revisit the film, to see if the pieces fit, unlike a simple twist ending, there is also room for interpretation. In short, *Spiral* becomes a psychological exercise in "did he or didn't he?" — the reason you've probably never heard of it is not because it's undeserving but because it's a slow burn that requires actual audience investment. Not the sexiest pitch in today's hard-sell, high-concept market.

But if there is any viewer that will "get" *Spiral*, it's one from the horror community. Usually seen as *different* by the mainstream, horror fans know something of the funny looks and awkward silences that ensue upon revealing their predilection for the dark heart of cinema. Before the advent of the internet, horror fans had no platform to access each other. Unless they happened to catch each other's eyes in a mom-and-pop VHS store, poring over the latest video nasties, it was all too easy to feel alone in one's viewing preferences. Who better to empathize with poor Mason and his inability to just be like everyone else?

Amanda Rose has lived her whole life in London, UK. A nudging-40 mother of four, she doesn't paint the stereotypical picture of a horror fan — looking more chick flick than chick dismemberment — but is passionate about the genre. This love led her to working for Frightfest, the UK's biggest horror film festival. She hopes for the days when horror will regularly blaze a bloody trail to the Academy Awards; for the mainstream recognition that some of the genre's offerings truly deserve.

THE SPIRAL STAIRCASE 1945

BY MARK EASTEADT

> **"YOU SHOULD RUN AWAY. LEAVE THIS HOUSE TONIGHT, IF YOU KNOW WHAT'S GOOD FOR YOU."**

I always enjoyed scary movies growing up, but I became a true horror fan in my early 30s. In the process of playing catch-up, I found myself exploring all kinds of subgenres and time periods. It was during a rush of older black-and-white horror films (during which I also came across future favorites *Gaslight*, *Curse of the Demon*, *The Haunting*, and *The Innocents*) that I first encountered *The Spiral Staircase*. The fine acting first drew my attention, followed by the stellar cinematography and haunting score. But as the story progressed, I kept noticing how far-reaching this unsung classic had been. From its early, almost elegiac murder sequence to its breathtaking finale, the film has exerted an enormous, but quiet, amount of influence.

The Spiral Staircase tells the story of Helen, a young woman mute due to a past familial trauma, who is employed at an eerie old mansion. As fate would have it, there is also a killer on the loose murdering women who have physical defects or afflictions. As she approaches the house to begin her shift, the rain starts to pour and she is pursued through the woods by a figure cloaked by darkness and a long, black raincoat. As she enters the house unaware and unscathed, with the killer watching from the trees, we know that she is in for a long night and we are in for some suspense. The house is peopled with family and household staff that all come under suspicion at one point or another. The scares and the fun come while trying to figure out, along with Helen, whom she should trust and whom she should flee.

First and foremost, this is a film held together by its wonderful acting. Whether it is Elsa Lanchester (best known as the titular *Bride of Frankenstein* 10 years earlier) as the brandy-stealing-and-swilling maid, Ethel Barrymore as the feisty and persnickety old dame of the house, or Gordon Oliver as the blunt, cold-hearted, black-sheep son, each actor builds an identifiable character with their own personality. While all the performances range from good to excellent, it is Dorothy McGuire's Helen that serves as our anchor. Her mute heroine is almost universally liked by everyone else onscreen and, in fact, they seem almost inordinately preoccupied with making sure she is looked after. At first, it seems odd that everyone is so concerned with her safety and well-being; such a "nice" character could easily come across as both cloying and fake. But thanks to McGuire's heartfelt, warm, and sincere performance, we believe her whether she's looking with wide-eyed admiration at the young doctor, smiling bemusedly at the tipsy maid, or silently screaming in fear or frustration. McGuire imbues the character with a slowly emerging core strength and determination

that undergirds her seeming fragility. Her nuanced portrayal makes the character not just likable, but real, and we find ourselves rooting for her right along with everyone else.

All of these great turns are given added depth by the great cinematography and fitting score by Nicholas Musuraca and Roy Webb, respectively. Musuraca and Webb—who also collaborated on such classic Val Lewton efforts as *Bedlam*, *The Ghost Ship*, *The Seventh Victim*, *Cat People,* and its sequel, *The Curse of the Cat People*—were artists who knew how to use shadows and light and musical instruments to deepen and heighten the audience experience. Bringing it all together is director Robert Siodmak, brother of *Wolf Man* creator Curt and director of such memorable horror and noir films as *Son of Dracula*, *The Killers*, and *Criss Cross*.

Even with all the quality on display, it is the little touches with long reaches that keep me coming back every few years. In the very first scene, we are treated to an extreme close-up of the killer's eye as he lays in wait for the right moment to spring out at his victim. I can remember immediately thinking of a *very* similar shot in Bob Clark's 1974 classic *Black Christmas*, even down to the killer hiding in a closet, his eye visible through the hangers and clothes. Intriguingly, we can follow the path of descent from *The Spiral Staircase* through *Black Christmas* all the way to the American slasher films of the late 1970s and 1980s. However, one first has to take a side trip to Europe, specifically Italy in the 1960s and 1970s, before coming back to America.

During that time, Italian filmmakers like Mario Bava, Dario Argento, and Umberto Lenzi popularized a genre of murder mysteries known as "gialli." Most shared some key features including first-person POV shots, a black-gloved murderer with psychosexual issues that inform his motive for killing, and artistically shot murder scenes, to name a few. One doesn't have to even pay close attention to find all these in *The Spiral Staircase*. Not only were these filmmakers inspired by Siodmak's 1945 feature, they often directly referenced it—both Argento (*Profondo Rosso*) and Fulci (*The New York Ripper*) featured a killer hiding in a closet while Lenzi essentially remade it in 1972 as *Knife of Ice*.

It is easy to see the giallo influences on *Black Christmas*, which in turn, inspired John Carpenter's *Halloween*, the first true slasher.

One final thought: It's possible that being made under the strict confines of the Hays Code actually benefited the *The Spiral Staircase*. The two truly memorable murder scenes are made so because Siodmak and Co. weren't allowed to show anything. While the Code often kept filmmakers from tackling subjects in an honest, straightforward way, it also forced them to find creative devices to inject and discuss ideas like violence and sex. These two scenes—much more so than if they had just showed a commonplace over-the-top strangulation and stabbing—inform us about the characters involved while adding thematically and symbolically to the movie overall. I'm not arguing for censorship, but rather for the idea that less *can* be more, or maybe more specifically, that sometimes having limitations forces artists to avoid the easy route and find a *better* way.

> *Mark Easteadt lives with his family in Lancaster County, PA. He could tell you what he does for a living, but he finds that to be one of the least interesting things about his life. Outside of work, he is a father, husband, Sunday school teacher, reader, movie and music lover, NY Giants fan, NY Yankees fan, and someday wants to grow a big, fluffy beard.*

SQUIRM 1976

BY JASON HIGNITE

"YOU GONNA BE DA' WORM FACE!"

Horror films quite often draw inspiration from sensationalized public sentiment. The 1970s infestation craze seemed to follow the environmental enlightenment of the late 1960s. As people were becoming aware of mankind's influence on nature, filmmakers responded with schlocky shockers like 1972's *Frogs* and *Night of the Lepus*, *Phase IV* (1974), *Bug* (1975), *Kingdom of the Spiders* and *Empire of the Ants* (both 1977), and the 1978 hat trick of *The Swarm*, *Piranha*, and *The Bees*. With its plot concerning hundreds of thousands of worms decimating a small town, *Squirm* was right at home nestled within this "animals attack" milieu, playing upon the widely held notion that Mother Nature was not happy...and ready to revolt.

The late '70s were also a pivotal point in film culture. Drive-in theaters were still going strong, with almost every indie film—including creepy crawly creature features—getting a theatrical release. But the local video store single-handedly changed the course for distribution of low-budget indie films. It was much cheaper to produce VHS tapes than 35mm prints, movies could circulate on and off rental shelves indefinitely, and (unlike the weather-dependent drive-ins) people could watch them year-round from the comfort of their home.

Thankfully, a nationwide audience got to experience writer/director Jeff Lieberman's full-scale nightcrawler nightmare in a crowded cinema or a dusty drive-in just in the nick of time. In a recent conversation, Lieberman divulged that he never intended any social message as subtext. "I was just attempting to make my first movie as entertaining as possible. My model was actually *The Birds*." Not only was this Lieberman's debut, *Squirm* also featured some of special effects makeup master Rick Baker's earliest work.

The story is simple: pummeled by a fierce storm, a high-tension power line transmission tower outside Fly Creek, Georgia, topples in the wind, sending a constant surge of electricity into the ground. This act results in Fly Creek being left without power or means of communication with the outside world. More importantly, the electricity is driving millions of carnivorous biting worms to the surface...and into town.

Geri (Patricia Pearcy) lives a quiet, small-town life with her mom and sister in Fly Creek, with the storm hitting just as her new "big city" boyfriend Mick (Don Scardino) is arriving via bus. As the agitated worms find their way into more populated areas, weird things begin to happen, such as the iconic moment where Mick finds a worm in his egg cream at the local diner. The event creates a big scene, but the worm manages to squirm away (see what I did there?) before anyone else sees it. The sheriff (Peter MacLean) labels Mick a trouble-maker and, as people begin to go missing and are ultimately found dead, the suspicious lawman becomes convinced that this urban outsider is the culprit.

Squirm culminates in a writhing invertebrate bloodbath of ridiculous pro-portions. How ridiculous? The production found itself ordering shipments of 250,000 worms at a time. "We not only wiped out the Glycera [blood worm, often used as fishing bait] population in New England that year," laughs Lieberman, "but also got thousands of other worms of varying species from other places and mixed them in figuring, hey, a worm's a worm, right? Who's looking that closely?" The footage of these frightening-looking creatures, in-tensely detailed and in-your-face, was captured the old fashioned way. "We used a macro lens mounted right on the floor, then shocked the worms with electricity to open their mouths."

Had casting taken a different route, this movie would likely be more talked about than it is. "Martin Sheen was actually cast for the lead of Mick, but when we met about the part it didn't seem that this material was right for him. Kim Basinger came in and read, but I thought she was too good-looking and nobody would believe she lived next to a worm farm. Although I loved Sylvester Stallone in *Lords of Flatbush*, I thought he'd be totally wrong for Roger once we re-set the movie down south, so we never brought him in."

Though these performances would

have been interesting, *Squirm* was cast perfectly. Pearcy, Scardino, and MacLean, as well as the rest of the cast, brought exactly what the story needed. To even come close to really "selling" a schlock film, the filmmaker needs to make as much of it as believable as possible to mitigate the outrageous. Using lesser-known actors who look, talk, walk, etc. just like people in your own town gives *Squirm* an honesty that allows the viewers to invest themselves in the story.

Over the years, the worm-infested flick has left its mark, hitting the drive-in culture's autumn years, gaining ground as an early video rental store favorite before going gangbusters with late-night horror-hosted programming. (*Squirm* was also one of the last features hosted/roasted on *Mystery Science Theater 3000*.) Additionally, throughout the 1980s, Atlanta cable giant TBS often played *Squirm* after its televised Braves baseball games, with announcer Skip Caray offering an autographed baseball to any fan that would watch *Squirm* and then submit a review to the station. TBS received literally thousands of reviews, making it one of the most-reviewed films in history.

Like many, I first encountered *Squirm* at home. Phoenix, Arizona, 1982, to be exact, lying on the living room floor watching *Friday Night Frights* with my dad. My mom had made pasta for dinner, and my dad thought it would be funny to play a little trick. Grabbing a handful of wet spaghetti, he dropped it on me right just as the worms started attacking some guy's face. With the wet, slimy noodles hitting my head, face, and neck, I came up swinging—sweating and pulse racing. Through the trauma, even at a young age, I realized that it wasn't dad's prank that scared me; it was this film. It was a magic moment for me—to realize that something captured by a camera from years before could climb inside and affect me like that. I was hooked.

Though it may not be one of the most well-known white-knucklers for today's generation, the low-budget wriggler's influence was far reaching. "Many guys your age, including Eli Roth and Guillermo del Toro, have told me that *Squirm* made a big impression on them," says Lieberman. "When making a silly, fun matinee-style movie like that, it never occurs to anyone that it will be taken for anything but that; certainly not that it will last in the public's mind longer than the few months it's in release. Don't forget, there was no home video yet, so

the idea of it being presented over and over to generation after generation was not on the radar." Thank the film gods for VHS!

Lieberman's rookie effort was not the first scary movie I ever saw (*Shriek of the Mutilated*), and it is by no means my favorite fright flick (countless, depending on my mood at any given time). But even though I spent my younger years growing up as a monster kid, it was *Squirm* that made me love horror films.

Jason Hignite is a writer for HorrorHound *magazine. He reviews independent horror films for the "Indie Spotlight" section, as well as penning the occasional article. He also serves as the director of the HorrorHound Film Festival at Horror-Hound Weekend Conventions in the spring and fall of each year. His affinity for horror stems directly from a childhood love for late night horror hosts.*

A TALE OF TWO SISTERS 2003

BY BRETT NEVEU

I first encountered *A Tale of Two Sisters* on one of those nights where fanatical recommendations call out from the digital ether. I was scouting a few movie-related internet sites, reading about various under-the-radar ghost movies, when its DVD cover image captured my attention. The artwork, a family portrait revealing two blood-soaked young girls slumped on an antique couch with their stiff-faced parents (or who I assumed were their parents) standing behind them, possessed the art direction of a horror connoisseur. I had recently been watching a number of other South Korean horror films, such as *I Saw the Devil* and *The Host*, and found them full of well-executed funhouse frights, dark humor, and iconic imagery, if lacking the clean psychological prodding and clear attachment to fable of other forms of Asian cinema. After further reading (successfully avoiding discussion about *The Uninvited*, the seemingly obligatory 2009 U.S. remake), I felt I had done the due diligence often required when deciding which new horror film to watch. My wife was out that night and my daughter was asleep in her bed; it seemed like the perfect time to learn the terrible backstory behind those blood patches on those sad, serious young girls.

As I watched, I confess I had no idea what the hell was going on the majority of the time. The reason for this WTF-state was not that it was

> "DO YOU KNOW WHAT'S REALLY SCARY? YOU WANT TO FORGET SOMETHING. TOTALLY WIPE IT OFF YOUR MIND. BUT YOU NEVER CAN. IT CAN'T GO AWAY, YOU SEE...AND IT FOLLOWS YOU AROUND LIKE A GHOST."

South Korean or that the plot was a mess or that relating to the characters was difficult. Quite the contrary. *A Tale of Two Sisters* was inspired by the Korean fairy tale "Janghwa Hongryeon jeon" ("The Story of Janghwa and Hongryeon"), a story of Rose and Lotus, sisters plagued by the murderous cruelty of an evil stepmother and haunted by the ghost of the village's mayor. The tale was first adapted in 1924 by Kim Yeong-han (and multiple times after that), but writer/director Kim Ji-woon's version takes a more psychological-horror, cinematographer-as-king approach to the modern riff of transforming oft-told children's bedtime stories into deep-seated adult mind-screws.

The basic framework of Kim Ji-woon's adaptation remains the same, with two sisters, a distant father and a cruel stepmother sequestered together in a dreary house with winding hallways and odd-shaped rooms. After an initial hospital therapy session with Soo-mi (Lim Su-jeong), the emotionally stronger of the sisters, a new telling of the fable begins to reveal itself. We learn the girls' mother is dead and a terrible apparition haunts the house. The ghost, its anger born of an experience both brutal and mysterious, is tied to both Soo-mi and her more timid sister, Soo-yeon (Moon Geun-Young). Odd occurrences begin to happen: a family relative has a violent, frothing seizure; a murdered bird is discovered in Soo-yeon's bed; a wild-eyed specter is spied under the kitchen sink; a drippy, blood-soaked bag is skidded down a long hallway. I would love to tell you how all this freaky imagery is linked together, but because these are only fragments of a complex (yet ultimately simple and human) plot, any explanation screams SPOILER ALERT! The joy of watching *A Tale of Two Sisters* is watching this psychological/supernatural mixture force-pressed together while being assaulted by some of the most chilling images K-horror has to offer. Gladly, the last ten minutes gently push most of the pieces into place, allowing for a satisfyingly creepy and heartbreaking ending to a story that remains true to its gothic fairy tale roots.

As Coralline Dupuy notes in her excellent (and exhaustive) analysis of the movie for *The Irish Journal of Gothic and Horror Studies*, "*A Tale of Two Sisters* features strong visual and thematic markers that point to the fairytale origins of the plot, such as an aesthetic obsession with flowers, the presence of ghosts, and the idyllic, yet isolated, lakeside location of the family home. All of these visual markers have strong symbolic values, echoing Jung's statement that 'in myths and fairytales, the psyche tells its own story.'" The story being told is one of mind and memory. Kim Ji-woon uses tactile, sensory-based imagery to conjure up a clear and tangible nightmare landscape. Color is used to connote emotional climates, such as red symbolizing dangerous situations and/or foreboding locations and green representing a more "safe" landscape and/or innocuous space. Sound is used to evoke a specific momentary mind-set, via the hum of a refrigerator or the rustling of leaves in trees, indicating a lull in the characters' (and our own) synaptic explosions. In contrast, the sharp pop-snap of the wooden floors, the treble-peaked screams of a frightened child, or the sharp echo of repeated and gushing knife-stabs vibrate as if born from the viewer's eardrums.

Beyond these subconscious elements, *A Tale of Two Sisters* also relies heavily on standard haunted house tropes, such as dimly lit corners, creaking doors, and dangerously heavy furniture. From the start of the film, when the family arrives at the house, the structure looms above them; a four-person coffin waiting to yank them inside. Much like the Western fairy tale, with its crumbling castles and candy-fortified witch cabins, this clapboard monster emanates brokenness and damage, a metaphor that reaches into the hearts of children and grownups alike the world over. A place of trust, warmth, and security that gradually becomes our tomb, the home holds secrets and doesn't mind sharing them in whatever way strikes its whim. The viewer wants to reach into the screen to pull the family from their fate, but the house has other ideas. There is no controlling the  cruel dwelling's consumption. We can only watch as those trapped within become eternally and tragically devoured again and again.

The movie also plays upon the standard horror-psychology of mental illness, reflected in its own up-is-down illogic. Multiple questions arise while watching: Does the entire story take place in a true reality? Do the ghosts roaming the house actually exist or are they born from some kind of twisted guilt? Do the ghosts represent a lack of feeling? Do they represent a broken love? Resentment? Sibling rivalry? Is the story meant to be truly understood at its end? Is the ending we're shown the real ending? Who is dead? Who is alive? WHAT THE HELL IS GOING ON??? The dream then wraps backward upon itself and we end up back in the same place where we began. Just like therapy (or a criminal interrogation), viewers of *A Tale of Two Sisters* must go over the evil deed repeatedly until it is labeled and understood. Labels and understanding are slippery constructs, however. Once a chosen path is taken, a traveler can get lost quite quickly. This "losing one's way" moves us back to the subconscious, leading us to what any *A Tale of Two Sisters* interpretation turns out to be—subjective. It's a film that requires you to join in its psychosis—adding in your own bit of personal turmoil—to deal with the muddled, muddy, and bloodstained ghosts therein.

Brett Neveu has had plays produced at A Red Orchid Theatre (where he's an ensemble member), The Goodman Theatre, Writers' Theatre, The Royal Court Theatre, The Royal Shakespeare Theatre and a bunch of other excellent spots. He's also been commissioned a number of times, developed plays all over and also writes film and television scripts. He currently teaches at Northwestern University.

TATTOO 1981

BY CHRIS ALEXANDER

"DON'T YOU KNOW THAT I HAVE COMMITTED MY LIFE TO YOU? THAT THIS IS A PROTECTIVE SHIELD? IT'S MY MARK, MADDY, IT'S ALL I HAVE TO OFFER YOU. NOW I'M NOT SURE ANYMORE WHETHER YOU'RE WORTHY OF IT."

Body modification is about as edgy these days as porn, which is to say not very. The mainstream has claimed the tattoo, along with various piercings, scars, and punctures as its own; it's now as common to see ink on your Aunt Sally as it is on a hardened biker. And yet, somehow, *Tattoo* is still a dangerous piece of cinema, a film so somber and sleazy and yet at the same time almost regal in its attitude that its cited detours into camp are only defaults of just how odd and wrong a viewing experience it is. A voyeuristic, outlandish and decidedly serious work of meditative terror....

Have you seen *Tattoo*?

If you were born after its release, chances are the answer is a defiant "no." See, *Tattoo* is a bona fide rare duck which, after causing some controversy upon release, faded into legend. As of this writing, it still lies trapped in the 20th Century Fox vaults, waiting for a chance to be unleashed like the sputtering ink from Bruce Dern's buzzing tat gun. Those of you who lived through its initial theatrical release or caught up with it in those early Wild West home video days are certainly aware of the strange power the picture oozes. But for those of you in the dark, allow me to illuminate.

In what may be his most intense performance, *Tattoo* stars the ever-fascinating Bruce Dern as a slowly-going-mad tattoo architect named—wait for it—Kinsky (not Kinski, though I'm sure there is some element of homage in the script to everyone's favorite Teutonic madman). So brilliant and dedicated an artist is Kinsky, so ingrained into his DNA is the myth of the tattoo (as endless slow-mo Asian tattoo ritual hallucinations hammer

home) that he is often approached by the world of *haute couture* to stencil temporary designs onto top models, a job he takes seriously, as seriously as everything centered around his profession. Too seriously, of course.

When his latest subject, an intelligent, physically immaculate model/actress named Maddy (the intelligent, physically immaculate double-time Bond girl Maud Adams) responds to his talent and intensity on a very basic, friendly level, Kinsky unravels into full-blown lunacy, kidnapping the woman and imprisoning her in a vacant home. His intent is not to defile her sexually, but rather something even more violating—to use her skin as his personal canvas, illustrating her physique with his serpentine, colorful mark. Attempts to escape are futile and the visceral relationship that evolves between captor and captive, while ugly in its S&M and sexual politics, is mesmerizing and unnerving on a primal level. Shades of 1965's *The Collector* are inevitable, but *Tattoo* has something dreamier on its mind, something more abstract, not surprising considering it was penned by Joyce Buñuel, the daughter of surreal cinema pioneer Luis Buñuel. On that familial tip, *Tattoo* is more kin to another surrealist's offspring's first work, that of Jennifer—daughter of David—Lynch's equally misunderstood and undervalued *Boxing Helena*.

The allegory in *Tattoo* is obvious and heavy-handed, suggesting that any kind of male/female connection is a kind of inking, a power play of the physical and psychological. Director Bob Brooks frames the film with such a gauzy, sensual yet aloof artiness that he himself may have thought the picture was deeper than it is. But whatever your read, *Tattoo* is an anomaly, a psycho-thriller that is more about mood, slow moments, and the act of possession than cheap shocks, gore, or easy thrills. One has to be patient for *Tattoo*'s rewards, which include its bizarre, haunting climax, the weirdest sex scene I've ever seen, with the brilliant, mad, vermin-faced Dern finally consummating his relationship with Adams' drugged and passive living painting before the very gun that sealed their fates. Dern has reveled in playing unstable, likably unlikable characters in films like *Hush...Hush, Sweet Charlotte*, *Silent Running*, *The 'Burbs*, and most recently, as the malevolent patriarch in HBO's *Big Love*. But here, Dern does psycho with a certain kind of dignity. There's an off-caliber moral code that Kinsky obeys, an absolute devotion to his craft and, like all of cinema and literature's great antiheroes, no matter how transgressive their acts, they are righteous in their purpose. Dern nails this dichotomy and creates a layered, fascinating, and complex character out of something that could have easily veered into cartoon.

Much has been cited about Adams' performance, or lack thereof. True, hers is a far less showy role, but what she lacks in provocative dialogue she makes up with an astonishing physical presence, one Adams pushes not only with her divine physique, but her wide eyes and deliciously full lips. See, Maddy is a bit of a cad. She is certainly plastic but that's the world she's ingrained in; what some critics have cited as "wooden," I see as a perfect reflection of that vast surface existence. She initially has a sexual interest and casual fascination with the intense Kinsky, but when she comes on to him, he recoils. She is married, after all, and the act of simple, impromptu "intercourse" out of wedlock is repugnant to him. This is the turning point of the picture and I like how Adams goes quietly from regal sophistication to slowly melting erotic victim/accomplice. It's a difficult role for anyone to play and Buñuel does not make Maddy easy to warm to nor identify with. Adams does a fine job wilting under Dern's operatic mania—she has to "earn" the right to have sex with him, and even though she becomes Dern's captive and victim, it's clear that a decent-sized part of her is trying very hard to please her new "master." Such a dynamic wasn't in fashion in Hollywood in 1981 and it's still a hot button now.

Director Brooks cut his teeth on British TV (including select episodes of the sparse, moody sci-fi show *Space 1999*) but it's his career as a photographer that gives *Tattoo* much of its textural presence. He understands this world, its shallow, predatory nature, its addiction to surface and maybe it's his empathy with Dern's plight—a man of substance (however skewed) in a

glossy, fake setting—that give the film an extra goose. Visually, it's flawless, with slow, long-take imagery of the beautiful Adams' equally flawless body and perfectly framed shots that are alternately lush and claustrophobic.

Pretentious? Perhaps. A masterpiece? Depends on your response. But whatever you take away from *Tattoo*, what's undeniable is that there is not a contemporary movie quite like it in existence (though Almodovar's *Tie Me Up! Tie Me Down!* shares a few kinky similarities). One viewing simply isn't enough to properly absorb its unique power. Here is a borderline horror movie rich with dark wonder, ripe for re-discovery.

> *Chris Alexander is a Canadian film journalist, filmmaker and music composer. He was a writer and columnist with critically acclaimed horror periodical* Rue Morgue *before joining the ranks of legendary NYC-based magazine* Fangoria, *a publication he has steered as editor-in-chief since 2010. As a filmmaker, Alexander made his feature writing/directing debut with 2013's* Blood for Irina, *for which he also composed the score. He lives in Toronto with his wife and three sons.*

THE TENANT 1976

BY FAWN KRISENTHIA

The Tenant is a quiet Parisian man named Trelkovsky (co-writer/director Roman Polanski) who finds a vacant apartment right as he is about to get evicted from his current one. It's available, he discovers, because the previous tenant, Simone Choule, threw herself out the window. Trelkovsky's celebration of his good fortune is short-lived when he realizes the apartment comes at a hefty price: He soon becomes convinced that his neighbors are the reason for Simone's attempted suicide, and they are driving him to the same fate.

> "AND NOW, IF YOU CUT OFF MY HEAD, WOULD I SAY 'ME AND MY HEAD,' OR 'ME AND MY BODY'? WHAT RIGHT HAS MY HEAD TO CALL ITSELF 'ME'?"

I discovered this brilliant movie, based on the novel by Roland Topor, a million and a half years ago, about the same time I moved alone into my first apartment. I was just coming out of my high school gothy stage of feeling that no one understood me, and feeling eyes on me wherever I went. My personal parallels to Trelkovsky's paranoia and self-consciousness struck a deep nerve that has not lessened over the years. I was no stranger to the sound of angry neighbors beating on the shared wall, and felt an acute sense of embarrassment and guilt whenever that happened. It is amazing how fast your behavior can be conditioned, even in a space as personal as your apartment.

Trelkovsky's fear that others are out to get him is an overarching theme of Polanski's horror films. I view *The Tenant* as the meat in Polanski's "Paranoia-in-an-Apartment" sandwich; while it's revealed in *Rosemary's Baby* (1968) that the neighbors *are actually out to get her*, conversely, it's made apparent in *Repulsion* (1965) that the madness Carol is experiencing is solely a product of her own mind. *The Tenant* strikes a balance between the two on the spectrum, where reality and paranoid fantasies meet.

Punctuations of terror are hauntingly and beautifully handled in this underrated masterpiece. As the opening credits flash onscreen, a camera shows Trelkovsky looking down, following his gaze to reveal broken glass roofing over the courtyard below him. When the camera pans back up, he has been replaced with a woman wearing a secretive expression...as well as a dress that we will come to recognize all too well by the bloody finale. In a scene where Trelkovsky is sick in bed, he deliriously reaches out to the water bottle and empty yogurt cups next to him, but his hands find that the items are as flat as a painting...an illusion. It's a subtle moment, one that I missed in my first few viewings. In another scene, Trelkovsky has just had the jarring experience of seeing himself from the bathroom window across the courtyard. Sitting near the entrance of his apartment, he suddenly gets up to stumble through the room in a brilliant shot that evokes Van Gogh's *The Bedroom*. The furniture, lamp, chairs, and even the water bottle seem to grow out of proportion while Trelkovsky appears to get smaller the closer he gets to the massive window. When he looks out across the courtyard into the bathroom, he sees Simone unwinding her bandages, a vulgar expression plastered on her revealed face.

If you are a Polanski fan that already has a relationship with *The Tenant* (and if you have not yet seen it, a fair warning of SPOILERS going forward), you will undoubtedly remember an early scene in which Simone is lying in a hospital bed wrapped in bandages. She screams when she sees Trelkovsky and Stella (Isabelle Adjani) and later dies. Near the end, after Trelkovsky has twice thrown himself out his apartment window in a suicide attempt, it is revealed that *he* is the wrapped hospital patient, watching the conversation between his friend Stella and his doppelganger unfold. Admittedly, I am not a fan of the twist because I feel it diminishes an otherwise haunting story of a man broken down by his own demons and injustices of the world. Trelkovsky's scream is perhaps his dismayed reaction to the junky *Twilight Zone* conclusion.

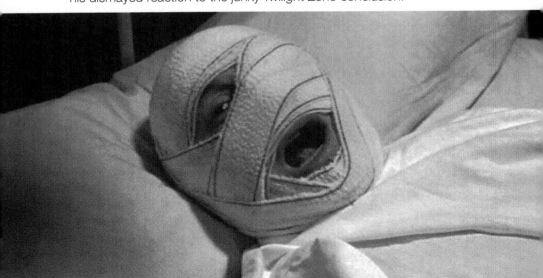

After re-watching, however, I discovered an intriguing layer that had not previously entered my mind, and even wondered if my understanding of the film over the years had been superficial (or perhaps I've watched David Lynch's *Mulholland Drive* too many times). But for any fan of *The Tenant*, I submit an interesting theory: Instead of being a story about a paranoid and obsessive man who slowly adopts the dress and psyche of a woman and is precipitated to suicide by his neighbors, I propose that the story is really about a troubled woman who, while on her death bed, dreams of a second chance with her secret love Stella and with an oppressive society. Monsieur Trelkovsky is a real man who comes to visit her in the hospital after learning of her apartment's availability, and bed-ridden Simone observes the awkward exchange between him and Stella. Perhaps her enraged scream is in response to realizing that Trelkovsky and Stella have hit it off, realizing the woman she secretly pined over will move on. She feels sharp jealousy and pain in the knowledge that it is with someone who will experience none of society's harsh judgment about lesbianism. She transports herself into Trelkovsky's shoes and fantasizes what it might be like to live as him, in her own apartment, amongst her own things, enjoying an unfettered sexual relationship with Stella. However, as time goes on, the cracks begin to show. Even the perfect male version of herself turns in on itself, punctuated by overwhelming anxiety, paranoia, and self-consciousness.

Subtle clues are peppered throughout, like Stella and Trelkovsky's conversation in the café about how Simone didn't like men, or during Trelkovsky's housewarming party when his guests have a conversation about homosexuality, which could be a projection of what Simone has had to deal with all her life. Or how the thieves only take Trelkovsky's belongings while none of Simone's things go missing (a subconscious removal of Trelkovsky from Simone's fantasy), and the ease in which Stella seems to return affection to Trelkovsky. Even the visit from Georges Badar serves as a symbol of Simone's frustration at never telling Stella how she truly felt. There is also Trelkovsky's wonderfully drunken "me and my head" soliloquy which point to Simone's feeling of disembodiment. The neighbors serve as harbingers of Simone's realization that she will never be accepted, not in any form, and not under any circumstances.

The denouement points to the conclusion that the Trelkovsky version of Simone is not immune to the judgments and oppression of society. Even her imagined version of herself commits suicide in order to "give the people want they want," i.e. her blood. Her scream at the end might be the beginning of an elaborate death dream. For aficionados of *The Tenant*, I suggest re-watching it with this theory in mind. Whether you agree or disagree, it's an excuse to have yet another engaged viewing of a brilliantly layered and ingeniously designed movie.

Fawn Krisenthia had her first horror movie experience at the age of four when she was taken to the theater to see The Entity. *She wants to thank her aunt for shaping what has become a deep love of the genre, although she hasn't quite shaken off the fear of being repeatedly assaulted by a demon ghost.*

TENEBRAE 1982

BY DUSTIN FREGIATO

"I WILL ELIMINATE THOSE WHO DISGUST ME, THE HUMAN PERVERTS, SOON NOW...THE CORRUPTER HIMSELF."

Does a film have to belong to a genre (or even a subgenre) to be considered great? Does a picture require a specific niche to end up with the respect it deserves? *Tenebrae* perfectly bridges the gap between Italian giallo films (possessing an intense whodunit plot) and American slashers (with its impressive gore and body count), yet it is often considered too "slasher" to be a great giallo and too "giallo" to be a classic slasher.

Worse, many have not even seen the film the way writer/director Dario Argento originally envisioned. Its sexualized violence was often censored to the point of non-recognition, shorn of the very elements that made it so special. Instead, these "offending" scenes saddled *Tenebrae* with the unenviable distinction of being on the UK's Video Nasties' list; it was ultimately one of the few pictures the British Board of Film Classification successfully prosecuted. For its 1987 United States release, re-titled *Unsane* and marketed as a sleazy slasher, ten additional minutes were trimmed, rendering it toothless and nearly incomprehensible. (For Americans who have only seen *Unsane*, I implore you to give the uncut version of *Tenebrae* a chance.)

After dabbling in the supernatural with his two biggest international hits, *Suspiria* (1977) and *Inferno* (1980), Argento returned to the format that had provided his early success. Meaning "yellow" in Italian, the term "giallo" references the yellow bindings of Italian mystery novels as well as the films they later inspired (which in turn influenced the U.S. slasher films of the 1980s). In the book *Dario Argento*, James Gracey described the giallo subgenre as one which "combines sex and violence, hyper-stylized and elaborate murders, lavish camerawork and set design, displaced protagonists who unwittingly stumble into the ensuing mayhem, ineffectual or nonexistent police and copious gore." Coming back to his roots, Argento maximized these elements in *Tenebrae* to pay tribute to the genre in a similar manner to what Wes Craven would do for the slasher with 1996's *Scream*.

The plot revolves around an American author, Peter Neal (Anthony Franciosa), during his latest book tour in Rome. While in the capital city, the writer is harassed by a man so infatuated with Neal's "perverse" writings that he begins gruesomely killing individuals and citing the writer's work as his inspiration. The Italian detectives eventually pull Neal into the investigation and all involved are brought to the brink of obsession and insanity.

The inspiration for the story sparked while Argento was visiting Los Angeles in 1980. Throughout his stay, he was called continuously by an obsessed fan who, after repeatedly explaining the impact *Suspiria* had on him, eventually threatened to kill the director. In a 1983 interview with Christophe Gans, Argento reasoned that "*Suspiria* had left its mark [on the man's] madness." The similarities between Argento's experience and that of his onscreen protagonist make *Tenebrae*'s plotline all the more frighteningly real. They also highlight the movie's major theme: we all have a little madness in us; it just takes a certain experience to bring it out.

The film begins with the following passage read aloud:

"The impulse had become irresistible. There was only one answer to the fury that tortured him. And so he committed his first act of murder. He had broken the most deep-rooted taboo, and found not guilt, not anxiety or fear, but freedom. Any humiliation which stood in his way could be swept aside by the simple act of annihilation: Murder."

This message is brought full circle in the final reel, concluding with the most intense eleven minutes you will ever spend watching a film, and featuring a shot that will amaze even the most jaded of critics. *Tenebrae* focuses on a man attempting to extinguish society's love for sex, gore, and violence, all the while tempting viewers to desire more of these forbidden fruits. This seeming contradiction between art and its effects registered strongly with me. Art can introduce us to the darkness it has the potential to create, desensitize us to it and perhaps ironically make us lust for that very darkness. Instead of being turned off by the violence and bloodshed that the film and its antagonist criticize, the viewer actually finds himself being turned on by it.

Even more impressive than *Tenebrae*'s textured themes or serpentine plot are its true strengths: the visuals. Lucio Fulci once said, "Violence is

Italian art." Like his countryman, Argento takes the art aspect of filmmaking very seriously. During production, "The Italian Hitchcock" spent three days on a two-and-a-half-minute sequence: an unbroken tracking shot in, over, and around a victim's house that voyeuristically displays a prowler's point of view and at the same time drives home the director's undeniable skill as a master of his craft. Argento has even described one of the final death scenes — where a woman splatters her blood across the walls — as the victim "painting," pointing out that he specifically filmed the scene in that manner to characterize himself as an artist rather than simply a merchant of the macabre. Regretfully, many censoring boards did not find his "artwork" appealing; the scene was absent for over a decade until Anchor Bay released their uncut DVD in 1999.

This stress that Argento places on the "film as art" makes *Tenebrae* not just a story told on screen, but a complete visceral experience. Though shot on location, this isn't the Rome that we recognize from the postcards. This city is extremely modern and unrecognizable. The colors employed are bathed in neutrals except for a few key instances of bright reds. Unlike many horror films, most of the action takes place during the day and features bountiful natural light, despite "*Tenebrae*" meaning "darkness" in Italian. This leads me to interpret the title as referring to the darkness of the human soul rather than the absence of light.

This personal abyss is brought out through the viewer's appreciation of the sexualized, almost dance-like death scenes of the beautiful women that Argento has handpicked to do away with onscreen. With the overt female objectification, copious amounts of violence, and perfect lighting, I found myself appreciating the work as a series of Italian Renaissance paintings played out at 24 frames per second than as a simple horror film.

But, as the saying goes, sometimes timing is everything. Following the successes of the vibrant and unique *Suspiria* and *Inferno*, *Tenebrae* was a financial flop. Argento diehards might have preferred he complete his "Three Mothers" trilogy instead of returning to his giallo origins. Additionally, as the

'80s slasher genre had a stranglehold on the horror market, an almost incoherent Italian giallo (due to censoring) featuring a lackluster body count was bound to get overlooked.

With actual character development, truly intense death scenes, and a constant air of anticipation regarding what is going to happen next (or more to the point, what Argento will show next), *Tenebrae* delivers the slasher goods while maintaining its cinematic respectability. I urge you to give this hidden gem two hours of your life. You won't regret it.

> *Dustin Fregiato is an attorney who resides in Indianapolis with his wife, Erica. Growing up, his favorite movie was* Creature from the Black Lagoon *(1954), and though his "favorites list" has grown over the years, not much has changed regarding his love of the genre. Dustin is an active staff member at HorrorHound Weekend's bi-annual horror conventions. When not watching a horror film in his man-cave, he can be seen at the local drive-in catching the latest flicks.*

TOMBS OF THE BLIND DEAD 1972

BY JIMMY SEIERSEN

After Virginia (María Elena Arpón, billed as Helen Harp) runs into her old friend Betty (Lone Fleming) in Lisbon, the two decide to spend a weekend in the country together with Virginia's love interest Roger

"DON'T SPEAK. THAT'S THE ONLY WAY YOU'LL BE SAFE."

(César Burner). While on the train, Roger's attention is drawn towards Betty and Virginia decides—in a fit of jealousy—to disembark in the middle of nowhere. Seeking shelter for the night, she explores a long-abandoned monastery. Big mistake! The cemetery nearby is the resting place of the legendary Knights Templar. After training in the occult in Egypt, their return to Spain was marked by sadistic rituals as they sought to unlock the mysteries of eternal life. Eventually excommunicated by the pope, the Templars were hung on crosses until crows devoured their eyes. Now more dangerous than ever, they leave their nightly resting grounds to hunt the living by sound alone.

Tombs of the Blind Dead, written and directed by Spanish filmmaker Amando de Ossorio, premiered in 1972, four years after George A. Romero's *Night of the Living Dead*. Producers didn't like Ossorio's script at first, since it didn't contain any famous horror characters such as Dracula or Frankenstein, but they changed their minds when Ossorio showed them some promotional images and masks. There still remained one problem: Spain was being promoted as the ideal destination for holiday getaways, and Franco's regime didn't want the country to be portrayed as superstitious...or as a place where the dead came out of their graves. The public relations concern was resolved by moving the story's setting from Spain to Portugal.

Ossorio's shuffling monsters were inspired by the real Knights Templar, medieval warrior monks who fought in the Crusades and indeed became too powerful for their own good. But the director was not the first to implement the Templars in a work of fiction. Spanish poet and author Gustavo Adolfo Bécquer used them back in the 1800s, though Ossorio denies that his movies were inspired by these earlier stories: "The Templars who appear in Bécquer's writings are phantoms, spirits of the dead. Mine are crumbling mummies." Ossorio did not consider his Templars zombies, but as "mummies on horse-back," attributing their slow movement to a displacement of time and space.

In truth, one could argue that the Templars' resurrection by use of occult sciences actually makes them closer to the original Haitian zombies (a living person controlled by a voodoo master) than Romero's inexplicably revived ghouls. If we are willing to extend the definition of the word "zombie" to include walking corpses, it's certainly not a stretch to also include the Blind Dead.

Though both movies focus on antagonistic walking dead and bleakly con-clude with still images, I believe Ossorio wanted to distance himself from *Night of the Living Dead* so people could assess his work on its own merit. But even if *Tombs of the Blind Dead* was inspired by its predecessor, it's far from a rip-off. One of the first modern undead films released after the 1968 game-changing classic, Ossorio invented an entirely new mythology surrounding the undead that distinguish his riding mummies from the brainchildren of Romero, Lucio Fulci, or any other filmmaker working within the zombie subgenre.

Ossorio developed several unique stylistic touchstones in addition to his original backstory. As the title would indicate, the Templars are also blind, accounting for their slow movement even without any time/space displacement (which is never really explained anyway). When they mount their nightmare steeds, the slow-motion photography lends these equestrian sequences an otherworldly feel. During their nightly resurrections, a layer of ground fog completes the scene. The perfect visualization of death, the skeletal Templars' frames are covered with a layer of dry, mummified skin. Just imagine a victim being alone with these things *slowly* moving in from all sides. Leaving the

ruins, in the mannequin factory where Betty works, there is a red light going on and off, giving an ominous feel to the building, like something bad is about to happen there.

The magnificent sound design is also an intrinsic characteristic of *Tombs of the Blind Dead*. In an incredible sequence, when the Templars surround Betty in the monastery, she tries to re-main quiet, but the silence is broken by a rhythmic thumping. The Templars are tracking their

victim by her very heartbeat! Antón García Abril's musical score, employing haunting choral moans and chanting, adds immeasurably to the atmosphere. In a 1990 *Gorezone* interview, the director said it was always his intent that these build-up scenes be the most horrific. "I used all my knowledge as a director and writer to make these scenes stick in the viewers' minds. I wanted them ready to faint. I don't know if anyone ever did or not, but there were plenty of screams coming from the audience. That made me feel great."

It was also common for sex and sensuality to figure prominently in European horror films of the '70s. In *Tombs of the Blind Dead*, we learn that Betty is a lesbian via a flashback of her and Virginia kissing. The heterosexual Fleming found the scene somewhat difficult to do, being solely attracted to men; she ultimately asked Ossorio for some wine, a bottle of which she and Arpón shared before completing the scene. Betty's homosexuality makes the characters' relationships a bit more interesting: Virginia likes Roger, who seems interested in Betty, who still wants Virginia. Some fans of '70s Euro-horror would probably prefer if the movie contained a bit more sleaze, while others might find these scenes purely gratuitous. I'll be honest; for me, any excuse for girl/girl kissing will do.

In all, Ossorio would make four official *Blind Dead* movies. In *Return of the Blind Dead* (1973), a 14th-century Portuguese village burns a group of Templars to death, with the unholy warriors returning to wreak havoc during a modern-day festival. The following year's *The Ghost Galleon* sent the slow-moving sightless to sea, as two models—traveling the Atlantic Ocean as a publicity stunt—encounter an abandoned old ship of legend and mystery. The series concluded with 1975's *Night of the Seagulls*, as a rural doctor arrives at a village where the locals—in exchange for peace— regularly sacrifice young women to the Templars. Though Templar mythology changes somewhat from film to film (in one they are unaffected by daylight, in another it kills them), the director explained that, "The Templar series is not meant to be a series in the true tradition of sequels as an American audience is trained to think, but a series of films containing the same sect of villains and nothing more."

Even with zombies enjoying more onscreen popularity than ever, *Tombs of the Blind Dead* continues to be overlooked by modern horror fans whose focus seem to be confined to the post-*Dawn of the Dead* '80s boom and the more recent spate of post-millennial gut-munchers. If the shoe fits, I'm urging you to dig a bit further. It would be a shame if the slow-creeping Templars (alongside other early '70s zombie movies), with their originality and charm, were to be buried even deeper in the cemetery of forgotten horror.

Jimmy Seiersen was born in the city of Lund, Sweden, in 1984. Being that horror and science fiction are his favorite film genres, it was only natural that he'd become involved in the local Lund International Fantastic Film Festival, and has been a short film programmer since 2010. He has also made a short film of his own, The Astral Projector. *Jimmy holds a Bachelor's degree in Media Studies from the University of Skövde.*

TOURIST TRAP 1979

BY MOLLY CELASCHI

"OH, YOU'RE SO PRETTY. IT'S A SHAME YOU HAVE TO DIE. IT WILL BE QUICK, BUT IT WON'T BE EASY. YOU'LL DIE OF FRIGHT."

You know the drill: a group of pesky kids gets lost in the countryside and stop to use the phone at the Slausen Oasis Museum, only to be terrorized by an unknown assailant. However, this is anything but your typical "teens terrorized, killer revealed, oh shock! horror! whodunit twist ending" horror fare. Starting with the opening credits, we're treated to Pino Donaggio's creepy musical score that warmly invites us to Mister Rogers' Creepy Country Neighborhood. Welcome to *Tourist Trap*.

What I truly love is how this film (a personal favorite of horror legend Stephen King) has the set-up of a conventional slasher flick, yet takes many, *many* unconventional turns throughout, throwing in everything but a killer kitchen sink. Besides some out-of-left-field paranormal activity, there is the strange psychotic backstory, a "you remind me of my wife" pseudo-rape scene, and human dolls littered everywhere. And the ending is more balls-out batshit crazy than any standard slasher fan could imagine.

As weird as the script is, it still plays by the introductory-horror numbers. You have the guy who wanders away from the group and promptly dies for his stupidity, the jiggly girl who leaves to investigate in darkness (let's be honest, it was more of an in*breast*igation), and the Final Girl survivor whose lily white vagina can conquer evil.

Let's introduce our victims, shall we?

Jerry (Jon Van Ness, also in *The Hitcher* and *Hospital Massacre*) is our kinda sorta hero. We'll say goodbye to idiot Woody (Keith McDermott) just as fast as we said hello. Robin Sherwood (*Death Wish II, Blow Out, Love Butcher*) plays Eileen, the cute but vain bimbo, while Becky is played by Tanya Roberts of *Charlie's Angels*, *The Beastmaster* and *Sheena: Queen of the Jungle* fame.

But from the moment the fantastic Jocelyn Jones, aka Molly, aka Final Girl, enters the picture, you know who you're dealing with. In contrast to the other clothing-allergic gals, Little Miss House on the Prairie sports a crisp white sundress and a white bonnet tied tightly under her presumably virgin neck. And her name is Molly! You know this sweet, sweet girl will kick big, big ass and her saintly womanhood will ultimately prevail after her hysterical screaming subsides.

Then we have TV's former *Rifleman* Chuck Connors as Mr. Slausen, the creepy, lumbering old guy who lives alone with his dead wife in a museum of mannequins and pistol-wielding puppetry. Graced with the imposing head of Frankenstein's Monster, Connors' military and professional sports backgrounds served him well in a variety of action roles for nearly 50 years. Genre fans will likely recall his appearances in *Soylent Green* and TV's *The Horror at 37,000 Feet*—in fact, Connors sought out the *Tourist Trap* role because he "wanted to be the Boris Karloff of the '80s." It is rumored that he and Jones did not get along well on set, mainly for their differing approaches to the craft—Connors being a more instinctive, physical performer while theatrical veteran Jones favored a more internal process. (The apple doesn't fall far from the tree either—Jocelyn's father is Henry Jones, the Tony Award-winning actor who starred in *The Bad Seed*, Alfred Hitchcock's *Vertigo*, and many more.) Even so, the behind-the-scenes conflict results in a very strong antagonistic relationship onscreen, making the two actors' scenes together that much more believable.

The guys (and some gals) will like the bimbos sporting tiny tops and even tinier shorts. I'm especially fond of Eileen who wants to "go check things out" in complete darkness and snuggles up in her holey wrap—essentially just a long piece of yarn—placed around her shoulders. While searching for her boyfriend, for no apparent reason, she also stops to put on a scarf she finds in the old house. (Sherwood says in an interview that this part made no sense to her but that she rationalized that her vain character wanted to look pretty for her missing boyfriend. Good enough for me.) She also gets a glass mirror smashed to shit in front of her face, an incident which sent Sherwood to the hospital with bleeding gashes in her side. (The experienced Connors had warned her to turn her face away during the shot, thus preventing more serious damage.)

As the dim-witted pretty chick, Roberts' Becky is not good for much more than providing bouncy tube-top teasing. (Sorry to disappoint, it never falls down. Did she superglue it on for her fight scene? So much struggling and no slippage.) Yet, despite *Tourist Trap*'s persistent bimbo-ism, there is a curious lack of sex and nudity, and in fact, there is no gore at all.

However, it's worth noting that one of the scariest films ever made, *The Texas Chain Saw Massacre*, was also devoid of nudity with minimal gore. *Tourist Trap* is an easy recommendation for Leatherface fans, with obvious parallels. In addition to a similar look and feel (courtesy of both films' art director, Robert A. Burns), there's the big hulking guy in masks made of human flesh, an older brother who plays nice guy, and stranded white kids in an old country house. But the twist isn't just that Davey, our havoc-wreaking lunatic, uses human faces—he turns his victims into mannequins! Oh yes, mannequins play a big part in this movie. Davey occasionally disguises himself as one, victims hide amongst them hoping to survive, dummies are rigged and puppets slide on pulley systems. Or sometimes they move on their own.

Wait, *whaaaat...?*

Yes, you read that correctly. Our villain is telekinetic! Charles Band Productions was smart enough to capitalize not only on *TCM*, but on Brian De Palma's *Carrie,* which had come out just three years prior. Genius. You can also see how this film influenced executive producer Band's future endeavors. Even the puppet at the beginning of *Tourist Trap* bears a striking resemblance to one of the tiny terrors in 1989's *Puppetmaster*. Not surprisingly, first-time director David Schmoeller (who co-wrote the script with J. Larry Carroll) would go on

to helm the first of the long-running series a decade later.

In addition to Schmoeller's well-cultivated atmosphere and Connors' quirky menace, the music and sound effects are key to what makes this movie so downright creepy. The incredibly talented Donaggio, whose extensive and impressive genre credits include *Don't Look Now*, *The Howling*, the aforementioned *Carrie*, and *Blow Out*, as well as dozens of Italian features, works miracles here. For example, the opening title credits melody resembles an eerie flute and violin sonata accented by clocks ticking, haunting piano tinkling, and twisting wind-up toys coming to life. Play this tune alone in the dark and you're sure to lose your mind.

If you haven't seen *Tourist Trap*, you need to have this in your life. Awesome soundtrack, cute juggie bimbos, and an ever-twisting ending — it succeeds as either a late-night fright flick (preferably seen alone in the dark upon first viewing) or a raucous party viewing with friends (there needs to be a "little girl" and "Isn't she pr-e-e-e-tty?" drinking game).

And remember the kindly Slausen hospitality the next time your car breaks down off the beaten path.

Molly Celaschi has produced several films including Mass Acre Hill, *Poca-Hauntus, and* X's & O's, *with her most recent being 2012's* Deliverance from Evil. *Molly is a writer for HorrorYearbook, FearZone, 2Snaps.TV, and Ultra Violent magazine. Contributions include the Spike TV Scream Awards, Fuse Fangoria Chainsaw Awards, EA Games Studio, Screamfest, Another Hole in the Head, and Dead by Dawn. Molly is now Executive Director at Malena Public Relations, a PR firm for filmmakers and authors.*

TREMORS 1990

BY ROB DENNEHY

Two handymen, Val (Kevin Bacon) and Earl (Fred Ward), pick the wrong day to finally move up in the world beyond their isolated tiny community of Perfection, Nevada. Heading out of town, they encounter several mysterious sights, including a dead

> "BROKE INTO THE WRONG GODDAMN REC ROOM, DIDN'T YOU, YOU BASTARD!"

body atop a power line and a human head buried underneath a hat. The trouble is revealed to be caused by underground monsters, enthusiastically dubbed "graboids" for their ability to seize and destroy. To make matters worse, the mutated snake-like creatures that initially menace our heroes turn out to be merely the tentacles of mammoth creatures hunting their prey through vibration. Val and Earl make multiple attempts to escape to find help, but come up short every time. Whenever a seemingly foolproof plan is devised, the creatures counter with a way to stop them.

Tremors began its existence under the working title *Land Sharks*, co-written by young-and-hungry scribes S.S. Wilson and Brent Maddock. Their partner Ron Underwood, with whom they had produced several educational films, was similarly working his way up the Hollywood ladder via Charles

Band's Empire Pictures. After toiling as second unit director on David Schmoeller's 1979 creepy classic *Tourist Trap* as well as associate producer on *Crawlspace* (1986, also directed by Schmoeller), Underwood was eager to begin directing himself and thought that this fresh spin on giant creature features would be an ideal debut feature. The three shopped the treatment around for several years to no avail, but a few revisions (and Wilson and Maddock's success with the *Short Circuit* movies) eventually got them through the door of Universal Studios.

Underwood's goal was to create something far different from your standard fright flick, a perfect combination of humor and horror. In addition to Wilson and Maddock's choice dialogue and plotting, plenty of action and well-developed characters, the story was primarily set in broad daylight—not an easy atmosphere in which to create suspense. Cinematographer Alexander Gruszynski's innovative camerawork really stands out, highlighting the barren desert surroundings as well as providing thrilling underground POV of the graboids chasing their prey. Meanwhile, composer Robert Folk was called in to punch up Ernest Troost's original efforts, the result being an impeccable musical score as effective as it is unconventional for a horror/sci-fi feature.

The film's secret weapon lies in the lived-in chemistry between Bacon and Ward, who take the screenwriters' well-crafted banter to a whole new level. With decision-making reduced to "rock-paper-scissors" as they attempt to save their fellow townsfolk's skins, the two bicker like an old married couple...which only further endears them to the viewer. The scene in which they discover the actual size of the creatures really sets the action into high gear; it always makes me laugh watching Bacon exuberantly point and shout, "Fuuuuck you!" at a dead graboid...just before realizing that there are more of the big boys lurking below the surface.

The rest of the cast deliver equally worthy turns. Best known for his seven-year run on TV's *Family Ties* as suburbanite dad Steven Keaton, Michael Gross does a fantastic job transitioning to a gung-ho survivalist. In addition to several amusing moments with Ward and Bacon, he has terrific rapport with legendary country/western singer Reba McEntire, who makes an impressive screen debut as his wife. The scene in which a graboid breaks into their basement is an instant classic; the variety of weapons and countless rounds of ammo they utilize to kill that motherhumper is quite a sight.

Yet, for all the rollicking humor, there are no less than a half dozen gruesome deaths during the film's first 30 minutes as the creatures' capactiy for sheer devastation is vividly displayed. Every time the humans formulate a plan to escape, the graboids have an answer and actually seem to grow smarter over time. Every time it appears the town might survive, things quickly go to hell, with even the most likable of characters meeting grisly ends. Underwood and his team create several clever scenarios for escape, with the monsters always game for a fresh assault. Hiding on top of rocks proves useless, since the buried behemoths are prepared to wait nearby for as long as it takes. Roof tops are only a temporary sanctuary, as the graboids learn how to bring a structure to the ground. Pole vaulting, bombs attached to lassos, escape via bulldozer, and a strategic awareness of one's surroundings ("Can you fly, sucker? Can you fly?") are all employed with varying degrees of success, but the monsters do not give up easily.

Speaking of our subterranean antagonists, FX legends Tom Woodruff and Alec Gillis did an amazing job of creating the practical effects. Having previously teamed under Stan Winston on *Aliens*, *Tremors* was the duo's first major effort with their newly created effects company, Amalgamated Dynamics. Their resulting wizardry, before the days of ubiquitous computer-generated imagery, still holds up decades later, especially the intricate tentacles emerging from the beasts' mouths. I truly prefer this method of monster making—with so many modern films using CGI, *Tremors* is a shining example of the good ol' days.

To be fair, most pictures of this type usually have some blunders throughout and *Tremors* is no exception. There is the obligatory love story between

Val and a college student named Rhonda (Finn Carter), conveniently in Perfection to study seismology. Though they prove worthy companions, each saving the other's life from precarious situations, the predictably smoochy ending is a little much. Similarly, we witness some questionable behavior from certain characters, such as the idiot who gets killed by lying on a big tire when people are shouting to get higher off the ground. Thankfully the poor choices are kept to a minimum and the majority of the decision-making is solid.

Whenever I think about *Tremors*, I can't help but smile at the multitude of elements that still click with me. Whether it be the homage to '50s monster movies, the comic chemistry between Bacon and Ward, or Gross' gun-toting weekend warrior, the entire film strikes all the right chords. Though not originally a box office success, it became a runaway word-of-mouth hit on home video, developing into a cult classic that spawned three sequels and a short-lived television series. During a time where movie studios milked slasher franchises dry, releasing an endless string of repetitive sequels, *Tremors* was and remains a breath of fresh air.

Rob Dennehy is from Frankfort, IL, and has been a horror fanatic for more than 25 years, his favorites being The Texas Chain Saw Massacre, Psycho, Halloween *and George Romero's* Dead *trilogy. He owns a mortgage company with his family and his hobbies include bowling, poker, fantasy sports and watching as many horror films as possible. Rob contributed the essay on* The Shining *for* HORROR 101: The A-List of Horror Films and Monster Movies. *He can be found on IMDb as BaseBallZombies.*

UZUMAKI 2000

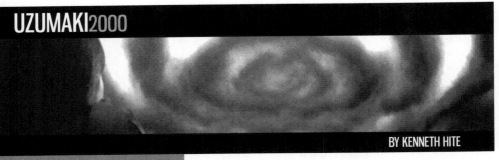

BY KENNETH HITE

"ISN'T IT LUCKY TO BE THE CENTER OF A FOCUS? LIFE IS MEANINGLESS IF NO ONE PAYS ATTENTION TO YOU. IT'S SUCH PLEASURE TO BE WATCHED. DON'T YOU THINK SO?"

I saw *Ringu* for the first time at a Canadian horror convention called Conthulhu; the experience sent me immediately to the dealer's room to hunt for it on DVD. Sadly, I wasn't the only person so inspired, and there were no more to be had. As a consolation prize to myself, I bought a (possibly pirated) copy of *Uzumaki* on VHS, tossed it into my duffel and watched it when I returned home. You'd think seeing *Ringu* would have taught me what happens when you watch strange videotapes of uncertain provenance. I didn't die, but I've been caught in a vortex ever since.

The director, the mononymic Higuchinsky (who until that point had mostly made music videos), based the film on a very popular manga by Junji Ito. He shot *Uzumaki* through a green filter, matching the coloring of some of Ito's pages, and he built shots of black shadow and white light reflecting the stark chiaroscuro of the manga panel. His characters emote not like Stanislavskian actors, but like anime icons, complete with bursts of humor and weirdness. Clearly Higuchinsky read—and better yet, absorbed and internalized—all of the manga there was to read, but Ito hadn't yet finished writing his story when the movie was filmed. Wonderfully, *nobody* knew the ending. The result is that happy rarity: a horror film that doesn't explain the horror. Indeed, Higuchinsky could no more explain the horrors on screen than his characters can. But he could, and does, re-create as many of Ito's disconnected set-pieces as he can, blending them into 88 minutes of film wrapped around that most archetypal of Japanese witness/victim/heroines, a teenage girl.

One or two of those set-pieces aside (I'm thinking of the millipede scene), *Uzumaki* isn't particularly scary. There are shocks, but nothing like the roller-coaster squeeze of tension and suspense in *Halloween* or the freezing sweat of *Ringu*. What *Uzumaki* is, in bushel basket loads, is uncanny. Its logic defies reason, its horrors defy exclusion. They are already here. Watching *Uzumaki* opens your eyes to the omnipresence of the threatening (now? suddenly? always?) in a way almost no movie does. It is a conspiracy movie with no conspiracy in it. Rather, it conspires with your pattern-matching instincts; it subverts your very desire to find rational calm. Finding the pattern reveals the horror—calm is just the eye of the storm. Freud may have been wildly wrong about what makes the "strangely familiar" so very unsettling, but he was right on the money about its effect: creeping dread.

Our viewpoint character Kirie Goshima (Eriko Hatsune) sums it up in her opening line: "Kurouzu-cho, the town of my birth. Let me tell you a story of the strangeness there." The town of Kurouzu is an isolated Everyplace, or at least Everyjapan, a Japanese version of a John Hughes or early-period Steven

Spielberg town, with only an attenuated connection to the world outside. (Specifically, a long tunnel. Freudian enough for you?) People in Kurouzu have become obsessed with uzumaki ("spiral" or "vortex" in Japanese), or perhaps the spirals have always been there and the residents have only now begun to notice these strangely familiar shapes, in snails and noodles and staircases and the oddly twisty pattern of the town's roads.

The other kids at Kirie's school become snail-like, or display spirals in their hairdos and outfits, while the gruesome spiral deaths mount up. As more and more attention is paid to the spirals, they grow more and more powerful: the smoke from the town's crematorium spirals across the sky, and outside news reports (of a spiraling typhoon) depict a spiral symbolically haunting Japan itself. An outside reporter, Ichiro Tamura (Masami Horiuchi) is drawn to investigate the town, perhaps uncovering hints of an appropriately Lovecraftian survival cult in the town's Dragonfly Lake. I say perhaps since he dies in yet another spiral and never reveals what he has learned, to Kirie or to the viewer.

We almost make a connection when we learn Kirie's father gathers clay for his pots from Dragonfly Lake; of course, those pots start displaying spiral characteristics. But then, Kirie's father heard about the spirals from the father of her would-be boyfriend Shuichi. Everything is interconnected, everything was already going to happen, everything has already started happening around you. Throughout these increasingly insane events, Kirie and Shuichi (Fhi Fan) talk, half-heartedly, about leaving the town, but they repeatedly abandon the notion, like someone turning over in the middle of a dream. At the end, with everyone around her twisted, deformed, and (usually) dead in the spirals' gravity, Kirie repeats her opening line, closing the circle.

It is something of a cliché to call surrealist movies, or those that don't stay fixed to the narrativist rails of an Aristotelian plot, "dreamlike," and although there is an undeniable oneiric quality to *Uzumaki*, it more resembles the

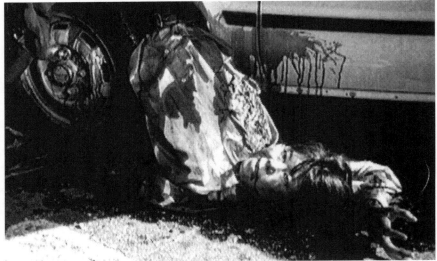

structure we attempt to impose on dreams recalled than it does the purely random free-association of an actual dream. Higuchinsky carefully builds his film as a spiral, emotionally and strategically twisting its coils around Kirie even as he revisits certain scenes (such as the washing machine suicide of Shuichi's spiral-obsessed father) from new perspectives. He spins his camera through 360-degree circles or widening pans, he connects segments with spiraling screen wipes, he reverses the action in one scene, in another he topologically re-creates a spiral in one bravura shot with a long fade from inside a car to outside it looking back in.

Just like Howard Hawks put Xs into every scene of *Scarface*, and Paul Thomas Anderson filled *Magnolia* with "8:2," Higuchinsky fills *Uzumaki* not just with the spirals of the plot—spinning pottery, stirring soup, the smoke-vortex in the sky above our Lovecraftian lake—but with other spirals for the viewer to notice: the repeated numbers 6 and 9, phone dials, twirling batons, the whorls of fingerprints. When our paranoia enters the film—as when a character slices off her fingerprints—we are, ourselves, caught in the vortex. Animated spirals spin and whirl in the background, the film itself twists in the corners.

Shuichi's father (Ren Ohsugi), a videographer, is introduced obsessively filming spirals, in snails, soup, and everywhere he can find them. As he explains, "The uzumaki is sublime. It is, in itself, the greatest work of art." Self-referentiality becomes horror, as Higuchinsky turns his own perspective inward, another spiral that only the viewer can perceive. High-concept meta-horror combines with brutal gore: a young boy who seemingly lives only to stalk Kirie winds up twisted around a car wheel, another character killed by his own monomaniacal gaze.

By now it should be apparent that the spiral-obsessed world of the film cannot be contained within its frames, its scenes, or its running time, no matter how neatly Higuchinsky joins the beginning and the ending. Just as Shuichi's parents cannot unsee the spirals that doom them, just as Shuichi and Kirie cannot escape Kurouzu's increasingly alien geometry, the viewer is likewise caught in the vortex. We cannot describe the horror without sounding weirdly obsessed with the quotidian—"It's about these spiral shapes, see, and they're everywhere." We are now inside, looking out at a world at once strange and familiar, a world uncanny.

Kenneth Hite has designed or written over 80 role-playing game books,
including GURPS Horror, The Day After Ragnarok, Trail of Cthulhu, *and* Night's
Black Agents. *Outside gaming, his works include* Tour de Lovecraft: The Tales,
Cthulhu 101, The Nazi Occult, *and a series of Lovecraftian childrens' books, as*
well as the "Lost in Lovecraft" column for Weird Tales. *He lives in Chicago with*
two Lovecraftian cats and his non-Lovecraftian wife, Sheila.

VAMPYR 1932

BY CHARLES M. KLINE

"WHY DOES THE DOCTOR ALWAYS COME AT NIGHT?"

The horror film comes in many flavors, each aiming to titillate the prospective viewer with twists of terror, dashes of death, sorbets of shock, and gourmets of grotesquerie. I've consumed many such cinematic feasts over the last 30 years, yet Carl Theodor Dreyer's *Vampyr* is one of the few to leave a hauntingly indelible impression after a single viewing. Merely in search of another 90-minute helping of violence and viscera at the time, I couldn't fully grasp what was happening. But in the years that followed I would recall the strange and fantastic imagery, the storyline's logic obscured in a mist-shrouded landscape where reason slept and nightmares roamed freely.

For those coming afresh to *Vampyr*, the surprises lie in how different it is from its bloodsucking celluloid cousins. Dreyer's hypnotic visuals hold viewers in their sway from the opening titles to the mesmerizing final frame 73 minutes later. The dialogue is sparse, with a narrative that relies more on looks and actions than on what characters actually say, and overt horror eschewed in favor of atmosphere. Of particular interest is the use of a book of lore concerning the undead as an expository device; *The Strange History of Vampires* contains an interesting variation on how these creatures deliver their victims into darkness—through suicide instead of transformation.

Based in part on *In a Glass Darkly*, Irish author J. Sheridan Le Fanu's 1872 collection of gothic mystery and supernatural fiction, *Vampyr* tells the story of a man's contact with occult forces in the French town of Courtempierre. Following the opening credits, scrolling text shares some background information about our protagonist: "This is the tale of the strange adventures of young Allan Gray, who immersed himself in the study of devil worship and vampires." Gray's arrival at a riverside inn is intercut with shots of a fisherman facing out towards the water, like Charon presiding over the River Styx. Holding the base of the long scythe extending past his shoulder, this ominous figure rings a bell, as if signaling the start of our protagonist's shadowy journey into the underworld.

Shown to his quarters by the proprietress, Gray soon hears ominous chanting from somewhere out past the hallway (made creepier by being in untranslated German). Investigating the source, he spies a blind man stumbling in an open doorway the next floor up (bringing to mind one of the purgatorial inhabitants of 1990's *Jacob's Ladder*). Gray hurries back to his room, locking the door before retiring to bed. Except sleep does not come easy, especially when another gentleman gains entrance in the middle of the night, declaring, "She must not die! You understand?" The intruder departs shortly thereafter, but not before leaving behind a package wrapped in paper, bound in twine, and sealed with wax. The words written upon it foreshadow tragedy: "To be opened after my death."

The remainder of the film represents an amalgam of imagery from Le Fanu's stories—most notably "Carmilla" and "The Room in the Dragon Volant"—and a metaphysical fever dream where the presence of the uncanny lurks at every turn. Shadows move independent of their subjects, a skeleton's outstretched hand reaches for a drowsing Gray with a bottle of poison in its grip, and a famous out-of-body sequence provides some of the eeriest footage ever captured on celluloid. Then there's the matter of the vampire herself who, a far cry from the beautiful seductress Carmilla, resembles an old hag out of a Goya painting. She is the main antagonist, preying on a young girl

named Leone (Sybille Schmitz, one of the cast's two acting professionals) at a chateau where Gray eventually winds up his quest. The vampire is aided by two henchmen in the carrying out of her nefarious deeds—a doctor and a peg-legged assassin in a soldier's uniform. In fact, the demise of one of these helpers is memorable for its inventiveness, and may have been the inspiration for a nasty little scene in Peter Weir's 1985 film *Witness*, where a dirty cop meets his end inside of a corn silo.

Of course Dreyer's journey in making *Vampyr* was perhaps more of a nightmare than the final result itself. Following the cool reception of his previous work, *The Passion of Joan of Arc* (1928), the director wanted to create something with broader audience appeal and decided to go the route of horror. A logical choice, given the popularity of the genre in Europe and the United States (sparked by the release of such early German 1920s expressionistic works as *The Cabinet of Dr. Caligari* and *Nosferatu*). Dreyer made his film entirely outside of the studio system, using mostly non-actors and shooting on location to save money; he even cast Baron Nicolas de Gunzburg (under the *nom de theater* Julian West) as Allan Gray in exchange for funding the production.

Unfortunately, contrary to the success of Tod Browning's 1931 smash *Dracula*, *Vampyr* was booed by audiences during an initial screening in Berlin in the spring of 1932, foretelling its ultimate commercial failure. Perhaps this was because *Vampyr* was originally conceived as a silent film and, as a consequence, much of the emphasis was placed on the visual elements. (What little dialogue the characters do speak—all recorded in post-production—seems more like an afterthought.)

Following the disappointing release of his talking picture debut—the previous nine had all been silents—Dreyer checked himself into a mental institution for a brief respite after a nervous breakdown in February 1933. He would not return to the director's chair for over a decade; *Day of Wrath* (1943) represents the first of four final titles in his filmography.

In Jorgen Roos' 1966 documentary *Carl Th. Dreyer*, the director commented on *Vampyr*'s ghostly look. "We had planned on a rather heavy style, but by chance we discovered something much better, so we changed our plans. Examining the first rushes…we stopped at a scene that seemed to have been shot in a fog, a muddle of grayish white." The finished product reflects this, presenting an exterior landscape where day and night blur into a perpetual kind of mist. Just as J. Sheridan Le Fanu created a masterpiece that forever changed the literary landscape of the vampire tale, so had Carl Theodor Dreyer done the same for the undead predator in cinema—through a camera lens darkly.

Charles M. Kline, a Maryland resident, grew up watching horror films instead of cartoons. Since then he's done special effects makeup for several low-budget indie film projects and is currently pursuing a BFA in Creative Writing from Full Sail University. His first short, Living with Lycanthropy, *won "Best Horror" at the 2012 IFQ Film and Webisode Festival in Los Angeles (http://vimeo.com/46138814).*

VENUS IN FURS 1969

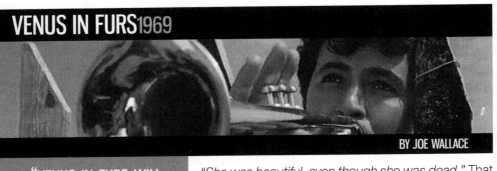

BY JOE WALLACE

"VENUS IN FURS WILL BE SMILING…WHEN THAT MOMENT ARRIVES."

"She was beautiful, even though she was dead." That quote from the opening scene of Jess Franco's *Venus in Furs* provides a fair impression of the journey one is about to take with this unusual, hallucinatory, surreal gem. While not as lurid or violent as other late '60s/early '70s genre films, *Furs* is an underappreciated masterpiece definitely worth your time.

Viewers' enjoyment likely depends on where they initially started within the extensive Franco filmography. If their first exposure was *Bloody Moon* (1981) or *Succubus* (1968), chances are they will rightly interpret *Venus in Furs* as one of the best—if not *the* best—of the lot. If the starting point was *The Awful Doctor Orloff* (1962), one might not be quite as impressed. No matter—suffice to say that regardless of which movie is his "best," this is Franco's *masterpiece*.

It's not unreasonable to view a good many of Franco's other productions as preparation for—or an attempt to live up to—this main event. *Furs* is the movie he's *trying* to make with *Vampyros Lesbos* (1971), *Virgin Among the Living Dead* (1973), and countless others. It's easy to find the film's key elements in much of what preceded and followed: the anything-goes surrealist atmosphere, a plot that works largely using dream logic, and bizarre left turns into "Is-it-real-or-not?" hallucination.

Venus in Furs begins on a beach, with jazz trumpet player Jimmy Logan (James Darren) digging his instrument out of the sand. Franco is telling us

from the outset that we'll be digging up the story along with Logan, but even if we understand this metaphor as such, the knowledge doesn't telegraph the plot or the revelations to come.

A story of obsession, lust, madness, and murder follows. Our trumpet player's been busy—sometimes busy doing nothing, other times chasing after a woman he's obsessing

over (Maria Rohm). He runs into her while gigging as a combo player for what seems to be the world's longest-running house party, but he's got a complication—his current girlfriend Rita (Barbara McNair).

Plus, this is no ordinary "other woman," as she looks exactly like someone Jimmy found in a bad S&M situation at a party. But that woman was dead… or so he thought. Who is this newcomer, and why is she here? He pursues her throughout the entire film; in the meantime, the pampered socialites involved in the S&M situation keep turning up murdered, one by one.

To say more about the plot involves major spoilers, but knowing the story does not in any way diminish the film's power, due to its surreal, psychedelic and (depending on who you ask) non-linear construction. Even so, *Venus in Furs* can also be discussed at length without talking spoilers; it's as mysterious an experience as the plot details themselves.

When contemplating the work of Jess Franco (aka Jesus Manera, Jesús Franco, Jesse Franco, A.M. Frank and too many other screen names to list), it's important to keep in mind that the director is, more or less, the Johnny Cash of his craft. It's possible to stereotype Franco as a horror director in the same way Cash was viewed as a country singer, but both men are completely unique. Franco is every bit as much his own genre as The Man in Black.

Furs could be considered a Franco acid test. If it doesn't resonate, chances are viewers won't have the patience or suspension of disbelief required for many of his other titles. On the flip side, it might not be weird enough for budding and enthusiastic Francophiles—these adventurous souls should proceed directly to *A Virgin Among the Living Dead* and go from there.

A running voiceover fills in important plot exposition and lends a noir feel, but even with Darren's haunted tones guiding us through the proceedings, things remain fairly mysterious. (How much more "out there" would this experience be if the voiceover was omitted and everything was left to the imagination?) From the outset, we understand this is going to be a detective story of sorts, albeit one with philosophical and even metaphysical questions attached.

There's more jazz music than dialogue. In the hands of a lesser director, this could be a severe liability, but here the music is a crucial part of the film's psychological makeup, very nearly a character all its own. All of the film's music is credited to Manfred Mann and Mike Hugg, with many sources giving a nod to an uncredited Stu Phillips. McNair sings the haunting title song on-screen—a motif echoed repeatedly throughout the film to great effect—but if you're enticed by her performance, good luck trying to chase down an official copy of the *Furs* soundtrack. There isn't one—not yet, at least.

On the technical end, having Harry Alan Towers as the film's producer likely kept Franco from indulging in certain excesses while allowing him free rein with others. For instance, if one expects hyperactive zoom lenses, zombies, extreme close-ups of drooling perverts (usually played by Franco himself), or extended tracking shots of nude vampires, they may be disappointed. That said, *Furs* is classic Franco with regard to its overt sexuality—from the implied group sex S&M scene to Rohm's seduction of Franco regulars Klaus Kinski and Dennis Price, there is plenty of flesh on display, living and dead.

Historically speaking, Franco went out on a limb by putting his protagonist into a bi-racial relationship. Originally he wanted his hero to be a black jazz player in love with a white woman; to the shame of all involved, this was vetoed as being too boundary-pushing for 1969. On the Blue Underground DVD, Franco explains that his producers felt "...the American public are not ready to see a black man and a white woman in bed. But they were fine with a white man sleeping with a black woman. We had to rewrite and tell another story."

Pushing the envelope in a more acceptable but still-controversial way, Franco reversed the racial love interest and tossed in a biting social commentary for good measure—McNair's character is the only decent human being within Darren's social circles of people. Most, if not all, of the others are spoiled socialites or hangers-on. McNair's involvement with Darren gives his character a place of retreat as he struggles with the mystery of seeing Rohm dead one moment and standing in the doorway the next.

Once McNair leaves, the film—and the trumpet player—begin drifting away into unending madness. Is it a bit of psychobabble to say she is Darren's bridge between the living and the dead? Perhaps. It's not good to elaborate on that notion any further—to reveal any more is to share too much.

After experiencing *Venus in Furs* firsthand, you'll discover its ghost in other Franco titles including his most infamous. (A notable exception being the following year's *Eugenie*, another entry that exists in the auteur's canon as wholly unique and practically unclassifiable.) This waking fever dream serves as the ideal place to begin (or continue) your journey into the mind and work of Jess Franco—the gateway to a lifelong obsession.

Joe Wallace is a writer, vinyl archivist, occasional filmmaker, and Euro-horror obsessive. He travels far and wide to buy record collections, meet fellow film/music fanatics, and eat exotic food. Joe sells hard-to-find vinyl and runs Turntabling.net.

VIOLENT MIDNIGHT 1963

BY DENISE LoRUSSO

Following the 1960 release of Alfred Hitchcock's *Psycho*, the flick that stopped a thousand showers, everyone from William Castle (*Homicidal*) to Hammer (*Scream of Fear*) to a young Francis Ford Coppola (*Dementia 13*) was determined to cash in on the psycho-thriller concept. In early 1963, Italian horror maestro Mario Bava introduced a stunning new genre, the *giallo*, by way of *The Girl Who Knew Too Much* (aka *The Evil Eye*). That same year, back across the Atlantic, a fun, delightfully murderous,

> "DON'T LOSE YOUR TEMPER, MR. FREEMAN, BECAUSE WHEN YOU DO, YOU KILL, DON'T YOU? ISN'T THAT RIGHT, MR. FREEMAN?"

and well-made feature was also making its debut, taking a page from Hitchcock, but also incorporating many elements closely identified with this new breed of Euro-terror.

With a black-gloved killer, one who creatively murders young female beauties while his/her identity remains a mystery until the final reel, is *Violent Midnight* (aka *Psychomania*) a *proto-giallo*? It's hard to say, as release-date documentation varies, but producer Del Tenney emphatically states that he had a finished product awaiting release in 1962. Both films' killers spare no viciousness, using a knife, ice pick, or something equally deadly (and sharp!) such as scissors, screwdriver, axe, and the like. All while a thorny screenplay keeps viewers guessing the identity of the psychopath. It's mind-blowing that

Violent Midnight and *The Girl Who Knew Too Much* came out so closely to one another—in different countries—and that neither knew of the other.

This suspenseful exploitation shocker, filmed entirely on location in Stamford, Connecticut, for a mere $42,000, proves a textbook example of excellent value extracted from a low production budget. Directed by Richard Hilliard and produced by first-timer Tenney (who went on to steer such B-movie standards as *The Horror of Party Beach*, *The Curse of the Living Corpse*, and *I Eat Your Skin*), *Violent Midnight* makes great use of the autumnal New England landscapes. Via Louis McMahon's crisp black-and-white photography, one can almost smell the pine-scented woods and musty wet leaves as characters make their way through breaking twigs and crackling brush.

Elliot Freeman (popular TV soap actor Lee Phillips) is an internationally renowned artist and handsome bachelor, which accounts for the bevy of semi-clad co-eds constantly competing for his attention. His favorite model, Dolores (Kaye Elhardt), is clearly infatuated, but despite wealth, success, and mounting fame, Elliot remains tense, moody, and quick to anger; when pushed, he viciously retaliates. Seems the young painter is a veteran of the Korean War, suffering from "battle fatigue." (We're told he "flipped his lid when somebody got it.") Is he capable of murder? Does the fact that Elliot's rich father went insane portend madness passing through the bloodlines? His eccentric lawyer and family friend Adrian Benedict (Shepperd Strudwick) certainly thinks so.

With surprisingly disturbing imagery and plenty of red herrings (courtesy of screenwriter Robin Miller) to keep you guessing whodunit, *Violent Midnight*

has a broad appeal for horror fans. The first murder sequence reveals a genuine understanding as to what made *Psycho*'s shower scene work, intercutting well-choreographed close-ups of blood and skin with violent silhouettes of the killer's blade in action. Hilliard and McMahon collaborate on some great camerawork here, with bloody hands smearing the wallpaper, a "walk through walls" dissolve (a Hitchcock hallmark), and a surprising—albeit corny—freeze-frame.

As luck would have it, more students of Belmont School for Girls start dropping dead at the hands of the muddy-booted killer—the same college where Elliot's estranged sister Lynn (Tenney's then-wife and collaborator, Margot Hartman) is starting classes. The siblings' touching and sweet meeting at the train station, their first in many years, is the first time we see the brooding Elliot smile and laugh. Meanwhile, breathy and busty young co-eds, despite the rampaging psychotic terrorizing the community, lack the sense to curtail their

naked, drunken, midnight paddles in the local lake. Their budding, swinging '60s sense of promiscuity appears to be a sign of the sexually permissive age to come, an era of anti-establishment and sex, drugs, and rock 'n' roll.

There's also the suggestion underlying *Violent Midnight* that "girls behaving badly"—sexual brazenness, nudity, wearing skin-tight clothing, vulnerable booziness—can stir up dangerous and uncontrollable passions in men that will potentially get them killed. In the film's only classroom scene, the biology teacher (and resident peeping tom on campus) pompously warns, "There is a lesson here, young ladies—do not let our lives be carried by passion beyond the bounds of good taste."

As a woman and a horror fan, the idea of "naughty girls" getting a raw deal doesn't hurt my sensitivities at all. I expect it and, dare I say, I want it! I love the scene with two half-dressed coeds dancing the twist in their dorm room, while their roommates' naked bodies are nearly visible through the frosted glass shower door. Tenney reveals that his distributors called for more risqué material; most of this sequence was shot later, as well as other mild nude scenes and a fairly explicit school utility closet seduction which contains the immortal line, "Hey, you smell of tobacco, beer...and animal!" cooed by a sexy vixen (Lorraine Rogers) to her motorcycle greaser paramour (a fresh-faced James Farentino).

Other characters include girl-next-door Carol (TV veteran Jean Hale), who happens to be in love with Elliot, desperate barfly Silvia (a sultry Sylvia Miles), who is hopelessly devoted to Farentino, and the "just gimme the facts" noir-copper Detective Palmer (Dick Van Patten), who has a list of suspects and corpses that both continue to pile up. Wilford L. Holcombe's musical score, a delightful mixture of jazz and rock 'n' roll, dispenses with the usual scene lilts while the moody "Black Autumn" song, with woeful lyrics sung by a beatnik college girl, provides an intriguing pause in the action.

Flipping channels on a dreary, rainy Saturday afternoon in the early 1980s, I stumbled upon *Violent Midnight*'s heart-racing opening scene, wherein a hunting outing turns tragic and fatal. By the time the final credits rolled, its suspenseful mystery and chilling climax having left me breathless, I wondered why I'd never heard of this obscure gem before. Worse yet, I couldn't remember the title! Over the following weeks, I went on a quest to find out more information about the film, writing television stations, hunting through old VHS cases at local thrift stores and music stores, flipping through cinema studies at the library hoping to see a name I remembered...all to no avail. With the advent of the internet, I still had no luck in my search, despite key words like "maniac," "schizo," "demented," "paranoia," "killer garbed in dark trench coat, black gloves, and muddy boots," etc. Even my trusty fiends on the IMDb horror message boards were stumped.

Then, one night a few years ago, while randomly tuning into Turner Classic Movies, the mysterious movie I had been desperately trying to find appeared before my eyes. There it was! *Violent Midnight* was found! Here's hoping you find it, too. And, since Dark Sky Films released the film on DVD in 2006, and you now know the title, your hunt will presumably bear fruit sooner than mine.

Denise LoRusso, aka "lennonforever" on the IMDb, is an avid horror aficionado, a staunch animal advocate and a devoted Beatles (especially John Lennon) fanatic. A retired OR registered nurse, she has plenty of time to watch horror! She is mom to a feline posse of five, and Grammy to four adored grandchildren.

WEREWOLF OF LONDON 1935

BY CRAIG J. CLARK

> "HERETIC! BRINGING A BEASTLY THING LIKE THAT INTO CHRISTIAN ENGLAND."

Like many horror movie buffs before me, I came to *Werewolf of London* thinking of it as an also-ran, the misfire Universal had to get out of its system before it went back to the drawing board and re-emerged six years later clutching *The Wolf Man* in its grubby paws. But approached on its own terms, it's quite an effective tale of obsession, echoing Robert Louis Stevenson's *The Strange Case of Dr. Jekyll and Mr. Hyde* with its warning about the dangers inherent in the heedless pursuit of knowledge. This is, of course, not to dispute *The Wolf Man*'s status as a classic—it is, after all, the film that launched a thousand fur-faced fiends—but to treat *Werewolf of London* as a footnote is to do it a great disservice. For without Henry Hull leading the pack as the silver screen's first two-legged wolf-man, who knows what his future kin would have looked like?

Made the same year as *Bride of Frankenstein*, *Werewolf of London* was Universal's attempt to add another monster to its stable, which by then also included the Phantom of the Opera, Dracula, the Mummy, and the Invisible Man. However, in lieu of an established literary source (Guy Endore's *The Werewolf of Paris* was published in 1933, but either the rights weren't obtained or it was found to be unsuitable for adaptation), several writers were charged with the task of concocting an original story. As a result, the script presented to contract director Stuart Walker bore little resemblance to existing werewolf lore and superstitions, but it's unique among tales of lycanthropy and the effect it has on those unlucky enough to be cursed with it.

In this case, the unfortunate one is Dr. Wilfred Glendon (Hull), a botanist who travels to Tibet in search of the *mariphasa lupina lumina*, described by one character as a "phos-

phorescent wolf flower." Upon finding it under the light of the full Tibetan moon, Glendon is attacked by a shadowy figure. He successfully fights off his hairy assailant, but not before being bitten on the arm. It is this bite that dooms him to become a beast himself at the next full moon, by which time he is back home in England, trying in vain to get the stubborn buds he collected to bloom. In the meantime, he's grown estranged from his wife Lisa (*Bride of Frankenstein*'s Valerie Hobson, playing house with a mad scientist for the second time that year) and troubled by the arrival of the mysterious Dr. Yogami (a subtly sinister Warner Oland) from the University of Carpathia, who turns out to know quite a lot about his work.

Curiously, the scenes in Dr. Glendon's laboratory push *Werewolf of London* in the direction of science fiction. Not only has he developed an artificial ray that replicates moonlight (capable of raising the hairs on the back of his hand), but he also has a remarkably sophisticated video-surveillance system for a private residence in 1935. Furthermore, one of the specimens in his well-stocked greenhouse is a giant carnivorous plant from Madagascar, which is the sort of bizarre detail that cropped up with some frequency during Universal's horror programmers and another handy reminder that, being in the vanguard of the movie monster business, they were essentially making things up as they went along.

For example, when Yogami introduces himself, he informs Glendon that his precious *mariphasa lupina lumina* is the only known antidote for "werewolfery," the medical term for which is said to be "lycanthrophobia." Then, of course, there's the fact that the full moon lasts for four consecutive nights (that's how many times Yogami and Glendon are condemned to change), which is a stretch no matter how you look at it. The film is also remarkably specific about how the curse is applied. When Glendon consults a reference book about his condition, it tells him that "transvection from man to wolf occurs between the hours of nine and ten at the full moon." Furthermore, a werewolf "must kill at least one human being each night of the full moon or become permanently afflicted." That means no locking oneself up and waiting it out—unless one has access to a certain Tibetan flower, which Glendon and Yogami wind up fighting over with deadly results.

For all its eccentricities, there are other ways in which *Werewolf of London* manages to be more consistent than its more famous descendant. One thing that goes unexplained in *The Wolf Man* is the way Lon Chaney Jr. is bitten by a four-legged werewolf (played by Bela Lugosi in human form), but becomes a two-legged wolf-man. Here, being attacked by a wolf-man and surviving turns you into the same. Accordingly, Hull's monster manages to retain more of his humanity and an unusual sense of refinement. (Note how he takes care to don a scarf, hat, and coat *after* his first transformation.) He's even capable of speech, although this trait doesn't manifest itself until the very end. What this does is allow him to thank the person who shot him "for the bullet" (which, it must be said, is not silver) and apologize to his wife, giving them some much-needed closure and her permission to move on after he expires.

One criticism that often gets lobbed in *Werewolf of London's* direction is that Hull plays such an unsympathetic character that it's difficult to care about what happens to him. While it's true that he's rather short-tempered and can

be exceedingly formal at times, he clearly has feelings for his wife and is genuinely concerned about her safety. True, he doesn't trust her enough to let her in on his monstrous secret, but I see this as his stereotypical English reserve coming to the fore, preventing him from reaching out. As far as I'm concerned, the characters who stick out like sore thumbs asking to be lopped off are the two Cockney landladies that Glendon encounters while looking for a room to let. Then again, this kind of broad comic relief was typical of Universal horrors of the period. Just think of Una O'Connor's turns in *The Invisible Man* and *Bride of Frankenstein*; the double act of Mrs. Moncaster and Mrs. Whack would have been right at home in those films, cackling and caterwauling alongside her.

Where *Werewolf of London* really shines is in its transformation sequences (there are four, including the final one where Hull reverts back to his human form, and all are handled differently) and Jack Pierce's always-distinctive makeup effects. Hull was decidedly not a fan of Pierce's original design for the monster, which he felt obscured too much of his face. As the actor later said, "Jack had a special talent for turning men into freaks." As a result, London's first werewolf wound up with a much less iconic, but still plenty feral-looking, visage (I certainly wouldn't want to meet him in a dark alley), and Pierce kept the excess yak hair at the ready when it came time to make *The Wolf Man* a half dozen years later. There's definitely something to be said for simplicity, though, as Hull proved by accentuating the man in the wolf-man. His intense performance makes *Werewolf of London* worth revisiting again and again.

Craig J. Clark hasn't seen every werewolf movie ever made, but he's working on it. His favorite is An American Werewolf in London, *which is a high standard to measure up to, but he'll give just about any hairy beast on two or four legs a chance. His 2,600+ reviews can be found on his website, Craig J. Clark Watches a Lot of Movies (dada.warped.com/movies), and he contributes the monthly "Full Moon Features" column to Werewolf News (werewolf-news.com).*

X: THE MAN WITH THE X-RAY EYES 1963

BY CHRISTIANNE BENEDICT

I sometimes think I learned everything I know about horror movies from Stephen King. I have an old copy of *Danse Macabre* that my parents gave me for Christmas in 1982. I've read it to tatters. One of the pieces of received wisdom found in that book is the notion that the most Lovecraftian film ever made is Roger Corman's *X: The Man with the X-Ray Eyes*. I would have eventually noticed it myself, given some seasoning in the genre. Lovecraft really leaps off the screen during the film's climax, in which Ray Milland's James Xavier raves about the all-seeing eye staring at him from the center of the universe. The film doesn't exactly depict Lovecraft's three-lobed burning eye of Yog-Sothoth, but it doesn't need to. Another arcanum found in *Danse Macabre* is the legend of a lost ending, in which Xavier, having plucked his eyes from their sockets, exclaims: "I can still see!" This is apocryphal. Corman himself debunks this particular legend—the scene was indeed discussed, but never filmed.

> "I'VE COME TO TELL YOU WHAT I SEE. THERE ARE GREAT DARKNESSES. FARTHER THAN TIME ITSELF. AND BEYOND THE DARKNESS, A LIGHT THAT GLOWS, CHANGES...AND IN THE CENTER OF THE UNIVERSE...THE EYE THAT SEES US ALL."

There *was* a lost beginning, though, that went out with the first theatrical prints only to be excised on re-release. It's on current DVD editions, and it's easy to see why Corman and A.I.P. would reconsider it. It plays like an educational film. Had it occurred to Corman and Sam Arkoff, I could see them shopping this footage to schools, though so far as I know that never happened. This lost beginning takes inventory of the senses, leaving sight for last, and then speculates about the dangers of enhancing them too much. It's the old, "There are some things that Man was not meant to know," trope. Then we get a shot of

Milland, his eyes a gold-in-black color, stumbling through the desert. The educational stuff makes for a stiff beginning while the footage of Milland telegraphs the end of the film. Corman was wise to remove it.

X (the subtitle "The Man with the X-Ray Eyes" does not appear on the film) follows Xavier, a surgeon who is looking into ways to expand the scope of human vision. He has developed drops that enable the human eye to see into other spectra of light beyond the narrow spectrum that is naturally visible. His experiments on monkeys show that the drug does indeed work. The monkeys, unable to process what they see, die of fright. Undeterred, Xavier moves ahead with human trials with himself as the subject. At first, the effects of the drops are temporary, and kind of fun, particularly when those around him seem

unclothed. Unfortunately, the foundation that has funded him pulls the plug on his research. He's left fuming, determined to prove himself. He intervenes—correctly—in a surgery where he can see that the doctor on the case has misdiagnosed the illness. This doesn't satisfy him. He is determined to see more. When his best friend tries to stop him, Xavier accidentally kills him.

He goes on the run, first finding employment as a carnival mentalist, then as a faith healer. When the authorities eventually catch up to him, he leads them on a merry chase that ends up at a tent revival where he raves about the things he sees in the light at the center of the universe....

Corman was on a roll when *X* was made. It's situated between the first few Poe films, in which Corman was still feeling his way around the Gothic horror playground, and the later Poes, which became increasingly daring formal experiments. Some of that experimentation can be seen taking shape in *X*. Early scenes look completely mundane. The dance party Xavier attends even descends into a goofy exploitation comedy when he sees through everyone's clothing. It swings close to a nudie film. Corman always liked his party scenes. When the point of view shifts to what Xavier is actually seeing in later scenes, though, the whole thing turns into a psychedelic light show. Tricky optical effects turn the familiar skyline of the Vegas strip into a multi-hued, skeletal nightmare city. Eventually, *X* veers into complete abstraction as the light at the center of the universe consumes Xavier's perceptions. It's a profoundly disorienting feature that anticipates the drug films Corman would produce later in the decade. The horror is different from the Poes, which are often painfully Freudian. *X* is both more abstract and more visceral. The premise itself preys on both the vulnerability of our eyes and on their strangeness as the only exposed viscera in the human body. It hides what is happening to Xavier's eyes behind dark glasses for much of its running time so it can provide a jolt to the audience when they're finally revealed.

Corman knew Lovecraft well, but only in *X* does he really "get" him. The director's next film, *The Haunted Palace*—converted into a Poe movie and given its title by A.I.P. when they acquired the production—is based directly on Lovecraft's "The Case of Charles Dexter Ward." But thematically, *The Haunted Palace* is all of a piece with the Poes, so there's some justification for this. Corman produced two later Lovecraft films, *The Dunwich Horror* and *Die, Monster, Die!*, both helmed by his frequent art director, Daniel Haller, and both completely missing the thrust of the author's specific brand of horror.

But then, the idea that thematic elements here are purely Lovecraftian is simplistic. *X* delves into another tradition of American horror. It's set in Tod Browning's universe of carnivals and con men. It's a portrait of the high and the low. It features the dark descent of film noir, in which the hero rises to the peak of his world only to stumble and fall. It's a steep drop. It has more in common with films like *Nightmare Alley* and *The Unknown* than it does with Corman's own Lovecraft films. A more apt comparison is Flannery O'Connor's novel *Wise Blood*, which features the same shady con men and faith healers. There are several identical plot points, in which James Xavier and O'Connor's Hazel Motes find themselves in the same metaphorical spot, including the ghastly climax of both O'Connor's book and Corman's film. Certainly, Don Rickles' con man, Crane, is the sort of grotesque who wandered through O'Connor's south, as is Xavier, for that matter. The movie even grants Xavier his moment of grace, his vindication, before shoving him down into the freak show. Xavier and Hazel Motes are also alike in their metaphorical blindness, even though both of them can "see" better than most. It's almost too similar to be an accident. Co-screenwriter Ray Russell was the fiction editor for Playboy—it's conceivable that he knew O'Connor's book and that the similarity is intentional.

There's one other thing concerning *X*'s ending. While the fabled "I can still see!" ending may not exist, it may not need to. After the final shot of Milland, the screen shifts to the multicolored nightmare of the X-ray Las Vegas as the credits appear. It's as if Xavier is being driven through the city by the police. Is this his point of view? If it is, then the film is even more horrible than its Grand Guignol ending lets on.

Christianne Benedict is a freelance graphic designer and illustrator. She blogs about movies at krelllabs.blogspot.com, among other places. Christianne lives in Central Missouri with her partner and her dogs.

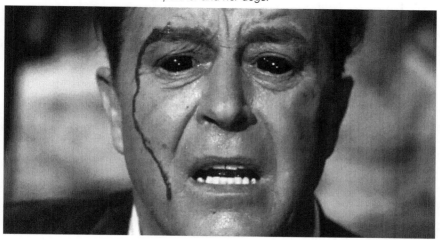

INDEX

COUNTRIES OF ORIGIN

Australia
Razorback

Brazil
At Midnight I'll Take Your Soul

Canada
The Changeling
Curtains
Pin

France
Fascination
Possession (co-production Germany)
The Tenant

Germany
The Hands of Orlac
Vampyr

Hong Kong
The Eye

Ireland
Isolation (co-production UK)

Italy
Blood for Dracula
City of the Living Dead
Dellamorte Dellamore
Django Kill
Kill Baby Kill
Tenebrae

Japan
Ichi the Killer
Kairo
Matango
Uzumaki

Mexico
Santa Sangre (co-production Italy)

New Zealand
Bad Taste

Russian
Dark Waters (co-production Italy/UK)

South Africa
Dust Devil

South Korea
A Tale of Two Sisters

Spain
Alucarda
The House That Screamed
The Hunchback of the Morgue
In a Glass Cage
The Living Dead at Manchester Morgue
Pieces
Tombs of the Blind Dead

UK
The Beast Must Die
Brimstone & Treacle
The City of the Dead
The Company of Wolves
Crimes at the Dark House
The Curse of the Werewolf
The Devil Rides Out
The Devils
Eden Lake
Event Horizon (co-production USA)
The Legend of Hell House
The Living and the Dead
Quatermass and the Pit
The Reflecting Skin
The Sender
Venus in Furs (co-production Germany/Italy)

USA

The Blob
Brain Damage
The Brotherhood of Satan
Carnival of Souls
Dark Night of the Scarecrow
The Entity
Evilspeak
Frailty
Frankenstein Meets the Wolf Man
The Gore Gore Girls
Habit
Halloween III: Season of the Witch
The Hills Have Eyes
The Hitcher
The Horror of Party Beach
Humanoids from the Deep
In the Mouth of Madness
Isle of the Dead
I Spit on Your Grave
Lemora: A Child's Tale of the Supernatural
Let's Scare Jessica to Death
Maniac
The Man Who Laughs
May
The Mothman Prophecies
A Night to Dismember
Night Warning
The Old Dark House
The Other Side
The Penalty
Phantom of the Paradise
Pretty Poison
Psycho II
Q
The Sadist
Season of the Witch
The Seventh Victim
Shock Waves
The Signal
Silent Scream
Society

Spider Baby
Spiral
The Spiral Staircase
Squirm
Tattoo
Tourist Trap
Tremors
Violent Midnight
Werewolf of London
X: The Man with the X-Ray Eyes

SUBGENRES

Art House
The Devils
Django Kill
Fascination
In a Glass Cage
The Reflecting Skin
Santa Sangre
Venus in Furs

Broken Minds
Let's Scare Jessica to Death
May
The Mothman Prophecies
Pin
Santa Sangre
Spiral
The Tenant

Cannibals
The Hills Have Eyes
Spider Baby

Comedy/Horror
Bad Taste
Brain Damage
The Old Dark House
Phantom of the Paradise
Society
Spider Baby
Tremors

Creature Features
Brain Damage
The Horror of Party Beach
Humanoids from the Deep
Isolation
Matango
Q
Razorback
Squirm
Tremors

Ghosts
Carnival of Souls
The Changeling
Dark Night of the Scarecrow
Django Kill
The Entity
The Eye

Kairo
Kill Baby Kill
The Legend of Hell House
A Tale of Two Sisters

Gore Galore
Bad Taste
Brain Damage
City of the Living Dead
Event Horizon
Evilspeak
The Gore Gore Girls
Humanoids from the Deep
Ichi the Killer
The Living Dead at Manchester Morgue
Maniac
Pieces
Tenebrae

Human Horror
The Devils
Eden Lake
Frailty
The Hands of Orlac
In a Glass Cage
I Spit on Your Grave
The Living and the Dead
May
Night Warning
The Penalty
Pretty Poison
The Reflecting Skin
The Sadist
Spiral
The Spiral Staircase
Tattoo

Mad Scientists
Frankenstein Meets the Wolf Man
The Hunchback of the Morgue
Werewolf of London
X: The Man with the X-Ray Eyes

Religious
Alucarda
At Midnight I'll Take Your Soul
Brimstone & Treacle
Dark Waters

The Devils
Frailty
The Other Side

Satanism/Occult
The Brotherhood of Satan
The City of the Dead
The Devil Rides Out
Evilspeak
Halloween III: Season of the Witch
In the Mouth of Madness
Season of the Witch
The Seventh Victim

Sci-Fi
Bad Taste
The Blob
Event Horizon
Evilspeak
Halloween III: Season of the Witch
Isolation
The Mothman Prophecies
Kairo
Quatermass and the Pit
The Signal

Silent
The Hands of Orlac
The Man Who Laughs
The Penalty
*Vampyr** (minimal dialogue)

Serial Killers/Slashers
Crimes at the Dark House
Curtains
Dust Devil
The Gore Gore Girls
The Hitcher
The House That Screamed
Maniac
A Night to Dismember
Pieces
Psycho II
Silent Scream
Tenebrae
Tourist Trap
Violent Midnight

Slow Burn
Brimstone & Treacle
Carnival of Souls
The Changeling
Isle of the Dead
Kairo
Let's Scare Jessica to Death
Matango
The Mothman Prophecies
Season of the Witch
The Seventh Victim
Spiral
Tattoo

Telekinetics
The Sender
Tourist Trap

Vampires
Blood for Dracula
Fascination
Habit
Isle of the Dead
Lemora: A Child's Tale of the Supernatural
Let's Scare Jessica to Death
Vampyr

Werewolves
The Beast Must Die
The Company of Wolves
The Curse of the Werewolf
Frankenstein Meets the Wolf Man
Werewolf of London

WTF Cinema
Ichi the Killer
A Night to Dismember
Possession
Santa Sangre
Society
The Tenant
Uzumaki
Venus in Furs

Zombies
City of the Living Dead
Dellamorte Dellamore
The Living Dead at Manchester Morgue
Shock Waves
Tombs of the Blind Dead

CONTACT

Comments? Questions? Drop us a line!

WWW.KITLEYSKRYPT.COM

6527128R00174

Printed in Great Britain
by Amazon.co.uk, Ltd.,
Marston Gate.